Praise f
Why the World N

"Ferrana treats China's place in the world within a sweeping exploration of the shifting contours of global imperialism from which the 20th century super-imperialism of United States springs. As China opened to the world during its post-1978 reform period, its global wealth grew [along with] its global power and influence. Yet, though China's global footprint manifested superficial similarities with that of neoliberal economic transformation and Western imperialism led by United States super-imperialism, Ferrana reveals China's often subtle, distinct differences in its relation with the world. Further, Ferrana debunks simple narratives of China's ruling class as capitalist. Notwithstanding real existing wealth disparities within China, the role of the state and the policy directions supported by the Communist Party continue to demonstrate ties of the latter to the socialist project of working-class power, Ferrana argues. Indeed, it is precisely China's distinguishing itself from U.S. super-imperialism in terms of its approaches to ecosustainability, international multipolarity, opposition to settler colonialism and so forth, concludes Ferrana, that has [made it] the object of relentless Western propaganda and misinformation."

—RICHARD WESTRA, University Professor at the University of Opole, Poland, Adjunct Professor in the Center for Macau Studies, University of Macau, and co-editor of *Journal of Contemporary Asia*. His most recent book is *The Political Economy of Post-Capitalism: Financialization, Globalization and Neofeudalism* (2024)

"Millions of people in the Global North are worried about war, austerity, environmental destruction, and climate change, but see nothing but more of the same coming from Western leaders. Most progressive writers of the Global North remain trapped in an updated version of 'Yellow Peril' Sinophobia, thinking of China as some kind of 'techno-dystopia,' an imperial power in its own right, or an adjunct of U.S. power. Kyle Ferrana's book is a methodical analysis of the unequal global economy led by the U.S., and of China's post-colonial struggle against this system and for sovereign economic development. Because only economic planning on a sovereign basis can save our planet, understanding recent Chinese history through *Why the World Needs China* is an antidote to both Sinophobia and to despair."

—JUSTIN PUDOR, host of the Anti-Empire Project, Associate Professor at York University's Faculty of Environmental and Urban Change, and co-author of *Extraordinary Threat: The US Empire, the Media, and 20 Years of Coup Attempts in Venezuela*

Praise *continued*

"With *Why the World Needs China,* Kyle Ferrana provides readers in the West with a hugely informative, readable and thought-provoking account of China's political economy and its relationship to the global process of ending imperialism and transitioning to a multipolar world order. Weaving together threads of history, economics and geopolitics, Ferrana creates a compelling and inspiring narrative about Chinese socialism and China's place in the world, and in so doing, demolishes a range of popular myths: that China has 'gone capitalist,' that it is an imperialist power, that it is a serial human rights abuser. Everyone will benefit from reading this book."

—CARLOS MARTINEZ, co-editor of *Friends of Socialist China* and author of *The East is Still Red: Chinese Socialism in the 21st Century*

"As the drumbeat for war with China is growing, Ferrana has written an incredible book showing why it is China that is the indispensable nation in the world. As Ferrana demonstrates, far from being an inevitable enemy, China is a country which should be courted as a friend and partner in building a better and more equitable world in which sustainable development is offered for all countries, and especially those of the Global South that the West has exploited for so long and is now intent on keeping down. Surely, this book is a much-welcome and much-needed antidote to the endless anti-China rhetoric being pumped out by the White House and regurgitated by the compliant mainstream press."

—DANIEL KOVALIK is a lawyer, educator, author and peace activist

"Kyle has written a beautiful book. In a time when we are bombarded with lies and propaganda, he offers us an exploration into China. Our efforts at China Is Not Our Enemy are for all of us to see each other in ways that lead to cooperation, appreciation and working together for a vibrant future for all. I felt at the core of Kyle's book is this offering; a pathway to peace."

—JODIE EVANS, co-founder CODEPINK and China Is Not Our Enemy

"Kyle Ferrana has done important work in this brilliant book. The scope of the work is ambitious; it analyzes the history of the evolution of imperialism, while convincingly showing how China is creating the conditions for a new world-system, one in which the Global South can finally reverse centuries of underdevelopment. Through careful and thorough research, Ferrana provides a useful corrective to the myth that China abandoned socialism. This book offers a much-needed update to historical-materialist theory of imperialism for the 21st century."

—BENJAMIN NORTON, founder and editor-in-chief
of *Geopolitical Economy Report*

"Emulating noted French sociologist Emmanuel Todd's rigor in relying on core data rather than ideology, Kyle Ferrana's *Why the World Needs China* thoroughly debunks Washington's trope that China is likely to initiate a conflict as unsubstantiated, as such leaving one to wonder whether U.S. elites aren't simply projecting onto Beijing their own pro-clivities to engage in warfare."

—ARNAUD DEVELAY, International Attorney at Law

WHY THE WORLD NEEDS CHINA

Development, Environmentalism, Conflict Resolution & Common Prosperity

KYLE FERRANA

Clarity Press, Inc.

ISBN: 978-1-949762-87-7
EBOOK ISBN: 978-1-949762-88-4

In-house editor: Diana G. Collier
Book design: Becky Luening

Library of Congress Control Number: 202493282

Clarity Press, Inc.
2625 Piedmont Rd. NE, Ste. 56
Atlanta, GA 30324, USA
https://www.claritypress.com

Table of Contents

Acronyms

AEI	American Enterprise Institute
AFRICOM	United States Africa Command
AFU	Armed Forces of Ukraine
ASPI	Australian Strategic Policy Institute
BBC	British Broadcasting Corporation
BJP	Bharatiya Janata Party
BOJ	Bank of Japan
BRI	Belt and Road Initiative
BRICS	Brazil, Russia, India, China, and South Africa
CBP	Customs and Border Protection
CEE	Central and Eastern Europe
CGTN	China Global Television Network
CIA	Central Intelligence Agency
CPC	Communist Party of China
CPN-M	Communist Party of Nepal (Maoist)
CSIS	Center for Strategic and International Studies
CSTO	Collective Security Treaty Organization
CSY	China Statistical Yearbook
DPRK	Democratic People's Republic of Korea
DRC	Democratic Republic of the Congo
Eximbank	Export-Import Bank
EU	European Union
FBI	Federal Bureau of Investigation
FDI	Foreign direct investment
GDP	Gross domestic product
GNP	Gross national product
GPCR	Great Proletarian Cultural Revolution
GWOT	Global War on Terror
HIPC	Heavily Indebted Poor Country
IMF	International Monetary Fund
IPO	Initial public offering
ISIS	Islamic State in Iraq and Syria

JSP	Japan Socialist Party
LDP	Liberal Democratic Party
MAS	Movimiento al Socialismo (Bolivia)
MRG	Minority Rights Group International
NATO	North Atlantic Treaty Organization
NED	National Endowment for Democracy
NGO	Non-governmental organization
NPR	National Public Radio
OAS	Organization of American States
OECD	Organization for Economic Co-operation and Development
PBS	Public Broadcasting Service
PDVSA	Petróleos de Venezuela, S.A.
PFLP	Popular Front for the Liberation of Palestine
PPP	Purchasing power parity
PRC	People's Republic of China
PSUV	United Socialist Party of Venezuela
RMB	Renminbi
SDR	Special drawing right
SRV	Socialist Republic of Vietnam
TAR	Tibet Autonomous Region
TNC	Trans-national corporation
TSMC	Taiwan Semiconductor Manufacturing Company Limited
UK	United Kingdom
UN	United Nations
UNCTAD	United Nations Conference on Trade and Development
UNICEF	United Nations Children's Fund
U.S.	United States
USAID	United States Agency for International Development
USD	United States Dollar
USSR	Union of Soviet Socialist Republics
UWSA	United Wa State Army
WST	World-Systems Theory
WTO	World Trade Organization
XUAR	Xinjiang Uyghur Autonomous Region

The Prius and the Frog

"There is no alternative."
—Margaret Thatcher, 1980[1]

*"Profound changes are afoot in the international
economic structure."*
—Xi Jinping, 2016[2]

At the turn of the twenty-first century, the first model of the Toyota Prius, the world's first mass-market hybrid-electric vehicle, was produced to much acclaim. Many in the United States bought the first Prius, yet in the following decades, the U.S. auto market was painfully slow in converting to electric; electric vehicles (EVs) of any kind remained at 1% or less of total vehicle sales until 2018. By 2021, sales rose to 5% of total—or about half a million new electric cars—a modest but significant step toward reducing the vast quantities of greenhouse gas emissions produced by transport in a country with one of the highest rates of automobile use in the world. There are, at the time of this writing, almost three hundred million motor vehicles in the U.S., or slightly less than one for each person.

The only country with a larger motor vehicle fleet, in fact, is China. In the year 2000, there were only about four million cars in China—one for every three hundred people[3]—but twenty years later, Chinese automobiles outnumbered those in the U.S., rising (given China's much larger human population) to about one for every four or five people. Chinese drivers were similarly slow to switch to electric; as late as 2014, for example, CNN reported that they were in fact "hesitant to adopt electric cars," buying only 7,000 such vehicles in the first quarter of the year.[4] The

---

1 A campaign slogan of the United Kingdom's Conservative Party, which has since become iconic as a justification and rationalization for neoliberal policy throughout the world.

2 Xi Jinping, *The Governance of China Vol. 2* (Shanghai Press, 2018), 276.

3 Tania Branigan, "China and Cars: A Love Story," *The Guardian,* December 14, 2012.

4 Zoe Li, "Chinese Drivers Hesitant to Adopt Electric Cars."CNN, April 14, 2014.

International Energy Agency reported EVs to account for no more than 1% of sales in China through 2016.

In the following six years, however, China's sales of electric vehicles were anything but modest. Its EV sales leaped to over three million—16% of total sales—in 2021,[5] and in the fall of 2022, was set to again nearly double at a projected *six million* new EVs that year, more than the rest of the world combined.[6] The cause of this dramatic shift lay not in any random vicissitude of the market; the country's skyrocketing EV industry, according to an analysis from the Paulson Institute in Chicago, had grown from scratch to become the world leader within a single decade due to a combination of "pilot programs, subsidies, government procurement, and some form of nontariff barriers."[7]

This demonstrates how, relatively speaking, the domestic policy of the People's Republic of China can and does turn on a dime. By now we are all acquainted with China's biggest problems; but even while being widely excoriated in the West for deficiencies both real and imagined, the Chinese government has become a remarkably efficient problem-solver. No matter how quickly you obtain them, specific descriptions of Chinese society will already be woefully obsolete by the time you begin reading. Where China is concerned, within virtually any milieu or level of education, the average Westerner—whether a loyal viewer of CNN or Fox News, a subscriber to *Le Monde* or the *Washington Post*, a stream-watcher or podcast-listener, a reader of supermarket tabloids, or a curator of social media feeds—is hopelessly stuck in the present. Even the most neutral treatments offer little more than a snapshot of a rapidly changing domestic and geopolitical environment.

Therefore, to remain as relevant as possible, this book, written in 2022 and 2023, attempts to suggest where China might go, and not simply describe where China is or where China has been. Though intended to be as brief as possible, the first three-quarters of the book still mostly does the latter. In fact, the first quarter barely even mentions China; but unfortunately, this can't be helped. "Men make their own history," said Karl Marx, "but they do not make it as they please; they do not make it under self-selected circumstances, but under circumstances

---

5 International Energy Agency, "Electric Car Registrations and Sales Share in China, United States, Europe and Other Regions, 2016–2021," May 23, 2022.

6 Daisuke Wakabayashi and Claire Fu, "For China's Auto Market, Electric Isn't the Future. It's the Present," *New York Times,* September 27, 2022.

7 Ilaria Mazzocco, "Electrifying: How China Built an EV Industry in a Decade," *MacroPolo,* July 8, 2020.

existing already, given and transmitted from the past."[8] Today we live in a world as interconnected as it is unequal and one more interdependent than any of our ancestors could imagine—a world-system, according to economic historian Dr. Immanuel Wallerstein and his school of thought. The capitalist world-system is not the sum of international law and multilateral institutions such as the United Nations and the World Trade Organization—institutions that the PRC has scrupulously respected—but the complex network of predatory trade relations and the global division of labor that has served to enrich the West at the expense of everyone else for centuries. Like every other country, the PRC is only comprehensible in relation to this world-system; and that relation can't be understood without accurately understanding the nature of the world-system, which can't be understood without accurately understanding its history.

Chapters One through Five introduce and explain the concept of super-imperialism—the latest, and most profitable system of exploitation that has yet been put into practice. In terms of economic policy, it is better known as neoliberalism, the ideology and practice of which UK Prime Minister Margaret Thatcher infamously sought to justify in the quote that begins this introduction. The super-empire, which currently consists of the United States and its junior partners in Europe and elsewhere, presently extracts enormous quantities of wealth from the rest of the world every year. It relies on four distinct mechanisms of control: 1) structural adjustments, 2) economic isolation, 3) military intervention, and 4) soft power. These are the supreme instruments of Western hegemony; as long as they can be exercised with impunity, the world-system cannot be changed.

Chapters Six through Ten consist of a thorough analysis of Chinese class society and economic life in the twenty-first century, ranging from the PRC's international relations and the Belt and Road Initiative, to the new campaign of wealth redistribution known as Common Prosperity, to the status and treatment of ethnic minorities in China's rural provinces. This part aims to explain why the PRC does what it does, how the Communist Party functions and has retained its legitimacy, and most of all what distinguishes China from other countries at every level in the world-system and why it is uniquely situated to facilitate a fundamental change to this system.

As these analyses will show, the PRC does not seek hegemony or the exploitation of others; yet increasingly, even if against its will, it must contend with the hostile and belligerent super-empire, which will

---

8 Karl Marx, *The Eighteenth Brumaire of Louis Bonaparte* (1913), Chapter I.

not quietly abandon its plunder of the world to make way for the PRC's vision of peace and shared prosperity. Chapters Eleven and Twelve are therefore an evaluation of this conflict. Predictions of the future are not easy, and should not be made lightly, or perhaps at all; but the price of not trying may be too high. Though China has grown stronger than ever and is now more independent than it has been in many generations, it is far from invincible, and there remain formidable forces that it must confront.

Escape from a world-system is not possible, since by definition it encompasses the world we must all live in. A new world-system—which may or may not retain the same institutions but does not include the hegemony and exploitation inherent to the current one—must instead be constructed to supersede it. The question of how this might be accomplished has plagued thinkers and revolutionaries for decades. We desperately need a working theory of change, which can only be built if we gain the proper perspective. That's what this book is for.

These are dangerous days. At the time of this writing, the wars in Ukraine and Palestine continue to escalate, and the world's two greatest nuclear powers grow ever closer to open conflict with one another. Tension between the world's economic titans—the U.S. and the PRC—is likewise increasing. The destruction of all human civilization in the near future has not been so likely for generations, whether through a nuclear conflict or through the slower burn of climate catastrophe; it may be likelier now than ever. According to the Western fable, we are all frogs in a pot, heedless that it is gradually coming to a boil.

But there's another frog-related fable they tell in the East. As the story goes, there was once a frog who lived at the bottom of a well. One day, he looked up and saw a sea turtle walking by overhead; the frog called out to the turtle, saying, "Won't you join me inside this well? The water is deep and the mud is comfortable. There is no finer place to live."

A frog at the bottom of a well cannot imagine the sea.

A Note on Sources, Statistics, and the First Rule of Reading Propaganda

It's customary for criticism to target an author's sources. Are they biased? Are they reliable? Are they propaganda? If they're secondary sources, are *their* sources trustworthy? Says who?

Those are all good questions. You might have them too.

"Just because you're paranoid doesn't mean they're not out to get you," goes the proverb. Similarly, just because it's propaganda doesn't mean it isn't true. In fact, some of the *most* effective propaganda is composed entirely or almost entirely of the truth! Crudely inventing a lie from whole cloth is rare in the propaganda racket because it seldom *convinces*. Propaganda is merely information, factual or not, that is deployed to further a political goal. There's no sense in lying if the truth will do; if a propagandist happens to have it on their side, the truth is the very best weapon in their arsenal.

So, it makes little sense to entirely disregard propaganda just because it is propaganda. If you do so, you'll never learn anything at all. "Seek truth from facts," advises the famous Chinese idiom—not least because facts are almost never told to us by someone (or some organization) with no agenda whatsoever.

How to sift truth out of propaganda? This rule of reading propaganda is the first because it's such a no-brainer: *if they admit it, it's probably true.*

If the head of the Strategic Air Command of the U.S. Air Force, for example, says that bombers under his command killed one million Korean civilians, we can safely assume that most likely, they did in fact kill at least that many. If a Turkish military strategy think tank estimates the current strength of the Kurdish nationalist insurgency at 50,000 fighters, one might be reasonably certain that there are in fact at least that many. On the other hand, if a top official of the anti-communist "Tibetan government in exile" publicly remarks that the number of Tibetans leaving China each year has declined, then we can be sure that Tibetan migration out of China has declined. In other words, failure, wrongdoing, or other information that is *contrary* to the established national or class interest of the organization producing or publishing it is more likely to be factual, while information that aligns with such interests is more likely to be fabricated.

Institutional bias in press organizations is generally not difficult to establish. In the case of the PRC, it's no secret that *Xinhua* and the *People's Daily* are organs of the Chinese government and the Communist Party, just as media like *Voice of America* and *Radio Free Asia* are instruments of the United States Congress, being funded and controlled by the U.S. Agency for Global Media. Though more neutral sources are preferred, and used wherever possible, in the course of this book's examination of domestic Chinese affairs, *both* governments' media will be used as sources of information—not just to glean truthful admissions using this heuristic, but to derive insight into the agenda and intent of each. (For example, the heavy censorship in the Chinese press of news regarding domestic terrorism, described at length in Chapter Eight, is a useful clue to the intent of the government's policy.)

There are of course limits to the first rule, which—as an investigation becomes more detailed and the subject matter more politicized, as any and all news regarding China now is in the West—become more obvious. No society, much less one of over one billion people, can be judged according to a handful of subjective anecdotes; any remotely accurate evaluation of the character and trajectory of Chinese policy must make use of systematically-gathered data—polls, scientific studies, statistics, &c., and there is a serious dearth of such data from Western or international sources. In each case, this book makes as much use of Western sources as possible; the anthropological studies of rural Tibet undertaken by Melvyn Goldstein and Cynthia Beall deserve special mention, as does the long-term polling of Chinese public opinion by the Harvard Kennedy School. Western academia, however, does not and certainly cannot be expected to operate as some kind of shadow Chinese census bureau. For obvious reasons, most studies of Chinese society are performed by Chinese academics from Chinese universities; and for information such as per capita income in the Chinese countryside,[9] data collected by the government must be used, usually in the form of regularly published statistical yearbooks.

How accurate are these? The quality of government census data must certainly vary from country to country, and perfect accuracy cannot be expected from any of them, but outright intentional fabrication is rare. Even the cruelest and most deceitful government needs accurate statistics at the highest level, for it must use them to tailor its own policies, whether oppressive and corrupt or not. It is far from unheard of for unscrupulous bureaucrats to doctor data they are responsible for reporting, but in doing so they runs the risk of the real data being leaked; the higher the level of government and the more officials involved in such a conspiracy, the more likely their deception is to be discovered.

Vladimir Lenin, who in the nineteenth century wrote extensively on the development of capitalism among Russian farmers, made enthusiastic use of what he called the "admirable material" provided by the Moscow Zemstvo,[10] an organ of the same Tsarist regime that had exe-

---

9 See Chapter Nine.

10 Vladimir Ilich Lenin, *What the "Friends of the People" Are and How They*

cuted his brother, and which Lenin later overthrew. The present-day Russian Federation—which the Western press considers "authoritarian" and regularly accuses of disinformation and election fraud—does not always produce census data that is positive. In recent years, for the sake of public image, it may have been in the interest of the Federation to lie about the unflattering rise in poverty and decline of real income in the Siberian Federal District, yet such data is available from Rosstat and has been the subject of studies published by Novosibirsk State University. If a government truly wishes to avoid admitting to the world the extent of its country's problems—or anything else unflattering that its official statistics might reveal—the typical recourse is not to fabricate, but to stop publishing a statistic altogether. For example, as of 2023, the Venezuelan Central Bank had not updated its GDP estimates for nearly five years.[11] According to American economist Dr. Michael Hudson with regard to the U.S. in 2003:

> A few years ago I sought to update my breakdown of the balance of payments to update the impact of U.S. military spending and foreign aid. But the Commerce Department's Table 5 from its balance of payments data had been changed in such a way it no longer reveals the extent to which foreign aid generates a transfer of dollars from foreign countries to the United States, as it did in the 1960s and 1970s. I telephoned the statistical division responsible for collecting these statistics and in due course reached the technician responsible for the numbers. "We used to publish that data," he explained, "but some joker published a report showing that the United States actually made money off the countries we were aiding. It caused such a stir that we changed the accounting format so that nobody can embarrass us like that again." I realized that I was the joker who had been responsible for the present-day statistical concealment, and that it would take a Congressional request to get the Commerce and State Departments to replicate the analysis that still was being made public in the years in which I wrote *Super Imperialism*.[12]

Fight the Social-Democrats, Part III (1894).

11 The catastrophic effect of the United States' sanctions on the Venezuelan economy are described in more detail in Chapters Two and Three.

12 Michael Hudson, *Super Imperialism: The Origin and Fundamentals of U.S. World Dominance* (Pluto Press, 2003), xiii.

The numbers printed in the PRC's statistical yearbooks, therefore, are generally very unlikely to be phony. Tangentially, Western institutions have tended to confirm, rather than refute,[13] the dramatic increases in income, infrastructure, and availability of services that western China has seen in the last twenty years, such as how in 2020, the *New York Times* reported on the World Bank's confirmation of the eradication of extreme poverty in the countryside.[14] According to an analysis published by U.S. think tank Center for Strategic and International Studies, unofficial estimates of China's GDP growth by Western banks and multinational institutions have matched the official PRC estimate almost exactly since 2010.[15] Reports going back decades show the remarkable consistency of the PRC's National Bureau of Statistics; the data are real.[16] More specific positive information, such as *Xinhua*'s claim in late 2020 that the last rural village in China had been connected to the country's paved road network,[17] may be viewed with suspicion, but can be accepted on a case-by-case basis—in this particular case, simply due to the fact that such a claim would be remarkably easy to expose, were it a lie. If there still were a village in China served only by dirt roads or footpaths, one of the intrepid satellite jockeys at the Australian Strategic Policy Institute in Canberra would certainly have found it by now.

---

13 But more often, of course, ignore.

14 Keith Bradsher, "Jobs, Houses and Cows: China's Costly Drive to Erase Extreme Poverty," *New York Times,* December 31, 2020.

15 Scott Kennedy and Qin (Maya) Mei, "Measurement Muddle: China's GDP Growth Data and Potential Proxies," *Big Data China,* September 13, 2023.

16 This is not to say there is no bias in their presentation. For example, the yearbooks have long published only total rural *employment*, with the government only measuring the *urban* unemployment rate, thus avoiding mention of the very large number of jobless peasants in Xinjiang in the early and mid-2010s. A rough estimate of rural joblessness, based on other demographic data, is calculated in Appendix D.

17 Xinhua, "Paved Road Links China's 'Last Village' with Outside World," *XinhuaNet,* July 1, 2020.

CHAPTER ONE

Five Stages of Imperialism: The Historical Evolution of Exploitation Thus Far

"Force, fraud, oppression, looting are openly displayed without any attempt at concealment, and it requires an effort to discover within this tangle of political violence and contests of power the stern laws of the economic process."
—Rosa Luxemburg, 1913[18]

"If money, according to Augier, 'comes into the world with a congenital blood-stain on one cheek,' capital comes dripping from head to foot, from every pore, with blood and dirt."
—Karl Marx, 1867[19]

Oppressed people cannot hope to liberate themselves without first identifying the source of their oppression. Since oppressors have no incentive to identify themselves, it therefore falls to others to correctly describe the present nature of oppression and its precise mechanisms of exploitation and control. Only with this understanding can the correct strategy be designed to throw off oppression, elevate the oppressed, and abolish all systems of exploitation once and for all.

The nature of oppression is always changing. Today, in its most organized and dangerous form, it is more complex, more widespread, and more international than ever before. It exacerbates all other forms of oppression and prevents at every turn their abolition. Though few can agree upon the definition, it has a name that everyone knows: imperialism.

The confusion surrounding this term is by design. It is in the interest of the ruling class of any empire to obscure the causes of the cruelty and exploitation that is foundational to its imperialism. If these rulers are to preserve the power and privileges to which they are accustomed, they

---

18 Rosa Luxemburg, *The Accumulation of Capital* (1913), Chapter 31.
19 Karl Marx, *Capital, Vol. 1: A Critique of Political Economy* (1867), Chapter 31, "Genesis of the Industrial Capitalist."

must at all costs prevent their subjects from clearly understanding the means by which their empire is imposed, for their subjects' ignorance and complicity is required to maintain it. Where this class cannot cover up its crimes, it blames others, sometimes its rivals or predecessors, but often its very victims; where it cannot blame others, it produces self-serving rationalizations. In 1883, when the British Empire was at its historical height, English historian John Robert Seeley famously wrote, "We seem, as it were, to have conquered and peopled half the world in a fit of absence of mind."[20] The mass murder and enslavement of millions that England had perpetrated in order to sit atop the world were apparently no more than unfortunate accidents, entirely without guiding hands or any ill intent.

1. Before Capitalism

Empires have existed as distinct centralized political entities for nearly all of recorded history. The Akkadian Empire in ancient Mesopotamia, which existed more than two thousand years before Christ, is widely considered the first; more well-known examples include the Roman Empire and the Macedonian Empire. For thousands of years, empires were created through military conquest of new lands—often, lands controlled by lesser or declining empires—the subjugation of their indigenous inhabitants, and the extortion or outright seizure of their possessions. The labor power of slaves and the loot of conquered lands were customarily taken by force or by the threat of force, a process that is best described as *dispossessive accumulation*. Such spoils are referred to as "super-profits"—wealth that is acquired coercively with the meanest possible compensation (or none at all) to its former owners.[21] Super-profits differ from the ordinary profits

---

20 John Robert Seeley, *The Expansion of England: Two Courses of Lectures* (Boston: Roberts Brothers, 1883), 8.

21 The "previous" or "primitive" accumulation that preceded capitalism was first described as such by eighteenth-century economist Adam Smith. Contemporary economists, who lived in a time in history when African slaves were worked to death on sugar plantations, somehow imagined the capitalists' "previous accumulation" as a peaceful process, in which a select few rose to control capital simply by virtue of working hard, or harder than the rest of the toiling masses from which they first arose. In *Capital, Volume I*, Marx dispels this rosy conception of "so-called primitive accumulation," describing how in reality it amounted to the violent theft of land and labor.

Moreover, "previous" or "primitive" imply that such a process was confined to the past. But neither this theft nor the associated violence ceased even long after capitalism became the dominant mode of production throughout the world. Therefore the concept must be generalized to reflect the fact that it is an ongoing, essential

that are generated by the labor of free domestic workers, which must be purchased with wages determined by market forces.

Who acquired these super-profits? Common soldiers won the plunder of such conquests, yet the wealth was always enjoyed primarily by a feudal or pre-feudal imperial aristocracy; a privileged minority that typically maintained its exclusivity through dynastic inheritance. The scale of their empires could be vast—the Mongolian Empire of the thirteenth century, for example, spanned nearly all of Asia—yet they were usually limited to a contiguous land area within a single continent.

This was the first, pre-capitalist stage of imperialism.

2. The Origin of the Colonies

By the sixteenth century, the capitalist mode of production began to develop, and over the next few centuries would eventually gain primacy in Europe. During this time, the feudal aristocracy still maintained its control, yet the scope of their empires steadily increased as the capitalist class grew stronger. Empires began to span multiple continents; capitalists, who by the nature of their enterprise accumulate and concentrate a surplus of wealth, were able to invest more and more of this surplus into the imperialist endeavor.

"At first," writes Wallerstein, "the Spaniards simply picked up the gold already mined by the Incas and used for ritual."[22] The European empires began to plunder not just the labor and the wealth possessed by its victims, but set up colonies in the conquered lands, harvesting resources through slave labor on cash-crop plantations. These colonial relationships, established so long ago, did not remain static, and nor have they ended; instead, they have continued to evolve throughout history, even to the present day.

This was the second, mercantilist stage of imperialism.

---

feature of not only feudalism and early capitalism, but modern society as well. Rosa Luxemburg, another political theorist in the Marxist tradition, explicitly defined this form of accumulation as such in the twentieth century, and modern Marxist economic geographer David Harvey expanded this concept in the twenty-first century to what he termed "accumulation by dispossession," to mean *any* coercive mechanism that extracts super-profits, past or present, including not only the conquest of land but the privatization of public resources, predatory trade agreements, &c. For the purposes of this book, it will be rendered as "dispossessive accumulation" for brevity.

22 Immanuel Wallerstein, *The Modern World-System I: Capitalist Agriculture and the Origins of the European World-Economy in the Sixteenth Century* (University of California Press, 2011), 170.

3. Colonialism and Inter-Imperialist Rivalry

Soon these empires developed the technological capability to extract raw materials from their colonies on a massive scale, primarily through industrial mining. This involved what is known as the *export of capital*—i.e., investments made by one country in another. Some expenditure was required to build the mines, the equipment, the refineries, &c., and therefore increase the flow of resources back toward the heart of the empire. These resources were then used for the production of commodities, the market trade of which, according to Wallerstein, became "fundamentally determinative" to the fate of these political entities.[23] Empires became truly global, as Britain, France, and other European countries seized and colonized overseas territories on every continent. The new period of history it inaugurated, often referred to as the New Imperialism or the Age of Imperialism, was characterized by quantitatively and qualitatively *greater* exploitation.

The beneficiaries of this new imperial system were the European capitalists, also called the bourgeoisie, who overtook the old feudal aristocracies to become the dominant force of class-based society. However, this class was not united; just as the pre-capitalist empires would war with and conquer each other, the bourgeoisie of Europe were divided by their respective nations, and competed, rather than cooperated, with one another to secure ever more spoils for their own empire.

In 1916, Vladimir Lenin, principal architect of the Bolshevik Revolution, summarized this new stage of imperialism as including five basic features:

1. the concentration of production and capital has developed to such a high stage that it has created monopolies which play a decisive role in economic life;

2. the merging of bank capital with industrial capital, and the creation, on the basis of this "finance capital," of a financial oligarchy;

3. the export of capital[,] as distinguished from the export of commodities[,] acquires exceptional importance;

4. the formation of international monopolist capitalist associations which share the world among themselves, and

---

23 Immanuel Wallerstein, *The Capitalist World-Economy (Studies in Modern Capitalism): Essays by Immanuel Wallerstein* (Cambridge University Press, 1975), 6.

5. the territorial division of the whole world among the biggest capitalist powers is completed.[24]

The iron law of capitalism is that profit must always increase. By locating the motor force of the new mode of imperial exploitation in these perpetually profit-hungry financial institutions, Lenin showed that modern empires were each *driven* to continually expand—and in a world that is finite, once all foreign lands had eventually been conquered, this expansion could only come at the expense of the other empires, leading inevitably to the First and Second World Wars.[25]

This was the third stage of imperialism: the stage of inter-imperialist rivalry.

4. Neocolonialism and the Inter-Imperialist Alliance

Lenin's definition of imperialism as *a special stage* of capitalism remains relevant today, given that the bourgeois financial oligarchy he described is still the dominant exploiter class of modern imperialism. Vast quantities of capital are also still being exported between countries.[26] However, after the end of the Second World War, conflict between empires seriously diminished, and the specific criteria of Lenin's definition became obsolete; most obviously, the fifth feature, which stipulates that the territory of the whole world be divided among the biggest capitalist powers, ceased to apply.[27] The colonies of Britain, France, and of the other capitalist empires gradually gained independence; within decades, colonialism in its traditional form—i.e., non-self-governing territories controlled by foreign governments—was relegated to only a few tiny regions of the world, such as American Samoa or New Caledonia. The prevailing forms of colonialism became either *settler-colonial*—self-governing territories controlled by a class of foreign settlers that have displaced and oppressed

24 Vladimir Ilich Lenin, *Imperialism, the Highest Stage of Capitalism: A Popular Outline* (Moscow: Progress Publishers, 1963), chapter 7.

25 Lenin, *Imperialism*. In the very same chapter within which he presented these five features, Lenin also wrote, "an essential feature of imperialism is the rivalry between several great powers in the striving for hegemony, i.e., for the conquest of territory, not so much directly for themselves as to weaken the adversary and undermine *his* hegemony."

26 Capital exports and their present purpose and condition will be revisited in further detail in Chapter Six.

27 Lenin himself warned against a dogmatic application of this definition beyond its specific historical circumstances; further details in Chapter Six.

the indigenous inhabitants—which today exists in a few countries such as the United States, Canada and Australia,[28] or *neo-colonial*, which remains prevalent throughout Africa, Latin America, and Asia, also collectively known as the Global South. The specific subset of the Global South that is presently dominated by neocolonialism (which is the vast majority) is also called the *periphery*—a geographic area where "the indigenous state is weak, ranging from its nonexistence (that is, a colonial situation) to one with a low degree of autonomy (that is, a neo-colonial situation)."[29]

In 1965, Dr. Kwame Nkrumah, the first prime minister and president of Ghana after its independence eight years earlier, offered his definition of neocolonialism:

> The essence of neo-colonialism is that the State which is subject to it is, in theory, independent and has all the outward trappings of international sovereignty. In reality its economic system and thus its political policy is directed from outside....
>
> The result of neo-colonialism is that foreign capital is used for the exploitation rather than for the development of the less developed parts of the world. Investment under neo-colonialism increases rather than decreases the gap between the rich and the poor countries of the world.[30]

In regard to any countries that resisted this arrangement, Frantz Fanon, famed anti-colonial political philosopher and member of Algeria's National Liberation Front, observed in 1961 that typically,

> ... you may see colonialism withdrawing its capital and its technicians and setting up around the young State the apparatus of economic pressure. The apotheosis of independence is transformed into the curse of independence, and the colonial power through its immense resources of coercion condemns the young nation to regression. In plain words, the colonial power says: "Since you want independence, take it and starve."[31]

---

28 Settler-colonialism and its specific characteristics will be described in Chapter Nine.

29 Wallerstein, *The Modern World-System I*, 349.

30 Kwame Nkrumah, *Neo-Colonialism, the Last Stage of Imperialism* (London: Panaf Books, 1965), ix–x.

31 Frantz Fanon, *The Wretched of the Earth* (New York: Grove Press, 1963), 97.

Why and how neocolonialism came to predominate is not immediately obvious. It is clear from the brutality of direct colonialism why the *victims* struggled to end it; to maintain or increase their rates of resource extraction, the European empires had often waged campaigns of mass extermination in their direct colonies, such as the "Rubber Terror" in the so-called Congo Free State and the genocide of the Herero in German South West Africa (now Namibia). But the ruling class of these empires also had an incentive for its abolition—on *their* terms.

Their total political dominance and the use of chattel slavery meant that empires could often absorb the entirety of colonial super-profits. However, administering a colony, defending it against rival empires, and subduing the insurrections that such oppression caused still represented a formidable expense. The wars and massacres that have since occurred in *neocolonial* Africa—which are often a consequence of imperial finance and economic pressures, as Chapter Two will show—have achieved the similar effect of ensuring that these neocolonies remain weak and exploitable in the long term, yet these are undertaken almost wholly by proxy and for only a fraction of the price. "Significantly," Nkrumah writes, "the neo-colonialist system costs the capitalist powers comparatively little, while enormous and increasing profits are made."[32] Neocolonialism was therefore overall a *more efficient* system of exploitation, serving the interests of the empire to greater degree.[33] Wallerstein agreed:

[southern Asia, the Middle East, and Africa] had to be decolonized in order to mobilize productive potential in a way that had never been achieved in the colonial era. Colonial rule had after all been an *inferior* mode of relationship of core and periphery, one occasioned

---

32 Kwame Nkrumah, *Handbook of Revolutionary Warfare* (New York: International Publishers, 1968), 13.

33 Lenin held a contrary view, referring to neocolonialism (or "semi-colonialism") as being a "middle stage" that finance capital would find less convenient, preferring to colonize directly. Yet the world's largest "semi-colonies" that Lenin referred to were Türkiye, Iran, and China, which shared the distinction of having never *yet* been directly colonized in the capitalist era. (Lenin, *Imperialism*, chapter 6.) The economies of these countries had therefore not yet been fully oriented toward resource extraction and exports—for example, their agriculture might have still produced more food for domestic consumption than cash crops—as had been the case in most of the world by the time of decolonization in the twentieth century. Lenin, Nkrumah, Wallerstein, and Arrighi may therefore all be easily reconciled with each other: neocolonization might maximize super-profits, but likely only after a period of direct colonization.

by the strenuous late-nineteenth century conflict among industrial states but one no longer desirable from the point of view of the new hegemonic power [the United States].[34]

These analyses have since been borne out conclusively by the economic data. In 1991, Professor Giovanni Arrighi modeled the economic performance of the Global South (divided, in his figures, into the specific regions and subregions of Latin America, Africa, the Middle East, South and Southeast Asia, and Indonesia and the Philippines) by measuring their gross national product per capita in proportion to the GNP per capita of the "organic core" of empire (North America, Western Europe, Australia and New Zealand), finding that in all such regions this proportion had decreased substantially since the Second World War.[35] Arrighi concludes that "... after more than thirty years of developmental efforts of all kinds, the gaps that separate the incomes of the East and of the South from those of the West/North are today wider than ever before."[36]

The ruling class of a neocolony, who collaborate with the empire to extract super-profits from their own country, are called *compradors*. Mao Zedong, the founder of the People's Republic of China, described them succinctly as "wholly appendages of the international bourgeoisie, depending upon imperialism for their survival and growth."[37] According to Fanon, Gabriel Léon M'ba, the first prime minister and president of Gabon, reassured Paris with the words, "Gabon is independent, but between Gabon and France nothing has changed; everything goes on as before."[38] Nkrumah elaborates:

In the first place, the rulers of neo-colonial States derive their authority to govern, not from the will of the people, but from the support which they obtain from their neo-colonialist masters. They have therefore little interest in developing education, strengthening the bargaining power of their workers employed by expatriate firms, or indeed of taking any step which would challenge the

---

34 Wallerstein, *The Capitalist World-Economy,* 32.
35 Giovanni Arrighi, "World Income Inequalities and the Future of Socialism," *New Left Review* 1, no. 189 (Sept./Oct. 1991): 10–12.
36 Arrighi, 40.
37 Mao Zedong, *Analysis of the Classes in Chinese Society* (1926).
38 Fanon, *The Wretched of the Earth,* 66–67.

colonial pattern of commerce and industry, which it is the object of neo-colonialism to preserve.[39]

Though compradors are typically bourgeois (i.e., they own capital themselves), they are not the only capitalists of their country. The function of the compradors is to dominate the political and especially the military establishment of their countries, and their true income is a percentage of the super-profits they secure for the imperialists. This income, while only a fraction of the surplus value of the neocolony's production, is essentially a bribe to diminish their drive for economic development, which, in an underdeveloped country, is in the class interest of the bourgeoisie as a whole. The other bourgeois classes of a neocolony (called the petit bourgeoisie and the national bourgeoisie) are distinguished by their relative exclusion from this bargain, which naturally gives rise to their wish to reclaim this *entire* surplus for themselves.

The privileged position of the compradors is therefore at odds with not only the interests of the peasants and workers of their country, but with other strata of their own class. The result is extreme instability, leaving the country prone not only to revolutions and armed insurgencies, but to even more bloody counterrevolutions, coups d'état, and interventions undertaken by the imperial powers, when they place a thumb on the scales to restore their puppets to power. Compradors, as Nkrumah explains, are often expendable:

In the neo-colonialist territories, since the former colonial power has in theory relinquished political control, if the social conditions occasioned by neo-colonialism cause a revolt the local neo-colonialist government can be sacrificed and another equally subservient one substituted in its place.[40]

Thus even where bribery does not suffice, a leader of a neocolonial state—even one democratically elected by a constituency that rejects imperial domination—may also be induced to collaborate with the empire by the threat, explicit or otherwise, that if he fails to govern according to its interests, he will likely be replaced, perhaps violently.[41]

---

39 Nkrumah, *Neo-Colonialism*, xv.
40 Nkrumah, *Neo-Colonialism*, xiv.
41 See the case study of Venezuela in Chapter Two.

Consequently, so long as a neocolony remains small and underdeveloped, escape from domination by the empire is all but impossible—unless, of course, an external force intervenes. Despite its advantages for the imperialists, neocolonialism could not become the dominant mode of exploitation under the inter-imperialist rivalry stage for the reason that as neocolonies, an empire's subjects would always be more vulnerable to conquest by a rival empire.[42] A prerequisite for a neocolonial world order was therefore a fundamentally different attitude of all the major imperial powers toward one another—one of peace and long-term cooperation rather than animosity. This prisoners' dilemma meant the novel phenomenon of persistent cooperation between the world's empires could not come about spontaneously. Instead, it emerged out of *necessity*, in response to the development of socialism.

In 1920, after the victory of the Bolsheviks and establishment of the Russian Soviet Republic, Lenin had also described the *national* dimension of imperialism in a speech to the Second Congress of the Communist International:[43]

The characteristic feature of imperialism consists in the whole world, as we now see, being divided into a large number of oppressed nations and an insignificant number of oppressor nations, the latter possessing colossal wealth and powerful armed forces. The vast majority of the world's population, over a thousand million, perhaps even 1,250 million people, if we take the total population of the world as 1,750 million, in other words, about 70 per cent of the world's population, belong to the oppressed nations, which are either in a state of direct colonial dependence or are semi-colonies, as, for example, Persia, Turkey and China, or else, conquered by

---

42 This contradiction existed throughout the inter-imperialist rivalry stage. Lenin chronicled the hypocrisy of the British imperialists, who would complain of the expense of their colonies even while continuing to expand them:

M. Beer, in an article, "Modern British Imperialism," published in 1898, shows that in 1852, Disraeli, a statesman who was generally inclined towards imperialism, declared: "The colonies are millstones round our necks." But at the end of the nineteenth century the British heroes of the hour were Cecil Rhodes and Joseph Chamberlain, who openly advocated imperialism and applied the imperialist policy in the most cynical manner! (Lenin, *Imperialism,* chapter 6)

43 Jay Tharappel, "Why China's Capital Exports Can Weaken Imperialism," 34.

some big imperialist power, have become greatly dependent on that power by virtue of peace treaties...

The second basic idea in our theses is that, in the present world situation following the imperialist war, reciprocal relations between peoples and the world political system as a whole are determined by the struggle waged by a small group of imperialist nations against the Soviet movement and the Soviet states headed by Soviet Russia. Unless we bear that in mind, we shall not be able to pose a single national or colonial problem correctly, even if it concerns a most outlying part of the world.[44] [45]

The new socialist bloc, being ruled by those representing the interests of the formerly-oppressed classes of workers (also called the proletariat) and peasants, was a potential ally to the many millions in the periphery who desired freedom from their colonial overlords. Traditional colonies, in which the brutality of dispossessive accumulation was more overt and the forces of national liberation were more easily united by the humiliation of foreign occupation, therefore became as vulnerable under the new conditions of imperialism as neocolonies had been under inter-imperialist rivalry, as Fanon describes:

> Strengthened by the unconditional support of the socialist countries, the colonized peoples fling themselves with whatever arms they have against the impregnable citadel of colonialism. If this citadel is invulnerable to knives and naked fists, it is no longer so when we decide to take into account the context of the Cold War.[46]

The European capitalists soon found neocolonialism to be not just the best but also the *only* option to maintain their empires. Those who resisted the new paradigm suffered severe consequences. When the Portuguese

---

44 V. I. Lenin, *Lenin Collected Works*, 213–63.

45 At the time, Lenin's assertion of the nascent socialist country's global importance was still premature; after the First World War, the political monopoly of the Western capitalist class had only *begun* to fracture, which neither precluded further inter-imperialist wars nor precipitated decolonization. However, by the time the Soviet Union emerged from the *Second* World War, it did so as a global superpower and the leader of a new bloc of socialist countries, shattering this monopoly decisively. A more thorough examination of the early Soviet Union's policy and the dynamic between it and the imperialist powers is presented in Chapter Twelve.

46 Fanon, *The Wretched of the Earth*, 79.

capitalist class refused to surrender political control over Angola and Mozambique, for instance, anti-colonial movements in both colonies sought the aid of the socialist bloc and for a time gained independence from both the imperialists and their compradors.

Socialism, therefore, represented a threat to the imperialist system itself. In response, the world's empires ceased to war with one another and were obliged to unite against their common enemy. Inter-imperialist alliances had existed in the past, either for the purposes of cooperating to subdue a victim that was too strong to be defeated by a single empire, or for mutual defense against other such inter-imperialist alliances;[47] yet these coalitions had always been temporary and unstable, liable to shift during peacetime or if a particular participant saw greater profit in switching sides. At stake in the Cold War against the socialist bloc was instead the preservation of the bourgeoisie as the dominant force of class society across the world. Therefore, the new inter-imperialist alliance was stabilized and solidified to a qualitatively different degree.

Nkrumah came to understand and describe this arrangement as "collective imperialism." Being motivated by class self-preservation on an *international* scale, this alliance required a mechanism to bring any errant individual empire into compliance should its actions not benefit the collective whole. Even France, having a large West African neocolonial empire, did not have sole control; instead, according to Nkrumah, it was subject to "a super State which can at times even override the policy wishes of the nominal neo-colonial master."[48] One empire—the United States—had become more powerful than any other, which led it to inhabit this role, but also allowed it to coerce its European (and Japanese) partners into unequal partnerships that they had no choice but to accept. As the hegemon of the imperial alliance, the United States acted to subdue its junior partners on several occasions, most notably during the Suez Crisis of 1956.[49] There, as in elsewhere in the periphery, the U.S. gradually both

---

47 For example, the alliance of France, Britain, and the Ottoman Empire against Russia during the Crimean War, or the Eight-Nation Alliance that defeated the Boxer Rebellion in China.

48 Nkrumah, *Neo-Colonialism*, 20.

49 When France and the United Kingdom invaded Egypt to restore their control over the Suez Canal, the U.S. used its influence with the International Monetary Fund to withhold any financial support and threatened to devalue the pound sterling through the sale of its government bonds, forcing the UK to withdraw its forces. The U.S., of course, intervened not for the sake of Egypt's liberation, but for its own imperial ambitions in the Middle East.

compelled its Western European allies to "decolonize" (i.e. transition to neocolonialism) and replaced them as the primary neocolonial overlord, reaping the greatest share of super-profits.[50] The United States' junior partners in the alliance nevertheless profited tremendously during the postwar era; when Arrighi further divided the "organic core" region of his model into subregions, while North America's GNP per capita remained well above the GNP per capita of the entire alliance throughout the mid-twentieth century, by 1991 Western Europe only lagged behind it by a margin of less than 17%.[51]

This was the fourth stage of imperialism, hereafter referred to as the Cold War stage.

5. Unrivaled Imperialist Unity, or Super-Imperialism

Nkrumah writes further:

The ideal neo-colonialist State would be one which was wholly subservient to neo-colonialist interests but *the existence of the socialist nations makes it impossible to enforce the full rigour of the neo-colonialist system.* [emphasis added] The existence of an alternative system is itself a challenge to the neo-colonialist regime.[52]

By the 1990s, geopolitical conditions had fundamentally changed once again. A socialist bloc no longer existed; the Soviet Union had been dismantled and itself neocolonized, and the People's Republic of China had become integrated into the capitalist world.[53] The Western bourgeoisie no longer faced a serious threat to their dominance of class society, yet their inter-imperialist alliance remained. The North Atlantic Treaty Organization, ostensibly a defensive alliance of Western countries against the Soviet Union, continued to exist after the Soviet Union's demise and even expanded, with the United States becoming an

---

50 In Iran, for example, the CIA organized a coup against Prime Minister Mohammed Mossadegh, who in 1951 had attempted to nationalize Iran's British-owned oil company. Once Mossadegh had been replaced with a comprador government, British Petroleum was restored to only a minority share of ownership, second to a consortium of U.S. oil corporations.

51 Arrighi, "World Income Inequalities and the Future of Socialism," 42–43.

52 Nkrumah, *Neo-Colonialism*, xiv–xv.

53 The details of this integration will be examined more closely in later chapters.

unchallenged superpower, supported by its European allies. Nor did the Western bourgeoisie reclaim their former direct colonies; as shown by Wallerstein and Arrighi's analyses, they had no interest in returning to this less-profitable form of dispossessive accumulation. Instead, facing no significant rivals, they were then free to bring *neocolonialism* to its highest and most exploitative stage, hereafter called super-imperialism.

While Cold War imperialism might best be summarized as global financial capitalist unity in the face of a socialist opposition, super-imperialism is global financial capitalist unity in the *absence* of opposition. "[M]odern neo-colonialism," Nkrumah had said in 1965, "is based upon the control of nominally independent States by giant financial interests. These interests often act through or on behalf of a particular capitalist State, but they are quite capable of acting on their own and forcing those imperialist countries in which they have a dominant interest to follow their lead."[54] During the Cold War, what had begun as an alliance between distinct countries had merged into something else entirely.

Under super-imperialism, the very worst aspects of neocolonialism have manifested all across the world. The Western bourgeoisie have grown even richer while poverty has increased nearly everywhere. According to Nkrumah, balkanization, or the fragmentation of a single country into smaller and weaker ones less able to resist domination by foreign powers, is "the major instrument of neo-colonialism,"[55] and, coinciding with the super-imperialist stage, there has been a profusion of new neocolonies. Since 1990, 34 new countries, together comprising nearly 20% of the world's current total, have been carved out of preexisting countries, most of them from the ruins of the Soviet Union and the Socialist Federal Republic of Yugoslavia.[56] The super-empire, consisting of the United States, its (mostly) Western subordinate countries, and their immense trans-national or multinational corporations, has dominated the periphery for decades with an iron fist.

Since it is the current stage, super-imperialism requires further and closer analysis. A wide variety of modern theorists, both within and outside the Marxist tradition, have recognized that imperialism has entered a qualitatively new stage, among them Bin Yu,[57] Cheng Enfu

---

54 Nkrumah, *Neo-Colonialism*, 22.

55 Nkrumah, *Neo-Colonialism*, 14.

56 Matt Rosenberg, "The World's Newest Countries Since 1990," *ThoughtCo.,* July 10, 2019.

57 Bin Yu, "Neo-Imperialism, the Final Stage of Imperialism," *International Critical Thought* 10, no. 4 (2020): 495–518

and Lu Baolin,[58] who refer to it as neo-imperialism; others refer to it as "unipolarity," the "unipolar world" being dominated by the United States. The term "super-imperialism" itself has also been notably used by Dr. Michael Hudson very similarly to describe the economic exploitation of other countries by the U.S. government. Professor Jiang Shigong, a prominent Chinese political theorist, remarked in 2021:

> It is deceptive and misleading to portray China and the United States as two equal sovereign states, ignoring the three faces of modern Western imperialism, and the fact that the imperial system of the United States is even more complex than the British Empire's ever was. The United States operates an imperial arrangement within its continental territory, followed by a second imperial core in the form of the Five Eyes alliance, followed by a system of vassal states in the guise of allies such as the military domination systems of Europe, East Asia, and the Middle East, operates Latin America as a "backyard," and, of course, it also has control over other supplementary "world-systems" such as the Internet, finance, and trade. Thus, the U.S.-China relationship is better characterized as China, a rising sovereign state, facing the U.S.-dominated world empire or world system. It's not a question of managing a relationship between two sovereign states, but a question of how China faces the U.S.-dominated world empire.[59]

All these conclusions about the nature of super-imperialism are similar, and yet there is a popular belief that it is increasingly unstable and unsustainable. Is this the case? How then will super-imperialism end, or how might it be ended? Any answer must first properly describe its features, its operation, and its quantitative and qualitative differences from previous stages.

---

58 Cheng Enfu and Lu Baolin, "Five Characteristics of Neoimperialism," *Monthly Review* 73, no. 1 (May 2021).

59 Jiang Shigong, "A History of Empire Without Empire," in Sun Feiyang and Nia Frome (eds.), *After Tamerlane: The Global History of Empire Since 1405* (Red Sails, 2021), sec. 5.

CHAPTER TWO

Mechanisms of Super-Imperialism

> *"To be sure, the use of force by one party in a market*
> *transaction in order to improve his price was no invention*
> *of capitalism. Unequal exchange is an ancient practice.*
> *What was remarkable about capitalism as a historical*
> *system was the way in which this unequal exchange could*
> *be hidden; indeed, hidden so well that it is only after five*
> *hundred years of the operation of this mechanism that even*
> *the avowed opponents of the system have begun to unveil it*
> *systematically."*
>
> —Immanuel Wallerstein, 1983[60]

Despite its continued existence for so much of history, imperialism is not a permanent phenomenon. A parasite cannot survive unless its host's efforts to remove it are frustrated; as engines fueled by exploitation, empires must always have a way to continually enforce that exploitation. There are therefore two mutually dependent features of any empire in *any* historical period: the empire must maintain control over its victims, and it strives to benefit at their expense. If it has no ability to coerce victims, it cannot profit from them; and if it does not benefit, then it would lose its incentive to exert control. The distinct methods by which each task is accomplished are outlined below.

The ways in which an empire may accumulate super-profits at its victims' expense are the *mechanisms of exploitation.* In previous stages of imperialism, these were more varied, including the forced labor of chattel slaves, the plunder of commodities by invading armies, and the payment of large war indemnities. Since capitalist finance and the performance of joint-stock corporations are by necessity transparent to the public, their mechanisms of exploitation are difficult for modern empires to fully conceal, and can be quantified by careful observers. For example, colonial state taxation—one such mechanism that primarily existed during the inter-imperialist rivalry stage—accounted for a total overall wealth transfer from India to Britain of about $1.9 trillion between 1765 and

---

60 Immanuel Wallerstein, *Historical Capitalism* (Verso, 1983), 30–31.

1900, according to economists Drs. Utsa and Prabhat Patnaik—which if cumulated at a low interest rate would amount to about $65 trillion in 2020.[61] The neocolonial era, in which empires no longer directly administer their victims, required different mechanisms of exploitation. Today, the majority of the transfer of wealth from the periphery to the core is accomplished through one such mechanism in particular: the unequal exchange underwriting international trade.

Unequal exchange is primarily driven by the vast disparity between the low cost of labor power in the periphery and the high price of commodities in the core. This represents a galactic yearly transfer of wealth. In 1966, economist Samir Amin estimated this transfer at 15% of the gross domestic product (GDP) of peripheral countries. When measured by the disparity between the exchange rate of each country's currency and its currency's purchasing power, this transfer is or has become far greater in the super-imperial era. Professor Gernot Köhler describes this process in the following way:

> When a low-income country (with a structurally distorted currency value . . .) trades with a high-income country, the high-income country gains a quantity of real value which does not show up in any account and the low-income country loses a quantity of real value which does not show up in any account. In colonial times, traders may have exchanged cheap glass beads for valuable ivory. Both sides agreed to the deal. Similarly, a low-income country may make a deal with a high-income country and the deal is balanced in monetary terms at the prevailing exchange rates. However, a quantity of real value has been extracted from the low-income country in this deal which does not show up in any account.

In 1995, shortly after the beginning of the super-imperial stage, Köhler measured this transfer at $1.8 trillion to Organization for Economic Cooperation and Development (OECD) countries (broadly: North America, Australia, Japan, and most of Europe) from non-OECD countries, or 24% of the non-OECD countries' GDP. By 2009, he estimated that the transfer totaled $4 trillion[62] between "Non-Advanced" and

---

61 Utsa Patnaik and Prabhat Patnaik, "The Drain of Wealth: Colonialism before the First World War," *Monthly Review* 72, no. 8 (February 2021). https://monthlyreview.org/2021/02/01/the-drain-of-wealth/

62 Both figures in 2009 dollars; in current (2023) dollars these totals would be

"Advanced" countries as defined by the International Monetary Fund (only a slightly more exclusive grouping than the OECD). As a percentage of the "Non-Advanced" victims' GDP, the total value extracted was similarly about 22.3%.[63]

In 2022, economic anthropologist Professor Jason Hickel and his colleagues criticized Köhler's approach as *under*estimating the scale of the total value transfer. Hickel et al. developed their own more comprehensive method, encompassing not only prices and exchange rates, but value added throughout the supply chain. According to their model, in 1990 the monetary amount that the IMF's "Advanced" countries "drained" from the rest of the world annually was approximately $4.5 trillion, and had increased to $10.8 trillion in 2015.[64] Between those years, they calculated a total transfer value of $242 trillion.[65]

There are multiple different forms of unequal exchange, which require lengthy analysis to properly describe; a simplified summary of one is detailed below, using the well-known example of the Apple iPhone. Another more detailed examination is presented in Appendix A.

It is commonly known that the production of the iPhone (and similar high-tech devices) has been almost entirely outsourced to a wide array of countries—from the mining of raw materials, to refining, to component manufacturing, to assembly, to packaging. By the end of the 2010s, the Apple Corporation reported hundreds of different suppliers for the manufacturing stage alone, which takes place mostly in mainland China, Southeast Asia, Japan, Taiwan, the Republic of Korea, and Vietnam. Over 150 suppliers had primary manufacturing locations in mainland China, while just 32 had any in the United States.[66] This continuing globalization of supply chains has naturally increased the cost of freight (the transport of products and materials from one stage of the supply chain to another), yet has also increased profits, sufficiently so that freight costs are superseded by an even more substantial *decrease* in the cost of production.

---

around $2.5 trillion and $5.7 trillion, respectively.

63 Gernot Köhler, "Estimating Unequal Exchange: Sub-Saharan Africa to China and the World," in Richard F. America (ed.), *Accounting for Colonialism* (Palgrave Macmillan, 2023), 297–315.

64 Both figures in 2010 dollars; in current (2023) dollars these totals would be around $6.2 trillion and $14.9 trillion, respectively.

65 Jason Hickel et al., "Imperialist Appropriation in the World Economy: Drain from the Global South through Unequal Exchange, 1990–2015," *Global Environmental Change* 73 (March 1, 2022).

66 Apple Inc., "Apple Supplier List, Fiscal Year 2020."

The base retail price of a new iPhone 6 upon its launch in September 2014 was $649,[67] which cost Apple an estimated $200 to produce.[68] In the first quarter of 2015, Apple reported a net profit margin of 24%, yielding an approximate net profit of $108 per iPhone sold.[69] Therefore, as a rough estimate, Apple gained $108 of surplus value throughout its supply chain per iPhone. This savings—the quantity by which the iPhone's globalized cost of production undercuts the (hypothetical) cost of production, were its supply chain entirely domestic—is derived from the low cost of labor in the periphery. According to an analysis in 2018 by Merrill, the Bank of America's wealth management division, if 100% of the iPhone's final assembly process were "reshored" to the United States, its retail price would have to increase by 20% to offset incremental labor costs.[70] Indeed, the surplus taken by ordinary wage-labor exploitation is largely *already extracted* by the time Apple must pay its total production costs—each stage of production is typically controlled by other capitalists who deduct a profit for themselves when selling their intermediate product to the next stage—therefore a large part of *Apple's* gigantic profit margin comes from the gross under-compensation of foreign labor. A factory worker in Southeast Asia can be paid far less than a worker in Europe or the United States, even if the labor performed by each is similar, resulting in a cheaper product. In an international market, Apple, along with a small coterie of other multinational technology firms, enjoys the ability to set the prices at which its suppliers sell intermediate components. These suppliers are comparatively too numerous to have any leverage to demand a higher price individually and are dispersed throughout so much of the world that neither can they do so collectively.

---

67 Protalinski, "iPhone Prices from the Original to iPhone X," *VentureBeat,* Sept. 12, 2017.

68 Ben Fox Rubin, "Costing $200 to Make, the iPhone 6 Should Offer Big Profits for Apple," *CNET,* Sept. 23, 2014.

69 Apple's reported net profit for the quarter was $18 billion, or about 24% of its total revenue of $74.6 billion. Unit sales of the iPhone, however, were a record 74.5 million, or approximately $48 billion, if they were sold at the $649 base price for the iPhone 6. This would account for about two-thirds of Apple's total quarterly revenue. (Apple Inc., "Apple Reports Record First Quarter Results.") If the iPhone itself is presumed to have the same margin as Apple's overall margin, this would amount to approximately $108 per iPhone sold, with the remaining $341 being spent on taxes and operating expenses, which presumably includes software, advertising, &c.

70 Tae Kim, "iPhone Prices Would Rise up to 20% If Apple Assembles in US like Trump Wants: Bank of America," *CNBC,* Sept. 10, 2018.

Many other quantitatively less severe mechanisms also exist. For example: the payment of rents in the form of intellectual property royalties (which are overwhelmingly paid to Western countries); transaction fees on remittances from immigrant workers; tax exemptions for Western multinational corporations; the payment of interest on debts. According to World Bank statistics, "Low & middle income countries" taken as a group paid over $1 trillion to service their external debts in 2020.[71] For many peripheral countries, a very large part of these payments, sometimes even a majority, is merely to cover interest,[72] and these debts must be repaid in foreign currency, meaning the debtor country must export goods in order to receive the cash to make payments, a process which is also subject to the unequal exchange described above.

A victim does not willingly and knowingly submit to be exploited, however. The enforcement of unequal exchange requires deception and coercion; equally relevant and necessary for the operation of empire are the *mechanisms of control*, enumerated below. In order, they are 1) structural adjustment, 2) economic isolation, 3) military intervention, and 4) soft power.

1. Structural Adjustment

> *"And ain't no gettin' up and movin' outside /*
> *The Repo Man got clientele worldwide"*
>
> —The Coup, 1994[73]

Ever since the 1980s, structural adjustment lending has been the preferred instrument of the super-empire's financial institutions (the International Monetary Fund and the World Bank, though officially independent international organizations, are disproportionately influenced by the United States),[74] and is the primary method by which the ideology

---

71 World Bank, "Debt service on external debt, total (TDS, current US$) - Lower middle income."

72 For example, during *La Década Perdida* [The Lost Decade] brought on by the super-empire's financial manipulations, the bulk of Mexico's debt service was made up of interest payments. Mohamed A. El-Erian, "VI Mexico's External Debt Policies, 1982–90," in Claudio M. Loser and Eliot Kalter (eds.), *Mexico: The Strategy to Achieve Sustained Economic Growth* (International Monetary Fund, 1992).

73 The Coup, *Repo Man* [song].

74 The World Bank, for example, admits on its website that "[a]s the only World

and practice of neoliberalism are forced upon the rest of the world by the Western bourgeoisie.

What is neoliberalism? Ostensibly, it is the ideology of the "free market," a belief that governments should spend little, regulate private business less, and privatize or eliminate every public service in the name of efficiency, and that the resulting state of affairs would somehow lead to wealth and prosperity. In practice, of course, it is merely the continuation of the dispossessive accumulation process, wherein the working class is robbed of services and subsidies, and wealth and prosperity is reaped by those who already had the most to begin with, at the expense of those who already had the least.

It is also the highest and most ruthless stage of neocolonialism. While working class Westerners suffered tremendously from neoliberal policy, in general, it fell hardest upon the periphery. "In fact," Hudson writes, "these privatizations reflect foreign government obedience to the Washington Consensus. The rhetoric is free enterprise, but the market is to be shaped and defined by bilateral diplomacy with U.S. planners. America would like to mobilize multilateral foreign aid through the IMF and World Bank to continue subsidizing client oligarchies and political parties whose policies serve U.S. interests rather than those of their own nationals."[75]

Starting in 1978, the World Bank repeatedly encouraged Mexico to take on more foreign debt to develop its industry and infrastructure, pre-dicting a large budgetary surplus by 1982. The Mexican government did so,[76] borrowing hundreds of millions from the World Bank and billions more from private banks in the United States and other junior exploiter countries in the West, yet the exact opposite occurred. In 1980, the U.S. Federal Reserve raised interest rates to a punishing record high of 20%, which quickly exhausted Mexico's currency reserves. Once the Mexican

---

Bank Group shareholder that retains veto power over certain changes in the Bank's structure, the United States plays a unique role in influencing and shaping global development priorities." World Bank, "The World Bank In United States." https://www.worldbank.org/en/country/unitedstates/overview)

75 Michael Hudson, *Super Imperialism*, xvi.

76 The Mexican government's decision may not have been due to simple naïveté. A CIA memo declassified by 2023 indicated that José López Portillo, the president of Mexico from 1976 to 1982, had been an informant for the CIA for several years, a relationship which may have influenced this policy. Zedryk Raziel, "Un documento desclasificado revela que el presidente mexicano José López Portillo fue un informante de la CIA" [A declassified document reveals that Mexican President José López Portillo was a CIA informant], *El País,* April 15, 2023.

government was nearly broke, U.S. banks withheld further loans and facilitated nearly $30 billion of capital flight by the Mexican comprador elite. By August of 1982, Mexico was squeezed by a massive $300 million bill with only half that much in its reserves. The IMF then helpfully offered a bailout—provided that Mexico use it to pay off its debt to private banks and implemented the IMF's structural adjustment program, which demanded the devaluation of the peso and the privatization of hundreds of state-owned companies. The Mexican government also nationalized private domestic banks, which was not done to redistribute anything to the people, but to redistribute all the assets—some $6 billion—to its U.S. creditors. By 1987, over $26 billion had been transferred from Mexico to foreign Western banks in *interest payments* alone.[77] Instead of merely acting as a tool to financially stabilize Western countries in a time of crisis (such as the confrontation over the Suez Canal or the 1973 oil embargo), the IMF had become a weapon.[78]

Throughout the 1980s, this weapon was honed in Latin America, where the socialist bloc had relatively little influence. Structural adjustment packages, or "shock therapy," were tested on Bolivia in 1985. What resulted followed a playbook that the IMF has repeated over and over across the world. The Bolivian government was forced to privatize state-owned companies, lay off tens of thousands of government employees, cut spending, and lift price controls. The government cracked down harshly on strikes and imprisoned union leaders. The product of these "reforms" was a financially stable comprador government that further impoverished its people and enriched the West. The same strategy was then used to chip away at the socialist bloc itself by ensnaring Poland and Yugoslavia[79] into the debt trap-IMF-austerity cycle: first enticing a country to take out loans from Western banks, then waiting for (or more often deliberately causing) it to fall into financial difficulties, and finally forcing the cash-strapped victim to submit to structural adjustments in exchange for IMF loans to repay the Western financial oligarchy.

---

77 Over the same time period, the IMF itself actually lost money in the deal—but that was irrelevant, because the IMF's purpose is not to make a profit for itself, but for the financial oligarchy. Rather than interest on loans, the IMF is mostly funded by subscription quotas, which are ultimately paid for with taxes, i.e., with money largely collected from the working classes of its member countries.

78 Éric Toussaint, "The Mexican Debt Crisis and the World Bank," *CADTM,* August 4, 2020.

79 Jeffrey D. Sachs and David Lipton, "How Yugoslavia Can Save Itself," *Washington Post,* December 31, 1989.

Debt owed *by* the United States *to* foreign governments, on the other hand, is of a completely different nature. Hudson writes:

> The stock and bond markets boomed as American banks and other investors moved out of government bonds into higher-yielding corporate bonds and mortgage loans, leaving the lower-yielding Treasury bonds for foreign governments to buy. U.S. companies also began to buy up lucrative foreign businesses. The dollars they spent were turned over to foreign governments, which had little option but to reinvest them in U.S. Treasury obligations at abnormally low interest rates. Foreign demand for these Treasury securities drove up their price, reducing their yields accordingly.[80]

The only thing bilateral debt owed by the U.S. government has in common with the bilateral debt owed by peripheral countries is that they are both in U.S. dollars, the supply of which is ultimately also in the hands of the U.S. government. According to Hudson, *U.S. government* debt represents in fact another aspect of this mechanism of control, wherein other countries are forced to finance U.S. deficit spending, and by extension, their own exploitation.

Financial coercion as a mechanism of control increased dramatically in the socialist bloc's absence. Between 1984 and 1989, the IMF disbursed an average of 4 billion "special drawing rights"[81] per year to its member countries. In an equal length of time after the collapse of the socialist bloc (1990 to 1995), this average doubled to 8.2 billion, and from 1996 to 2001 further increased to 14.6 billion. In 2020, the IMF disbursed a record of nearly 37 billion SDRs.[82] While only some disbursements are considered "structural adjustment facilities" by the IMF, *any* loans may come with varying preconditions that include neoliberal policy changes such as the elimination of price controls, budget austerity in the form of limits on social spending, increasing the "independence" of central banks (i.e. placing victim countries' own financial policy in the hands of the Western oligarchy), focusing industry on resource extraction

---

80 Michael Hudson, *Super Imperialism*, 19.

81 The SDR is not a currency, but an asset issued by the IMF with a value relative to the current values of the world's major currencies. SDRs may only be held by member countries and may be exchanged for currency when needed.

82 International Monetary Fund, "Past IMF Disbursements and Repayments for All Members from May 01, 1984 to July 31, 2022."

and direct exports, &c.[83] A victim country is typically required to begin restructuring before it can even be considered for a loan.[84] Facing no real global competition, let alone resistance, the IMF continued to expand its activity, absorbing the former socialist countries and subjecting them to its relentless austerity as well.

In analyzing data between 1980 and 2014, a study in *Social Science & Medicine* found that the labor "reforms" of IMF structural adjustment programs decreased access to healthcare and increased infant mortality in developing countries throughout the world.[85] A similar study in the *Journal of International Relations and Development* using data from 1986-2016 indicated that structural loan conditions increased poverty rates in a sample of 81 developing countries.[86] Structural adjustments are not only a worldwide driving factor in obscene wealth inequality, the undermining of labor unions, the decline of real wages (despite increases in productivity), and environmental degradation; they have also prevailed in "de-developing" some peripheral countries that had been successful in building the infrastructural, industrial, and—especially—the agricultural capacity needed to resist neocolonial domination. In 1993, Argentina's state-owned railways were privatized; by 2020, according to the president of the Argentine Institute of Railways, 75% of the network remaining in operation was in "regular or poor condition, or has closed or impassable sectors."[87] The removal of farm subsidies led to the collapse of domestic food production and increased dependency on imports in Côte d'Ivoire (due to conditions for structural adjustment loans from the World Bank), The Gambia (through an IMF agreement), and many other countries across

83 For example, all of the IMF's disbursements to Poland between 1990 and 1995, totaling 1 billion SDRs, are listed as "stand-by arrangements" or other standard types rather than "structural adjustment facilities," (International Monetary Fund, "IMF Financial Data Query Tool") yet negotiations nevertheless required comprehensive economic restructuring by the Polish government in exchange for debt relief and new loans. Steven Greenhouse, "Poland Is Granted Large Cut in Debt," *New York Times,* March 16, 1991.

84 Éric Toussaint, *Your Money or Your Life! The Tyranny of Global Finance* (Pluto Press, 1999), 138.

85 Forster et al., "Globalization and Health Equity: The Impact of Structural Adjustment Programs on Developing Countries," *Social Science & Medicine* 267 (December 2020): 112496.

86 Glen Biglaiser and Ronald J. McGauvran, "The effects of IMF loan conditions on poverty in the developing world," *Journal of International Relations and Development* 25 (June 7, 2022): 827.

87 Pablo Martorelli, "Transforming Argentina's railway, driven by a plan for recovery," *Global Railway Review,* June 25, 2020.

the Global South.[88] According to Hudson, as early as the 1945 congressional hearings on the creation of the World Bank, U.S. government officials were primarily concerned with its ability to protect domestic agricultural production and expand the global market for U.S. food exports.[89] In 1987, Thomas Sankara, the president of Burkina Faso, said in an interview why his country refused food aid from the West:

> They have not helped us to develop. They have instead created a beggar mentality. We hold out our hands to receive food. That is not a good thing. Our farmers have stopped producing, because they cannot sell what they produce. The surplus from farmers in other countries is brought in here. We want something else. Those who really want to help us can give us plows, tractors, fertilizer, insecticide, watering cans, drills, dams. That is how we define food aid. Those who come with wheat, millet, corn or milk, they are not helping us. They are fattening us up like you do with geese, stuffing them in order to be able to sell them later. That is not real help.[90] [91]

In former Yugoslavia and across the African continent, structural adjustments proved to be strong catalysts for immensely destructive military conflict. Sudan, for example, which after half a century of British colonial domination had become entirely reliant on cash crop exports, was convinced by Western banks in the 1970s to take out loans to develop its agriculture to produce a food surplus again; when that project encountered difficulties, Sudan could not pay its debt and was compelled to agree to structural adjustment in 1978. The World Bank then offered a rehabilitation plan, not to cultivate food, but to return to cash crops, specifically cotton. With fresh loans provided by the World Bank, private commercial farmers forced smallholding peasants off their land, which they then farmed unsustainably for export crops. Declining

---

88 William G. Moseley, Judith Carney, and Laurence Becker, "Neoliberal Policy, Rural Livelihoods, and Urban Food Security in West Africa: A Comparative Study of The Gambia, Côte d'Ivoire, and Mali" *PNAS* 107, no. 13 (March 25, 2010). https://doi.org/10.1073/pnas.0905717107

89 Michael Hudson, *Super Imperialism*, 185–86.

90 Göran Hugo Olsson (Director), *Concerning Violence: Nine Scenes From the Anti-Imperialistic Self-Defense,* coproduced by Louverture Films (2014).

91 Only months after this interview, President Sankara was overthrown and killed in a coup d'état and replaced by a comprador. His death went uninvestigated for decades. Ruth Maclean, "Who Killed African Icon Thomas Sankara? Trial Opens, 34 Years After His Death," *New York Times,* Oct. 11, 2021.

domestic food production left Sudan in an especially precarious position; a drought in 1983-1984 had disastrous consequences, triggering a famine, mass starvation among the peasantry, and contributed to a new civil war that lasted for decades.[92]

In the twenty-first century, structural adjustments would seem to be less commonly used by the IMF and the World Bank—yet this is only an exercise in rebranding. The same policies and loan conditionalities have continued under different names. Sudan, again unable to pay its debts, was compelled to undergo "reforms" by the IMF *again* in 2021, which entailed devaluing its currency and ending fuel subsidies.[93] [94] Membership in the IMF remains unofficially compulsory—out of 193 countries in the United Nations, 190 are also members of the IMF, making even the victims of the organization participate in their own oppression and the oppression of other countries in the periphery. For such victims, the "bitter pill" of structural adjustments is preferable to the alternative; *leaving* the IMF, as Cuba did in 1964, can bring even worse consequences.

2. Economic Isolation

"If such a policy is adopted, it should be the result of a positive decision which would call forth a line of action which, while as adroit and inconspicuous as possible, makes the greatest inroads in denying money and supplies to Cuba, to decrease monetary and real wages, to bring about hunger, desperation and overthrow of government."

—*Memorandum From the Deputy Assistant Secretary of State for Inter-American Affairs* (Mallory) *to the Assistant Secretary of State for Inter-American Affairs* (Rubottom), April 6, 1960[95]

The IMF has of course encountered considerable resistance in the periphery. In many peripheral countries, anti-imperialist political parties

---

92 John Prendergast, "Blood Money for Sudan: World Bank and IMF to the 'Rescue,'" *Africa Today* 36, no. 3/4 (1989): 44.

93 Nafisa Eltahir, Karin Strohecker, and David Lawder, "Sudan Approved for Debt Relief, \$2.5 Billion Funding by IMF," *Reuters,* June 29, 2021.

94 This reform agreement, and the IMF's more recent versions of structural adjustments, are described in more detail in Chapter Six.

95 U.S. Department of State, "Memorandum From the Deputy Assistant Secretary of State for Inter-American Affairs (Mallory) to the Assistant Secretary of State for Inter-American Affairs (Rubottom)," Washington, April 6, 1960, *Foreign Relations of the United States, Cuba 1958–1960, Vol. VI.*

or aspiring leaders promising to challenge austerity often gain considerable momentum. Where they do come to power, however, they are subjected to an even cruder and harsher mechanism of control: sanctions and trade embargoes, which isolate their countries from the global economy.

Often, even an implicit threat of economic punishment can be enough to force an uncooperative government to turn comprador against its will. The case study of Venezuela during the first decade of the super-imperial era is particularly illustrative.

In the 1970s, Carlos Andrés Pérez and Rafael Caldera each served non-consecutive terms as president,[96] during which their administrations made improvements to Venezuela's development and social welfare. In Caldera's first term, he re-established diplomatic ties with the socialist bloc, granted amnesty to the left-wing guerrillas, legalized the Communist Party, and made considerable investments in public infrastructure. Pérez, who succeeded Caldera in 1974, nationalized oil production and spent billions expanding social welfare and state-owned industry, presiding over the most prosperous (though exceptionally corrupt) period theretofore in Venezuelan history. This prosperity, however, was undone the following decade; on February 18, 1983—known as the *Viernes Negro*, or "Black Friday"—Pérez's successor devalued the bolívar by 70%, destroying the savings, wages, and pensions of the Venezuelan working class overnight.[97]

Both Pérez and Caldera won second terms in 1988 and 1993 respectively, running on explicitly anti-neoliberal platforms and their legacies of abundance and prosperity. Yet only weeks after his victory, Pérez accepted over $2 billion in IMF loans in exchange for the privatization of public utilities and the liberalization (increase) of fuel prices. The Pérez Administration suppressed unrest against these policies with extreme force, killing hundreds.[98] During his own second term, President Caldera

---

96 Despite their successes and relative popularity, neither could serve consecutive terms as president due to Article 184 of the Constitution of the Republic of Venezuela, which stated that no incumbent may run for re-election. (Republic of Venezuela, "Constitution of the Republic of Venezuela," art. 184.)

97 Juan Francisco Alonso, "Qué fue el Viernes Negro y por qué marcó el fin de la 'Venezuela saudita'" [What was Black Friday and why it marked the end of "Saudi Venezuela"], *BBC News Mundo,* February 17, 2023.

98 Contemporary scholars considered the *Caracazo* uprisings of 1989 to be the most massive social revolt against austerity—and the government response to be the most repressive—in Latin American history. [Fernando Coronil and Julie Skurski, "Dismembering and Remembering the Nation: The Semantics of Political Violence in Venezuela," in Jo-Marie Burt and Philip Mauceri (eds.), *Politics In The Andes: Identity, Conflict, Reform* (University of Pittsburgh Press, 2004), 291.] The coup

signed an agreement with the IMF in 1996 to implement even more austerity measures.

From their history, one would guess that neither Caldera nor Pérez had any wish to so blatantly become tools of imperialism. But when confronted with the full power of Western finance, they had little choice. Caldera's successors provide a clear example of the alternative; when President Hugo Chávez followed through with his own anti-austerity platform in 2002 and 2003 by re-nationalizing the oil industry, the United States responded by sanctioning Venezuela in 2004, depriving his government of access to development loans.[99] Over the next two decades, the United States escalated its economic war with Venezuela, with appalling consequences. According to a report written by Venezuelan economist Luis Oliveros and published by the Washington Office on Latin America in 2020, U.S. sanctions deprived Venezuela of between $17 billion and $31 billion in revenue over a period of three years, and reduced imports by approximately 75%;[100] another Washington D.C.-based think tank estimated the sanctions had caused 40,000 excess deaths in only a single year.[101]

After structural adjustments have robbed the neocolonies of the agricultural capability to feed their population, economic isolation can then selectively rob them of the food imports upon which they have grown to depend. The United States government ostensibly crafts its sanctions to exempt humanitarian supplies such as food and medicine; yet in practice, and by design, sanctions cause shortages of both, by reducing access to the money, tools, and raw materials that the victims might have used to buy or produce them. This has been admitted by the authors of the sanctions themselves; a secret U.S. government memorandum from 1960 declared that the goal of the economic embargo on Cuba was "to bring about hunger, desperation and overthrow of government."[102] This memo

---

attempt led by Hugo Chávez in 1992 was largely a reaction to this massacre.

99 "Venezuela Says Sanctions by U.S. Are Part of Anti-Chavez Campaign," *Baltimore Sun,* September 26 (updated September 30), 2021.

100 Luis Oliveros, *Impacto de las Sanciones Financieras y Petroleras sobre la Economia Venezolana* [Impact of Financial and Oil Sanctions on the Venezuelan Economy], WOLA, October 2020.

101 Mark Weisbrot and Jeffrey Sachs, *Economic Sanctions as Collective Punishment: The Case of Venezuela* (Center for Economic and Policy Research, April 2019).

102 U.S. Department of State, "Memorandum From the Deputy Assistant Secretary of State for Inter-American Affairs (Mallory) to the Assistant Secretary of State for Inter-American Affairs (Rubottom)."

was not declassified until 1991—just after the dissolution of the Soviet Union.[103] In its most desperate hour, the Cuban government gave in and requested technical assistance from the IMF in 1993—only for the United States to veto any such assistance, conditional or not.[104]

The use of economic isolation as a weapon has increased tremendously since the collapse of the socialist bloc. In 2000, an analysis published by scholars at the University of Notre Dame called the 1990s "The Sanctions Decade," recording fifty new applications of sanctions, the majority of which were imposed by the United States or the European Union.[105] Through 2022, every successive U.S. administration has issued a higher yearly average of new sanctions designations.[106]

Cuba, and the Democratic People's Republic of Korea, being the last two holdouts of the traditional socialist system, have been subjected to some of the worst and most prolonged policies of economic isolation that the super-empire has ever applied. But while sanctions, embargoes, and blockades have had devastating effects on the people of Cuba, the DPRK, Venezuela, Iran, Iraq, Afghanistan, Yemen, &c., they are seldom able to bring about regime change by themselves. Their primary purpose is to *prevent further development* by depriving the victim country of capital and starving its labor force. If such policies bring about the *conditions* for a successful counterrevolution or coup by U.S.-backed opposition forces within the country, so much the better for their architects; but if not, it is enough that the victims' poverty and starvation serve as an example to others, and to limit the spread of any anti-imperialist ideology that might interfere with the dispossessive accumulation process elsewhere in the periphery.

---

103 Ricardo Alarcón de Quesada, "The Truth About the 'Embargo' on Cuba," *CounterPunch,* October 5, 2006.

104 James M. Boughton, "Will Cuba Rejoin the IMF?" *Project Syndicate,* January 8, 2015.

105 David Cortright and George Lopez, "Sanctions Decade: Assessing UN Strategies in the 1990s," Carnegie Endowment for International Peace, Washington, D.C., April 18, 2020.

106 Simon Kennedy, "Sanctions Statecraft," *Bloomberg,* February 24, 2023.

3. Military Intervention

> *"Our strategy must now refocus on precluding the emergence of any potential future global competitor. But because we no longer face either a global threat or a hostile, non-democratic power dominating a region critical to our interests, we have the opportunity to meet threats at lower levels and lower costs...."*
>
> —Defense Planning Guidance for the Fiscal Years 1994–1999
> (draft document), U.S. Department of Defense, 1992[107]

Karl Kautsky, another Marxist theorist and contemporary of Lenin, predicted on the eve of the First World War that financial monopolies could ultimately merge into a system he called "ultra-imperialism" which would then exploit the world in a unified fashion. This hypothesis strongly resembles what is known of the super-imperialist stage; but the "perils" of Kautsky's ultra-imperialism, he theorized, would "lie in another direction, not in that of the arms race and the threat to world peace."[108] In his famous essay "The End of History?" Professor Francis Fukuyama predicted:

> The developed states of the West do maintain defense establish-ments and in the postwar period have competed vigorously for influence to meet a worldwide communist threat. This behavior has been driven, however, by an external threat from states that possess overtly expansionist ideologies, and would not exist in their absence.[109]

With the collapse of the socialist bloc now several decades in the past, it is clear just how badly these forecasts have missed the mark. Though inter-imperialist wars did cease, the latest stage of imperialism, being both unified and unopposed, instead became even *more* warlike.

Unconstrained by any significant counterbalancing force, the United States no longer needed to rely on proxies such as Cuban exiles (as it had during the Bay of Pigs invasion) or the Nicaraguan Contras to make new conquests. During the 45-year period between the end of the Second

---

107 "Excerpts From Pentagon's Plan: 'Prevent the Re-Emergence of a New Rival.'" *New York Times,* March 8, 1992.

108 Karl Kautsky, "Der Imperialismus" [Ultra-Imperialism], *Die Neue Zeit* (September 1914).

109 Francis Fukuyama, "The End of History?" *The National Interest* No. 16 (Summer 1989): 3–18.

World War and the collapse of the socialist bloc in 1989, the United States military was significantly involved in conflicts in Korea, Vietnam and its immediate neighbors, Lebanon, the Dominican Republic, Grenada, and Libya. With the exception of the Vietnam War, all such conflicts were either relatively short in duration[110]—or conducted cautiously, at the "independent" request of an existing comprador regime. In just the first 25 years after 1989, however, the U.S. military openly intervened in Panama, Somalia, Haiti, Bosnia, Kosovo, Afghanistan, Sudan, Iraq, Yemen, Pakistan, Libya, and Syria. (Panama, the first such victim, was invaded only one month after the opening of the Berlin Wall.) Even in the decade before the "War on Terror" policy further accelerated this process, the U.S. had invaded Iraq in 1991, intervened in Somalia and Haiti, and bombed Sudan, Afghanistan, the former Yugoslavia in multiple wars, and Iraq once again in 1998. By the 2000s, several countries were subjected to prolonged "targeted killing" aerial bombing campaigns, and Afghanistan and Iraq experienced decades of direct military occupation by U.S. forces. As of the Biden Administration, every U.S. president to take office since 1989 has ordered airstrikes on Iraq, and by the 2010s, the U.S. was openly conducting combat operations in seven foreign countries at once.

Occasionally, these attacks were justified by the invitation of comprador regimes, yet more often the victim countries were invaded on whatever pretext the U.S. government found convenient at the time; sometimes, a country was invaded simply for being suspected of developing advanced weapons—weapons of which the United States itself had plenty, but forbade the rest of the world from obtaining. The true reasons, of course, were to maintain and expand the process of dispossessive accumulation in the periphery by toppling anti-imperialist governments that threatened its regional influence (such as Libya's), by defending its compradors from armed uprisings, or by forcibly replacing neocolonial regimes that had grown uncooperative (such as Panama's). On average, before the collapse of the socialist bloc, the United States began one new significant direct military intervention every five years; afterward, this frequency increased to one new significant intervention every two years. A research article published in the *Journal of Conflict Resolution* found that of the almost 400 *total* military interventions of any kind that the United States had ever conducted (based on data from between 1776 and 2019), over 25%

---

110 The Korean War, the second-longest, was (*de facto*) three years long, while the invasions of the Dominican Republic and Grenada lasted only months and days, respectively.

of them had been carried out in the period after the end of the Cold War, i.e. the most recent 12% of its history.[111]

The United States military was transformed from its former role as a global deterrent against the spread of socialism into a global occupying force. Hundreds of thousands of soldiers (mostly stationed in West Germany, just in case the Cold War ever turned hot) were recalled and hundreds of installations were closed, yet U.S. military spending doubled as it increased its reach everywhere else. According to David Vine, a Professor of Political Anthropology at American University, in 1989 the United States maintained military bases in approximately 40 different foreign countries; by 2021, he estimated this number had doubled to 80 different foreign countries.[112] In 2008, AFRICOM, an entirely new strategic command devoted to operations on the African continent, was created.

On the mechanics of enforcing unequal exchange, Wallerstein writes:

> The enormous apparatus of latent force (openly used sporadically in wars and colonization) has not had to be invoked in each separate transaction to ensure that the exchange was unequal. Rather, the apparatus of force came into play only when there were significant challenges to an existing level of unequal exchange. Once the acute political conflict was past, the world's entrepreneurial classes could pretend that the economy was operating solely by considerations of supply and demand, without acknowledging how the world-economy had historically arrived at a particular point of supply and demand, and what structures of force were sustaining at that very moment the 'customary' differentials in levels of wages and of the real quality of life of the world's work-forces.[113]

While military force is the most powerful mechanism of control available to the super-empire, it is wielded at great expense, and even at its highest point of technological advancement can only target a handful of victim countries at once. It must therefore exercise considerable practical expediency in choosing these targets. In 2009, George Friedman, the

---

111 Sidita Kushi and Monica Duffy Toft, "Introducing the Military Intervention Project: A New Dataset on U.S. Military Interventions, 1776–2019," *Journal of Conflict Resolution* 67, no. 4 (2023): 752–779. http://doi.org/10.1177/00220027221117546

112 David Vine, "Lists of U.S. Military Bases Abroad, 1776–2021," American University online resource posted August 4, 2023. https://doi.org/10.17606/7em4-hb13

113 Immanuel Wallerstein, *Historical Capitalism*, 32–33.

founder and chairman of STRATFOR, the U.S. geopolitical think tank that News Corp subsidiary *Barron's* called "the Shadow CIA,"[114] wrote:

The United States had to be prepared for regular and unpredictable interventions throughout the Eurasian landmass. After the fall of the Soviet Union, it did engage in a series of operations designed to maintain the regional balance and block the emergence of a regional power. The first major intervention was in Kuwait, where the United States blocked Iraqi ambitions after the Soviets were dead but not yet buried. The next was in Yugoslavia, with the goal of blocking the emergence of Serbian hegemony over the Balkans. The third series of interventions was in the Islamic world, designed to block al Qaeda's (or anyone else's) desire to create a secure Islamic empire. The interventions in Afghanistan and Iraq were both a part of this effort. ...

Rhetoric aside, *the United States has no overriding interest in peace* [emphasis added] in Eurasia. The United States also has no interest in winning a war outright. As with Vietnam or Korea, *the purpose of these conflicts is simply to block a power or destabilize the region*, [emphasis added] not to impose order. In due course, even outright American defeat is acceptable. However, the principle of using minimum force, when absolutely necessary, to maintain the Eurasian balance of power is—and will remain—the driving force of U.S. foreign policy throughout the twenty-first century. There will be numerous Kosovos and Iraqs in unanticipated places at unexpected times. U.S. actions will appear irrational, and would be if the primary goal is to stabilize the Balkans or the Middle East. But since the primary goal will more likely be simply to block or destabilize Serbia or al Qaeda, the interventions will be quite rational. They will never appear to really yield anything nearing a "solution," and will always be done with insufficient force to be decisive.[115]

---

114 Jonathan R. Laing, "The Shadow CIA," *Barron's*, October 15, 2001.

115 George Friedman, *The Next 100 Years: A Forecast for the 21st Century* (Doubleday, 2009), 45–46.

4. Soft Power

> *"By vote, the Amana abandoned the system of living together and moved in stride to the system of free enterprise that surrounded them. Church and state were separated.... Amana eventually chose the dominant values of the United States because it was too weak, politically, economically and culturally, to overcome modern capitalism, which was stronger than it in every way."*
>
> —Wang Huning, *America Against America*, 1991[116]

The fourth and final mechanism of control involves counterrevolution. Though one of the most crucial tools in the super-empire's arsenal, it is also the most obscure and least apparent, and therefore requires closer examination.

In his 1997 book *Blackshirts and Reds: Rational Fascism and the Overthrow of Communism*, Dr. Michael Parenti lays bare the inadequacies of the socialist system practiced within the Eastern Bloc countries that "seemed to inhere in the system itself":

... People complained about broken toilets, leaky roofs, rude salespeople, poor quality goods, late trains, deficient hospital services, and corrupt and unresponsive bureaucrats ...

... If fired, an individual had a constitutional guarantee to another job and seldom had any difficulty finding one. The labor market was a seller's market. Workers did not fear losing their jobs but managers feared losing their best workers and sometimes overpaid them to prevent them from leaving. Too often, however, neither monetary rewards nor employment itself were linked to performance. The dedicated employee usually earned no more than the irresponsible one. The slackers and pilferers had a demoralizing effect on those who wanted to work in earnest ...

... With rigorous price controls, there was hidden inflation, a large black market, and long shopping lines ...

... There was strong resentment concerning consumer scarcities: the endless shopping lines, the ten-year wait for a new automobile, the housing shortage that compelled single people to live at home

---

116 Wang Huning, *America Against America* (2022), 28–29.

or get married in order to qualify for an apartment of their own, and the five-year wait for that apartment. The crowding and financial dependency on parents often led to early divorce.[117]

Parenti argues that despite the success of socialism in guaranteeing employment and satisfying the people's basic material needs such as housing, healthcare, and food security, the often-low quality of products and services created widespread disillusionment. By the 1980s, the sharp contrast between the socialist system and the privation that had preceded it were quickly fading from public consciousness. He concludes:

> The human capacity for discontent should not be underestimated. People cannot live on the social wage alone. Once our needs are satisfied, then our wants tend to escalate, and our wants become our needs. A rise in living standards often incites a still greater rise in expectations. As people are treated better, they want more of the good things and are not necessarily grateful for what they already have. Leading professionals who had attained relatively good living standards wanted to dress better, travel abroad, and enjoy the more abundant life styles available to people of means in the capitalist world.[118]

The term "color revolution" in popular parlance is mostly synonymous with the protest movements that brought about the collapse of the Eastern Bloc. Among Marxists, it is more commonly used to describe any such movement that is not in the interests of the working class. Yet in the revolutions of 1989, just as in other color revolutions that have taken place all across the world since then, it should not be forgotten that these movements could not exist in the absence of significant material grievances among the proletariat. To what extent Western imperialism and its economic siege weapons of sanctions and debt helped to create these conditions should of course be the topic of careful study, but hundreds of thousands of people do not assemble in protest in the streets of major urban centers for weeks, as they did all across the socialist bloc, if all is well with their lives. Nor could they achieve such numbers were they not composed strongly of urban proletarians.

---

117 Michael Parenti, *Blackshirts and Reds: Rational Fascism and the Overthrow of Communism* (City Lights, 1997), 62–65.

118 Michael Parenti, *Blackshirts and Reds,* 65–66.

What then distinguishes a color revolution, or counterrevolution, from a progressive revolution?

The first, most relevant question is which organizations are playing the greatest role in the direction and development of the revolution. A movement composed of and influenced by organized workers' collectives might create dual power structures, as did the Iranian Revolution, the Bolivarian Revolution, or the February Revolution in the Russian Empire in 1917. For an uprising against a bourgeois or colonial government to seize state power for the proletariat, the leadership or at least the participation of a communist vanguard is required, often in the form of an established Marxist-Leninist party or similar revolutionary organization, such as the Bolshevik Party in the October Revolution, or the National Liberation Front of South Vietnam. The degree of support a revolution receives from external forces is not only a major factor in its success or failure but may help indicate the character of the new system it inaugurates—not only by the benefactor's choice of a client most likely to become an ally, but by the material incentive of a client to adopt its benefactor's ideology. Fidel Castro, for example, did not profess his Marxist-Leninism until the Soviet Union and the People's Republic of China had extended their aid and friendship to his revolutionary government in Cuba.

On the other hand, a revolution led or exclusively aided by Western non-governmental organizations (NGOs), or funded by the governments of the super-empire, is most likely to be or become a reflection of very different values.

Solidarność, the "independent" trade union that played a critical role in ending socialism in Poland and whose leader Lech Wałęsa became president in 1990, had been funded by over $30 million from the CIA and other U.S. government agencies.[119] In *Time* magazine in 2001, journalist Carl Bernstein wrote that Solidarność had been chosen as a weapon to destroy socialism in Poland by a secret alliance between U.S. President Ronald Reagan and Pope John Paul II. Together, the U.S. government and the Vatican conspired to smuggle "[t]ons of equipment—fax machines (the first in Poland), printing presses, transmitters, telephones, shortwave radios, video cameras, photocopiers, telex machines, computers, word processors" to Solidarność to disseminate propaganda, and provided "strategic advice" to the organization that "reflected the thinking of the Vatican and the Reagan Administration."[120]

---

119 Carl Bernstein, "The Holy Alliance," *TIME,* February 24, 1992.
120 Carl Bernstein, "The Holy Alliance."

The propaganda that cost the U.S. government a fortune to saturate the Eastern Bloc with sometimes proved decisive. A small group of anticommunist intellectuals known as Charter 77[121] had an outsized influence in the weeks-long "Velvet Revolution" that resulted in the end of socialism in Czechoslovakia. The revolution began with a demonstration on International Students' Day,[122] and was inflamed when members of Charter 77 supplied Radio Free Europe with a news story of a student's alleged death during the protest. In fact, not only had no one died in the protest, but the student in question, "Martin Šmíd," was entirely fictitious. Without attempting confirmation, Radio Free Europe (a media organization created by the CIA and funded by the United States Congress) immediately propagated the fake story throughout the country, generating outrage among the population.[123] Václav Havel, a wealthy playwright from a bourgeois family and a signatory of Charter 77, became the first president of post-socialist Czechoslovakia, and other members of the group were elevated to key positions in the government.

Overall, the revolutions that destroyed the majority of the socialist bloc were financed with many millions of dollars from not just the CIA and other appendages of the U.S. government, but from Western capitalists' private "philanthropic" organizations. In fact, as the socialist bloc fractured, it became less important for the United States to keep its undermining of foreign governments secret. In 1991, just a month after Boris Yeltsin's administration survived the Soviet military leadership's last-gasp attempt to preserve the Soviet Union by means of a coup, a co-founder of the National Endowment for Democracy blithely told the *Washington Post* that "A lot of what we do today was done covertly 25 years ago by the CIA."[124]

Indeed, the NED is a private but not very secretive entity—which just happens to be funded by the U.S. government, a detail that its operators today would have you believe has no effect on the nature of its activities.[125] Yet these very operators and staff "experts" are largely drawn from

---

121 An organization named for, and formed from, the signatories of a dissident manifesto.

122 November 17, 1989.

123 Victor Sebestyen, "The Accidental Uprising: How 'corpse' Killed Communism," *The Independent,* November 22, 2009.

124 David Ignatius, "Innocence Abroad: The New World of Spyless Coups," *Washington Post,* September 21, 1991.

125 According to the NED's website, it receives an annual appropriation from Congress, and its "continued funding is dependent on the continued support of the

former U.S. government officials. On its website, the NED lists among its team President George W. Bush's chief of staff,[126] the Director of the Information Security Oversight Office,[127] members[128] and multiple Senior Directors of the National Security Council,[129,130] a U.S. ambassador and Director of the U.S. government-funded Wilson Center,[131] former[132] and sitting members of U.S. Congress,[133,134,135] and members of the U.S. State Department.[136] Some of its more infamous experts include (or included) Cold War-era National Security Advisors Henry Kissinger[137] and Zbigniew Brzezinski,[138] and former U.S. Secretary of State Madeleine Albright.[139] Members of the NED's staff and Board of Directors who were *not* members of Congress or previously employed at the highest levels of the U.S. government are typically wealthy capitalists, or else drawn from the vast Beltway ecosystem of think tanks, lobbyists, and government consultants that are so interconnected with the political establishment that it is often difficult to determine where they end and the government begins.

Naturally, the "democratic" forces that the NED supports line up with the United States' imperial interests again and again. During the 1980s, it funded free-market organizations, dissident groups, and propaganda

---

White House and Congress" (National Endowment for Democracy, "Frequently Asked Questions"). Moreover, it admits that "NED is answerable to a wide array of overseers in both the Executive and Legislative Branches" and "frequently consults with relevant policy makers about its work" (National Endowment for Democracy, "History.").

126 National Endowment for Democracy, "Andrew H. Card, Jr. (Chairman 2018-January 2021)."

127 National Endowment for Democracy, "National Endowment for Democracy Names Edmung M. Glabus Chief Operating Officer," March 26, 2019.

128 National Endowment for Democracy, "Dr. Nadia Schadlow."

129 National Endowment for Democracy, "Damon Wilson."

130 National Endowment for Democracy, "Elliott Abrams."

131 National Endowment for Democracy, "Ambassador Robert H. Tuttle (Treasurer)."

132 National Endowment for Democracy, "The Honorable Peter Roskam (Vice Chairman)."

133 National Endowment for Democracy, "The Honorable Karen Bass (Vice Chairman)."

134 National Endowment for Democracy, "The Honorable Ileana Ros-Lehtinen."

135 National Endowment for Democracy, "David E. Skaggs (Vice Chairman)."

136 National Endowment for Democracy, "Dr. Michele Dunne (Secretary)."

137 National Endowment for Democracy, "Henry Kissinger."

138 National Endowment for Democracy, "Zbigniew Brzezinski."

139 National Endowment for Democracy, "Madeleine Albright."

publications in Czechoslovakia, Poland, Hungary, Bulgaria, and Romania as well as the Soviet Union.[140] "Pro-democracy" organizations in Cuba and Venezuela—the two Latin American countries who have most consistently opposed the United States over the last twenty years—are also now some of the largest recipients of NED cash in the region. The opposition protests that established a veneer of legitimacy for the 2002 coup attempt on Chávez were led by organizations that had received nearly $1 million in NED funding the previous year,[141] and in 2010, an NED-funded think tank disclosed that over $40 million was being spent annually on "civil society actors" in Venezuela by the external "donor community."[142] In Haiti, student protests and a three-week armed rebellion against President Jean-Bertrand Aristide in 2004—that provided the justification for the United States to intervene and remove him from power—were guided and agitated by organizations such as Convergence Démocratique and the Group of 184, both of which were funded by the NED[143] and its intermediary, the International Republican Institute.[144] In the 1980s the NED spent nearly $16 million to undermine the Sandinista government in Nicaragua, and between 2014 and 2018 spent a further $4 million on 54 different organizations to "[lay] the groundwork for insurrection" according to its own associated media organization, Global Americans.[145]

Nor are the oppositional forces supported by the NED democratic in any sense. Multiple studies of the NED's and other U.S. government-controlled soft-power organizations' activities have yielded no positive correlation between them and the levels of democracy or human rights—however measured—within the countries so targeted. For example, a data regression analysis of all NED activity between 1990 and 1999 published in the *Democratization* journal found that "NED aid neither produces

---

140 David Ignatius, "Innocence Abroad."

141 Christopher Marquis, "U.S. Bankrolling Is Under Scrutiny for Ties to Chávez Ouster," *New York Times,* April 25, 2002.

142 Susanne Gratius, "Assessing Democracy Assistance: Venezuela," FRIDE Project Report (May 2010), 1.

143 Anthony Fenton, "U.S. Gvt. Channels Millions Through National Endowment for Democracy to Fund Anti-Lavalas Groups in Haiti," *Democracy Now!,* January 23, 2006.

144 Joshua Kurlantzick, "The Coup Connection," *Mother Jones,* November/December 2004.

145 Benjamin Waddell, "Laying the Groundwork for Insurrection: A Closer Look at the U.S. Role in Nicaragua's Social Unrest," *Global Americans,* May 1, 2018.

democracy nor follows democratization." In fact, they found a *negative* relationship between NED grants and measured democracy scores.[146]

Since the collapse of the socialist bloc, the National Endowment for Democracy and the convoluted ecosystem of "charitable" foundations and "civil society" NGOs that revolve around Washington have greatly expanded their operations. In 1989, the NED's yearly expenditures totaled just $21 million;[147] by 2008, they had increased more than sixfold to $135 million.[148] Wherever mass protests, insurrections, or civil wars broke out, NED grants or money and other forms of support from U.S. government agencies could very often be traced to organizations involved in the unrest.

The Hong Kong protest movement of 2019-2020 provides a well-documented example of how the NED functions in relation to a mass uprising. The protests were sparked by a new extradition bill in the local Hong Kong legislature, which had been introduced in response to a high-profile case in which a man named Chan Tong-kai had allegedly murdered his pregnant girlfriend in Taiwan and fled back to Hong Kong to escape justice. Supposedly the protests were rooted in concern that the bill would lead to greater influence over Hong Kong by Beijing, yet it soon became clear that the protesters' actual primary motivations had little to do with the bill or with Chan Tong-kai.[149] Within a week, massive demonstrations—estimated at between hundreds of thousands and one million Hong Kongers—had forced the government to concede and suspend the bill from becoming law, yet afterward these demonstrations only increased in size.

The materialist axiom that people do not take part in massive, sustained protests if all is well with their lives most certainly obtained in Hong Kong in 2019. According to a report by The Economist Group, by that year Hong Kong was the *most expensive* city to live in worldwide.[150] The

---

146 James Scott and Carie Steele, "Assisting Democrats or Resisting Dictators? The Nature and Impact of Democracy Support by the United States National Endowment for Democracy, 1990–99," *Democratization* 12, no. 4 (August 2005): 439-460.

147 National Endowment for Democracy, *Annual Report 1989*, 43.

148 National Endowment for Democracy, *2008 Independent Auditor's Report*, 174.

149 As of October 2021, Chan Tong-kai is quietly living free in Hong Kong, according to local newspapers. ("Chan Tong-Kai Has Left Police's Safe House: Sources," *The Standard*, October 13, 2021.)

150 Actually, a three-way tie with Paris and Singapore. (The Economist Intelligence Unit, "Worldwide Cost of Living 2019," October 22, 2019.)

Hong Kong economy, once far stronger than that of any other Chinese city, was falling behind relative to the mainland; well-paying industrial jobs were steadily disappearing,[151] and the homeownership rate had fallen below 50%.[152] According to *Forbes* magazine in 2016, the home-ownership rate in China overall was 90%, with only 18% of households having a mortgage, and a home mortgage-to-GDP ratio of only 15%;[153] but at the end of 2015, the Hong Kong government reported a 70% home mortgage-to-GDP ratio.[154] The working class of Hong Kong was under increasing pressure by the wealthy bourgeoisie in the bloated real estate industry—yet during the protest movement, housing issues remained well in the background, scarcely appearing in Western press coverage at all. The famous "five demands" of the protesters that were widely covered by the Western news media did not even mention housing, wages, or any other economic difficulties, instead focusing exclusively on greater voting rights and the police brutality that some previous demonstrations had experienced.

Though nominally a "leaderless" movement, the protests were greatly influenced by many well-established groups that participated in organiz-ing them. Starting in 1995, the NED has spent hundreds of thousands of dollars yearly to strengthen the "independent" Hong Kong Confederation of Trade Unions,[155] [156] which was heavily involved in the movement, and since then its co-founder and general secretary Lee Cheuk-yan has spoken at NED events[157] and in 2019 testified before the U.S. Congress, praising the "Hong Kong Human Rights and Democracy Act" that placed unilat-eral sanctions on Hong Kong.[158] In 2020, the NED spent $1.9 million on

---

151 According to the United Nations' International Labour Organization statistics, industrial jobs in Hong Kong had steadily declined between 1991 and 2019, resulting in an overall drop from 34% to 14% of total employment. (World Bank, "Employment in Industry (% of Total Employment) (Modeled ILO Estimate) - Hong Kong SAR, China.")

152 Research Office, "Socioeconomic Implications of Home Ownership for Hong Kong." *Research Brief,* No. 2 (2020–2021), March 2021.

153 Wade Shepard, "How People In China Afford Their Outrageously Expensive Homes," *Forbes,* March 30, 2016.

154 Benny Lui and Clara Liu, "An Overview of the Household Debt Situation in Hong Kong" (December 2015), 1.

155 National Endowment for Democracy, *Annual Report 1995,* 32.

156 Not to be confused with the Hong Kong Federation of Trade Unions, the largest, oldest, and more pro-Beijing labor union federation in Hong Kong.

157 National Endowment for Democracy, "New Threats to Civil Society and the Rule of Law in Hong Kong."

158 "Hong Kong's Future in the Balance: Eroding Autonomy and Challenges

"pro-democracy" organizations in Hong Kong,[159] and according to *Time*, another $2 million from the U.S. Agency for Global Media had been earmarked to assist the protesters in evading government surveillance (though these funds were later frozen).[160] Lacking any cohesive leadership and direction, the movement was given one by Western-funded NGOs. U.S. and British flags appeared prominently in the demonstrations, some of which appealed to the West and their former colonial overlords— who for a century prior to 1997 had directly ruled over a considerably less-democratic Hong Kong—for deliverance.

While there is some genuine desire for more democracy in Hong Kong, statistically, it is unlikely to have been the largest or even a very significant factor behind the mobilization; according to the Berlin-based Latana Democracy Perception Index Report, by the spring of 2022 a two-thirds supermajority of Hong Kongers believed that Hong Kong did not need more democracy,[161] and most held a positive view of mainland China.[162] During the same year as the protests themselves, a *Reuters* poll found that while a majority supported the protests, only 8% expressed a strong desire for Hong Kong's independence from China (out of a total of 17% who expressed any desire for it whatsoever), and only 12% blamed the central government in Beijing for the unrest.[163] Yet this tiny minority seemed to have greatest control over the movement; the protesters' rage had been primarily caused by the Hong Kong bourgeoisie that had thrived under the "one country, two systems" arrangement forced upon the People's Republic of China by the United Kingdom, but was somehow redirected away from the primary source of their misery and toward the mainland instead.

The NED's general insistence that their activities are unrelated to actual protests is true only in the most direct sense. In 2021, a group of Russian activists surreptitiously recorded senior NED officials taking credit for supporting the protesters against the Belarussian government

---

to Human Rights."

159 National Endowment for Democracy, "Hong Kong (China) 2020."

160 Billy Perrigo, "Trump Administration Freezes Funds Intended to Benefit Hong Kong Protesters." *TIME*, June 26, 2020.

161 Latana, *Democracy Perception Index Report 2022*, 11.

162 Latana, 49.

163 James Pomfret and Clare Jim, "Exclusive: Hong Kongers Support Protester Demands; Minority Wants Independence from China - Reuters poll," *Reuters*, December 31, 2019.

that year.[164] The U.S. Agency for International Development is even less subtle about its political agenda—in 1999, it openly acknowledged that its willingness to invest in Central and Eastern Europe is due to "the significance of these regions to the United States."[165]

The 2004 "Orange Revolution" in Ukraine ushered President Viktor Yushchenko into power, who according to both the *American Conservative* and U.S. diplomat Michael McFaul had NED and U.S. government support.[166] [167] A decade later, only months before the Euromaidan protest movement in Ukraine which overthrew the new pro-Russian President Viktor Yanukovych (who had been elected in 2010), the president of the NED called Ukraine the "biggest prize" of Eastern Europe in a *Washington Post* op-ed and urged engagement with "civil society in Ukraine."[168] During the uprising, U.S. Ambassador and State Department spokesperson Victoria Nuland claimed in a speech that the United States had spent a total of $5 *billion* to "assist Ukraine" in "build[ing] democratic skills" among other goals since 1991—an average of over $200 million per year.[169] If this number is accurate, the NED—which according to its website in 2021 had recently spent around $5 million in Ukraine[170]—is only the tip of a very large iceberg.

Lenin once remarked that "revolution is impossible without a nation-wide crisis";[171] history has since shown that this is also true of counter-

---

164 Marc Bennetts, "We Fund Russian Democracy Protesters, Boasts US Group," *The Times,* May 19, 2021.

165 Gerald Sussman and Sascha Krader, "Template Revolutions: Marketing U.S. Regime Change in Eastern Europe," Westminster Papers in Communication and Culture 5, no. 3 (August 2008): 93.

166 Daniel Lazare, "The National Endowment for (Meddling in) Democracy," *The American Conservative,* March 8, 2018.

167 Additionally, McFaul claimed in 2007 that "Both the United States and the European Union spend roughly $1.5 billion a year on democracy promotion," that the U.S. government had spent more than $18 million in "election-related assistance efforts in the two years leading up to the 2004 presidential vote" in Ukraine, and that the U.S. Agency for International Development and other Western organizations had provided funding, organization, and technical assistance to "independent media." Michael McFaul, "Ukraine Imports Democracy: External Influences on the Orange Revolution," *International Security* 32, no. 2 (Fall 2007): 45–83.

168 Carl Gershman, "Former Soviet States Stand up to Russia. Will the U.S.?" *Washington Post,* September 26, 2013.

169 *Victoria Nuland's Admits Washington Has Spent $5 Billion to "Subvert Ukraine,"* YouTube video [8:46], February 9, 2014.

170 National Endowment for Democracy, "Ukraine 2020."

171 Lenin, *"Left-Wing" Communism: An Infantile Disorder,* sec. "Left-Wing" Communism in Great Britian.

revolution. Shortly after the Orange Revolution, Lorne Craner, the head of the NED-funded International Republican Institute and former State Department official, responded to criticism of the United States' involvement by stating "There's this myth that the Americans go into a country and, presto, you get a revolution.... It's not the case that Americans can get 2 million people to turn out on the streets. The people themselves decide to do that."[172] He is, of course, entirely correct. No amount of money, training, supplies, or propaganda will create a revolution by itself, or the super-empire would have already swept away its adversaries in Cuba, Iran, Russia, and everywhere else; only the material realities faced by the people can bring them into the streets or induce them to take up arms in large numbers. But when these ingredients—money, training, supplies, and propaganda—are provided by an external force, especially one as wealthy, powerful, and globally unopposed as the United States, any such uprising once begun can easily be controlled, manipulated, and directed to serve whatever agenda that force wishes it to manifest.

An important dimension to the super-empire's "democracy" rhetoric and reliance on NGOs to undermine foreign governments that is commonly remarked upon by the left is its hypocrisy. According to an analysis by the nonprofit news organization Truthout, as of 2015, Freedom House (a Washington-based NGO funded by the State Department) had classified 49 countries in the world as "dictatorships," nearly all of whose governments the NED and similar soft-power organizations are devoted to undermining. Yet with its other hand, the U.S. government was providing military support to 73% of these regimes.[173] To explain this apparent contradiction, it is useful to examine another prominent wave of revolutions that have occurred since the fall of the socialist bloc—the so-called "Arab Spring" of 2010 and 2011.

The super-empire employed nearly every mechanism of control at its disposal to manipulate the events of the Arab Spring. First, the conditions for the protests had been created in the preceding years largely by the IMF's structural adjustment programs, which for example in the 1990s required the privatization of the Egyptian textile industry, leaving half the workforce unemployed.[174] Egypt, Tunisia, Morocco, and Jordan—all

---

172 "U.S. Money Helped Groups That Joined Opposition in Ukraine," *Nevada Appeal*, December 9, 2004.

173 Rich Whitney, "US Provides Military Assistance to 73 Percent of World's Dictatorships." *Truthout*, September 23, 2017.

174 Austin Mackell, "The IMF versus the Arab Spring," *The Guardian*, May 25, 2011.

flash points for mass demonstrations and great social upheaval during the Arab Spring—had been praised in 1999 for "successfully" implementing structural adjustment policies.[175] This "success" entailed not only mass unemployment and a widening gap between the rich and the poor, but the stagnation of wages while the cost of living increased.[176] The peasantry and working class were steadily squeezed throughout the following decade, as conditions grew increasingly desperate.[177]

Second, U.S. government agencies and NGOs had invested in the region in order to be able to direct the protests when they inevitably occurred. In the spring of 2011, the *New York Times* and the *Washington Post* discovered through interviews and leaked U.S. diplomatic cables that not only had the State Department itself covertly given millions of dollars to Syrian opposition groups between 2006 and 2010,[178] but that "key leaders of the movements" throughout the Arab region had been trained and financed by the International Republican and National Democratic Institutes (both NED-funded) and Freedom House.[179] Hosni Mubarak, Egypt's comprador president who was militarily supported by the U.S. government, viewed these operations with deep suspicion, and ultimately with good reason; when the massive demonstration (estimated to be well over a million strong) centering on Tahrir Square in Cairo had gained too much momentum for Mubarak to crush, President Obama turned on his own comprador and insisted that he resign.

In general, the United States government had not been dissatisfied by Mubarak's rule. But in the final analysis, his presence, like any comprador ruler of a neocolony, was not indispensable. If Mubarak's replacement was unsatisfactory, U.S. control of the Egyptian military establishment and ability to direct popular protests made further regime change easy.[180] What was one comprador more or less?

---

175 Karen Pfeifer, "How Tunisia, Morocco, Jordan and Even Egypt Became IMF 'Success Stories' in the 1990s," *Middle East Report* No. 210 (Spring 1999): 23–27.

176 Austin Mackell, "The IMF versus the Arab Spring."

177 Gilbert Achcar, "On the 'Arab Inequality Puzzle': The Case of Egypt," Development and Change 51, no. 3 (May 2020): 746–770.

178 Craig Whitlock, "U.S. Secretly Backed Syrian Opposition Groups, Cables Released by WikiLeaks Show," *Washington Post*, April 14, 2011.

179 Ron Nixon, "U.S. Groups Helped Nurture Arab Uprisings," *New York Times*, April 15, 2011.

180 Indeed, his replacement Mohamed Morsi had barely been president for one year before another protest movement and coup d'état removed him as well. U.S. military aid to Egypt, and Egypt's cooperation with the IMF and U.S. foreign policy

Finally, while the Arab Spring presented some inconveniences for the empire, on balance it was well worth the investment for the challenges it posed to anti-imperialist states in the Middle East and North Africa, which were then helped along through military intervention. Though the super-empire allowed protests to be crushed in Bahrain and Saudi Arabia with a shrug, when the movement encountered difficulties in Libya and Syria, the U.S. and its NATO allies launched airstrikes on the Libyan government and armed the rebel forces in both countries.

In the aftermath, a few reforms were conceded by some governments, such as Jordan's and Morocco's, but where governments had been over-thrown, the conditions for most Arab workers and peasants had not changed for the better. Comprador governments that had fallen were replaced with new comprador governments, which were forced to submit to even more structural adjustments by the IMF and the World Bank.[181] Economic development not only hadn't increased, but it had gone backwards as the horrors of civil war enveloped Libya, Syria, and Yemen for many years. No new anti-imperialist governments had emerged,[182] one that already existed had fallen, and the proletariat had not taken state power anywhere. Thus was the full rigor of the neocolonial system enforced—business as usual for the United States and the financial oligarchy.

The second major criteria by which revolutions may be judged, in the cases where they succeed in toppling the governments to which they are opposed, are the outcomes for the poor and working class who provide the engine and fuel for the uprising.

In the era immediately following the Second World War, when social-ism had reached its historical peak, revolutions had almost always had net positive effects. Countries such as Vietnam and Laos threw off the shackles of colonial domination and achieved a degree of real independence from the West for the first time in generations. China emerged from its Century of Humiliation, abolishing once and for all both the old

---

continued under the next president, Abdel Fattah el-Sisi.

181 Éric Toussaint, "The World Bank Did Not Foresee the Arab Spring Popular Uprisings and Still Promotes the Very Same Policies That Triggered Them," CADTM, April 12, 2021.

182 With the potential exception of the Ansarallah movement and the Supreme Political Council in northern Yemen; after nearly a decade of civil war and struggle against the Saudi intervention, a cease-fire was reached in 2022, and after some interruptions, negotiations for peace began in April 2023. Though the results are not yet known as of this writing, it is highly likely that Ansarallah will dominate Yemen's political future.

structures of feudal oppression and the cruel comprador regimes of servitude and drug addiction imposed on it. Land reform liberated millions of peasants, infant mortality rates dropped, and average life expectancy skyrocketed. The Cuban Revolution transformed a poor agrarian country that lacked basic sanitation into a healthier, cleaner, more educated, and more dignified society; the "Castro regime" that the U.S. media so frequently excoriated brought basic medical care to the rural population for the first time, and advanced to the point of not only treating disease but preventing it. 91% of the rural population in Cuba had been malnourished in the years before the revolution, and while afterward food security was slow to develop due to the U.S. embargo, the countryside finally received a fair share.[183] In 1969, according to a former official of the UN Food and Agriculture Organization, since the revolution "more schools and hospitals" had replaced poverty and misery in the countryside, and 70% of the Cuban people lived better than they ever had before.[184] A 1986 study published in the *American Journal of Public Health* found that even according to the World Bank's own statistical data, socialist countries outperformed capitalist countries in similar income categories on nearly every criterion related to physical quality of life.[185]

When the socialist bloc disappeared in 1989, however, so did this trend. This was immediately obvious in the first wave of counterrevolutions; shock therapy and neoliberalism enforced by IMF lending led to disaster in the former Eastern Bloc after only a few years. Agricultural output declined precipitously after privatization; by the mid-1990s, Hungary's farm output had fallen by 40%,[186] and Bulgaria was suffering a bread shortage—seeing the potential for greater profit outside the country, the new private firms had exported their grain rather than sell it at home.[187] Rents increased from only a few percent of income to well over fifty percent of income. Homelessness, almost unheard of under socialism,

183 Nelson P. Valdés, "Health and Revolution in Cuba," Science & Society 35, no. 3 (Fall 1971): 314.

184 Erich H. Jacoby, "Cuba: The Real Winner Is the Agricultural Worker," FAO: *Ceres* 2 , no. 4 (July–August 1969): 32.

185 Shirley Cereseto and Howard Waitzkin, "Economic Development, Political-Economic System, and the Physical Quality of Life," *American Journal of Public Health* 76, no. 6 (June 1986): 661–666.

186 Carol J. Williams, "Taste for Capitalism Slips in Nation Once Fed on 'Goulash Communism': Hungary: Formerly at the Forefront of Eastern Europe's Transition to Free Market, It Has Failed to Exploit Advantages," *Los Angeles Times,* January 29, 1994.

187 Veselin Toshkov, "Bulgaria Suffers Bread Shortage."

became a harrowing new fact of life all across Eastern Europe, the former Soviet Union, and Mongolia; during the 1990s, an estimated 20,000 children were living on the streets in Romania.[188] Infant mortality increased in Bulgaria by 25%.[189] Human trafficking and sexual slavery reappeared in Eastern Europe. Real incomes shrank, pensions vanished, unemployment increased, unions were weakened or destroyed, and organized crime and corruption became commonplace. In Russia, a new batch of compradors was created almost overnight, which proceeded to plunder the large state-run economy, privatizing 90% of industries at vastly undervalued prices. The subsequent economic crash led to a massive increase in poverty and a six-year drop in Russian life expectancy—the greatest drop ever recorded anywhere in history in the absence of war or natural disasters, according to a study from the Berlin-based Dialogue of Civilizations Research Institute.[190] In 2001, the United Nations Children's Fund (UNICEF) estimated that in all "transition countries" excluding Bosnia and Herzegovina, there had been a total of approximately 3.2 million excess deaths between 1990 and 1999 (i.e. deaths that would not have occurred had mortality rates remained at their 1989 levels).[191] A study published in the *Cambridge Journal of Economics* in 2023 estimated this figure to be *much* higher, around 7 million.[192] Another 2019 study from the IZA Institute of Labor Economics in Bonn found that surviving adults who had been born during the period of shock therapy grew up to be nearly one centimeter shorter than the preceding generation on average.[193]

Eastern Europe having thus been conquered, the Arab Spring shows how the super-empire wielded the weapon of revolution in the absence of a significant bloc of "enemy" countries: like a blunt instrument, crushing friendly and hostile regimes alike, confident that its soft-power NGO network and system of global finance would prevent any new hostile regimes

---

188　Edet Belzberg (Director), *Children Underground*, Romanian documentary film [1h 44m], 2001.

189　Elwood Carlson and Sergey Tsvetarsky, "Birthweight and Infant Mortality in Bulgaria's Transition Crisis," Paediatric and Perinatal Epidemiology 14, no. 2 (April 2000): 159–162.

190　Vladimir Popov, *Mortality and Life Expectancy in Post-Communist Countries,* June 5, 2018.

191　Innocenti Research Centre, *A Decade of Transition,* sec. Executive Summary.

192　Gábor Scheiring et al., "Deindustrialisation and the Post-Socialist Mortality Crisis." *Cambridge Journal of Economics* 47, no. 2 (March 2023): 341–372.

193　Alicia Adserà *et al.,* "Transition from Plan to Market, Height and Well-Being" (IZA Institute of Labor Economics, September 2019): 15–16.

from rising out of the ashes. The National Endowment for Democracy became a geostrategic gambler, placing bets on every number of the roulette wheel. According to its website in 2021, it had invested in every region of the world—except, of course, North America, Western Europe, and Australia, where "democracy" apparently needs no encouragement.

So far, this strategy has been a tremendous success. Exceptions such as the Bolivarian Revolution, which empower the proletariat to some extent,[194] are very few and far between in the new age of super-imperialism. In the neocolonies, those who wish to overthrow the comprador establishment face not only the challenge of organizing their countrymen, but of doing so with none of the vast resources the color revolutionaries enjoy. Often, the most that can be reasonably hoped is that the new comprador rulers that a revolution inevitably inaugurates will be less brutal than the last. There is little fear among the Western bourgeoisie that they might fail to gain control of a new uprising—i.e., fail to co-opt and "color" a revolution—wherever it may appear. After all, where is their competition? By far, the greatest exporter of revolution in the twenty-first century has not been Venezuela, nor Cuba or Russia; it has certainly not been the PRC, which maintains a careful policy of noninterference in foreign political affairs; nor is it even the Islamic Republic of Iran. It is the United States of America. Today, wherever and whenever the oppressed rise up in search of justice, the agents of injustice are always there among them, ready to lead them astray.

---

194 See Chapter Three.

Peasant and Proletarian Anti-Imperialism

> *"[W]hen Mr. Khrushchev brandishes his shoe at the United Nations, or thumps the table with it, there's not a single ex-native, nor any representative of an underdeveloped country, who laughs. For what Mr. Khrushchev shows the colonized countries which are looking on is that he, the* moujik, *who moreover is the possessor of spacerockets, treats these miserable capitalists in the way that they deserve. In the same way, Castro sitting in military uniform in the United Nations Organization does not scandalize the underdeveloped countries. What Castro demonstrates is the consciousness he has of the continuing existence of the rule of violence. The astonishing thing is that he did not come into the UNO with a machine-gun; but if he had, would anyone have minded?"*
>
> —Frantz Fanon, 1961[195]

Given the present super-imperial world order and how it is enforced, the question arises: what forces remain opposed to it? What modes of resistance exist, what are their goals and limitations, what are the conditions for success, and what are their paths to victory?

Just as the super-empire's exploitation is driven by the interests of the Western capitalist class, resistance to it is driven by the interests of the classes that do not benefit from this exploitation. But since not every class is exploited or excluded in the same manner, not every class employs the same mode of resistance and to the same ends. Resistance by each class or group of classes will therefore be examined according to their similarity, the first being the peasantry and the proletariat of the global periphery, who are grouped together by their commonality of being the objects of the super-empire's dispossessive accumulation.

A victory by these groups over their oppressors, in Marxist terms, would result in a *proletarian state*—a political organization of and for the workers and peasants, which attains control and sovereignty over

---

195 Fanon, *The Wretched of the Earth*, 78.

their country, and acts in their collective interests to end or defend against oppression and imperialism. Toward such a goal, these groups employ two main modes of resistance.

The Popular Front

Venezuela and the *chavismo* movement provide perhaps the best example of the proletariat in a former colony achieving a measure of lasting success in creating and influencing an anti-imperialist state during the stage of super-imperialism. Though modern Venezuela has commonly been called socialist after the election of Hugo Chávez in 1998, the character of his and subsequent administrations defy a straightforward class analysis.

The accomplishments of Chávez's United Socialist Party of Venezuela (PSUV) in the interests of the working class of Venezuela speak for themselves: the constitutional reform of 1999, which enshrined indigenous rights and representation in government, a promise of social security benefits for domestic labor, and a guarantee of housing, healthcare, and employment to the entire population;[196] the nationalization of several industries, banks, and other key sectors of the economy;[197] the replacement of traditional elites as directors of museums, galleries, and other cultural institutions;[198] and the effective re-nationalization of Venezuela's state oil company—which for decades had been run like a private corporation by Venezuelan compradors—so as to reallocate its profits to fund social programs. Chávez himself was unabashedly a revolutionary, heavily influenced by communists throughout his military career,[199] and even leading an attempted coup d'état of the brutally repressive neoliberal government in 1992, for which he was imprisoned. Marxist Professor

---

196 Gregory Wilpert, "Venezuela's New Constitution," *Sendika.Org,* November 2, 2007.

197 "Factbox: Venezuela's Nationalizations under Chavez," *Reuters,* October 7, 2012.

198 Ludmila Vinogradoff, "La 'revolución cultural' de Hugo Chávez escandaliza a los intelectuales venezolanos" [Hugo Chávez's 'cultural revolution' scandalizes Venezuelan intellectuals], *El País,* January 29, 2001.

199 Chávez's close personal friendship with Fidel Castro and his public ideological alignment with revolutionary Cuba began well before his election to the presidency. "Latin American youths came here to Cuba many times in our dreams," said Chávez in Havana in 1994 after his release from prison (*Hugo Chávez Speech in La Habana. 1994*), though he mostly avoided applying the label of "Marxist" for himself, instead preferring the banner of "Socialism for the Twenty-First Century."

José Rafael Núñez Tenorio, Chávez's mentor and director of ideology of his Fifth Republic Movement party (PSUV's predecessor), is regarded as a principal architect of *chavismo* and in his writings stressed the need to unite the leftist uprising within the military with the popular movement of the working class.[200] It was precisely this proletarian movement that mobilized after Venezuela's comprador oligarchy (aided by top-level U.S. government officials)[201] launched their own coup d'état against Chávez in April of 2002, replacing him with Pedro Carmona, the president of Fedecámaras, Venezuela's main business federation. Within 48 hours, tens of thousands of Chávez's supporters marched in the streets of Caracas, surrounded the presidential palace and several military bases, took over the state television station, and forced his reinstatement.

This mass movement of the poor and working class was undeniably the source of Chávez's political strength. By 2004, according to Steve Ellner, a prominent American historian specializing in Venezuela, mass demonstrations in Caracas regularly organized by the *chavistas* numbered in the "hundreds of thousands."[202] The events of April 2002, and the failure of the opposition's capital strike later that year, made it clear that he possessed both the power and public support needed to punish the capitalist class, nationalize or dismantle their corporations, and expropriate their tremendous wealth. The desperately impoverished Venezuelan workers long demanded that Chávez subject the capitalist elite to *la mano dura*.[203] But he never did.

In practice, the defining characteristic of Bolivarian Revolution was and has ever been—first with Chávez, then with President Nicolás Maduro—political compromise. Chávez and Maduro always sought to make peace with the wealthy oligarchs, despite the multiple coup attempts and the other frequent, often violent attacks upon them[204] and their supporters.[205] Ellner wrote in 2001, "On numerous occasions

---

200 Steve Ellner, "The Radical Potential of Chavismo in Venezuela: The First Year and a Half in Power," *Latin American Perspectives* 28, no. 5 (Sept. 2001): 11.

201 Ed Vulliamy, "Venezuela Coup Linked to Bush Team," *The Guardian,* April 21, 2002.

202 Steve Ellner, *Rethinking Venezuelan Politics: Class, Conflict, and the Chávez Phenomenon* (Lynne Rienner Publishers, 2008), 120.

203 The "heavy hand."

204 In August of 2018 there was an attempt on President Maduro's life. (Carla Herreria Russo, "Venezuelan President Unharmed After Assassination Attempt By Explosive Drones," *Huffpost,* August 4, 2018.)

205 In 2017, for example, there were several high-profile lynchings of Black *chavistas*, or Afro-Venezuelans suspected of being *chavistas*, by opposition

[Chávez] threatened institutions under the sway of his adversaries with dissolution or mobilizations to pressure them into accepting new rules that facilitated radical structural change. He then typically backed off and offered a compromise arrangement."[206] Even during the most radical phase of the Revolution in the mid-2000s, despite the impressive program of nationalization and land redistribution accomplished by Chávez, the statistics published by the Venezuelan Central Bank show that more than half of the Venezuelan economy never left private hands.[207] During the self-declared term of "Interim President" Juan Guaidó (the United States' opposition puppet whose 2019 coup attempt ended in failure), Maduro's administration did not arrest him, or charge him with a crime.[208]

There are two significant, mutually reinforcing reasons for their lack of action. The first that is the class composition of the Bolivarian Revolution has never been homogenous. *Chavismo* represents a balance of class interests; in one crucial dimension—anti-imperialism—these interests are united, while in others they remain at odds. No matter how much legal or moral authority a leader may have, that leader does not govern according to his whim, but by the consent and will of the class forces that support him.

Within the Venezuelan military, whose staunch support of Chávez and Maduro has saved the Revolution from total disaster on more than one occasion, most officers, Ellner writes, were from "middle- and lower-middle-class backgrounds"[209]—relatively less privileged than the officer corps of other countries in Latin America, yet significantly drawn from petit bourgeoisie families, particularly those desiring greater social mobility. Furthermore, Ellner notes that "Most Chavista military officers

---

militants. ("Venezuela Man Set Alight at Anti-Government Protest Dies," *BBC,* June 5, 2017. Lucas Koerner, "Venezuela: Soldier Killed, Three More Burned Alive," *Venezuelanalysis,* June 27, 2017.)

206 Steve Ellner, "The Radical Potential of Chavismo in Venezuela," 12.

207 Only in 2018 did the public sector first account for more than half of GDP. Most likely, capital flight, rather than any new initiative to nationalize existing production, was responsible for this statistic; in 2018 the private sector contracted while the public sector did not significantly expand. (Banco Central de Venezuela, "Producto interno bruto por sector institucional" [Gross domestic product by institutional sector].)

208 The Venezuelan authorities finally did move to issue a warrant for Guaidó's arrest, but only in 2023, the year after his "interim government" was dissolved, and not for treason, but for the misappropriation of PVDSA's resources. (John Yoon and Orlando Mayorquin, "Venezuela Seeks Arrest of Juan Guaidó, Former Opposition Leader," *New York Times,* October 6, 2023.)

209 Steve Ellner, *Rethinking Venezuelan Politics,* 3.

favor the soft-liners' pragmatic approach,"[210] i.e., a minimal program of consolidating existing gains and maintaining state power rather than the pursuit of further nationalization or expropriation supported by the "hard-liner" *chavistas*. This is entirely consistent with a national-bourgeois class interest, wherein private property and profits are shielded from both foreign and proletarian control. In effect, the "civilian-military alliance" envisioned by Núñez Tenorio that propelled Chávez to power and kept him there also entailed a popular front against imperialism consisting of an alliance between the proletariat and a less prosperous faction of the Venezuelan bourgeoisie.[211] [212]

---

210 Several of these, Ellner notes, were elected to state governorships in the elections of 2004 (*Rethinking Venezuelan Politics*, 141).

211 In a 1996 speech at the Central University of Venezuela, Núñez Tenorio described even more explicitly how the strategy for revolution should incorporate not only workers, students, and intellectuals, but that "we must even call on the medium and small agricultural producers and industrial entrepreneurs so brutally struck by the crisis." (J. R. Núñez Tenorio, *Estrategia y Táctica: ¿Cómo hacer? ¿Cuál es la salida?* [Strategy and Tactics] [Fondo Editorial de la Asamblea Nacional William Lara 2014], 35). Frequently, the analyses of foreign Marxists contemporary to Chávez also identified the bourgeois ingredient of *chavismo*. Alan Woods, even in defending the International Marxist Tendency's involvement in the Bolivarian Revolution from criticism by some of these, wrote frankly in 2005, "The standpoint of Hugo Chavez is that of petty-bourgeois revolutionary democracy." (Alan Woods, "Foxes and Grapes: Sectarian Stupidity and the Venezuelan Revolution," *In Defence of Marxism*, July 19, 2005.) Nevertheless, both the IMT and the Communist Party of Venezuela joined Chávez's coalition, recognizing in *chavismo* the opportunity to empower the working class to eventually take control of the state.

212 The complexity of the lower bourgeoisie's relationship to *chavismo* is even more apparent when the racial divisions of Venezuelan society are taken into account. The wealthy comprador elite is overwhelmingly white (Arlene Eisen, "Racism Sin Vergüenza in the Venezuelan Counter-Revolution," *Black Agenda Report*, April 8, 2014.) and the reaction to *chavismo* has been highly racialized. According to Ellner, "members of the opposition used racial slurs against the chavistas, while racism also manifested itself in graffiti in wealthy zones and even occasionally in the media...." (Steve Ellner, *Rethinking Venezuelan Politics*, 6–7). Both Hugo Chávez and Evo Morales, the former president of Bolivia whose election in 2005 was also the result of an anti-neoliberal movement, had the support of a multiracial coalition that explicitly prioritized indigenous rights and the struggle of non-white South Americans. The Statutes of the PSUV state, above any reference to economic class, the party's values and principles to be "... mestizo socialism, full of Africanity, of the elements of our indigenous peoples ..." (Partido Socialista Unido de Venezuela, "Estatutos del Partido Socialista Unido de Venezuela (PSUV)" [Statutes of the United Socialist Party of Venezuela], art. 3.) Non-white Venezuelans of all classes, including the urban mestizo petit bourgeoisie, faced with a long history of deep racial hostility from the opposition, were overwhelmingly more likely to align themselves with Chávez.

In December of 2002, their coup having just been decisively defeated by the *chavistas*, the opposition changed tactics and launched a general capital strike against the government. Fedecámaras and the pro-opposition union and management of PDVSA, the state-owned oil company, called for businesses to close indefinitely until Chávez resigned. A majority of PDVSA workers refused to support the strike. Chávez biographer Bart Jones writes, "Like Venezuelan society in general, PDVSA was polarized between a well-heeled elite who despised Chávez and lower-paid workers who supported him or at least did not want to use PDVSA as a political weapon." Chávez's support from workers, and the *chavistas'* willingness to endure shortages, eventually undermined and broke the strike, yet Jones also notes that "Many small businesses never joined the walkout in the first place," particularly in the barrios of western Caracas, where most business owners were also pro-Chávez.[213] According to Ellner, not only did "the vast majority of workers [reject] the strike call," but "in nonaffluent neighborhoods throughout the nation, a majority of commercial establishments remained open."[214]

Luis Miquilena, a Venezuelan entrepreneur who for a time served in Chávez's cabinet and was considered a leader of the pro-business right wing of the Revolution, more overtly supported a class alliance with even the larger bourgeoisie, advocating that the party establish ties with "progressive" or "honest" capitalists, and used his connections with wealthy businessman Tobías Carrero Nácar to secure funding for Chávez's first election campaign.[215] [216] There were distinct limits to the influence of this faction—in 2002 Miquilena resigned, objecting that Chávez's administration had too little respect for private property, and in 2009, the government confiscated agricultural land from Carrero's estate despite his objections.[217] Yet the alliance limited the left wing of *chavismo* as well. Ellner writes that "By spelling out the ideals of the Chavista movement

213 Bart Jones, *Hugo!: The Hugo Chávez Story from Mud Hut to Perpetual Revolution* (Steerforth, 2007), chap. 23, "Oil Strike."

214 Steve Ellner, *Rethinking Venezuelan Politics,* 119.

215 Steve Ellner, 164.

216 In Miquilena's point of view, the 2002 coup against Chávez had failed not just because of the protests, but because the bourgeoisie involved in the coup were not unified in their economic interests, and many of them did not support another puppet government that would do the United States' bidding. Thus, according to Miquilena, when Carmona announced a program of neoliberal austerity immediately upon ascending to the presidency, this faction withdrew their support.

217 Michael Fox, "Venezuela News Summary #77" (March 11–March 17, 2009), *Venezuelanalysis,* March 18, 2009.

while avoiding reference to the specifics of revolutionary socioeconomic change, class struggle, or socialism, the Constitution lends itself to the soft-line view. Indeed, the proposal to reform the Constitution in 2007 in order to radicalize its contents led to the defection of the soft-line Podemos party."[218] The dissent from moderate *chavistas* made all the difference; the referendum to rewrite the Constitution to include explicit references to the class struggle—essentially, a step towards proletarianizing the state—ended up failing by a margin of less than one percentage point.

There is also a second principal reason why the PSUV, whether under either Chávez's or Maduro's leadership, has not advanced the interests of the Venezuelan proletariat through a serious program of expropriation: Venezuela's relative international isolation.

A strikingly illustrative historical parallel to the Bolivarian Revolution may be found only a few hundred miles to the north and west. Indeed, the Venezuelan opposition often tried to draw attention to Chávez's association with his close friend and ally Fidel Castro, attempting to stoke fear among the people by invoking the specter of Cuban communism spreading to the continent. When the Cuban Revolution was won, the U.S. puppet leader Fulgencio Batista fled the country on New Year's Day of 1959; yet it was not until two years later that the character of the revolutionary government was firmly established in favor of the workers and the peasants. Just like Chávez, Castro had joined a broad coalition of competing class forces, in his case including petit-bourgeois anti-Batista dissidents,[219] and liberal anticommunists such as José Miró Cardona, who served as the revolutionary government's first prime minister.[220] However, after only a few months, Castro's faction won this competition decisively. By the summer of 1959, he had replaced Miró Cardona as prime minister and began confiscating land from the bourgeoisie. By the end of October 1960, the Cuban government had nationalized the majority of all industries, utilities, and private businesses, and expropriated foreign capital from all U.S. corporations such as Shell Oil and Coca-Cola—in short,

---

218 Steve Ellner, *Rethinking Venezuelan Politics*, 142.

219 Fidel Castro, *Fidel Castro Speaks on Marxism-Leninism: Dec. 2, 1961* (Fair Play for Cuba Committee, 1962), 34.

220 Of his alliance with Miró Cardona, Castro later said "... there were the opinions of the Prio-Miro Cardona group, that whole bunch in the Front, who were in Miami, opposed to a broad, complete unity. They all were in favor of excluding the Socialist Party from that unity. We defended the inclusion of the Socialist Party." (Fidel Castro, 27.)

precisely what a great many poor and working class Venezuelans had wished of Chávez's government.

In the 2000s, at the height of super-imperialism, for consumers of Venezuelan and U.S. bourgeois media alike, the anti-imperialist rhetoric that Chávez so frequently reveled in probably seemed only a hair's breadth from provoking a U.S. military invasion. And indeed, the possibility of such an intervention, either *de jure* or by proxy, has ever been a Sword of Damocles over his and Maduro's heads. Yet a vast material difference exists between Chávez's public condemnation of the United States and its leaders, and a program of radical expropriation and redistribution to fundamentally change Venezuela's intensely stratified society. And while the United States is already engaged in the highest levels of economic warfare against Venezuela, through the crushing sanctions that have done tremendous damage to the health and prosperity of the Venezuelan people, the escalation to a military intervention would represent a significantly greater commitment, one that the U.S. oligarchy would not make lightly—and not solely over the exchange of harsh words.

Just as Chávez knew well which lines could and could not be crossed under the conditions he faced, Castro's actions upon taking power were also not without careful thought. A U.S. response to the creation of a new socialist state, especially one next door in the Caribbean, was inevitable.

A popular view of the Bay of Pigs invasion is that it was doomed to failure, either by the weakness of the invasion force (only 1,500 men), the leak of the invasion plans to the media, the lack of U.S. air support, the strength and unity of the Cuban defenders, or by some combination of these. It must be noted, however, that most likely, the intended purpose of the invasion force that landed at Playa Girón was not to conquer the island, but merely to establish a stable beachhead. Once this had been accomplished, Miró Cardona—who had become a leader of the Cuban exiles in Miami—was to be flown in and installed as the president of a provisional comprador government that would then appeal to the U.S. for a *de jure* military intervention.[221] When taking the full measure of this strategy into account, the idea that the invasion's failure was a foregone conclusion is less certain; but more importantly, none of the reasons

---

221 Pat Holt, the former Chief of Staff of the Senate Foreign Relations Committee, detailed this plan together with the Committee's Chairman James William Fulbright in a memo to President Kennedy the month before the invasion, describing it as the most effective strategy for overthrowing Castro's government. (Pat M. Holt, Chief of Staff, Foreign Relations Committee, *Interview #5: Fulbright and the Bay of Pigs,* United States Senate Historical Office—Oral History Project, 149–54.)

traditionally given for its failure preclude the potential success of subsequent attempts to overthrow the revolutionary government by the vastly stronger and better-equipped U.S. military.

"Without the existence of the Soviet Union," Castro remarked two years later, "Cuba's socialist revolution would have been impossible."[222] On the afternoon of April 18th, 1961, while the invasion force was engaging the Cuban defenders, the Soviet embassy telegrammed the U.S. State Department threatening to defend Cuba by military force.[223] As evidence of U.S. involvement mounted and was brought to the United Nations, it became clear that the U.S. could neither bring its own troops into the equation without risking nuclear war nor continue its subterfuge in front of the international community. Over the following decades, the Soviet Union's military and economic support, existence, and deterrent to U.S. aggression prevented the gains of the revolution from being destroyed. Recognizing this, Castro could implement his program with the hope and confidence of victory.

But while Cuba had the Soviet Union, in 2004 Venezuela had no protector, and the Venezuelan proletariat could count no foreign country but Cuba as an ally. Chávez reportedly said, on the question of the feasibility of Venezuela adopting the Cuban economic model, that Castro himself advised him, "remember, this isn't 1960."[224]

Armed Struggle

General Võ Nguyên Giáp is widely considered one of the greatest military strategists in history, sometimes called the "Red Napoleon" by the Western press. In his long military career, he led the Vietnamese army to victory over the Empire of Japan, the French Fourth Republic, and the United States, liberating his country from colonialism and reuniting it under a socialist government. Later his army defeated the Khmer Rouge in Cambodia, and even forced the People's Liberation Army of China to withdraw within only a few weeks of battle along Vietnam's northern border in 1979. In December of 1971, at the height of the resistance against the U.S. invasion, Giáp said in a speech to Soviet leaders in Moscow:

---

222 Fidel Castro, "Speech at Red Square," April 28, 1963.

223 Nikita Khrushchev, Telegram From the Embassy in the Soviet Union to the Department of State, April 18, 1961.

224 Ian James, "Despite Chavez, Venezuela Economy Not Socialist," *The San Diego Union-Tribune,* July 18, 2010.

"We would like to carry on this mission together with the Soviet Union, because no one can do it without the Soviet Union."[225]

Indeed, throughout the war, the state in north Vietnam had received an extraordinary amount of military and economic aid from both the PRC and later the Soviet Union, including not just weapons and ammunition, but vehicles and fuel, raw materials, food, fertilizer, and other supplies. Soviet military advisers trained Vietnamese troops and even participated in combat themselves, operating anti-aircraft batteries that shot down U.S. bomber planes, and over 300,000 Chinese troops were deployed to fight U.S. forces.[226] The DPRK sent hundreds of fighter pilots,[227] and most other countries in the socialist bloc provided some level of economic or technological assistance.

After the United States was defeated on the battlefield, the imperial alliance resorted to economic warfare, isolating the new Socialist Republic of Vietnam from trade with the international community. Again the Soviet Union helped sustain the fledgling socialist state, canceling all its war debts and giving it over $11 billion in aid over the next two decades.[228] Without it, the SRV's hope of rebuilding or even surviving seems staggeringly unlikely.

General Curtis LeMay, President Lyndon Johnson's Air Force Chief of Staff until 1965, had advocated "[bombing] them back into the Stone Age." The U.S. invasion had included the largest aerial bombardment in history, dropping twice as much ordnance on Vietnam, Laos and Cambodia than had been used in all of the Second World War.[229] Due to the indiscriminate use of the Agent Orange chemical weapon to defoliate nearly a quarter of the entire forest area in southern Vietnam,[230] even

---

225 Sergey Radchenko, "Why Were the Russians in Vietnam?," *New York Times,* March 27, 2018.

226 Reuter, "China Admits Combat in Vietnam War," *Washington Post*, May 17, 1989.

227 Kham Nguyen and Ju-min Park, "From Comrades to Assassins, North Korea and Vietnam Eye New Chapter with Trump-Kim Summit," *Reuters,* February 15, 2019.

228 Sergey Radchenko, "Why Were the Russians in Vietnam?"

229 Cooper Thomas, "Bombing Missions of the Vietnam War: A Visual Record of the Largest Aerial Bombardment in History." https://storymaps.arcgis.com/stories/2eae918ca40a4bd7a55390bba4735cdb

230 "Agent Orange: What Efforts Are Being Made to Address the Continuing Impact of Dioxin in Vietnam?," Hearing before the Subcommittee on Asia, the Pacific and the Global Environment of the Committee on Foreign Affairs, House of Representatives 111th Congress, June 4, 2009.

today, Vietnamese children are still born with birth defects from exposure
to Agent Orange in the groundwater that researchers estimate will persist
for another "six to twelve generations."[231] Unexploded ordnance remains
a hazard, limiting agricultural development and killing several people in
neighboring Laos each year, even as late as 2021.[232] A socialist Vietnam
had needed to be rebuilt from virtually nothing.

Every Marxist-Leninist state—as well as several other "non-aligned"
countries—that came into existence during the Cold War era had military
and economic support from a large part of the socialist bloc. The Chinese
revolution was aided and directed by the Soviet Union; the PRC then
defended the DPRK against the United States. Elsewhere in Africa, Asia,
and Latin America, oppressed peoples seeking liberation from the imperial alliance invariably turned to either the Soviet Union or the PRC for
assistance. They needed it—any such movement for liberation inevitably
came under siege by the U.S. and Western Europe.

The stage of super-imperialism resulted in barely mitigated disaster
for the entire socialist world. After the counterrevolutions of 1989, the
proletariat in socialist states faced a hard choice: either give up state power
or endure a period of tremendous hardship. Ruling communist parties in
Cambodia, Mongolia, Angola, and much of the Eastern Bloc abandoned
Marxism-Leninism. The German Democratic Republic (GDR) and the
People's Democratic Republic of Yemen (PDRY) gave up their independence.[233] A few others—in China, Laos, and Vietnam—weathered the
storm by submitting to integration with the global capitalist economy,
giving up many of the gains of the revolution and allowing a degree of
exploitation by foreign and domestic capitalists as the price of retaining
political authority.[234] The DPRK and Cuba, who alone refused either

---

231 Ash Anand, "Vietnam's Horrific Legacy: The Children of Agent Orange,"
NEWS.COM.AU, May 25, 2015.

232 "UXO Kills Three, Injures Two During Clearance Operation in Southern
Laos," *Laotian Times,* December 6, 2021.

233 In the case of the PDRY, the initial surrender was on relatively favorable
terms; they retained their state organizational structures and combined with the North
in a unity government. Yet this was ultimately unacceptable to the new super-imperial
world order. The North antagonized and provoked the South into a civil war in 1994
in which the remaining vestiges of the socialist state were brutally destroyed with the
tacit approval of Western governments. [Carlos A. Parodi, Elizabeth Van Wie Davis,
and Elizabeth Rexford, "The Silent Demise of Democracy: The Role of the Clinton
Administration in the 1994 Yemeni Civil War," *Arab Studies Quarterly* 16, no. 4 (Fall
1994): 65–76.]

234 See Chapter Seven for a more complete analysis of this path.

course, suffered the most. Deprived of their largest trading partner and source of development aid, they experienced famine and economic crisis throughout the 1990s as the economic siege of their countries reached a level of total encirclement. In much of the former socialist bloc, Marxist groups were banned and Marxists were persecuted and sometimes executed or massacred by the new comprador elites.[235]

Since 1989, as of this writing, no new specifically Marxist governments have been created, and the working classes have not seized state power anywhere. Armed national liberation movements, led by the peasantry and proletariat (or else at the very least openly claiming the mantle of class-based leadership) have similarly declined overall. Several, such as the Irish Republican Army and the Farabundo Martí National Liberation Front (FMLN), made deals with the governments they had fought against; having failed to achieve national liberation they settled for amnesty and a place in the "legitimate" political arena. The Communist Party of Nepal (Maoist), or CPN-M, now known as the Communist Party of Nepal (Maoist Centre), has been perhaps the most successful in this regard as of this writing, remaining one of the largest parties in the Nepalese parliament, which is alternately dominated by it and other communist organizations. The FMLN, despite later gaining power through elections in 2009, subsequently all but vanished from the Salvadoran legislature. As of the 2022 parliamentary elections, the Revolutionary Armed Forces of Colombia, which eventually negotiated a peace deal with the Colombian government in 2017, had not gained representation in the Colombian legislature beyond the ten seats automatically guaranteed by the agreement until 2026.[236] For the most part, non-ruling Marxist political parties faded into political irrelevance around the world, performing abysmally in elections and in some countries ceasing to exist entirely—a long decline that only very recently may be reversing.[237]

Some armed struggle has continued, but with little success, and more often facing complete disaster, such as befell the Communist Party of Peru

---

235 When Yeltsin disbanded the Supreme Soviet in 1993, the Russian Army at his direction stormed the parliament building and massacred the occupants. Yeltsin's government admitted that "only" 147 people were killed and hundreds more were injured.

236 Angela Barajas, "Colombia Clears Path for Former FARC Members to Hold Office," *CNN,* April 28, 2017.

237 The emergence and growth of new Marxist political formations around the world, such as the Communist Party of Kenya or the Economic Freedom Fighters in South Africa, for example, may be signs of a turning point.

(also called the Shining Path). In 1993, several thousand of the remaining rebel forces surrendered, and as of this writing only a few remnants remain active.[238] A few peasant movements such as the Zapatista Army of National Liberation in Mexico, the United Wa State Army in Myanmar, and most notably Ansarallah in Yemen, have managed to establish *de facto* independent territories within their respective countries, yet still lack sovereignty and international recognition as of this writing.[239] Other remaining communist insurgencies, despite at times gaining impressive strength,[240] have not drawn closer to victory after over thirty years of armed struggle.

In Mao Zedong's lectures on protracted war, he identified three distinct stages of conflict:

> The first stage covers the period of the enemy's strategic offensive and our strategic defensive. The second stage will be the period of the enemy's strategic consolidation and our preparation for the counter-offensive. The third stage will be the period of our strategic counter-offensive and the enemy's strategic retreat.[241]

As of this writing, with the exception of the CPN-M, not one self-appellated Maoist insurgency has reached even the second stage since the fall of the Soviet Union.[242] It cannot be said that any such surviving orga-

---

238 "Abimael Guzmán: Peru's Shining Path Guerrilla Leader Dies at 86," *BBC*, September 11, 2021.

239 However, in the case of Ansarallah, this may soon change as a result of the peace process that is ongoing as of this writing, as noted in Chapter Two.

240 In 2010, for example, even the Center for Strategic and International Studies (a Washington-based think tank) gave a large estimate (140,000 fighters) of the size of the Naxalite militias in India. (William Magioncalda, "A Modern Insurgency: India's Evolving Naxalite Problem," *South Asia Monitor* no. 140, CSIS, April 8, 2010.)

241 Mao Zedong, "On Protracted War," May 1938.

242 It is naturally uncommon for an organization engaged in a military conflict to publish details about the progress of their struggle. The most optimistic, pro-Maoist estimates are typically written by international supporters or veterans of these struggles, but even these analyses do not indicate that this critical stage has yet been reached. For example, Jose Maria Sison, the former Chairman of the Communist Party of the Philippines, whose armed New People's Army has been waging guerrilla war against the government for over half a century as of this writing, declared that the Party's five-year plan from 2017 to 2021 aimed to "bring the protracted people's war to the advanced phase of the strategic defensive, in order to reach the threshold of the strategic stalemate." (Jose Maria Sison, "The Filipino People's Revolutionary Armed Struggle for National and Social Liberation in the Past 50 Years," *Philippine Revolution Web Central*, March 28, 2019.) However, by 2021, according to Sison,

nization does not have the will to fight. When viewed in the context of the current stage of imperialism, their lack of progress is instead quite explicable: they must make do without an external supply of needed resources.

This unfortunate reality has not escaped those still engaging in armed struggle. Three quotations from the Popular Front for the Liberation of Palestine's *Strategy for the Liberation of Palestine*, written during the Cold War, best describe how such movements must take into account the geopolitical context they inhabit to have any hope of victory:

> If we remember the enemy camp and recall its size and nature, we will immediately realise that any strategic thinking about the Palestinian liberation struggle must cover the mobilisation of all forces of the revolution on the Arab and world levels, because it is only through such mobilisation and concentration that we can create the power capable of confronting Israel, Zionism, world imperialism and Arab reaction. *The Palestinian revolution which is fused together with the Arab revolution and in alliance with world revolution is alone capable of achieving victory. To confine the Palestinian revolution within the limits of the Palestinian people would mean failure, if we remember the nature of the enemy alliance which we are facing.* [emphasis added][243]
>
> World imperialism at this time has circumstances and conditions which distinguish it from what it was in previous times, and is exercising the process of exploitation of peoples by new methods which differ from its old ones. On the other hand, the camp of the anti-imperialist forces has in respect of size and power, a new position and level which differ from those before the Second World War. The liberation movements of the world should realise the basic international facts which govern this period of history. *The Palestine and Arab liberation movement does not move in a vacuum. It lives and fights in the midst of specific world circumstances which affect and react with it, and all this will determine our fate. The international ground on which national liberation*

---

protracted war in the Philippines remained in the strategic defensive phase. (Jose Maria Sison, *Specific Characteristics of People's War in the Philippines* (1974).

243 The Popular Front for the Liberation of Palestine (PFLP), *Strategy for the Liberation of Palestine* (1969), 24–25.

movements move, has always been, and will remain, a basic factor in determining peoples' destinies. [emphasis added][244]

The revolutionary army will be able to triumph over the enemy's superiority through the following conditions: be politically aware and coalesce with the organised masses that support it and supply it with its human and material requirements; *ally itself with world revolutionary forces who will furnish it with support and reinforcements;* [emphasis added] gain experience and efficiency through its struggle and coalesce with the revolutionary party which provides it with a clear view and an organic connection with all revolutionary forces at all levels.[245]

The PFLP recognized that against the entire Western imperialist alliance—the full force of which is invariably brought down upon *any* attempt by the working class to gain state power—a revolutionary vanguard, even if led by the proletariat with popular support, was *not sufficient* to accomplish their goals:

The mobilisation and concentration of the revolutionary forces on the Palestinian level, even through a political organization adhering to and guided by scientific socialism, mobilising the downtrodden classes on the greatest scale and forming with the petit bourgeoisie a united front, *will not suffice to create a revolutionary camp capable of gaining superiority over the enemy camp consisting of a strong and wide front which includes Israel, the Zionist movement, imperialism and Arab reaction.* [emphasis added][246]

Throughout its history, the PFLP has worked tirelessly to ally itself with the most powerful anti-imperialist forces that existed beyond Palestine. During the Cold War, it sought to maintain a connection with both the PRC and the Soviet Union, as well as the anti-imperialist governments that existed in Egypt, Syria, and Iraq. Later, it forged ties with the Islamic Republic of Iran. By the end of the twentieth century, victory as defined by the PFLP—a single "democratic national state in Palestine in which both Arabs and Jews will live as citizens with equal rights and

---

244 PFLP, *Strategy for the Liberation of Palestine*, 34.
245 PFLP, *Strategy for the Liberation of Palestine*, 40.
246 PFLP, *Strategy for the Liberation of Palestine*, 26.

obligations"[247]—had grown even further away than it had been in 1969, given that the greatest possible alliance with anti-imperialist forces on a global scale was so diminished. The conditions of super-imperialism force upon armed national liberation movements an unhappy choice: negotiate for peace or continue to fight an uphill struggle for survival until these conditions become more favorable. Without "a clear perspective of the enemy and a clear perspective of the revolutionary forces," the PFLP wrote that "national action becomes an impetuous gamble which soon ends in failure."[248]

It is not a coincidence that the most successful peasant- and proletarian-led movements of the super-imperial era tended to have some connection with a large and powerful state sponsor. The UWSA, in particular, is most likely the last remaining proxy of the PRC,[249] and with 20,000 soldiers is considered the largest, best-equipped, and most powerful faction in Myanmar's multi-sided civil war—as of this writing, the longest ongoing civil war in the world.[250] In 2022, *Asia Times* considered the UWSA an "early winner" of the renewed hostilities between rebel groups following the military coup of the previous year.[251] Of armed national liberation movements that are *not* unambiguously led by the peasant or proletarian classes, the most successful have typically also received significant material support from a powerful existing state.[252]

Overall, religion has replaced Marxism as the most vital anti-imperialist ideology, which sometimes obscures the class struggle to the advantage of the petit bourgeoisie and to the detriment of the proletariat, as it has within Iran, even as it provides the proletariat with the most practical avenue for resistance. Revolutionary Shi'ism forms the basis of both Ansarallah and Hezbollah, and the PFLP's current orientation in the struggle for Palestinian liberation is as a subordinate partner to Hamas—which given the current balance of anti-imperialist forces, is the

---

247 PFLP, *Strategy for the Liberation of Palestine*, 43.

248 PFLP, *Strategy for the Liberation of Palestine*, 2.

249 Due mostly to the UWSA's proximity on the Chinese border and its cooperation in preventing a refugee crisis, it is an unofficial exception to the PRC's non-interference foreign policy.

250 Bertil Lintner, *The United Wa State Army and Burma's Peace Process* (United States Institute of Peace, 2019).

251 Anthony Davis, "Wa an Early Winner of Myanmar's Post-Coup War," *Asia Times*, February 22, 2022.

252 Lebanon's Hezbollah, for example, receives weapons, money, and training from the Islamic Republic of Iran.

only path available to it.[253] According to the PFLP's General Secretary Ahmad Sa'adat:

> The development of Islamic organizations throughout the world is a direct consequence of the collapse of the Soviet Union. It weakened the organizations of the Left that fought against imperialism in the Arab world. The communist forces in the Arab world have applied the viewpoints of the Soviet Union by the book and have never developed their own theoretical and political "flavor." That would have enabled them to analyze the contradictions in the Arab world. After the collapse of the Soviet Union, most left parties were shocked and confused and started to quarrel. They lost their confidence in Marxist-Leninist theory. Their weakening left a gap that is being filled by the Islamist movements....[254]

Even where these ideologies are a progressive force against neocolonialism and the weight of the super-empire, they are not sufficient to liberate the working class. Materially, they are closest to the popular front model—i.e., based on class collaboration with the petit and national bourgeoisie, and subject to all the instability, contradiction, and class antagonism such an alliance entails. Proceeding to the next highest stage in Marxist terms—proletarian control of the state—requires a global unification of resistance that in the past was provided only by an already-existing bloc of proletarian states ready to support others in revolution.

In fact, without a vital socialist bloc—i.e. a return to the Cold War stage—even the creation of new anti-imperialist states of a *bourgeois* character has become extraordinarily more difficult. Between 1989 and 2022, Nkrumah's dream of a united Africa drifted further from realization than it had been during his lifetime. Neocolonialism was restored in Angola, Mozambique, Somalia and Libya one way or another; ethno-religious

---

253 Catholic Liberation Theology has also been a strong component of the Bolivarian Revolution; Hugo Chávez frequently attacked the conservative Catholic Church leadership in Venezuela on religious grounds and used religious rhetoric in his speeches. In 2006, he compared President Bush to the Devil (David Stout, "Chávez Calls Bush 'the Devil' in U.N. Speech," *New York Times,* September 20, 2006), and once famously said of the revolution, "Either you are with God or you are with the Devil, and we are with God." (Larry Rohter, "Now Chavez Takes On the Church in Venezuela," *New York Times,* December 19, 1999.)

254 Ahmad Sa'adat, Interview with Ahmad Sa'adat in Jericho Prison – February 2006.

conflict exacerbated by comprador governments and imperialist finance split Sudan and has recently threatened to split Ethiopia. The trend has been toward division and not unity, and until a sufficient counterbalance or disruption to the super-empire's mechanisms of control exists, the reversal of this trend is unlikely.[255] Chapters Eleven and Twelve will explore what form such a disruption is likely to take, and to what degree one might now, at long last, be emerging.

---

255 There is an obvious "chicken-and-egg" problem raised by this conclusion, namely, if a revolution must depend upon international support from a socialist bloc, how this bloc constructed—and how it might be reconstructed—in the first place must be determined. If all remaining socialist countries—the PRC, Vietnam, Laos, Cuba, and the DPRK—are in effect descendants of the Bolsheviks, originating long ago from their first uprising in Petrograd, it is essential to make a close analysis of the conditions of the Revolution of 1917. An attempt to determine the factors in the Bolsheviks' success, both in taking state power and in retaining it, along with their relevance to the present, can be found in Appendix C.

CHAPTER FOUR

Bourgeois Anti-Imperialism

> *"We agreed to shrink. We began to worship Hayek as fiercely*
> *as we had worshiped Marx. We slashed the demographic,*
> *industrial and military potential by half. We turned our backs*
> *on the other Soviet republics and were about to say good-bye*
> *to the autonomies. ... But even a downsized and humble Russia*
> *proved unable to negotiate the turn towards the West."*
>
> —Vladislav Surkov, "The Loneliness of the Half-Breed," 2018[256]

Chapter One identified the divisions in the global periphery between the comprador bourgeoisie who collaborate with an empire to extract resources from their own country, the national bourgeoisie who seek to retain these resources for their own exclusive benefit, and the lower bourgeoisie or petit bourgeoisie who aspire to join one of the other groups by attaining greater capital. Just as they did in Venezuela, the less prosperous bourgeois classes have a strong incentive to eliminate the restrictions on development that comprador rule enforces upon a neocolony. This chapter will explore *their* goals and limitations, their relationship with the other classes, and the nature of their conflict with the super-empire.

The Development of the National Bourgeoisie

In a 1961 report to the British Foreign Office, the UK's ambassador to Iran described how this aspirational attitude had begun to produce revolutionaries:

> Throughout the upper and middle classes, there are professional people, politicians, economists, planners, bankers, architects, journalists and writers who have been highly educated abroad. ... Although most of these people belong to privileged or prosperous families, whether of the upper or upper middle classes, they comprise a number of the real Iranian reformers and even

---

256 Vladislav Surkov, "The Loneliness of the Half-Breed," *Russia in Global Affairs,* May 28, 2018.

revolutionaries. Many indeed would readily connive at revolution, if they judged that it would serve to amputate the "dead hand" of social and bureaucratic tradition and would offer a hope of more efficient administration and fulfilment of their own ideas whether political and economic aspirations or personal ambitions. These people have seen what is going on in more highly developed societies. They are well read, they have been members of students' unions and debating clubs; and above all they have escaped for a few years from the autocratic system of domestic relations of Iranian family convention. They are acutely conscious, not so much of the absence of political freedoms in their own country, as of social injustice, nepotism, corruption and incompetence.... The bulk of them are not more than 45 years old, and some of them together constitute virtually a corporate intellectual elite...[257]

The Iranian Revolution of 1978 is commonly oversimplified, often called the "Islamic" Revolution due to the theocratic system that eventually emerged. More fundamental to the Revolution's development, however, was the ongoing class struggle. Under Shah Mohammad Reza Pahlavi's reign, the population of Iran had doubled, and the working class became the most numerous—particularly in Tehran and other urban areas, as many peasant sharecroppers, unable to purchase enough farmland to live off following the Shah's land reform program in the early 1960s, migrated by necessity to the cities.[258] Without their support, the popular movement would have been unable to overthrow the comprador Shah. Rather than ideology—religious or communist—the essential causes of the urban proletariat's mass mobilizations were low wages, rising rents, severe income inequality, and the insufficiency of the Shah's reforms. Workers began a massive strike wave in 1978, culminating in a general strike in October and November which paralyzed oil production; 35,000 oil workers had gone on strike demanding wage increases.[259] The Resolution of the Ashura March of December 1978, which the *New York*

---

257 Ansari, "The Myth of the White Revolution: Mohammad Reza Shah, 'Modernization' and the Consolidation of Power," *Middle Eastern Studies* 37, no. 3 (July 2001): 4.

258 Ervand Abrahamian, *A History of Modern Iran* (Cambridge University Press, 2008), 131–32.

259 Jonathan Kandell, "Iran's Oil Workers Told to End Strike or Face Discharge," *New York Times,* November 13, 1978.

Times reported was attended by "several million" protestors,[260] demanded "the right of workers and peasants to the full benefit from the product of their labor."[261] The Shah fled the country the following month, never to return.

As a remnant of feudalism, the landholding clergy were quite naturally conservative, yet by 1979 it was a demographic inevitability that feudalism would never be restored as the prevailing mode of production in Iran. The millions of new city-dwellers could not return to the countryside even if they wanted to, and reversing land reform was politically impossible even for a figure of Ruhollah Khomeini's considerable influence. However, decades of repression by the Shah's secret police had severely diminished every potentially revolutionary organization (liberal and communist alike), leaving only the clerics relatively untouched (with the exception of Khomeini himself, who had been arrested and exiled). At the height of the Revolution, the clergy therefore found itself in command of a broad alliance of classes—everyone, really—that had mobilized against the Shah.

This alliance quickly destroyed the Iranian comprador class and redistributed much of its wealth. Many wealthy pro-Western business owners followed the Shah, or else fled after the Islamic Republic was officially declared by referendum in April 1979. That summer, the revolutionary government moved to expropriate their assets, as well as nationalize all private or foreign-owned banks,[262] insurance companies, and large-scale industry,[263] all without compensation.[264] Between 1979 and 1980, the nominal minimum wage was tripled,[265] and when the rural peasantry

---

260 The article cites Iranian opposition sources placing the attendance at 7 million, or one-fifth of the entire population, as well as the Shah's government, which admitted a total of nearly 2 million. (Nicholas Gage, "Protesters March for 2d Day in Iran; Violence Is Limited," *New York Times,* December 12, 1978.)

261 Sohrab Behdad, "Winners and Losers of the Iranian Revolution: A Study in Income Distribution," *International Journal of Middle East Studies* 21, no. 3 (August 1989): 327.

262 William Branigin, "Iran Announces Takeover of All Private Banks," *Washington Post,* June 8, 1979.

263 Youssef M. Ibrahim, "Iran Taking Over More Industries; General Motors Affiliate Affected," *New York Times,* July 6, 1979.

264 Sohrab Behdad, "Winners and Losers of the Iranian Revolution," 328.

265 According to a 1989 paper in the *International Journal of Middle East Studies* by Sohrab Behdad, a Professor of Economics at Denison University in Ohio, the minimum wage was first increased from 210 rials to 567 rials in 1979, then was increased by another 12 percent in 1980. ("Winners and Losers of the Iranian Revolution," 332.)

seized 800,000 hectares of farmland from large private landholdings, the government was either unwilling or unable to return the confiscated land to its former owners.[266]

Nevertheless, once their common enemy had been eliminated, the alliance gave way to the class struggle between bourgeoisie and proletariat. While Khomeini's government gave to workers with its left hand, it ruthlessly crushed their independent revolutionary leadership with its right. All Marxist parties were banned and their leaders arrested. Even the Tudeh Party, a Marxist-Leninist organization which had supported Khomeini, was eventually suppressed in 1983. Throughout the 1980s, the government executed several thousand political prisoners, including not just the Shah's former secret policemen and loyal military officers, but members of the People's Mujahedin of Iran,[267] and many communists as well. Workers' councils, which had seized factories and organized local proletarian resistance to the Shah, were gradually disbanded or replaced by Islamic Councils more loyal to the government.[268] Meanwhile, Iran's secular national legislature became dominated by the petit bourgeoisie. In *A History of Modern Iran*, Iranian-American historian Ervand Abrahamian writes: "the Majles, which had been a debating chamber for notables in the distant past and a club for the shah's placemen in more recent years, was now filled with the propertied middle class. For example, more than 70 percent of the deputies in the First Islamic Majles [elected in 1980] came from that class. Their fathers included 63 clergymen, 69 farm owners, 39 shopkeepers, and 12 merchants."[269]

Today, there can be little doubt that the Iranian bourgeoisie has developed and holds state power with a grip that is stronger now than it has ever been. In 2006, the Islamic Republic's constitution was amended to allow the privatization of 80% of shares of government businesses (excepting the National Iranian Oil Company and several other key state-owned entities).[270] Though implemented at a slower pace than neoliberal shock therapy, privatization has nonetheless proceeded over the last two decades, even despite strikes and protests by the affected workers. Within a few

---

266 Sohrab Behdad, "Winners and Losers of the Iranian Revolution," 329.

267 A militant organization that had attempted to overthrow the Islamic Republic, it joined the Iraqi side during the Iran-Iraq War, and has since become a willing tool of U.S. regime-change efforts.

268 Sohrab Behdad, "Winners and Losers of the Iranian Revolution," 335.

269 Ervand Abrahamian, *A History of Modern Iran*, 179.

270 The Islamic Republic of Iran, "Principle 44 of the Constitution of the Islamic Republic of Iran," art. C.

years of the constitutional amendment, the government began gradually privatizing the banking sector, including Bank Saderat Iran, one of the largest state-owned banks.[271] According to the *Tehran Times* in 2014, hundreds of state-owned businesses had been privatized or were slated to be privatized;[272] by 2017, the government had privatized over half the country's power plants, and further planned to privatize at least 80% in total.[273] By 2019, the government formally held only a minority share—which it pledged to sell entirely by 2021—in Iran Khodro and SAIPA, two of the largest domestic car manufacturers.[274] Poverty has declined considerably since the Revolution, recently aided in large part by substantial direct cash transfers from the government during the early 2010s;[275] yet hard limits to this willingness to redistribute wealth have emerged. A combination of U.S. sanctions, declining oil prices, and the COVID-19 pandemic caused economic disaster in Iran during the latter part of the decade. GDP per capita plunged;[276] in 2020, the World Bank downgraded Iran back to its "lower-middle income" classification,[277] and despite the still-existing welfare state, inflation likely outpaced wage increases, according to analysis from Iran's Ministry of Finance and Economic Affairs.[278] Yet Iran's new rich went unharmed; while two decades of progress in reducing rural poverty were erased,[279] the government's priority during the crisis was to support the stock market with large infusions of cash from its sovereign wealth fund,[280] in effect sustaining private fortunes with public money.

---

271 "Bank Saderat Iran IPO Today," *Tehran Times*, June 10, 2009.

272 "Iran to Privatize 186 State-Run Companies: Official," *Tehran Times*, May 11, 2014.

273 "Power Plant Privatizations Reach 55%, More to Come," *Financial Tribune*, August 16, 2017.

274 "Gov't Reiterates Plan to Privatize IKCO, SAIPA," *Financial Tribune*, June 24, 2019.

275 Djavad Salehi-Isfahani, "Poverty and Income Inequality in the Islamic Republic of Iran," *Revue Internationale Des Études Du Développement*, no. 229 (2017): 113–36. https://www.jstor.org/stable/26452360

276 World Bank, *GDP per Capita (Current US$) - Iran, Islamic Rep.*

277 World Bank, *The World by Income and Region.*

278 Maziar Motamedi, "Humour, Resignation, Despair: Living with Inflation in Iran," *Al Jazeera*, October 5, 2020.

279 Djavad Salehi-Isfahani, "Rising Poverty and Falling Living Standards in Iran in 2020," *Tyranny of Numbers* [blog], August 28, 2021. https://djavadsalehi.com/2021/08/28/rising-poverty-and-falling-living-standards-in-iran-in-2020/

280 "NDF to Inject over $595m into the Stock Market by Late March," *Tehran Times*, January 9, 2021.

During the Cold War stage of imperialism, this was a possible path of development from neocolonialism to a national-bourgeois state that, as described in Chapter Two, is now largely precluded by the super-empire's mechanisms of control. However, it is not the only path.

In the decade after the dissolution of the Soviet Union, Russia was ruled by a new comprador elite, enabled by President Yeltsin and the U.S. government[281] to plunder the former Soviet state-run economy. Throughout the 1990s, this comprador bourgeoisie siphoned billions from the Russian public into Western banks,[282] and facilitated the export of raw materials, removing quantitative restrictions and reducing export taxes.[283] In the 2000s, however, the plunder of Russia changed in character after Vladimir Putin succeeded Yeltsin as president and struck a "grand bargain" with Russia's new rich. Thereafter, oil and gas production were renationalized,[284] new taxes were levied to create the federal Stabilization Fund, and Russia began to recover economically. The Russian Federation also began to reassert itself as a regional power—often, and increasingly, against the wishes of the United States.

Both President Putin and Ayatollah Khomeini (or now, Khamenei) are sometimes deemed "bonapartists" who stand somehow above the class struggle, mediating between antagonistic classes so that the neither bourgeoisie nor proletariat gain a decisive advantage. But while the "bonapartist" concept is derived from Marx's description of Louis-Napoléon Bonaparte and his seizure of power that ended the Second French Republic in 1852, Marx himself did not employ the term as his ideological descendants have. In his work *The Eighteenth Brumaire of Louis Bonaparte*, Marx wrote:

---

281 In an interview in 1997, the coordinator of U.S. assistance to the former Soviet Union remarked, "If we hadn't been there to provide funding to [privatization architect and Russian Deputy Prime Minister Anatoly] Chubais, could we have won the battle to carry out privatization? Probably not." (Peter Reddaway, "Beware the Russian Reformer," *Washington Post,* August 23, 1997.)

282 See Chapter Two for a more detailed description of the disaster this process caused for the Russian working class.

283 Glenn E. Curtis, *Russia: A Country Study* (Washington, D.C.: Federal Research Division, Library of Congress, 1998), sec. "Foreign Economic Relations," 372–379.

284 Marin Katusa, "Vladimir Putin Is The New Global Shah Of Oil," *Forbes,* October 29, 2012.

And yet the state power is not suspended in the air. Bonaparte represented a class, and the most numerous class of French society at that, the small-holding peasants.[285]

Bonapart*ism*,[286] if it means anything, must refer instead to the political strategy determined by the specific crossroads in the development of class society that was unique to mid-nineteenth century Europe, in which the feudal aristocracy was declining but still powerful, and the bourgeoisie and proletariat were ascending but still weak. Yet no matter the balance of class power, the idea that an executive unsupported by any class might rule over a country of millions for decades is as nonsensical today as it was two centuries ago.

The Iranian clergy's base of class support was always the traditional bazaari merchant class, i.e., the urban lower bourgeoisie. Khomeini's choice for prime minister—Mehdi Bazargan, the managing director of a construction company, who had once been the chairman of the National Iranian Oil Company after it was nationalized by Prime Minister Mohammed Mossadegh in 1951—though not technically bourgeois himself was clearly a representative more friendly to capitalists than to workers. In advance of Bazargan's appointment, the *New York Times* described how he negotiated an end to the oil workers' strike and "confronted and overcame a Marxist element among the strikers."[287]

It is equally clear from Putin's rise to power that his base of support was not any other class than the bourgeoisie. Not only was Putin Yeltsin's handpicked successor, who had served in Yeltsin's government, but when he became the interim president after Yeltsin resigned in 1999,[288] he was still virtually unknown to the public. He had only become prime minister—the fifth prime minister in the space of a year—in 1998, appointed by a vote of the State Duma rather than by referendum. In what passed

---

285 Karl Marx, *The Eighteenth Brumaire of Louis Bonaparte,* Chapter VII (1852).

286 Marx did not even use this word in *The Eighteenth Brumaire*; "Bonapartist" he used only to denote supporters of Louis Bonaparte himself, and perhaps of the original Napoleon Bonaparte.

287 R.W. Apple Jr., "Engineer, 73, Might Head a Khomeini Rule," *New York Times,* January 23, 1979.

288 Yeltsin, after a decade of his horrific pro-Western policies, suffered the fate of many comprador leaders. By November, a poll showed he was so unpopular that if an election were held that month, he would receive no more than 0.2% of the vote. [Stephen White, "The Russian Presidential Election, March 2000," *Electoral Studies* 20, no. 3 (September 2001): 484–489.]

for his political platform in the next election, Putin made strongly-worded but vague promises to be tough on crime and corruption, and to fight poverty, yet he also pledged that "It is our duty to secure property rights and protect entrepreneurs against arbitrary and illegal interference in their activities" and did not mention any specific policy in the interests of workers.[289] The proletarian demographic of the Russian electorate was instead targeted by his opponent and strongest contender, Gennady Zyuganov, who stood for the Communist Party (KPRF) and ran on an explicit platform of re-expanding the public sector, raising wages, and reducing the cost of housing.[290] [291]

Putin's "grand bargain" itself, rather than the act of a "dictator" or a "bonapartist" unilaterally subordinating or manipulating an entire ruling class to his individual will, was in fact first proposed by the oligarchs themselves, in an arrangement to be brokered by Prime Minister Yevgeny Primakov. According to political scientist Gerald Easter, Primakov attempted to negotiate a deal in which big business would cease tax evasion if the state granted an amnesty on wealth redistribution. Such offers had been rejected both by Yeltsin and—initially—by Putin.[292] The agreement Putin eventually reached with the business elite involved more political concessions and a more comprehensive tax reform—but not a redistribution of their existing wealth. His administration did severely punish a few of the Yeltsin-era robber barons, in particular Mikhail Khodorkovsky and Boris Berezovsky—who were not coincidentally among the most prominent and egregious compradors.[293] After Khodorkovsky—the richest man in Russia at the time—attempted to sell a large stake of his oil company Yukos to Chevron in 2003, he was arrested by federal officials and

289 Vladimir Putin, "Open Letter to Voters," published in the newspapers *Izvestia, Kommersant,* and *Komsomolskaya Pravda,* February 25, 2000.

290 Stephen White, "The Russian Presidential Election, March 2000."

291 The KPRF has remained the largest opposition party, but thereafter, Putin's government created its own controlled opposition to reduce the KPRF's influence. According to Wood, "[A Just Russia] was the Kremlin's own confection, set up in 2006 to siphon votes from the Communist Party (KPRF)." (Tony Wood, *Russia Without Putin: Money, Power and the Myths of the New Cold War* (Verso Books, 2020), sec. Chapter 1: The Man and the System.)

292 Gerald M. Easter, *Capital, Coercion, and Postcommunist States* (Cornell University Press, 2012), 81.

293 In 1996, they had been ringleaders of the "Davos Pact," a conspiracy among the Russian delegation to the World Economic Forum to influence the upcoming election and guarantee Yeltsin a second term. (Matthew Bodner, "Russia's 8 Most Memorable Davos Moments," *The Moscow Times,* January 22, 2014.)

sentenced to nine years in prison.[294] However, the majority of the Russia's new bourgeoisie were untouched, and instead enriched further. Most of the Yeltsin-era billionaires—for example Roman Abramovich,[295] Oleg Deripaska, Alisher Usmanov, Viktor Vekselberg, Mikhail Prokhorov, and Vagit Alekperov—later benefited from their association with Putin.[296] The assets of Yukos, for example, were seized and redistributed—not just to the state directly, according to Easter, but also to other, "more politically compliant tycoons."[297]

Many new billionaires were minted since Putin became president, and the overall wealth of the Russian bourgeoisie has only increased. Though tax evasion was curtailed, under Putin's leadership, Russia's top corporate income tax rate fell to 20%, below both the global average and the European average.[298] Historian Tony Wood writes:

> [Putin introduced] a series of measures designed to extend the reach of private capital: in 2001, a flat income tax set at 13 per cent; in 2002, a labour code scaling back workers' rights; tax cuts for businesses in 2002 and 2003.[299]

What explains the willingness of Yeltsin's robber barons to compromise at all? Most likely, they knew they could not proceed as they had indefinitely. A key feature of neocolonialism has been the control of the neocolony's own military forces by a foreign empire; in nearly every Latin American country, for example,[300] the comprador establishment has become entrenched within the military over many generations. Russia, however, was not so underdeveloped. Managers of the large former Soviet military and state apparatus—now broadly referred to as the "siloviki"—had no such loyalty to the West and no history of their patronage.

---

294 David Black, "Kremlin Threat to U.S.-Yukos Deal," *The Guardian*, August 3, 2003.

295 Abramovich is rumored to have recommended Putin to Yeltsin as a potential successor, and in 2012 fought a bitter legal battle against the exiled Berezovsky in a London court. (Luke Harding, "Is Abramovich at Last Paying the Price for Being Too Close to Putin?," *The Guardian*, May 21, 2018.)

296 Blake Schmidt and Scott Carpenter, "Who Are Russia's Oligarchs and Can They Sway Putin?" *Bloomberg*, March 21, 2022.

297 Gerald M. Easter, *Capital, Coercion, and Postcommunist States*, 82.

298 Sean Bray, "Corporate Tax Rates around the World, 2021," *Tax Foundation*, December 9, 2021.

299 Tony Wood, *Russia Without Putin*, sec. Chapter 1: The Man and the System.

300 With a few exceptions such as Venezuela (see Chapter Three).

Rather than become the victims of a new cycle of neocolonialism in Russia, Yeltsin's robber barons had chosen—for their own protection, and for most, their own interest—to centralize and thus stabilize state power, allowing their class to expand to include the siloviki and develop into a true national bourgeoisie.

Nevertheless, the financial interests of the developing Russian bourgeoisie alone did not alienate them from the West. When the stage of super-imperialism began, national-bourgeois states at first sought not to resist the super-empire, but to join it—on their own terms, rather than as subservient compradors.

Imperialist Exclusivity

Khomeini's successors attempted not only to privatize state-owned enterprises and infrastructure but to attract investment from the West. In 1995, the Iranian government signed a contract with a French company to develop oil fields in the Persian Gulf.[301] The Tehran Stock Exchange was revived. Under President Akbar Hashemi Rafsanjani, Iran first applied to join the World Trade Organization. In 1999, President Mohammad Khatami went even further, proposing a "total restructuring" of the economy, and spoke of the importance of making Iran safe for foreign capital.[302] In spite of Colonel Muammar Gaddafi's socialistic rhetoric, in 2008 the Libyan government also began to embrace private enterprise.[303] In 2010, it announced that half of the state-run economy would be privatized, and that foreign investment would no longer face any limitations, other than in the banking sector and in oil and gas exploration.[304]

Similarly, with Putin as president, the Russian Federation at first remained oriented toward the West. According to Wood:

> After 1991, the Russian elite tended to see the country's future as lying either alongside or within the liberal internationalist bloc led by the United States. This commitment first gained ascendancy

301 Sen. Alfonse D'Amato (R-NY), S.1228 — 104th Congress (1995-1996): *Iran Oil Sanctions Act of 1995.*

302 Agence France-Presse, "Iran President's 5-Year Plan Would Privatize Major Industries." *New York Times,* September 16, 1999.

303 Tom Pfeiffer, "Gaddafi Reform Heralds Private Sector Push," *Reuters,* March 26, 2008.

304 Lamine Ghanmi, "Libya Aims to Privatise Half of Economy in Decade," *Reuters,* March 31, 2010.

in the Kremlin under Gorbachev, and reached its peak during the Yeltsin years; but it remained substantially in place under Putin and Medvedev too—lasting much longer than is assumed by the general run of Western media commentary. It was only finally undone in the wake of the Ukraine crisis [of 2014], to be succeeded by a more combative vision.[305]

This assessment was echoed by none other than Vladislav Surkov, a key figure in the Russian Presidential Administration and one of Putin's personal advisors. In a 2018 article titled "The Loneliness of the Half-Breed," Surkov declared that as of 2014, ". . . Russia's epic westward quest is finally over ... attempts to become part and parcel of the Western civilization, to get into the 'good family' of European nations have ground to a final halt." Russia's cultural and geopolitical identity was that of "[a] half-blood, a cross-breed ..." belonging to neither East nor West; the famous quote questionably attributed to Tsar Alexander III that "Russia has only two allies: its army and navy" seemed to Surkov to best describe the "geopolitical loneliness which should have long been accepted as our fate."[306]

The new Russian national bourgeoisie, having secured their country against dispossessive accumulation, anticipated and expected greater integration with the West as junior partners to the super-empire, rather than as its subjects. Many of the Yeltsin-era billionaires who had raised Putin up still kept their massive fortunes in Western tax havens (and in early 2022, with the most to lose from sanctions, they were the most reluctant among their class to support the military intervention in Ukraine).[307] According to Amin in 2006,

> the dismemberment of the Russian Federation, following that of the USSR, is a major strategic objective for the United States. Until now the Russian ruling class does not appear to have understood this. It seemed convinced that, having lost the war, it could go on to win the peace—as Germany and Japan did before it. What it

---

305 Tony Wood, *Russia Without Putin*, sec. Chapter 5: After the Maidan.

306 Vladislav Surkov, "The Loneliness of the Half-Breed," *Russia in Global Affairs*, May 28, 2018.

307 For example, in March 2022—only a week after the intervention began—*Reuters* reported that several of the "so-called oligarchs who built fortunes in the chaos of the 1990s" were publicly calling for peace. (Guy Faulconbridge, "Russian Billionaire Fridman to Contest 'groundless' EU Sanctions," *Reuters*, March 1, 2022.)

forgot was that Washington needed the recovery of its two wartime enemies, precisely in order to face down the Soviet challenge. The new conjuncture is different, as the United States no longer has a serious rival.[308]

Perhaps, had the Russian bourgeoisie not been so young and immature as a class, and had it not held such a rosy view of its one-time benefactors, it would not have taken so long to learn the lesson that had been drilled into Iran's ruling class during the preceding decades. Despite its desire for reconciliation and development, the Islamic Republic has continually experienced rejection and aggression. In 1996, the United States blocked its application to the WTO, and the one time (more recently) that it applied for a loan from the IMF, it was also denied due to U.S. influence.[309] Even during Rafsanjani's relatively reform-minded presidency, in which the Islamic Republic pursued integration into the global economy, new sanctions on Iran were imposed both by President Clinton's executive orders[310] [311] and by the U.S. Congress.[312] In 2002, President George W. Bush declared Iran to be part of an "Axis of Evil." When the United States and the Islamic Republic finally agreed upon the Joint Comprehensive Plan of Action in 2015 to ease sanctions in exchange for guarantees regarding the Iranian nuclear program, the U.S. reneged almost immediately. In 2020, on orders from President Trump, the U.S. military assassinated the Islamic Republic's most celebrated military leader, General Qasem Soleimani. Just as it had with regard to Gaddafi's Libya, the super-empire designated the Islamic Republic to be its enemy, and nothing less than its destruction could ever suffice.

The super-empire, continually driven to increase profits by the Western financial oligarchy, cannot permit the loss of a profitable neocolony. When a national bourgeoisie develops to the point of attaining sole control of state power, and moves to end foreign dispossessive accumulation within

308 Samir Amin, *Beyond U.S. Hegemony? Assessing the Prospects for a Multipolar World* (Zed Books, 2006), 10–11.

309 Ian Talley and Benoit Faucon, "U.S. to Block Iran's Request to IMF for $5 Billion Loan to Fight Coronavirus" *Wall Street Journal,* April 7, 2020.

310 President William J. Clinton, "Executive Order 12957—Prohibiting Certain Transactions With Respect to the Development of Iranian Petroleum Resources," March 15, 1995.

311 President William J. Clinton, "Executive Order 12959— Prohibiting Certain Transactions With Respect to Iran," May 6, 1995

312 Rep. Benjamin A. Gilman (R-NY-20), H.R.3107 — 104th Congress (1995-1996): *Iran and Libya Sanctions Act of 1996.*

its own country, this means less super-profits for the imperialists; and if this national bourgeoisie were to join the group of exploiters, there would be more imperialists among which to divide even less loot. To sustain its rate of profit, the super-empire must therefore remain an exclusive club, and finds it preferable to annihilate, rather than embrace, any potential new partner—especially one so large as Russia.

According to former National Security Advisor and National Endowment for Democracy board member Zbigniew Brzezinski in 1994:

> The politically decisive fact is that Russia bulks too large, is too backward currently and too powerful potentially to be assimilated as simply yet another member of the European Union or NATO. It would dilute the Western character of the European community and the American preponderance within the alliance.[313]

Even when the other former Soviet republics were subtracted from it, Russia retained a large and highly educated population, developed infrastructure, nuclear weapons, and the formidable military that the Soviet Union had been forced to create to compete with the United States during the Cold War. This both made Russia impossible for the super-empire to dominate for long, and, when it became clear to Russia that it would not be allowed to join as a junior exploiter either, enabled it to rebuild a sphere of influence over former Soviet republics in Eastern Europe, Central Asia, and the Caucasus.

Could this mean, as so many Western commentators and political theorists now breathlessly predict, that the Russian Federation has or will become an empire in its own right—one opposed to the United States, and thus returning world imperialism to the stage of inter-imperialist rivalry?

The Russian bourgeoisie is quite well-established. Of the selection of large countries measured by Credit Suisse's Global Wealth Report in 2020, wealth inequality in Russia was higher than in any other except Brazil.[314] According to *Forbes*, Russia's billionaire population reached a peak of 117 in 2021,[315] 17% of which had made their fortunes in the financial sector—the upper echelon of a burgeoning financial oligarchy, which is a necessary condition of imperialism according to Lenin's 1916 definition. In comparison with Western corporations, however, such

---

313 Zbigniew Brzezinski, "Normandy Evasion," *Washington Post,* May 2, 1994.
314 Credit Suisse Research Institute, *Global Wealth Report 2021,* 24.
315 Forbes, "World's Billionaires List: The Richest in 2021."

an oligarchy would appear to be profiting but little. In January 2019's *Monthly Review*, Stansfield Smith thoroughly explored Russia's financial position among the international community, finding that according to *Forbes Global 2000* list of richest corporations in the world, only 25 were Russian—a proportion which had in fact declined since the early 2010s—and collectively accounted for less than 1% of the list's collective assets.[316] As of 2022, the highest-valued Russian corporation, Gazprom, ranked 49th on the list.[317]

In 2020, only one of the world's 100 largest banks by total asset value was Russian, ranking 60th.[318] Raw materials, rather than capital or consumer goods, still constitute the majority of Russian exports.[319] Indeed, it is difficult to argue that Lenin's other principal requirement—that the export of capital driven by an empire's financial oligarchy takes on "exceptional importance"—applies to the Russian Federation. According to a recent study in the *Herald of the Russian Academy of Sciences*, Russians' direct investment abroad was not likely to significantly increase overall this decade, in large part due to the slow pace of technological modernization caused by sanctions.[320] Since its publication in early 2022, these sanctions only increased to unprecedented heights following the Russian intervention in Ukraine. Russia's aggregate total foreign direct investment (FDI) exceeded $400 billion during the early 2010s, but stood at less than that by 2022, according to the external sector statistics published by the Central Bank of the Russian Federation.[321] By comparison, in 2021 the United States held almost $10 *trillion* in foreign investment stock; the United Kingdom, Germany, and Japan approximately $2 trillion each; and Switzerland and France $1.5 trillion each. Among the super-empire's lesser partners, several—such as Spain and Italy (approximately $600 billion each)—had a much higher position, and even satellites such as the Republic of Korea and Sweden had aggregate totals greater than Russia's.[322] Despite the Russian Federation's relatively great size and

---

316 Stansfield Smith, "Is Russia Imperialist?" *Monthly Review online*, January 2, 2019.

317 Forbes, "The Global 2000."

318 Zarmina Ali, "The World's 100 Largest Banks, 2020," *S&P Global,* April 13, 2020.

319 Stansfield Smith, "Is Russia Imperialist?"

320 A. V. Kuznetsov, "Direct Investment from Russia Abroad: Changes since 2018," *Herald of the Russian Academy of Sciences* 91 (2021): 700–707.

321 Central Bank of the Russian Federation, "Direct Investment Cumulative Positions of the Russian Federation by Instrument (Directional Principle)."

322 U.N. Conference on Trade and Development, "UNCTAD/WIR/2022," 214.

wealth, by any objective measure, its capital exports are quite modest even for the lowest tier of imperial powers, with signs not of growth but of decline[323]—and given how brazenly Western governments have been confiscating Russian assets abroad since 2022, it is little wonder that Russian capitalists are even more reluctant to invest in other countries than before.

Though the Russian Federation has the military capability to intervene and settle conflicts within its sphere of influence to its own advantage, such as in Syria, Kazakhstan, &c., Russian finance capital has struggled to dominate even its closest neighbors. In 2014, at the height of Russian political influence in Ukraine since the dissolution of the Soviet Union, five major Russian financial institutions accounted for 16.8% of the Ukrainian banking sector's market share (slightly more than half of the 31% total market share of foreign-owned banks), according to the CEE Banking Sector Report from Austrian banking group Raiffeisen.[324] By 2020, this share had declined to 7.4%, held by only two major Russian banks (Alfa and Sberbank), while Western banks' share had increased to 17%.[325] In 2019, over four years after the beginning of the Russian intervention in Syria, the pro-Russian Syrian government had been sta-bilized, but approximately 70% of Syria's oil fields were still controlled by the Syrian Democratic Forces, the Kurdish-dominated and U.S.-backed militia coalition.[326] According to CNN, the following year a U.S. corporation was given a contract (by the U.S., rather than the Syrian, government) to develop 60% of these oil fields, which were expected to produce billions of dollars.[327] Even Kazakhstan, which has such close ties

---

323 Furthermore, as of 2022, over *half* of Russia's aggregate total of foreign direct investment ($224 billion) was invested in a *single country*, Cyprus! (Central Bank of the Russian Federation, "Dashboards 'Direct Investment Positions by Geographical Region, Partner Country, Instrument and Industry.'") Cyprus has a population of scarcely more than one million. *These* exports surely represent capital flight—i.e., the profits of the Russian bourgeoisie squirreled away in an international tax haven—rather than any project to extract an even greater amount of super-profits in Cypriot labor or natural resources. (Note that this does not imply that capital exports *in general* are not at the root of imperialism. The complex relation between capital exports and imperialism will be explored further in Chapter Six.)

324 VTB, Alfa, Sberbank, as well as Prominvestbank (then owned by a Russian state-owned enterprise) and Ukrsotsbank (a subsidiary of the Alfa Group). (Raiffeisen Research, "CEE Banking Sector Report 2014," 51.)

325 Raiffeissen Research, "CEE Banking Sector Report 2020," 43.

326 Reality Check team, "Syria War: Who Benefits from Its Oil Production?," *BBC News,* November 20, 2019.

327 Kylie Atwood and Ryan Browne, "Former Army Delta Force Officer, US

that it hosts Russia's space program and anti-ballistic missile tests, and is part of the Russian Federation's Collective Security Treaty Organization, has been far more thoroughly penetrated by Western capital, which owns its largest oil field through TengizChevroil, a consortium dominated by Chevron and ExxonMobil.[328] As of January 2022, Russian oil company LukArco accounted for a paltry 5% share in the consortium, to Chevron and ExxonMobil's collective 75% share.[329] In their initial research quantifying the rate of unequal exchange, Hickel and his colleagues determined that as of 2018, Russia was in fact among the most *exploited* countries, losing an amount of value through trade several times greater than India or Indonesia on an annual per capita basis.[330]

As shown in Chapters One and Two, Lenin's 1916 definition of imperialism is both obsolete and incomplete. Yet of the criteria he identified that *are* still relevant under the current stage of imperialism, the Russian Federation fulfills them only on a quantitatively minuscule and qualitatively irrelevant level. If it were to be called an empire, it would be a fourth rate empire, and in recent years has been declining. Of the super-empire's mechanisms of control, the Russian Federation can compete with none of them save military force; and even then, the success that the Russian war machine has achieved against the United States' proxy in Ukraine has cost the Russian bourgeoisie enormously. In April of 2022, *Forbes* reported that Russian billionaires had lost 27% of their wealth on average since 2021 due to the super-empire's aggressive economic sanctions.[331] Though the Western press may be viewed with some suspicion when it reports upon Russian losses, the Russian government's own economic data revealed initial symptoms of serious hardship. In the summer of 2022, Rosstat recorded a decline in Russian auto manufacturing of over 60% compared with 2021,[332] and the Russian Ministry of Economic

---

Ambassador Sign Secretive Contract to Develop Syrian Oil Fields," *CNN*, August 5, 2020.

328 KazMunayGas, "Oil and Gas Sector."

329 Pat Davis Szymczak, "Tengizchevroil Production Rebounds After Antigovernment Protests Curtailed," *Journal of Petroleum Technology*, January 10, 2022.

330 Jason Hickel, Dylan Sullivan, and Huzaifa Zoomkawala, "Plunder in the Post-Colonial Era: Quantifying Drain from the Global South Through Unequal Exchange, 1960–2018," *New Political Economy* 26, no. 6 (2021): 1030-1047.

331 David Dawkins, "Here's How Big A Hit Russia's Billionaires Have Taken In The Past Year," *Forbes*, April 5, 2022.

332 Paul Hannon, "Russian Car Makers Hit Hardest as Factory Output Falls After Ukraine Sanctions," *Wall Street Journal*, June 1, 2022.

Development later estimated that overall Russian GDP would contract by 7.8% by the end of the year.[333] [334]

With Russia's wealthiest capitalists' fortunes in free fall as a consequence, it would appear to make little sense for the national-bourgeois Federation to have launched its intervention in Ukraine for economic reasons. If it *had* been an imperialist venture, months later, when Russia's economic pain due to the initial onslaught of sanctions became undeniable, there would seem to have been even less sense in continuing it.

Though there is a near-universal chorus in the Western press attributing the Russian intervention to ideological, expansionist, or imperialist agendas, Western *military* analysis must by necessity have a more grounded perspective. According to an article published in the University of Calgary's *Journal of Military and Strategic Studies* in December 2022, for example, the intent of the intervention was "to prevent Ukraine from becoming an ever-stronger and threatening NATO bridgehead on Russia's borders." At the heart of Putin's reasoning was not the hope of any immediate gain, but the need to prevent "an imagined future in which Russia would confront an existential threat."[335,336]

If Ukraine had joined NATO—fulfilling the intent that was openly announced and written into its very constitution in 2019[337]—the United

---

333 IANS, "Russia Forecasts 7.8% GDP Contraction in 2022; Unemployment Rate at 6.7%," *Business Standard,* May 18, 2022.

334 The pessimism of the Russian government has since been proven incorrect, however; the economy ultimately contracted by only 2% and returned to growth in 2023. For a more detailed accounting, see Chapter Eleven.

335 Geoffrey Roberts, "'Now or Never': The Immediate Origins of Putin's Preventative War on Ukraine," Journal of Military and Strategic Studies 22, no. 2: Special Issue on the War in Ukraine (December 2022): 4.

336 The article continues in further detail: "Some see Putin's actions as driven by an underlying geoideological ambition, such as the restoration of the Soviet/Tsarist empire or Orthodox Russia's pursuit of a civilizational struggle with a *decadent* West. Others view it is part of a persistent pattern of centuries-long Russian aggression, authoritarianism and expansionism. More parochial explanations include the idea that war served to shore up Putin's domestic regime and popularity. Or perhaps, as some argue, it was the decision of an isolated, egoistical dictator, surrounded by fawning courtiers, who believed Russia's invasion would be welcomed by his Ukrainian blood-brothers. The limitation of all these explanations is their lack of definite documentary evidence. They attribute reasons for Putin's actions for which there is no proof except a perceived pattern of events that is deemed to fit the assumed motivation." (Geoffrey Roberts, 5–6.)

337 Українське Незалежне Інформаційне Агентство Новин, "Ukraine's Parliament Backs Changes to Constitution Confirming Ukraine's Path toward EU, NATO," *UNIAN,* February 7, 2019.

States would have been free to install missiles within Ukrainian territory. According to Putin, this would grant NATO the capability to strike Moscow and Russia's most densely-populated southwestern urban centers within five minutes of launch, too quickly to be detected in time for a retaliatory strike to be marshaled.[338] This logistical reality, combined with NATO leaders' policy of strategic ambiguity on the question of Ukraine's accession to NATO,[339] and of refusing to make a no-first-strike pledge regarding nuclear weapons, produced a threat to Russian nuclear deterrence. If deterrence were weakened or eliminated, the super-empire could then dictate any terms to the Russian Federation that it pleased, including its dissolution and balkanization into easily manageable neocolonies that the United States could dominate in perpetuity—as was indeed the West's intention.

It is obvious that such a scenario would entail the end of national-bourgeois rule in Russia. The Russian capitalists, if they survived, would be de-developed, and could at best hope to become compradors again; less powerful, less wealthy, and serving again at the whim of Western masters. But perhaps more likely, they would be liquidated—meeting the same fate as Gaddafi and Saddam Hussein, for example—and replaced with more subservient clients. For the national bourgeoisie, escaping this fate is worth any price. They had gone to war not to gain *more* wealth, but to avoid losing what they had.

Though the Western press was always careful to avoid giving an honest assessment of the super-empire's ambitions in Ukraine and their ultimate outcome had the Russian Federation not intervened, there is nevertheless complete agreement between the Western media establishment and the Russian leadership on the consequences of a Russian defeat. "Prepare for the disappearance of Russia" announced the headline of a May 2022 article in the *Hill*, which called it "probable" that the Federation would "metamorphose into 10 or more states."[340] Similar predictions were made

---

338 Humeyra Pamuk et al., "Putin Hits Back as NATO Warns Moscow against Attacking Ukraine," *Reuters,* November 30, 2021.

339 In an interview aired on CNN in March 2022, Ukrainian President Volodymyr Zelenskyy said that NATO leaders had privately told him Ukraine would not be allowed to join, but that "publicly the doors will remain open." [*Volodymyr Zelensky. Big interview for CNN (2022) News of Ukraine,* Odesa Film Studio video (36:13), premiered Mar 21, 2022.

340 Alexander J. Motyl, "Prepare for the Disappearance of Russia," *The Hill,* May 13, 2022.

by the American Enterprise Institute[341] and the *Atlantic*, which advocated that Russia be balkanized into a multitude of smaller neocolonies,[342] later asserted in a headline following the Russian Armed Forces' retreat from Kherson that "The Russian Empire Must Die."[343] According to European think tank Geopolitical Intelligence Services, the most likely outcome of a Russian defeat would see the Federation dissolved into multiple independent countries, with significant territory being claimed by its neighbors, and possibly a civil war.[344] The Brookings Institution concluded that even if the Federation survived a loss in Ukraine, its Caucasus region at least would be balkanized, and its neighbor and only European ally Belarus would be forced to become a Western neocolony.[345] Regardless of the Russian national bourgeoisie's motives in pursuing intervention in the first place, it is now undisputed that the conflict is for them existential— and for the other classes of Russian society, the only thing preventing the horror and misery of the 1990s from repeating itself, should the Federation be balkanized as the Soviet Union was then.[346]

The Islamic Republic had on a similar basis become the leading exporter of armed revolution against the super-empire's hegemony. By the early 2000s, the super-empire had fully encircled Iran. To the east and west, the United States' military had invaded and occupied Iran's closest neighbors. To the north and south lay willing collaborators (Türkiye and Saudi Arabia). The U.S. government had openly announced to the world that Iran was its enemy, and perhaps the next to be invaded. Lacking a nuclear deterrent, the Islamic Republic, out of self-defense, had to heavily invest in anti-imperialism, by arming and bankrolling national liberation movements throughout the Arab world.[347]

---

341 Michael Rubin, "Putin's War in Ukraine Could Mean the Collapse of Russia," *American Enterprise Institute,* Feburary 27, 2022.

342 Casey Michel, "Decolonize Russia," *The Atlantic*, May 27, 2022.

343 Anne Applebaum, "The Russian Empire Must Die," *The Atlantic,* November 14, 2022.

344 Stefan Hedlund, "Scenarios for a Postwar Russia: Survival or Collapse?," *GIS Reports,* October 10, 2022.

345 Pavel K. Baev, "Time for the West to Think about How to Engage with Defeated Russia," *Brookings,* November 15, 2022.

346 See Chapter Two.

347 Unbiased estimates of the volume of Iranian aid to Hezbollah and Ansarallah are difficult or impossible to find, but the U.S. government at least considers them significant, for example in 2018 alleging that the Islamic Republic provided Hezbollah with $700 million per year. (Joyce Karam, "Iran Pays Hezbollah $700 Million a Year, US Official Says," *The National News,* June 6, 2018.)

Deterrence, of course, only works if an aggressor believes in its target's commitment to carrying out a threat; therefore the Iranian national bourgeoisie tied itself as closely as possible with the "Axis of Resistance,"[348] both materially and ideologically. Article 154 of the Islamic Republic's constitution states:

> The Islamic Republic of Iran has as its ideal human felicity throughout human society, and considers the attainment of independence, freedom, and rule of justice and truth to be the right of all people of the world. Accordingly, while scrupulously refraining from all forms of interference in the internal affairs of other nations, it supports the just struggles of the freedom fighters against the oppressors in every corner of the globe.[349]

Under the conditions of super-imperialism, these national bourgeoisies are essentially stuck—perpetually unable to develop into imperialists, and frequently threatened with either annihilation or de-development. This is both a boon and a curse for the global proletariat. The workers and peasants in the neocolonies find national-bourgeois states to be their strongest allies in the struggle for liberation, yet within these countries, they are similarly stuck.

The Lesson of Libya

The Socialist People's Libyan Arab Jamahiriya had been an inconsistent force in regional politics over the decades preceding the Arab Spring, at times supporting or opposing the socialist bloc and later cooperating to a degree with the United States' "War on Terror." Despite this, however, Libya was at the time the wealthiest, most developed, and most economically independent country in Africa. Before Gaddafi and his cadre overthrew the comprador King Idris I in 1969, Libya had been exporting over 3 million barrels of oil per day at one of the lowest prices in the world;[350] but by 2011, through the protection of its oil supply and

---

348 A broad anti-Western alliance of states and regional paramilitary groups such as Syria, Hezbollah, and Ansarallah.

349 The Islamic Republic of Iran, "The Constitution of The Islamic Republic of Iran," art. 154.

350 Ronald Bruce St. John, "The Changing Libyan Economy: Causes and Consequences," *Middle East Journal* 62, no. 1 (Winter 2008): 75–91.

the redistribution of its revenues, their country had no foreign debt, the highest life expectancy, and lowest infant mortality rate in Africa.

Moreover, it represented a persistent threat to the Western financial oligarchy's control of the continent. Colonel Gaddafi had frequently urged Libya's neighbors to reject foreign aid and loans from the West, and in a speech before the UN General Assembly, condemned Western governments and demanded they pay trillions in reparations for their role in the colonization of Africa.[351] Under his leadership, Libya had promoted Gaddafi's pan-Africanist vision by funding an independent telecommunications satellite network,[352] and had invested heavily in providing an alternative to the IMF and the World Bank. According to *Reuters*, Libya had granted more than $2 billion in loans to other countries in the developing world, many of which were interest-free.[353]

By the late 2000s, however, its government had begun privatizing the state-run economy. In February, on the eve of the civil war, the IMF praised the Libyan government for its "progress on enhancing the role of the private sector. . . ."[354] This naturally led to a deterioration of the conditions faced by poor and working-class Libyans. Libya's first protests of 2011 were rooted not in a desire for Western style "freedom and democracy" but in class struggle. They emerged first in the less-developed eastern city of Darnah, motivated by disputes over housing.[355]

The government had seriously miscalculated but attempted to correct course. A few weeks later, it announced a reduction of food prices and a new $24 billion fund for new housing.[356] However, this was too little, too late. As with the other Arab Spring movements, the unrest in Libya initially lacked direction and leadership, and received them from the

---

351 Ed Pilkington, "UN General Assembly: 100 Minutes in the Life of Muammar Gaddafi," *The Guardian,* September 23, 2009.

352 Before Gaddafi's satellites were launched, African countries had been paying Europe half a billion dollars per year to use their telecommunications network. (Honourable Saka, "Africans Will Remember Gaddafi For One Important Achievement," *Modern Ghana,* November 17, 2012.)

353 Ali Shuaib, "Libya's Gaddafi Uses Loans to Flex Global Muscle," *Reuters,* February 9, 2011.

354 International Monetary Fund, Public Information Notice (PIN) No. 11/23: "IMF Executive Board Concludes 2010 Article IV Consultation with the Socialist People's Libyan Arab Jamahiriya," February 15, 2011.

355 Al-Masry Al-Youm Staff, "Libyans Protest over Delayed Subsidized Housing Units," *Egypt Independent,* January 16, 2011.

356 "Libya Sets up $24 Bln Fund for Housing." *Reuters,* January 27, 2011.

super-empire's soft power networks and Al Qaeda.[357] The February uprisings were mobilized mostly from Western Europe, by the National Conference for the Libyan Opposition, a coalition of Libyan émigré groups created in London.[358] Any doubt regarding the opposition's Western orientation was swiftly erased a few weeks later, when a group called the Libyan National Transition Council emerged as the leader of the rebel forces, declared itself the legitimate government of Libya, and immediately called for a military intervention in the conflict.[359] The French government quickly began supplying the NTC with weapons,[360] and NATO forces started bombing Libya by mid-March, with devastating and long-lasting results.

Since the NATO intervention and Gaddafi's murder, Libya's foreign debt has increased from zero to over $3 billion. The CIA World Factbook summarizes the economic situation in Libya since the Arab Spring:

> The Libyan dinar has lost much of its value since 2014. . . . The country suffers from widespread power outages, caused by short-ages of fuel for power generation. Living conditions, including access to clean drinking water, medical services, and safe housing have all declined since 2011.[361]

After decades of independence, Libya had been de-developed and transformed back into a neocolony—and even more importantly, it had lost the ability to help its neighbors escape neocolonialism.

It is clear that the Libyan national bourgeoisie were badly mistaken that they could reconcile with the West and survive. But it is equally

---

357 Despite its "War on Terror" rhetoric, the U.S. government was all too happy to look the other way as Al Qaeda took on a significant role in sustaining the violence of the revolution; while Western media ridiculed Gaddafi for his claims of Al Qaeda involvement in the Civil War, leaked State Department cables and the U.S. military's own internal analyses both indicated that eastern Libya had the highest per capita concentration of Al Qaeda fighters in the world. (Alexander Cockburn, "Libya Rebels: Gaddafi Could Be Right about al-Qaeda," *The Week*, March 24, 2011.) The true enemy of the United States, after all, was always the national-bourgeois state in Libya and the threat it posed to the neocolonial world order.

358 Sabina Henneberg, "The Libyan National Transition Council," chapter 4 in *Managing Transition: The First Post-Uprising Phase in Tunisia and Libya* (Cambridge University Press, 2020), 115.

359 CNN Wire Staff, "Rebel Leader Calls for 'immediate Action' on No-Fly Zone," *CNN*, March 10, 2011.

360 Sabina Henneberg, "The Libyan National Transition Council," 131.

361 Central Intelligence Agency, "Libya," *The World Factbook*.

clear that while the super-imperialist stage continues, a real revolution against a national-bourgeois state is likeliest to leave the peasantry and working class considerably worse off than before. Unless and until conditions change more fundamentally, neither the Russian Federation nor the Islamic Republic will soon develop either into empires or into a new socialist bloc (which could end super-imperialism in favor of either a new inter-imperialist rivalry or a new Cold War stage, respectively). The war in Ukraine is not an inter-imperialist proxy war, but an inter-capitalist proxy war, since the super-empire's enemy remains in the national-bourgeois stage. Though some regard it as a decisive conflict that heralds a new era of "multipolarity,"[362] the outcome of the war, and its ultimate effect upon the structure of the global economy, still remain to be seen.

---

362 The concept of the "multipolar world," and to what degree it does or will exist, will be explored in more detail in Chapter Eleven.

CHAPTER FIVE

Compromising with Capitalism: The Terminal Decline of Western Social Democracy

> *"Throughout history there has been only one thing that ruling classes have ever wanted—and that is everything: all the choice lands, forests, game, herds, harvests, mineral deposits and precious metals of the earth; all the wealth, riches, and profitable returns; all the productive facilities, gainful inventiveness, and technologies; all the surplus value produced by human labour; all the control positions of the state and other major institutions; all public supports and subsidies, privileges and immunities; all the protections of the law with none of its constraints; all the services, comforts, luxuries, and advantages of civil society with none of the taxes and costs. Every ruling class has wanted only this: all the rewards and none of the burdens."*
>
> —Michael Parenti, "Global Rollback: After Communism," 2002[363]

So far, this book has only examined resistance to the super-empire by victims beyond its borders. Within the core of the empire, however, there also exists a variety of groups besides the financial capitalist oligarchy that face varying forms of its oppression.

The most desperate of these are disenfranchised minorities, for example the remaining indigenous inhabitants of Western settler-colonies, who face forms of dispossessive accumulation similar to those in the periphery.[364] Due to the severe nature of this exploitation, this group is likeliest to pursue the forms of resistance described in Chapter Three, but as minorities, they are a marginal force in Western class society overall. Disproportionately overlapping this group are those who have been forced

---

363 Michael Parenti, "Global Rollback: After Communism," *CovertAction Quarterly,* Spring 2002.

364 A more thorough accounting of settler-colonialism will be provided in Chapter Nine.

to secure a living outside the traditional wage-labor economy, e.g., people who are incarcerated, and those with informal or proscribed professions.

There are few peasants within the core of the super-empire; a majority or a sizable plurality of Westerners are proletarians, whether urban or rural, selling their labor power in exchange for a living. Though some live in extremely dire conditions, their relationship with the capitalist class is primarily one of wage-labor exploitation, qualitatively less severe than dispossessive accumulation.

The capitalist class itself is more developed in the West than in anywhere else in the world yet is also considerably stratified. Adjacent to (and interspersed with) the financial oligarchy, there is an upper crust of millionaires, nearly all of whom are capitalists;[365] according to Credit Suisse's Global Wealth Report, millionaires in the United States numbered 22 million in 2020,[366] or almost 7% of the total U.S. population and almost 40% of all millionaires worldwide. Also numerous are a comfortable middle bourgeoisie, consisting of modestly successful business owners and investors, small- or medium-scale landlords, &c.; and below them are the petit bourgeoisie, generally consisting of small business owners, non-profit executives, artists, performers, consultants, and other self-employed workers. Of all the classes, the petit bourgeoisie are the most nebulous, often considered to also include the wealthiest layer of proletarians such as managers, engineers, and other white-collar professionals, who receive much greater compensation and have greater autonomy than the average worker.

Among the political left there is considerable disagreement over to what degree each class in the core countries benefits from the imperialist system. For those living in the United States, for example, the high value and stability of the dollar relative to other currencies may be considered an indirect benefit. The high wages Western workers earn in comparison with workers in the periphery, as explained in Chapter Two, are a key basis for unequal exchange; and even if prices are correspondingly higher in the core of the empire, these workers have relatively greater mobility.

It cannot be denied, however, that *relative to the other classes*, the Western upper and middle bourgeoisie absorb the overwhelming majority

---

365 Note that a large volume of wealth alone is not sufficient to determine an individual's class. A few millionaires, such as highly-paid celebrity performers or athletes, are still not capitalists if they do not own capital (though they are almost universally supporters of the capitalist system, and are often deployed in this role in one way or another).

366 Credit Suisse Research Institute, "Global Wealth Report 2021," 19.

of the super-profits taken from the periphery, and that the petit bourgeoisie (however defined) receive a mere trickle of this plunder, while the others may at best see a drop (regardless of how significant a sum that drop might be for those living in the most abject poverty). The overall wealth held by the United States continues to grow steadily; yet the real incomes of the poorest 50% of its population have declined throughout the super-imperial era.[367] Whatever measure of plunder the United States *does* redistribute to its population is becoming outstripped by the amount that is extracted from its own working class through traditional wage-labor exploitation.

The orientation of the Western proletariat with respect to imperialism is therefore ambiguous, and the petit bourgeoisie's even more so. For the most part, they are not—or not yet—the targets of the worst forms of dispossessive accumulation, and so have no urgent or direct motive to abolish it, even though some *individuals* among them find it abhorrent and may wish to do so. The *class* interest of Western workers can only be awakened and shaped by the most powerful and immediate form of exploitation they *do* experience. Therefore, their struggle is first and foremost one of anti-capitalism, and not one of anti-imperialism. Consequently the most useful analysis from an anti-imperialist perspective is to measure how the class struggle within the core of the super-empire has developed or is likely to develop, and determine what the implications of that development are for the liberation of the rest of the world.

The kind of workers' revolution Marx and many others predicted and hoped for—destroying the bourgeois state and overthrowing the capitalist relations of production entirely—might hypothetically undo the imperialist relations as well. However, such a revolution has not yet occurred in any Western country, nor in any developed industrial power. Imperialism, as this book has so far shown, is an increasingly and overwhelmingly international phenomenon, and as such a successful revolution must be international as well. To date, proletarian-led revolution has only ever had lasting success in the periphery, where the chain of imperialism was weakest,[368] and not in the countries with the most concentrated urban population or the most developed industry or any other such quality. If revolution in the core was unlikely during the previous stages of imperialism, such as in the early twentieth century United States when openly

---

367 Facundo Alvaredo et al., "Global Inequality Dynamics: New Findings from WID.World," *American Economic Review* 107, no. 5 (May 2017): 6.

368 J. V. Stalin, *The Foundations of Leninism* (1953), chap. 3.

revolutionary political parties such as the Socialist Party of America or the Communist Party USA were at their historical peak, it can only be less likely during super-imperialism, when the chain of imperialism is stronger than ever.

Instead, the prevailing anti-capitalist ideology and practice within the core has become one of reform and compromise, or as it is commonly known: social democracy.

Nearly as much confusion and disagreement exists over the meaning of the term *social democracy* as there is over *socialism* or *communism*. For the purposes of this book, it will suffice to define social democracy as a system of governance in which the greatest possible share of the profits of the capitalists are redistributed to the lower (i.e. less prosperous or unpropertied) classes without fundamentally altering the relations of production. Wealth in a social democracy is not *created* any differently than in the most neoliberal state, but under a social-democratic system wealth is *concentrated* more slowly.

As a definition this is uncontroversial; the confusion instead arises from the differences in the ideology and motivation among social democracy's many supporters. The compromise inherent in social democracy attracts advocates from every class; indeed, even Bill Gates and Warren Buffet, two of the very wealthiest capitalists in the world, have called for more and greater taxes on themselves and the other mega-rich, to be used to pay for increased healthcare, pensions, and support for those with low incomes.[369] There are those who believe that the super-empire could be transformed into a type of "compassionate capitalism," i.e. an economy that retains free enterprise yet has eliminated poverty. The most cynical of the petit bourgeoisie might be content with social democracy even if dispossessive accumulation in the periphery would continue, thus relying on the state to redistribute to them a greater share of the plunder than they would otherwise have taken. Still others view social democracy as only a temporary but necessary stage of development in political economy, that might lead to socialism and an eventual "gradualist" overthrow of class society. Such a transformation, according to their ideologies, might take place at the ballot box or through mass demonstrations and other expressions of class struggle; U.S. Senator Bernie Sanders, whose recent repeated grassroots campaigns to become president galvanized great numbers of working class supporters with the promise of redistributing

---

369 Emmie Martin, "Warren Buffett and Bill Gates Agree That the Rich Should Pay Higher Taxes—Here's What They Suggest," *Yahoo!Finance,* February 26, 2019.

wealth, spoke frequently of the need for a ("political") revolution involving labor unions, strikes, and collective bargaining tactics.[370]

Despite their very different hopes and ultimate objectives, all these groups are united in their most immediate goal of reducing the vast inequality that exists in Western class society, and since their informal coalition represents the largest organized opposition to the Western financial oligarchy from within the core, an analysis of their prospects—both present and historical—is called for.

The State and Reform

Modern social democracy came about as a reaction to the excesses of capitalist dominance of class society during the inter-imperialist stage, but did not see considerable success until well into the twentieth century. The so-called "Progressive Era" that began around the turn of the century is often considered the origin of the social-democratic movement in the United States. The reforms and redistribution it promised, however, were long in coming. Child labor—which was common in mills, coal mines, farms, factories and many other workplaces—was not abolished in the U.S. until 1938.[371] President Theodore Roosevelt, the first "Progressive" president, did expand worker protections and impose some modest regulations on business, but failed to levy any new taxes upon the wealthy. Both he and his successor, President William Howard Taft, are known for their frequent "trust-busting" or intervening to break up capitalist monopolies, which may have marginally slowed the development of the U.S. financial oligarchy, but did not redistribute anything to the workers or the poor.[372] Similarly, social reformers in the United Kingdom had only modest accomplishments. The Progressive Era was mirrored by a long period of Liberal Party governments in the UK that succeeded in establishing a thin social safety net involving a pension, health insurance, and meager welfare payments. In 1910, after a considerable legislative battle, the

---

370 Gregory Krieg, "Bernie Sanders Introduces Labor Plan to Broaden Union Power," *CNN*, August 22, 2019.

371 According to the census, the total participation of 10–15-year-olds in the workforce only began declining after 1910 and by 1920 was still over one million. [United States Census Bureau, *1920 Census: Children in Gainful Occupations* (1924), 11.]

372 Antitrust laws were in fact often enforced targeting labor unions rather than monopoly corporations. Eugene V. Debs, the Socialist Party candidate for president in the 1912 election against both Roosevelt and Taft, did not support trust-busting for these very reasons, adopting a platform of nationalizing large corporations instead.

government's "People's Budget" finally imposed a progressive income tax on the wealthy—of only twenty pence per pound, or about 8%.[373] Prior to the First World War, the vast incomes—and colossal fortunes—of the richest capitalists were left almost entirely untouched.

This changed in 1917, when the marginal federal income tax rate on the wealthiest category in the United States saw its largest increase to date with the War Revenue Act. The super-rich went from scarcely paying anything to handing over two-thirds of every excess dollar almost overnight. The top income tax rate reached a maximum of seventy-seven cents per excess dollar in 1918, then steadily declined; by 1925, the wealthy paid only 25%.

The years immediately following the Great Depression also saw massive increases in taxation to fund the welfare, jobs programs, and redistributive policies of the New Deal. The Depression is generally considered to have lasted the entire decade of the 1930s; the top marginal income tax rate soared once again throughout this period, reaching 79% on the wealthiest category by the end of the decade. The United States' entrance into the Second World War coincided with even further increases to the marginal tax rate, reaching the all-time high of 94% on all income past $200,000 per year in 1944. This tax rate then remained in place—not falling below 90%—for almost twenty years afterward.[374]

Similarly, while capitalist rule was overthrown in Eastern Europe at the end of the Second World War, Western Europe experienced a triumph of social democracy. Aided in large part by the United States' increased spending via the Marshall Plan, France, West Germany, and the United Kingdom recovered from the extreme devastation of the war and built welfare states of unprecedented magnitude. In 1945, the British Labour Party won its first majority government in a landslide, and swiftly built new public housing, created the National Health Service, entirely new systems of welfare, and nationalized the railways, utilities, and one-fifth of the entire economy. Top marginal tax rates in Western Europe remained at or near wartime levels, over 90% in the UK and West Germany and 70% in France. Even non-belligerent Sweden, which had suffered relatively little, increased taxes on the wealthy tremendously during the war to arm itself against potential threats; afterward, those taxes remained high,

373 Ian Packer, "1909 People's Budget," *Journal of Liberal History.*

374 The Tax Foundation, "Historical U.S. Federal Individual Income Tax Rates & Brackets, 1862-2021," August 24, 2021.

with top marginal rates exceeding 60%.[375] The social-democratic nature of the Scandinavian countries was officially established with the "grand compromises" between capitalists and workers in Denmark, Norway and Sweden during the Depression of the 1930s, yet was only significantly realized during the post-war years. After its liberation from Nazi occupation, the Norwegian state seized and nationalized all German business assets, eventually resulting in a public sector that accounted for a majority of GDP.[376] Its most comprehensive reforms were then established during the next two decades of virtually uninterrupted Labour Party governance, including social security, child and disability benefits, and unemployment and sickness insurance; in all, a "cradle to grave" welfare system that seemed to serve as a shining example of gradualism, and one that social democrats everywhere aimed to follow.[377]

The remarkable history of social democracy in the twentieth century reveals, more than anything, its parallels with armed proletarian revolution. Both socialist countries and social-democratic systems struggle to make progress in typical years, but in times of extreme crisis both can expand quickly. The first socialist countries were established as a result of the two world wars; the first social democracies were created at the same time, or else during the Depression as a desperate gamble by capitalists to prevent the socialists from taking over. If social democracy can only be established as a response to economic or humanitarian disaster, however, the gradualist ideology is thoroughly discredited. As the welfare state lessens the pain of wage-labor exploitation, the class struggle becomes less acute; when conditions improve, the working class then has less motivation to seek further wealth redistribution, and over time, the capitalists may take back what they surrendered.

The top marginal income tax rate in the United States fell to 70% in 1965, then to 50% in 1982. By the end of the Cold War, it had fallen below 40%—where it has remained, as of this writing.[378] The top effective corporate tax rate also dropped from a height of 50% in the mid-twentieth century to less than 40% by the 1990s. Today, it stands at less than 26%.

---

375 Torregrosa-Hetland and Sabaté, "Income Tax Progressivity and Inflation during the World Wars," *European Review of Economic History* 26, no. 3 (August 2022): 311–339.

376 "The Rich Cousin," *The Economist*, January 31, 2013.

377 Even Lange, "The Development of the Norwegian Welfare State, 1945-1970," Aarhus University, *nordics.info*, August 19, 2020.

378 The Tax Foundation, "Historical U.S. Federal Individual Income Tax Rates & Brackets, 1862-2021."

Though about half of the U.S. federal government's annual budget is still spent on "entitlements" or welfare state programs such as Medicare and unemployment insurance, almost none of it is financed by the upper strata of the capitalist class. Social Security, the largest such category remaining, consists of around one-fifth of all federal spending yet is mostly paid for by a tax on workers and the petit bourgeoisie.[379] The United States' system of taxation has also become infamous for its corruption, allowing billionaires and large conglomerates innumerable loopholes to avoid paying anything. According to a study by the Institute on Taxation and Economic Policy, 55 of the largest U.S. corporations paid $0 in taxes in 2020 despite substantial profits.[380] In the 2023 fiscal year only 8% of federal tax revenue came from corporate income taxes and 1% from estate taxes.[381]

Western Europe experienced a corresponding erosion of social democracy in the latter half of the twentieth century. In the UK, most nationalized industries were once again privatized during the 1980s; by the 1990s the public sector's share of GDP had fallen to 2%.[382] In the late 1980s, privatization increased in Spain and the Netherlands; by the time it reabsorbed the formerly socialist East, the West German government had already sold the majority of its own industrial shareholdings to private investors. Top marginal income tax rates slowly declined across the region. An attempt by the French Socialist Party[383] to reverse the trend in 1981 was partially successful, but most reforms were short-lived; new

---

379 Though the payroll tax that funds Social Security is levied equally on employees and employers, self-employed workers (or petit-bourgeois, if strictly defined as neither working for a wage nor employing others) must pay double. At approximately 10% of the labor force (Rakesh Kochhar, "The Self-Employed Are Back at Work in Pre-COVID-19 Numbers, but Their Businesses Have Smaller Payrolls," Pew Research Center, November 3, 2021) the self-employed therefore pay an outsized share to fund Social Security, leaving traditional employers responsible for a minority of the total cost.

380 Matthew Gardner and Steve Wamhoff, "55 Corporations Paid $0 in Federal Taxes on 2020 Profits," Institute on Taxation and Economic Policy, April 2, 2021.

381 U.S. Department of the Treasury, "How Much Revenue Has the U.S. Government Collected This Year?" U.S. Treasury *FiscalData.*

382 David Parker, "Privatization in the European Union: A Critical Assessment of Its Development, Rationale and Consequences," *Economic and Industrial Economy* 20, no. 1 (Feb. 1999): 10.

383 At this time, the Socialist Party was generally considered to be social-democratic in ideology and practice.

taxes on the wealthy were quickly repealed and new nationalizations were reversed before the end of the decade.[384]

In hindsight, the Achilles' Heel of the social democrats is all too obvious: even at their most successful, they had never truly bargained from a position of strength. Convincing—or even coercing—the state to redistribute wealth is not necessarily the same thing as controlling it. Wherever, and as long as there are classes, the class struggle always continues. If the capitalists retain their fortunes, their factories, and their systems of patronage, they can always recoup their profits later, whether all at once or one dollar at a time. The gradualists were wrong. Once built, welfare states tend not to grow, but to crumble. The only thing gradual about social democracy in the latter twentieth century has been its death.

Social Democracy under Super-Imperialism

Just as the destruction of the socialist bloc was a disaster for the proletariat around the world, it significantly accelerated social democracy's decline. Between 1989 and 1991, the top corporate income tax in Sweden was cut in half, and Denmark and Austria's fell by almost as much in the same time period, as did Norway's in 1992.[385] One of the greatest symbols of social-democratic achievement, the tax on net wealth, was soon abolished in Denmark and Germany, later followed by Finland, Luxembourg, Sweden,[386] and eventually France;[387] in Europe today, only Norway, Spain and Switzerland still retain a tax on net wealth.[388] During the 1990s, income inequality steadily rose throughout nearly all of Europe, along with deregulation, privatization, and austerity.

The welfare state's vulnerability to neoliberalism, however, did not fully discount the more moderate social democrats' view that a gentler, more compassionate form of capitalism could yet be forged; or at the very least, that with sufficient class struggle and given the right opportunity, the proletariat might reuse the same strategy to regain what it had lost. If it is an axiom that social democracy is born out of crisis, could another crisis bring it back?

---

384 Parker, "Privatization in the European Union," 10–11.

385 Sean Bray, "Corporate Tax Rates around the World, 2021."

386 David Ibison, "Sweden Axes Wealth Tax," *Financial Times*, March 28, 2007.

387 In 2018 the French tax on wealth was downgraded to a property tax.

388 Cristina Enache, "Wealth Taxes in Europe," *Tax Foundation | Europe*, May 9, 2023.

Japan stands out as a notable, but extremely brief, exception to the decline of social democracy in the super-imperialism stage, in a very large part in response to a severe domestic economic crisis. In 1991, the asset price bubble burst, crashing the Japanese economy and swiftly halting its meteoric rise that had commanded the world's attention during the latter twentieth century.[389] In the next election, the conservative Liberal Democratic Party lost power in the National Diet for the first time in four decades, ushering in a coalition of social-democratic parties that had languished in the opposition. The next year, the LDP regained power, but only weakly, in a "grand coalition" with the Japan Socialist Party,[390] whose representative Tomiichi Murayama became prime minister. Murayama was the first prime minister to offer an official apology for Japan's actions during the Second World War,[391] and during his and the previous coalition's ministries the Diet passed numerous reform policies, including a large expansion in elder care services under its "New Gold Plan,"[392] greater welfare provisions for disabled persons, more labor rights, new workplace safety regulations, and family care leave.

These reforms, however, were the result of an extremely short-lived political anomaly, and one even less likely than it seemed. The LDP had elevated Murayama, a 70-year-old elder statesman, expecting that he would govern for a short time as a respected but weak-willed figurehead. If in this expectation the LDP miscalculated, it correctly anticipated the interregnum to be brief. The position of the JSP in the Diet's governing coalition, born of the its inertia as the largest traditional opposition party, concealed a precipitous decline that had begun years earlier. In the 1993 general election, before it had even gained power, the JSP lost nearly half its seats in the lower house of the Diet. A poll of the Japanese public found that the most popular explanation for the JSP's defeat was that "the

---

389 The crisis in Japan will be explored in further detail in Chapter Twelve.

390 Not to be confused with the Japanese Communist Party, which was not part of either coalition.

391 Sheryl Wudunn, "Japanese Apology for War Is Welcomed and Criticized," *New York Times,* August 16, 1995.

392 In 1989, the LDP government had formulated its "Gold Plan" to expand these services by the year 2000, in response to Japan's looming aging crisis. The "New Gold Plan" in 1994 greatly increased funding for these services, revised targets for much wider-scale improvements by 2000 and set new targets for 2010. (Ministry of Foreign Affairs of Japan, "Second Periodic Report by the Government of Japan under Articles 16 and 17 of the International Covenant on Economic, Social, and Cultural Rights.")

reason for the party to exist had disappeared."[393] Labor unions, the JSP's base of support, became politically diffuse after the LDP's temporary loss of legitimacy, spreading their support across an increasing number of other left-wing opposition factions, and the JSP's compromises with the LDP further disenchanted its most radical members. In 1996, the JSP was officially disbanded, and the LDP regained its traditional role as the dominant party in government. Though their accomplishments were not inconsiderable, Japan's traditional social democrats, after waiting so long for their opportunity to take power, had doomed themselves by grasping it.[394]

Again, the stage of super-imperialism had changed the rules. But what about the United States, which experienced ample economic growth during the 1990s while Japan and Europe stagnated? According to Hudson in 2003:

No one anticipated that America's federal budget deficit during the 1990s would be financed by China, Japan and other East Asian countries rather than by American taxpayers and domestic investors. Yet this international exploitation was implicit in the U.S. Treasury bill standard. Since 1971 it has freed the U.S. economy from having to do what American diplomats insist that other debtor countries do when they run payments deficits: impose austerity to restore balance in its international payments. The United States alone has been free to pursue domestic expansion and foreign diplomacy with hardly a worry about the balance-of-payments consequences. Imposing austerity on debtor countries, America as the world's largest debtor economy acts uniquely without financial constraint.[395]

Yet the domestic expansion of social democracy did not continue. Though not as severe as the Great Depression or a world war, the Great Recession of 2008 was the worst global economic crisis since. It too had

---

393 Sarah Hyde, *The Transformation of the Japanese Left: From Old Socialists to New Democrats* (Nissan Institute/Routledge Japanese Studies, 2009), 91–92.

394 A similar attempt was made in the aftermath of the Great Recession, when the new Democratic Party of Japan defeated the LDP in the 2009 general election, also with mixed results. The LDP regained power in the following election, and the DPJ was disbanded a few years later. A more detailed account of the DPJ's brief rule can be found in Chapter Twelve.

395 Michael Hudson, *Super Imperialism*, xii.

the same effect as the dissolution of the Soviet Union, further curtailing and not expanding social democracy. Wealth inequality only further increased after the crisis. In 2014, Credit Suisse found that its metric of inequality—the ratio of wealth to household income—had risen in the United States to the same level as just before the Great Depression.[396] According to statistical data from the U.S. Federal Reserve in 2019, the richest 1% had seen a 300% increase in wealth since 1989.[397] Subsequently, a report by Inequality.org, a project of the Institute for Policy Studies think tank, found that U.S. billionaires even further increased their wealth by 70% during the height of the COVID-19 pandemic, from a total of $3 trillion to $5 trillion.[398] By 2015, the real income of the poorest 50% of the U.S. population was lower than it had been in 1978. Wealth in the U.S. *was* being redistributed more in the aftermath—but *from* the working class *to* the capitalist class, and not the other way around.

After 2008, some European social-democratic political parties were voted into power, but largely failed to make progress, and often found themselves supporting austerity instead. Soon after President François Hollande was elected in 2012, his administration moved to *increase* workers' pension contributions;[399] his approval rating consequently cratered, and the French Socialist Party garnered no more than a single-digit percentage of the vote in later elections. Others faced similar electoral disasters throughout Europe, such as the Labour Parties in Ireland and the Netherlands. Social democrats in Germany and Luxembourg managed to make the most of their declining support by joining increasingly-broad coalition governments, but even the parliamentary pluralities commanded by the most powerful social-democratic parties in Norway and Sweden have slowly shrunk. The Czech Social Democratic Party, which had been the strongest political force in the country at the beginning of the 2010s, lost all its seats by the end of the decade. PASOK in Greece, which as the ruling party implemented austerity at the behest of the IMF and the European Commission, within a decade also ceased to exist as an independent party. Its anti-austerity successor SYRIZA was then forced

396 Credit Suisse Research Institute, "Global Wealth Report 2014," 6.

397 Raksha Kopparam, "The Federal Reserve's New Distributional Financial Accounts Provide Telling Data on Growing U.S. Wealth and Income Inequality," Washington Center for Equitable Growth, August 22, 2019.

398 Chuck Collins, "Updates: Billionaire Wealth, U.S. Job Losses and Pandemic Profiteers," *Inequality.org,* November 21, 2022.

399 Catherine Bremer and Emmanuel Jarry, "France's Hollande in Tight Spot on Pension Reform," *Reuters,* July 21, 2013.

to implement even more austerity by the EC, leading to its own decline after 2015.[400] Just as in the periphery, the super-empire's mechanisms of control were deployed to crush any new political movements promising to resist neoliberalism in Europe as well. In the inner core, attempts by the old guard to radicalize the center-left establishment in the U.S. and the UK similarly failed. By the end of the 2010s, Sanders and his British counterpart Jeremy Corbyn both lost electoral campaigns promising to revitalize social-democratic programs after being vilified in the national presses.

On the topic of Western social democracy, Nkrumah wrote in 1968:

> Threatened with disintegration by the double-fisted attack of the working class movement and the liberation movement, capitalism had to launch a series of reforms in order to build a protective armour around the inner workings of its system.
>
> To avoid an internal breakdown of the system under the pressure of the workers' protest movement, the governments of capitalist countries granted their workers certain concessions which did not endanger the basic nature of the capitalist system of exploitation. They gave them social security, higher wages, better working conditions, professional training facilities ... .[401]

Upon the destruction of the Soviet Union two decades later, this "double-fisted attack" lost a fist. There was therefore little reason for the capitalist class to continue to compromise; after its greatest enemy without had been dealt with, its alliance with its enemy within was no longer needed. Dispossessive accumulation, once reserved for the periphery, began to advance in the core as well—and Western workers who have not yet been subject to it soon will be.

The Rise of the Political Far-Right

The unraveling of the welfare state will have grim consequences that are only beginning to be felt. Due to their obvious popularity among the people, social-democratic reforms themselves tend to be relatively durable, and often take time and considerable class struggle for neoliberal

---

400 Alexander Kazamias, "Syriza Betrayed Its Principles – and the Greek People. Its Days Are Numbered," *The Guardian,* July 5, 2019.

401 Nkrumah, *Handbook of Revolutionary Warfare,* 3–4.

forces to undo, even after the parties that institutionalized these reforms are no more. OECD statistics indicate that the ruin of the social-democratic left has not yet translated into a large decline in social spending; indeed, the activation of existing safety nets in 2009 resulted in an OECD-wide *increase* in public social expenditures of about 3% of GDP (from 17.8% to 20.8%), and only declined about by about 1% of GDP since then, as of 2019.[402]

As the Western bourgeoisie continue to shed their own responsibility for these payments, however, the working class will eventually only be "redistributing" its own money back to itself. The age of retirement is increasing in nearly every country in Europe—perhaps an inevitable consequence of an aging and declining population, yet pension systems (the largest category in public social expenditures in the OECD) are also being "reformed" to collect more from workers in taxes or pay out less in benefits. By the mid-2010s, income inequality in Sweden was growing at one of the fastest rates in the EU.[403] In 2020, the *New York Times* reported that the proportion of "nonregular employees" in Japan (employees that were excluded from Japan's traditional system of lifetime employment, and thus earned lower wages and retirement allowances for the same work), which during the 1980s was only 16% of the labor force, had reached nearly 37%.[404] A report by Statistics Norway in the same year showed that despite a top marginal income tax rate of nearly 40%, the richest 1% in Norway actually paid much less than nearly every other income group due to their increasing practice of sheltering income in corporate profits.[405] A study published in the *Journal of Epidemiology & Community Health* attributed over 300,000 excess deaths to the UK's austerity policies between 2012 and 2019.[406] "Europeans Are Becoming Poorer," a *Wall Street Journal* headline announced in the summer of 2023, as real wages and consumption declined across the continent.[407] In September, the

402 Organization for Economic Co-operation and Development (OECD), "Compare Your Country."

403 Patricia Nilsson, "Swedish Society's Big Divisions—in 6 Charts," *Financial Times,* August 29, 2018.

404 Makiko Inoue and Ben Dooley, "A Job for Life, or Not? A Class Divide Deepens in Japan," *New York Times,* May 18, 2021.

405 Bård Amundsen, "The Richest Norwegians Pay the Least Taxes," *sciencenorway.no,* September 30, 2020.

406 David Walsh et al., "Bearing the Burden of Austerity: How Do Changing Mortality Rates in the UK Compare between Men and Women?," *Journal of Epidemiological Public Health* 76, no. 12 (December 2022): 1027–1033.

407 Tom Fairless, "Europeans Are Becoming Poorer. 'Yes, We're All Worse

U.S. Department of Housing and Urban Development reported that the elderly—those aged 65 and older—were the fastest-growing segment of the homeless population, a phenomenon so severe the *Journal* said it was being called a "silver tsunami."[408] By the end of the year, homelessness in the U.S. overall had reached its highest reported level ever.[409]

Meanwhile, the void left by the collapsing social-democratic establishment is being filled by the nativist far-right. In France, the xenophobic National Rally (RN) has risen from relative obscurity to become the largest single opposition party as of the 2022 elections, receiving about one-fifth of the vote.[410] In 2023, after massive, sustained protests against plans to raise the pension age from 62 to 64, the French government enacted the "reform" anyway, using its special executive power to bypass a vote in the National Assembly; Marine Le Pen, RN's perennial candidate for president, was one of the loudest voices against the procedure.[411] The Brothers of Italy, which favors a blockade of immigrants from northern Africa, now leads the Italian government.[412] The right-wing Sweden Democrats have become the second-largest party in the Riksdag; other right-wing movements have become entrenched in Hungary and are gaining ground in Germany and the Netherlands.[413] History is poised to repeat itself as fascism strains to return to Europe.

Such political formations aim to collect voters disillusioned with the social democrats; their rhetoric has become carefully calibrated to appeal to the anxiety felt by the working class at the weakening of the social safety net. Instead of contemptuously opposing the welfare state, as RN's former leader Jean-Marie Le Pen had during the 1980s,[414] nativist leaders now cynically and falsely promise to save it—not through redistribution

---

Off,'" *Wall Street Journal,* July 17, 2023.

408 Shannon Najmabadi, "Why More Baby Boomers Are Sliding Into Homelessness," *Wall Street Journal,* September 12, 2023.

409 Kevin Freking, "US Homelessness up 12% to Highest Reported Level as Rents Soar and Coronavirus Pandemic Aid Lapses," *AP,* December 15, 2023.

410 Tom Wheeldon, "'A Seismic Event': Le Pen's Party Makes Historic Breakthrough in French Parliament," *France 24,* June 20, 2022.

411 Hugh Schofield and Paul Kirby, "France's Macron to Force through Pension Reform with No Vote," *BBC,* March 16, 2023.

412 Chico Harlan and Stefano Pitrelli, "Right-Wing Victory in Italy Expected to Bring Swift Changes to Migration," *Washington Post,* September 26, 2022.

413 Mike Corder and Raf Casert, "In a Shock for Europe, Anti-Islam Populist Geert Wilders Records a Massive Win in Dutch Elections," *AP,* November 23, 2023.

414 Elsa Conesa, "How Marine Le Pen Gave up Economic Liberalism for a 'social-Populist' Agenda," *Le Monde,* April 21, 2022.

by raising taxes on the wealthy, but through chauvinist consolidation, by denying benefits and entry to minorities and immigrants.

Hungary's new redistributive model, for example, is largely a propaganda myth. Under the Fidesz political party, the top corporate income tax rate in Hungary fell to 9%, the lowest in the OECD; the value-added tax[415] rose to 27%, the highest of any country in Europe; the system of progressive personal income taxes was replaced with a regressive flat tax.[416] The last increase in Hungary's public social expenditures mostly came while Fidesz was in the opposition (2002-2010); from 2009 to 2019 they *declined* by over 5% of GDP.[417] What social programs that do exist are an unsustainable façade, funded by external aid from the EU[418] and by the working class themselves, including remittance payments from Hungarians working elsewhere in Europe, which in the first three years since Fidesz took power in 2010 doubled as a percentage of GDP, amounting to three or four times the EU average.[419] Concurrently, the Hungarian government has adopted relatively extreme anti-migrant rhetoric and policies, rendering asylum procedures virtually inaccessible and fencing its Serbian border with barbed wire.[420]

The crisis model of social democracy has therefore become obsolete. Once beneficiaries of the increased neocolonial plunder during the Cold War stage, the Western working class is now increasingly victim of the

---

415 A consumption tax which the wealthy may pay at a higher absolute rate but pay less as a percentage of their income.

416 The Tax Foundation, "Taxes in Hungary."

417 Organization for Economic Co-operation and Development (OECD), "Compare Your Country (Hungary)."

418 As of 2022, the European Commission has stopped publishing statistics on member states' net positions (i.e. contributor or recipient), but according to a recent estimate by the German Economic Institute using the same method of calculation used by the EC in previous years, Hungary was the third-largest net recipient of EU funds, exceeded only by Greece and Poland. [Berthold Busch, Björn Kauder, and Samina Sultan, *Wer finanziert die EU? Nettozahler und Nettoempfänger in der EU* (Who finances the EU? Net contributors and net recipients in the EU), IW-Report 55/2022.] Fidesz is well-aware of the reality of Hungary's dependence; the crisis in 2022 induced President Orbán to plead for subsidies and a large loan from the European Commission, in addition to the billions in EU funds Hungary has already been receiving. (Brückner Gergely, "Orbán Is Requesting the EU Loan: After Four Big Blows, Hungary Has Decided That Cheap Money Is Better than Expensive Money," *telex*, March 25, 2022.)

419 The World Bank, "Personal Remittances, Received (% of GDP) - Hungary, European Union."

420 Daniel Nolan, "Hungary Orders 100-Mile Serbia Border Fence to Keep out Migrants," *The Telegraph*, June 17, 2015.

same capitalist oligarchy. Compromise between worker and capitalist is inherently unsustainable; social democracy in the core of the super-empire will not flourish in economic adversity, but be stamped out. The upper bourgeoisie of the West will have what they consider their due—everything—whether through cruel austerity or through cruel austerity cloaked in racial chauvinism. Social democracy in the periphery, or the closest thing to it, is even more quickly destroyed or else suffers under perpetual economic siege as described in Chapter Two. Presently, out of every region in the world, social democracy is significantly expanding in only one place.

CHAPTER SIX

China and the World

*"Whether you like it or not, the global economy is the big ocean that
you cannot escape from. Any attempt to cut off the flow of capital,
technologies, products, industries and people between economies, and
channel the waters in the ocean back into isolated lakes and creeks is
simply not possible."*

—Xi Jinping[421]

"If you want to get rich, first build a road."

—Chinese proverb

To summarize the conclusions of the preceding chapters:

1. World imperialism is currently in the "super-imperialism" stage, in which a single unified and unrivaled empire controlled by the Western capitalist class has a neocolonial relationship with most of the world.

2. Super-imperialism is characterized by one primary mechanism of exploitation (unequal exchange) and four mechanisms of control (structural adjustment, economic isolation, military intervention, and soft power).

3. Either the development of a socialist bloc or the development of a rival empire are possible conditions for an end to the super-imperialist stage, yet in general, the mechanisms of control suppress both proletarian revolution and pre-imperial rivals while exporting counterrevolution.

With these in mind, a proper analysis of the People's Republic of China and its relation to world imperialism can now be made. It is undeniable that the PRC is a rising superpower that has overtaken the United States in some respects and will soon in still more. As the world's second-largest country by population, and the world's second-largest economy, the status and orientation of China will naturally be the most consequential to world affairs throughout the next several decades. Yet the nature of the

---

421 "Xi at Davos: Also a Master of Metaphors," *Xinhua*, January 17, 2017.

PRC, its behavior, and the intentions behind such behavior are all poorly understood around the world, especially by Westerners. Has capitalism been restored in China? Which class or classes hold state power? Is the PRC currently an empire? Will it form an empire, or a new socialist bloc, or neither? There is no consensus; therefore, this and succeeding chapters will attempt to answer these questions and demystify modern China in as much detail as possible.

We begin at the highest level, the PRC's relations with the rest of the world, which will be analyzed below. Following chapters will examine China's governance, the class struggle within China, and the dynamics of the Chinese ethnic groups. This chapter, however, will treat China itself as a "black box" whose intentions and internal decision-making processes are opaque and unknowable, and focus solely on what can be deduced from its international relations.

China and Unequal Exchange

Since the beginning of the PRC's period of Reform and Opening Up, its relations with the periphery have been the source of considerable controversy. A narrative of ruthless Chinese exploitation of helpless African nations has since emerged, popularized by the Western press. The PRC has been accused of stealing African land and resources, stealing jobs from native Africans, spying on African governments and their citizens, discriminating against African people, and many other crimes. Terms such as "imperialism," "debt-trap diplomacy," and "neocolonialism"— all real phenomena described at length in Chapters One and Two—have been weaponized against China, used to denigrate any and all bilateral agreements between the PRC and peripheral countries and cast suspicion upon whatever gifts or gestures of goodwill the PRC has offered to them.

Any objective quantitative analysis cannot help but show that even if the very worst allegations against the PRC have merit, the exploitation of Africa by the West is orders of magnitude more severe. According to the Institute for Security Studies, an African non-profit organization, as of 2019 over 7,000 French troops were active in independent (i.e. non-United Nations) operations across the African continent, superseded only by the United States Africa Command, which operated a total of 34 military outposts in Africa.[422] The PRC, in contrast, maintains only

---

422 Andrews Atta-Asamoah, "Proceed with Caution: Africa's Growing Foreign Military Presence," Institute for Security Studies, August 27, 2019.

a single military base near Djibouti City, which also hosts bases for multiple other foreign powers, including the U.S., France, Italy, Japan, and recently Saudi Arabia.[423] War on Want, a London-based anti-poverty charity organization, wrote in 2016 that one hundred companies listed on the London Stock Exchange collectively controlled over $1 trillion worth of the most valuable natural resources in Africa, notably gold, platinum, diamonds, copper, oil, gas, and coal.[424]

Nevertheless, the PRC's relations with African countries are not above reproach. With respect to trade, its approach does not qualitatively differ from the West's; though it has become the majority trading partner of nearly every country on the continent, wages in these countries—particularly those paid to workers who must extract raw materials, as described in Chapter Two and Appendix A—and export prices have remained artificially low, maintaining the rate of unequal exchange, and Africa continues to experience a net loss of several billion dollars each year through capital flight and the repatriation of profits to foreign entities.[425] In some cases, bilateral economic agreements are conducted in secrecy or produce results slanted in favor of Chinese companies and interests. For example, in 2007, in a barter exchange for commitments by a Chinese consortium to spend an estimated $6.5 billion in loans from China Eximbank constructing roads, railways, hospitals and other badly-needed infrastructure in the Democratic Republic of the Congo, the DRC guaranteed the consortium long-term access to 8,050,661 tonnes of copper, 202,290 tonnes of cobalt, and 372.3 tonnes of gold, wherein the Chinese partners received a two-thirds majority stake in joint mining concern Sicomines, which was to be exempt from taxes until the loans were repaid from the mining proceeds. The world market prices of these commodities of course rise and fall over time, but if this entire amount had been sold at a high point in the 2010s, the revenue would likely have been in excess of $80 billion.[426] Though depending on the rate at

423 Michaël Tanchum, "China's New Military Base in Africa: What It Means for Europe and America," European Council on Foreign Relations, December 14, 2021.

424 Mark Curtis, *The New Colonialism: Britain's Scramble for Africa's Energy and Mineral Resources* (War on Want, July 2016), 1.

425 Mark Curtis and Tim Jones, "Honest Accounts 2017: How the World Profits from Africa's Wealth," Committee for the Abolition of Illegitimate Debt (CADTM), June 6, 2017, 2.

426 At its 2019 annual average price of $6,010 per tonne, the total amount of copper (by far the cheapest of the three metals) alone would be equivalent to nearly $50 billion. [The World Bank, "World Bank Commodities Price Data (The Pink

which subsequent production is taxed by the DRC once the loans are paid off, with profits split two-to-one, it is clear that the terms of this barter relationship could result in long-term profits much greater for the Chinese than the Congolese, i.e. so slanted that they would amount to the dispossessive accumulation of Congolese natural resources by a foreign power.[427]

Given its complicity in the most significant mechanism of exploitation, it must therefore be asked if the PRC has become a partner of the super-empire, seizing for itself its own neocolonies? At the time of the initial Sicomines arrangement (which will be reexamined later on in this chapter) the answer was negative. In his study based on 2009 world trade flows and exchange rates, Köhler found that the unequal exchange between Africa and the group of "advanced economies" lay between 16% and 20% of the victim countries' GDP, whereas the unequal exchange between those countries and the PRC—which by 2009 had become the largest trading partner to nearly every country in that region[428]—amounted to 0.5% of their GDP.[429] According to Köhler's conclusion:

> On the other hand, exports from Sub-Saharan Africa to China do not embody significant amounts of transfer value. In other words, Sub-Saharan Africa's trade with China (in 2009) is fairly equitable, as defined here. That observation is based on estimates for the year 2009. Should China's currency appreciate in relation to U.S. and other high-income country currencies in the future, Africa-China trade could become more unequal.[430]

Sheet)," August 2022, 2.]

427 Democratic Republic of the Congo, "Protocole d'accord entre la République Démocratique du Congo et le groupement des Entreprises Chinoises" [Memorandum of Understanding between the Democratic Republic of Congo and the group of Chinese companies].

428 Roland Rajah and Alyssa Leng, "Chart of the Week: Global Trade through a US-China Lens," *The Interpreter,* December 18, 2019.

429 Though the model published by Hickel et al. in 2022 was more comprehensive than Köhler's, it did not aim to measure the exchange between China and other "non-advanced" economies; however, it did conclude that in 2015 the "advanced" countries siphoned $2.4 trillion from China through unequal exchange, or nearly a quarter of the entire value transferred from all "non-advanced" countries. [Jason Hickel et al., "Imperialist Appropriation in the World Economy: Drain from the Global South through Unequal Exchange, 1990–2015," *Global Environmental Change* 73 (March 22).]

430 Gernot Köhler, *Estimating Unequal Exchange: Sub-Saharan Africa to China and the World,* March 2022.

Throughout 2009, the U.S. dollar was worth approximately 6.8 Chinese yuan; in 2020, it was worth 6.9 yuan. During the 2010s, it ranged between a maximum value of 6.9 yuan and a minimum of 6.1 yuan.[431] An updated calculation for the year 2016, using both Köhler's formula and his sources, yields an increase in unequal transfer value from the same group of African countries[432] to China, yet the total was just 0.76% of their GDP.[433] Today, as mentioned above, with only a few exceptions, the PRC is the largest trading partner of every African country, yet overall, the terms of this trade are likely thus far only very slightly in favor of China.

How could the PRC extract a great volume of raw materials from the periphery, yet not also drain a significant amount of value through unequal exchange? To return to the example of the early-2010s iPhone from Chapter Two, economist Dr. Sean Starrs writes contemporarily:

Nor does the fact that China exports virtually all iPads and iPhones necessarily mean that Chinese firms reap the largest profit from the sale of these iPads and iPhones, or electronics more generally. In fact, it does not even mean that a Chinese firm is performing final assembly. On the contrary, it is a *Taiwanese* firm, Hon Hai Precision Industry, that employs over one million Chinese workers (China's largest private employer) to conduct final assembly of electronics such as iPads and iPhones in China, but the profit from this final assembly largely goes to Taiwanese shareholders, especially to the Taiwanese billionaire founder Terry Gou. Even still, the profit that Hon Hai Precision Industry makes from the assembly of iPads and iPhones in China is peanuts compared with the profit that Apple ultimately makes from owning the proprietary design and brand.[434]

Despite becoming the world leader in electronics manufacturing, Chinese companies received only a small fraction of the total profit

---

431 World Bank, "Official Exchange Rate (LCU per US$, Period Average) - China."

432 "Sub-Saharan Africa" as categorized by the IMF, which includes all African countries except Mauritania, Morocco, Algeria, Libya, Tunisia, Egypt, Sudan, and Djibouti.

433 See Appendix B for the updated calculation.

434 Starrs, "American Economic Power Hasn't Declined—It Globalized! Summoning the Data and Taking Globalization Seriously," *International Studies Quarterly* 57, no. 4 (December 2013): 819.

generated by the world's top electronics firms. In 2016, according to Starrs' research, in its largest category of manufactured exports ("Office & Telecom Equipment"), China accounted for 32% of all world exports by value while the U.S. accounted for 8.3% by value; but of the total profit share of the global top 2000 firms that were in this category, China received only 1.6% while the U.S. took 60%.[435]

The PRC's principal sin, therefore, is that its industry has taken a step up in the economic value chain. It buys raw materials at the same grossly undervalued prices (i.e., extracted in African mines with vastly under-compensated labor) that the West does, yet the super-profits of this exchange still flow almost exclusively to the West, as Chinese manufacturing transforms those materials into commodities and sells them *also* at grossly undervalued prices. Indeed, the PRC cannot acquire these materials much more dearly, for its market dominance in commodity manufacturing has only been possible by underselling Western manufacturing. The price gap between cheap Chinese goods and expensive Western goods can only be derived from an equivalent gap in the price of labor power, meaning that China's newfound wealth has come from the labor of Chinese workers, and not at the expense of African workers—whose exploitation is severe but unchanged—but at the expense of Western domestic industry. Thus, through this cycle of relationships Africa has remained poor, China has grown gradually richer, and the Western financial oligarchy have seen no reduction in their obscene super-profits.

The importance of trade to exploitation during the two most recent stages of world imperialism—as well as the relative decline of Marxism-Leninism—have necessitated new forms of analysis during the twentieth century, one of the most thorough being World-Systems Theory (WST), most notably advanced by Wallerstein. WST provides a structural model of international economic relations based upon the worldwide division of labor, which explains the new role of the PRC and its constraints therein. Accordingly, in his recent analysis based in WST, Professor Minqi Li places China in the "semi-periphery,"[436] an intermediate category between the periphery and the imperial core, the natures of which have already been described.

Wallerstein clarifies the features of this category in the following way:

---

435 Sean Starrs, *Signs of the Times #3 - On U.S. Decline, with Sean Starrs*, Sage4Age YouTube video [36:41; loc. 15:17], June 3, 2022.

436 Minqi Li, "China: Imperialism or Semi-Periphery?," *Monthly Review*, July 1, 2021.

The semiperiphery, however, is not an artifice of statistical cutting points, nor is it a residual category. The semiperiphery is a necessary structural element in a world-economy. These areas play a role parallel to that played, *mutatis mutandis*, by middle trading groups in an empire. They are collection points of vital skills that are often politically unpopular. These middle areas (like middle groups in an empire) partially deflect the political pressures which groups primarily located in peripheral areas might otherwise direct against core-states and the groups which operate within and through their state machineries.[437]

The application of WST would seem to indict the Chinese government as a sort of slightly-more-privileged comprador to the super-empire. Indeed, Li's conclusion remains studiously neutral on the question of the PRC's intentions and motivations, noting only that its structural position within the capitalist world is in fact currently far lower than Western media often allege, and that China cannot advance to the core without causing complete environmental ruin—implicitly presupposing that the Chinese capitalist class, if they are indeed at the helm of the Chinese government, are somehow more farsighted and conscientious than the Western bourgeoisie, whose unchecked political power and pursuit of increasing profits are bringing such ruin anyway![438]

WST in its orthodox form, however, is even grimmer and more totalizing. The structural determinism of Wallerstein's model, in fact, cannot distinguish between revolution and counterrevolution. Describing the Bolshevik Revolution, Wallerstein writes:

The Russian Revolution was essentially that of a semiperipheral country whose internal balance of forces had been such that as of the late nineteenth century it began on a decline towards a peripheral status. This was the result of marked penetration of foreign capital into the industrial sector which was on its way to eliminating all indigenous capitalist forces, the resistance to the mechanization of the agricultural sector, the decline of relative military power (as evidenced by the defeat by the Japanese in 1905). The Revolution brought to power a group of state managers who reversed each

---

437 Wallerstein, *The Modern World-System I*, 349–50.
438 Minqi Li, "China: Imperialism or Semi-Periphery?"

one of these trends by using the classic technique of mercantilist semiwithdrawal from the world-economy.[439]

Though Wallerstein considered the national liberation movements in Vietnam, et al., to be part of a "long-run process of social transformation," he regarded it as a dialectical process, which also further integrated Vietnam into the capitalist world-economy.[440] "If tomorrow U.S. Steel became a worker's collective in which all employees without exception received an identical share of the profits and all stockholders expropriated without compensation," Wallerstein asks, "would U.S. Steel therefore cease to be a capitalist enterprise operating in a capitalist world-economy?"[441] In other words: not only China—both after Reform and before—but Vietnam, the Soviet Union, and any revolution where state power is taken from the bourgeoisie cannot develop further except through the continued oppression of the periphery, and could then (perhaps) only advance into the core, where they would become indistinguishable from the Western empires.

How can liberation be achieved given such a dialectic? In Marxist terms, under what conditions could this contradiction be resolved? What alternatives might exist? For all his considerable diagnostic prowess, Wallerstein had no answers. The most he offered on this score, unfortunately, were vague and inconsistent predictions that a new socialist world-system will eventually replace the capitalist one, through undefined "movements and forces."[442] The "future world order," he suggested passively, "will construct itself slowly, in ways we can barely imagine, let alone predict."[443]

To Marx, the purpose of his political and economic science was not merely to explain the world, but to change it.[444] For those who pursue liberation in seriousness, movements and forces must first be defined and imagined, if they are to later be embodied, and even the most comprehensive diagnostic analysis must also indicate a mechanism of change in order to truly be useful. For the purposes of *this* analysis, a deeper look at the PRC's international relations will demonstrate the shortcomings of an orthodox World-Systems approach.

---

439 Wallerstein, *The Capitalist World-Economy*, 30–31.
440 Wallerstein, *The Capitalist World-Economy*, 63–65.
441 Wallerstein, *The Capitalist World-Economy*, 34.
442 Wallerstein, *The Capitalist World-Economy*, 34–35.
443 Immanuel Wallerstein, *Historical Capitalism*, 93.
444 Karl Marx, "Theses On Feuerbach."

China's Export of Capital

China's ascent to its current status as a major economic actor began in earnest during the 1990s, yet it was not until 2001 that the PRC joined the World Trade Organization and the exponential curve of the Chinese economy's growth started to have large-scale effects upon the world. With the Soviet Union gone and Western finance plundering Eastern Europe and Southeast Asia (during the crisis of 1997), the United States' control over the world economy at this time was absolute. From 1995 to 2001, the United States accounted for over 100% of net global GDP growth.[445] In 2002, however, this trend changed rather dramatically. Over the next six years—until the recession of 2008—global GDP doubled, not just in the U.S., or in the core of the super-empire, but in every region of the world. The U.S. economy, in fact, only increased at the same more-or-less steady rate it had been during the previous decade.[446]

Many different factors, of course, accounted for the global prosperity of the early twenty-first century, and under the regime of neoliberalism this increase in GDP often corresponded to a rise in income inequality rather than better living standards for the global proletariat, as the Arab Spring quite decisively demonstrated in 2011.[447] Yet it is clear that during this period—known among economists as the "commodities boom"—an extraordinary amount of wealth was created, both directly and indirectly, by China's meteoric growth and rapid industrialization. Oil-exporting countries in particular benefited enormously from a massive increase in demand for energy and raw materials, exporting more crude oil at higher and higher prices; the economies of national-bourgeois- and popular front-controlled oil exporters such as Venezuela, Libya, Iran, and Russia all more than tripled—a rate of increase only exceeded by China's.[448] According to the World Investment Report by the United Nations Conference on Trade and Development (UNCTAD), the PRC's capital exports by 2008 were relatively negligible; in fact, the PRC had

---

445 That is to say, for this seven-year period, GDP grew in some countries other than the United States, but fell so much elsewhere that the net global increase was smaller than the increase in just the U.S. World GDP grew from $31 trillion to $33.6 trillion while U.S. GDP grew from $7.6 trillion to $10.6 trillion, according to World Bank statistics.

446 The World Bank, "GDP (Current US$) - World, United States."

447 See Chapter Two.

448 The World Bank, "GDP (Current US$) - Russian Federation, Libya, Venezuela, RB, Iran, Islamic Rep., China."

no more than $100 billion in outward foreign direct investment stock, well behind the Russian Federation, Finland, or Norway. (FDI stock held by the United States at that time, for reference, was nearly $3 trillion.)[449] China, it seemed, had suddenly risen to become the world's second-largest economy without fulfilling a principal criterion of Lenin's 1916 definition of imperialism.

Today, of course, the PRC is one of the leading capital exporters in the world, holding an aggregate total of nearly $2.2 trillion in direct investment abroad made between 2005 and 2021 according to the American Enterprise Institute,[450] or over $2.5 trillion in 2021 according to UNCTAD.[451] Though still well behind the United States' $10 trillion, this places the PRC in rarefied company, on an equal footing with the United Kingdom, i.e. equivalent to a major subordinate partner within the super-empire. This would seem to classify the PRC as a significant imperialist power according to Lenin's third criterion. So, is it?

That the PRC fails other key criteria set down by Lenin will be shown later on; however, it is precisely in the character of the PRC's foreign direct investments that the deficiencies of his century-old definition of imperialism can be found. Again according to the AEI data until 2021, the biggest single recipient country of Chinese investment, with nearly $200 billion, was none other than the United States! The next two largest recipients were the United Kingdom and Australia, each with around $100 billion. Could these investments represent an exploitation or dispossessive accumulation by the PRC of the super-empire itself? The vast discrepancy in per capita income between these countries and China makes it quite challenging to answer this question other than in the negative. Certainly, few if any of these investments can be imagined to be driving dispossessive accumulation of U.S. labor or natural resources; the largest such transaction between the PRC and the U.S. recorded by AEI, for example, was the $10 billion acquisition of an airline leasing company by a subsidiary of the HNA Group—a Chinese aviation conglomerate—in 2017.[452]

---

449 United Nations Conference on Trade and Development, "UNCTAD/ WIR/2008," 259.

450 American Enterprise Institute, "China Global Investment Tracker."

451 United Nations Conference on Trade and Development, "UNCTAD/ WIR/2022," 215.

452 Avolon, "Avolon Completes US$10.38 Billion Acquisition of CIT Group Aircraft Leasing Business," April 4, 2017.

Even a high-level examination of world investment statistics shows that today, the relationship between capital exports and imperialism is anything but direct and transparent. It is not just the PRC which has invested heavily in the Western imperial countries; the constituents of the super-empire also invest in each other, even more than they do in the periphery! In 2021, three-quarters of the world's total foreign direct investment stock was invested in the category of "developed economies" that included Europe, the U.S., Canada, Australia, and Japan, and around the same amount of FDI stock was also *held* by those countries. Clearly, Western countries invest most of their capital in either themselves or each other; but as their average wages and per capita income figures indicate, they cannot—with some exceptions—be each other's victims in terms of dispossessive accumulation.[453]

Li also suggests that Lenin's analysis is either obsolete or incorrect, citing instead the work of more recent Marxist economists, including Arghiri Emmanuel and Samir Amin, principal contributors to the theory of unequal exchange.[454] Later in 2021, Dr. Jay Tharappel, an economic historian at the University of Sydney, proposed an alternative theory of imperialism involving what he terms "national exploitation" that directly contradicts Lenin's 1916 definition. The capital exports of the British Empire had been almost exclusively (more than 80%) directed at its settler-colonies in North America, South Africa, and Australia; yet the super-profits of the British capitalist class were taken mostly from India through colonial state taxation. In contrast, British capital exports to the American colonies had had the effect of accelerating capitalist development, eventually to the point where they became so rich as to replace Britain as the strongest imperial power in the world.[455] The brief analysis in Appendix A yields the conclusion that while Western capital exports facilitated some forms of unequal exchange (in the example of the super-empire's corporations building factories in Southeast Asia, wherein workers are super-exploited to produce artificially cheap goods), other forms were facilitated by a chronic *absence* of capital (in the example of artisanal gold mining).

Though briefly described in Chapter Two, a more detailed examination of the mechanisms of exploitation of modern empires is needed. The

---

453 United Nations Conference on Trade and Development, "UNCTAD/ WIR/2022," 214.

454 Minqi Li, "China: Imperialism or Semi-Periphery?"

455 Jay Tharappel, "Why China's Capital Exports Can Weaken Imperialism," 34.

five stages of imperialism have already been partially reconciled with Tharappel's theory of national exploitation, or at least his example of India: as a mechanism of exploitation, colonial state taxation is no longer possible under the latter two stages due to the replacement of direct colonialism with neocolonialism. The primary mechanism of exploitation is now unequal exchange through international trade.

Emmanuel, who in the 1960s codified the theory of unequal exchange, did so by integrating, with the phenomenon of international trade, both Karl Marx's theory of value and nineteenth century British economist and politician David Ricardo's theory of comparative advantage, which has repeatedly been used by other capitalist economists to justify unequal exchange under the guise of "free trade" for centuries. By the twentieth century, it had become abundantly clear that Ricardo's prediction that profits and wages would equalize between countries as a natural process arising from a lack of barriers to trade had not come to pass. According to Emmanuel, the conditions under which Ricardo's equalization process might not take place, and under which Marx's model of price equalization allowed for an exception, fit the present-day reality:

> Sufficient *mobility of capital* [emphasis added] to ensure that in essentials international equalization of profits takes place, so the proposition regarding prices of production remains valid; sufficient immobility of labor to ensure that local differences in wages, due to the socio-historical element, cannot be eliminated, so that a modification of the proposition regarding prices of production is made necessary.[456]

In other words: the combination of the immobility of labor (i.e., workers are largely unable to emigrate to more prosperous cities or countries that pay higher wages) with the mobility of capital (i.e. the export of capital) is the very force that maintains the vast international disparity in production costs and prices that persists in the world. Not much is new under the sun; though neocolonialism has further obscured their relationship, capital exports are still at the root of super-profits taken from one country by another.

The payment of interest on debt, a secondary mechanism of exploitation under super-imperialism described in Chapter Two, is by definition

---

456 Arghiri Emmanuel, *Unequal Exchange: A Study of the Imperialism of Trade*, xxxiv.

nothing but a consequence of capital exports (loans). Therefore, in total, the export of capital is even more fundamental to imperialism today than ever! Lenin's third criterion has not been invalidated, merely shown to be incomplete: the export of capital is a *necessary* condition of imperialist exploitation, but not a *sufficient* one.[457] Thus while the Russian Federation can be easily categorized as a non-imperialist or pre-imperialist power due to the insignificance of its capital exports, the function and character of the PRC's *significant* capital exports must be examined carefully before it can be categorized at all.

Li finds that according to investment income statistics, the average rate of return on the PRC's new overseas assets was relatively quite low:

> From 2010 to 2018, the rates of return on China's overseas assets averaged about 3 percent and the rates of return on total foreign investment in China varied mostly in the range of 5 to 6 percent. An average rate of return of about 3 percent on China's overseas investment obviously does not constitute "superprofits." Moreover, foreign capitalists in China are able to make about twice as much profit as Chinese capital can make in the rest of the world on a given amount of investment.[458]

A similar—or perhaps even slightly larger—disparity exists between the PRC's and the *global* average rate of return on outward direct investment; the latter ranged between 5.3% and 6.6% at the end of the 2010s, and in the years just before the 2008 recession had averaged 10.5%.[459]

---

457 To Lenin's credit, it must be noted that in the same breath as his analysis of imperialism as a special stage of capitalism in 1916, he warned against a dogmatic application of his five criteria to define it. In the paragraph immediately following his definition, he writes:

"We shall see later that *imperialism can and must be defined differently* if we bear in mind not only the basic, purely economic concepts—to which the above definition is limited—*but also the historical place of this stage of capitalism* in relation to capitalism in general, or the relation between imperialism and the two main trends in the working-class movement. The thing to be noted at this point is that imperialism, as interpreted above, undoubtedly represents a special stage in the development of capitalism." [emphasis added] (Lenin, *Imperialism,* chapter 7.)

Lenin obviously could not foresee the Cold War and super-imperialist stages during the time of his writing, but he did recognize that the nature of capitalism—and by extension, imperialism—was to continuously change and develop, requiring any analysis of imperialism to correspondingly change and develop to remain accurate.

458 Minqi Li, "China: Imperialism or Semi-Periphery?"

459 United Nations Conference on Trade and Development, "UNCTAD/

As Li further notes, the PRC's net investment income from abroad is negative; in fact, according to World Bank statistics, with the relatively modest (around $13 billion) exception of 2014, the PRC has not had a positive net primary income from abroad (that is, all income from the PRC's investments in other countries minus payments on foreign investments in China) in any year since it first became a major capital exporter in 2008, and had an overall loss of more than $700 billion over the entire period recorded by the World Bank. In 2018, a typical year for the decade, the PRC's net primary income stood at negative $61 billion; in contrast, in the same year France had almost $65 billion in positive primary income, and the United States—which has never had a negative net primary income from abroad in any year recorded by the World Bank—had nearly $300 billion.[460] China, it seems, is home to some of the richest finance capitalists the world has ever seen—but also either the most patient or the most blundering. They have made enormous and increasing investments in the rest of the world, but so far turn only an abysmally low profit from them. Whether in their strategy or their objectives, it is clear Chinese investments qualitatively differ from those of other major capital exporters.

In terms of social and economic development, there is a large and growing body of scholarship indicating that Chinese capital exports have had net positive effects on the periphery. Despite a loud chorus of Western NGOs and newspapers alleging that Chinese infrastructure projects harm partner countries' economies by importing Chinese workers rather than giving jobs to locals, the data often inconveniently disagree. A 2017 study of such projects in eight African countries by global management consultant McKinsey & Company found that Chinese enterprises "overwhelmingly" employ and train local workers;[461] in Nigeria, for example, Johns Hopkins researchers also surveyed fifteen Chinese manufacturing companies, finding that on average they employed 84.9% local workers.[462] A more recent study of Tajikistan and Kyrgyzstan found that every

WIR/2022," 39.

460 The World Bank, "Net Primary Income (Net Income from Abroad) (Current US$) - China, United States, France."

461 Kartik Jayaram, Omid Kassiri, and Irene Yuan Sun, "Dance of the Lions and Dragons: How Are Africa and China Engaging, and How Will the Partnership Evolve?" McKinsey & Company, June 2017, 40.

462 Yunnan Chen, Irene Yuan Sun, Rex Uzonna Ukaejiofo, Tang Xiaoyang, and Deborah Brautigam, *Learning from China?: Manufacturing, Investment, and Technology Transfer in Nigeria,* China-Africa Research Initiative Working Paper 2 (Johns Hopkins School of Advanced International Studies, January 2016), 20.

major Chinese company had localized their workforces by 2020.[463] According to a 2018 paper from a research lab at the College of William & Mary, Chinese development projects reduced economic inequality in their respective regions;[464] a 2021 special report by the South African Institute of International Affairs based on case studies in Kenya, Ethiopia, and Nigeria concluded that the PRC's Belt and Road projects, despite their expense and unevenness, had both direct and indirect net positive effects;[465] a long-term case study in Ethiopia conducted by the London School of Economics and Political Science found that Chinese foreign direct investment had "significant and persistently positive effects after 6-12 years."[466] A 2022 study published in *Social Sciences & Humanities Open* found that the PRC's FDI had a positive effect on African countries' economic and social development;[467] even a recent study by researchers at Jiangsu University in Zhenjiang, while criticizing negative aspects of PRC-Africa trade relations, nevertheless found that Chinese FDI had improved economic growth in middle- and low-income African coun-tries.[468] And according to Tharappel:

> China transformed into a net-exporter of capital in 2000 . . . and since 2015 has grown to become the largest net-exporter of capital in the world, but like the exports of capital by Britain these exports are an *industrialising* force in the countries they are exported to, rather than a *deindustrialising* force, which is what defined the national exploitation of India, China, and African nations by Britain. That Africa is rapidly industrialising as a consequence

---

463 Dirk van der Kley, "Chinese Companies' Localization in Kyrgyzstan and Tajikistan," *Problems of Post-Communism* 67, no. 3 (2020).

464 Richard Bluhm, Axel Dreher, Andreas Fuchs, Bradley Parks, Austin Strange, and Michael Tierney, *Connective Financing: Chinese Infrastructure Projects and the Diffusion of Economic Activity in Developing Countries,* AidData Working Paper no. 64 (Williamsburg, VA: AidData at William & Mary, September 2018), 30.

465 Adedeji Adeniran et al., *Estimating the Economic Impact of Chinese BRI Investment in Africa* (South African Institute of International Affairs, June 2021).

466 Riccardo Crescenzi and Nicola Limodio, "The Impact of Chinese FDI in Africa: Evidence from Ethiopia (Institute of Global Affairs, The London School of Economics and Political Science, January 2021).

467 Debongo Devincy Yanne Sylvaire et al., "The Impact of China's Foreign Direct Investment on Africa's Inclusive Development," *Social Sciences & Humanities Open* 6, no. 1 (2022).

468 Emma Serwaa Obobisa et al., "The Causal Relationship Between China-Africa Trade, China OFDI, and Economic Growth of African Countries," *SAGE Open* 11, no. 4 (October 2021).

of Chinese investment is widely acknowledged. According to the IMF, "Sub-Saharan Africa is the second-fastest-growing region of the world today, trailing only developing Asia" (Sayeh 2013); according to the American Enterprise Institute (AEI), "the value of China's overseas investment and construction combined since 2005 exceeds $2 trillion" (AEI 2020), with $304 billion invested in sub-Saharan Africa alone. Chinese investment is rising, while U.S. and European investment is falling in Africa—since 2011, China represents 40% of the investment for developing Africa's infrastructure, whereas the U.S. share declined from 24% to 6.7%, while the European share fell from 44% to 34% (Huang 2016). According to Dr. Parag Khanna, author of *The Future Is Asian*, the reason why China established the Asian Infrastructure Investment Bank (AIIB) was because the World Bank turned away from financing major infrastructure projects more than five decades ago (Khanna 2019). Therefore, by aiding the industrialisation of Africa, China's capital exports perform a similar role to British capital exports to its settler-colonies and to Western Europe, insofar as it results in the diffusion of industrial production.[469]

Xinhua reported that during the 2000-2020 period, the PRC had helped African countries build 13,000 kilometers of railways, 100,000 kilometers of highways, 1,000 bridges, and 100 ports.[470] The Western press, as of this writing, has neither published its own estimates on the volume of infrastructural development by the PRC, nor disputed *Xinhua*'s. In a 2019 article, *Forbes* described how "[t]he central players in many of Africa's biggest ticket infrastructure projects—including the $12 billion Coastal Railway in Nigeria, the $4.5 billion Addis Ababa-Djibouti Railway, and the $11 billion megaport and economic zone at Bagamoyo—are being developed via Chinese partnerships." The article quoted Daan Roggeveen, founder of international urban planning research center MORE Architecture, in calling Chinese infrastructural projects on the African continent "ubiquitous," estimating that ". . . any big project in African cities that is higher than three floors or roads that are longer

---

469 Jay Tharappel, "Why China's Capital Exports Can Weaken Imperialism," 43–44.

470 Xinhua, "Sino-African Cooperation Eyes More Benefits," *China Daily,* December 20, 2022.

than three kilometers are most likely being built and engineered by the Chinese."[471]

Overall, the West has reacted strongly but inconsistently to the PRC's rise as a competing capital exporter. Consumers of the Western press have heard that infrastructure projects undertaken through the Belt and Road Initiative cost too much, that they are too "risky" for Chinese investors, that they are prone to corruption, that they displace communities, and that they are bad for the environment; such projects that fail, are canceled, or that have experienced delays are widely publicized and eagerly portrayed as representative of the BRI as a whole. Implicit in such criticism is the assumption that there is a "right" approach to building a road or railway or hydroelectric dam—an approach that has no environmental impact, chooses the proper location, is completed quickly, and has no negative consequences to speak of. Given the option of the "right" approach and another approach that suffers any or all of the above, Chinese firms and financiers are presumed to have always chosen the latter, instead. It is assumed that firms engaged in the construction of new infrastructure are cutting corners—using improper materials, perpetrating labor violations, or foregoing proper environmental impact studies—to *save* money; yet simultaneously, the nefarious intent behind these projects is supposedly to incur the greatest possible expense, so that the partner country will be saddled with unpayable debts. A typical Western think tank or newspaper will give an overwhelming impression of the BRI as a colossal scam, certain to produce no good results at all—while alternately promoting schemes by increasingly anxious Western governments aimed at *competing* with it.

The BRI was launched in 2013; by 2017 the U.S. government published plans to revive its own similar "New Silk Road" infrastructure plan to "counter" the PRC's initiative.[472] The New Silk Road had in fact been announced before the BRI, in 2011; but the United States had failed to follow through with it, revoking its funding before it had begun even a single project. Its revival fared no better; as of this writing, no NSR projects have been reported. In 2022, the U.S. introduced plans to create the nebulous Indo-Pacific Economic Framework, an anti-PRC economic alliance between the U.S., India, Japan, Australia, and other Southeast

---

471 Wade Shepard, "What China Is Really Up To In Africa," *Forbes,* October 3, 2019.

472 "US Revives Two Infra Projects in Asia to Counter China's OBOR," *The Economic Times,* May 24, 2017.

Asian countries—which, admitted CNBC, expert analysts considered to be "more symbolic than it [was] effective or real policy."[473] In 2021, the G7 announced the "Build Back Better World Partnership" that again, according to the U.S. government, would "counter" the BRI by investing in five-to-ten large infrastructure projects around the world by January of the following year.[474] By April of 2022, however, it had not funded any such projects, and National Public Radio reported (generously) that there had been "little tangible progress to herald" and that instead, President Biden planned to relaunch the initiative at the 2022 G7 conference under yet another name.[475] In June, it was rebranded as the "Partnership for Global Infrastructure and Investment" and G7 countries pledged to spend $600 billion to finance infrastructure in developing countries. Similarly, the European Union's "Global Gateway" initiative had promised in 2021 to spend over $300 billion on infrastructure in the periphery as a "true alternative" to the BRI, yet when questioned by the press at the end of 2022, the European Commission could not name a single new project even being *planned* as part of the program.[476]

Only time will tell if Western governments and financiers will ever actually spend this money, whether under the Partnership for Global Infrastructure and Investment, Global Gateway, or yet another successor organization, and what the outcome of such investments will actually be,[477] but present trends paint a very uncertain picture. Another study by McKinsey in 2020 found that United States investors had by far the greatest potential "appetite" for infrastructure investment in Africa of any country, yet in practice, of all planned infrastructure projects in general, less than 10% were actually funded.[478] A survey of over one thousand policymakers in 25 African countries by the Inter Region Economic Network think tank in Kenya found that the PRC held a "substantial lead over

473 Su-Lin Tan, "The Indo-Pacific Economic Framework: What It Is—and Why It Matters," *CNBC,* May 25, 2022.

474 Reuters, "U.S. Plans January Rollout of Projects to Counter China's Belt and Road Initiative, Official Says," *CNBC,* November 9, 2021.

475 Tamara Keith, "Biden Said the G-7 Would Counter Chinese Influence. This Year, He'll Try Again," *NPR,* June 24, 2022.

476 Finbarr Bermingham and Jevans Nyabiage, "1 Year on, EU Alternative to China's Belt and Road Fails to Deliver," *South China Morning Post,* December 31, 2022.

477 Su-Lin Tan, "G-7's Infrastructure Plan Offers an Alternative to China's Belt and Road Initiative in a 'Deliberate Way,'" *CNBC,* June 28, 2022.

478 Kannan Lakmeeharan et al., "Solving Africa's Infrastructure Paradox," McKinsey & Company, March 6, 2020.

the EU" in the "timely completion of projects in Africa" such as roads, hydroelectric dams, railways, and bridges.[479] Typically, Western finance finds other ventures far more profitable. When Alhaji Momodu Koroma, Sierra Leone's Minister of Foreign Affairs between 2002 and 2007, was asked to compare the PRC with other foreign donors to his country, he said:

> There is a difference, and it is huge. What they want to help you with, is what you have identified as your need. With Britain, America, *they* identify your needs. They say: "Look, we think there is a need *here*." The German President visited. They promised €12.5 million [$17.5 million] for assistance. President Kabbah said we will use this for rural electrification. But a few months later, GTZ [the German aid agency] said it would be used for their human security project.[480]

According to the most recent OECD data from 2018-2021, the G7 member with the largest foreign direct investments in construction (as a percentage of total FDI) was Italy, at 7.7%. Investments in finance and insurance were more than 20% of total FDI in every G7 country, and for the United States was 64.8%, while its percentage of FDI in construction was just 0.1%.[481] The AEI data for the PRC, on the other hand, classified over $500 billion in investments as construction-related, out of $838 billion total BRI spending and $2.2 trillion in total foreign investment.[482] Despite poor returns on investment during the first decade, the PRC has shown no signs of reducing its overall commitment to the Belt and Road.

What has made Western investors so reluctant, and Chinese investors so eager, to finance large infrastructure projects in the periphery? Individually, Western finance capitalists are motivated by returns on investment, and as a class, to keep the periphery underdeveloped so as to maintain the rates of unequal exchange with the imperial core. Even when solely entertaining the former motivation (return on investment), financing the construction of a railway or power plant in a poor African

---

479 Purity Gitau, "Africa Prefers Chinese Infrastructure Projects - IREN Study," *The Star*, July 22, 2022.

480 Deborah Brautigam, *The Dragon's Gift: The Real Story of China in Africa* (Oxford University Press, 2009), 139–40.

481 Organization for Economic Co-operation and Development Data, "Outward FDI Stocks by Industry."

482 American Enterprise Institute, "China Global Investment Tracker."

neocolony is typically considered a risky endeavor; the project may not be completed or require much more funding than originally estimated, a significant percentage of the money may be lost to corruption, and the local government may default on their debt. The Belt and Road Initiative, however, has not only consistently taken on such projects, but has continued to do so for *ten years* and is still expanding. If the Belt and Road has been an albatross for the PRC financially, it is only reasonable to conclude that it is not principally motivated by profit.

China as a Creditor

The narrative frequently expressed in the Western press that the PRC is perpetrating "debt-trap diplomacy" is one of the more pernicious falsehoods surrounding Chinese investment abroad. In essence, the PRC is seen as a duplicitous moneylender, providing loans to poor countries that they cannot afford, ostensibly to aid in their development, but actually for its own gain. When the victim country must default on the loans, Chinese banks would be ready to seize what they truly wanted—the land, precious minerals, or infrastructure—in recompense. In other words, it is the idea that Chinese finance operates in exactly the manner of Western finance, whose role in maintaining underdevelopment and exploitation was thoroughly examined in Chapter Two.

It has already been shown that the motivations behind Western and Chinese finance differ fundamentally. This chapter will further show that over the entirety of the PRC's dealings with the periphery, the "debt trap" narrative has struggled to establish even a single point of contact with reality. Yet an investigation into the operation of Chinese finance will nevertheless suggest that there *is* a hidden agenda behind it—one that will go a long way toward demystifying the poor financial performance discovered earlier in this chapter; and one that is concealed not from its clients but from its Western competitors.

The PRC is not only a terrible investor; it is also a poor debt collector, and an utter failure as a repo man. "China does not always collect its debts on time," admitted a headline in the *Economist* in 2022, citing a study by World Bank economists.[483] In 2019, when due to its declining oil output Venezuela fell behind on its oil-for-loans commitment to the PRC, rather than seizing Venezuelan assets or demanding

---

483 "China Does Not Always Collect Its Debts on Time," *The Economist*, February 12, 2022.

painful economic restructuring, the Chinese side instead restructured the agreement, postponing Venezuela's obligations by two years and in the meantime buying Venezuelan oil for cash.[484] In 2015, the Chinese side agreed to concessionary interest rates (1.6% or less) for infrastructure loans to Pakistan, offered another loan at a 0% interest rate,[485] and converted a $230 million loan for the construction of the new Gwadar International Airport into a grant.[486] In 2006, one of China Eximbank's first concessional loans—to fund the Sino-Zimbabwe Cement Plant in Gweru District as a joint venture between a Chinese and a state-owned Zimbabwean corporation—was restructured, lowering the interest rate to 2%. Professor Deborah Brautigam of Johns Hopkins University, one of the leading scholars of Chinese foreign development policy, identified this as a pattern in Chinese finance even during the 2000s.[487] During the 2010s, the repayment schedules of several billion dollars' worth of loans from Chinese financial institutions to Chad, Mozambique, Ethiopia, the Republic of the Congo, and several other African countries were extended, often with reduction of interest rates. In 2016, China Development Bank's commercial loans to Angola totaling $7.5 billion were refinanced. According to a paper co-authored by Brautigam and two of her peers in 2020, though more than 30 Chinese banks and companies had provided credit to African governments and loan renegotiations were generally conducted on a case-by-case basis, there was a notable trend "toward real net present value (NPV) reductions, mainly through lower interest rates, longer grace periods, and substantially longer repayment periods."[488]

More careful anti-China propaganda publications will avoid the "debt trap" phrasing and instead cite peripheral countries' "unsustainable debt" to the PRC, or accuse the PRC of contributing to their overall "debt distress." But even then, is a debt truly a debt if it is never repaid? Simply having a large account with the PRC—as many countries in the periphery now do—is not in itself equivalent to exploitation or the extraction of super-profits. The actual transfers of wealth—the *servicing* of the debt

---

484 Deborah Brautigam, "A Critical Look at Chinese 'Debt-Trap Diplomacy': The Rise of a Meme," *Area Development and Policy* 5, no. 1 (2020).

485 Naveed Butt, "Economic Corridor: China to Extend Assistance at 1.6 Percent Interest Rate," *Business Recorder,* September 3, 2015.

486 Mehtab Haider, "China Converts $230m Loan for Gwadar Airport into Grant," *Geo News,* September 23, 2015.

487 Brautigam, *The Dragon's Gift,* 129–30.

488 Kevin Acker, Deborah Brautigam, and Yufan Huang, "Debt Relief with Chinese Characteristics."

with interest, or the coercion of other concessions using the debt as leverage—must occur before Chinese lenders can ultimately benefit from the numbers in their ledgers.

That Africa is presently the least wealthy continent on Earth is undisputed, and foreign banks encounter few obstacles and plentiful opportunities to take unfair advantage of most countries within it. An actual debt trap is profoundly easy both to set and to spring, and nearly impossible to escape; for example, according to financial records released recently, Sudan received loans totaling scarcely more than a few hundred million pounds from the United Kingdom during the twentieth century, which by 2021 had ballooned to nearly a billion pounds through the accrual of interest alone.[489] In order to obtain relief from the IMF, the Sudanese government was compelled to end fuel subsidies, devalue its currency, and normalize relations with Israel.[490] When dealing with Western lenders, even the *forgiveness* of debt is conditional upon enacting harsh austerity measures, as the IMF and the World Bank made clear in their initiative to cancel loans to countries it classified as "Heavily-Indebted Poor Countries" (HIPC), who must show willingness to "manage public finances and monetary policy" before being considered.[491] Chinese lenders, however, are not loan sharks; they do not take opportunities to exploit a foreign debtor's inability to pay, require no structural adjustments, and instead of exploiting decades-old debt, they are often likely to forgive it unconditionally. Though Chinese lending to foreign countries was relatively marginal before the twenty-first century, and consisted mainly of interest-free aid loans, scarcely any of that debt still exists. Brautigam writes:

> At first, when many of its aid loans started to come due in the early 1980s, China rescheduled them, sometimes just for a year or two. Repayments for the Tan-Zam railway were put off for ten years. Payments in Ghana and Niger were stretched out over twenty years instead of fifteen. Other countries simply did not pay ...[492]

---

489 Mattha Busby, "Four-Fifths of Sudan's £861m Debt to UK Is Interest."

490 Nafisa Eltahir, Karin Strohecker, and David Lawder, "Sudan Approved for Debt Relief, $2.5 Billion Funding by IMF."

491 International Monetary Fund, "IMF Support for Low-Income Countries."

492 Brautigam, *The Dragon's Gift*, 128–29.

Later, in parallel with the HIPC initiative, the PRC began forgiving debt as well—but unconditionally:

Most of China's public pledges were consciously couched as debt relief for "highly indebted" and "least developed" countries. This does not mean, however, that China followed all the rules of the HIPC debt relief regime negotiated in Washington and Paris. Chinese debt cancellation was non-conditional. They did not require governments to prove their ability to manage their economies or to develop strategies to use the canceled debt for poverty reduction. This meant that China canceled debt for at least six countries that qualified for the HIPC initiative because of their high levels of debt and poverty (Comoros, Côte d'Ivoire, Eritrea, Somalia, Sudan, and Togo), but which had failed to follow the steps of the World Bank/IMF dance, and so were stuck in what the HIPC program called the "pre-decision point," the purgatory of high debt, but no relief...

Countries with the most pressing problems were handled first. The Ministry of Commerce sent a delegation to discuss the debt with the Chinese embassy in the country and the local Ministry of Finance. Figures on overdue debts were carefully compared and reconciled, loan by loan. A Chinese professor who advised the Ministry told me: "These zero-interest loans were rescheduled so many times, the countries couldn't even find the agreements anymore!" Debts were written off for each individual loan. The pledges focused specifically on the overdue, interest-free foreign aid loans (not on other debt—export credits, for example). Ultimately, 376 separate "mature debts" would be written off.[493]

By 2019, $9.8 billion of these remaining old loans—the vast majority—had been forgiven.[494] In August of 2022, China's State Councilor announced that the PRC would waive a further 23 interest-free loans to 17 African countries that had matured the previous year.[495] For loans either old or new, Brautigam and her colleagues found no evidence of asset

---

493 Brautigam, *The Dragon's Gift*, 128–29.
494 Kenneth Rapoza, "China Has Forgiven Nearly $10 Billion In Debt. Cuba Accounts For Over Half."
495 Wang Yi, "China and Africa: Strengthening Friendship, Solidarity and Cooperation for a New Era of Common Development."

seizures, penalty interest rates, or indeed any negative consequences to a borrower country failing to repay Chinese banks or companies—the worst that has ever happened in the (frequent) case of default, they conclude, is that Chinese creditors have sometimes imposed moratoriums on any new lending.[496] Interest rates on Chinese loans to Africa have also remained low—only about half what is charged by Western lenders (2.7% as compared to 5%) according to a 2022 report by British charity organization Debt Justice.[497]

In another 2020 article, Brautigam calls Chinese "debt-trap diplomacy" a "meme" perpetuated by Western media institutions repeating dubious and since-debunked rumors enough times that it has entered the public consciousness despite having no original factual basis.[498][499] Numerous studies and publications by her peers since the latter 2010s are in nearly universal agreement. The Chatham House policy institute in London, for example, wrote in 2020 that scant evidence of Chinese "debt traps" existed, and disputed the idea of any "geopolitical strategy" of Chinese developmental finance.[500] In 2019, New York-based think tank the Rhodium Group analyzed 40 recent cases of Chinese external debt renegotiation, concluding that in nearly all cases, the debts were written off or restructured. Only in a single case did the report identify a possible asset seizure, that of the Hambantota Port in Sri Lanka.[501]

Indeed, the "debt trap" narrative has since derived its remarkable longevity from this single data point. The PRC had lent the Sri Lankan government the money to build the port, and later when Sri Lanka became

---

496 Kevin Acker, Deborah Brautigam, and Yufan Huang, *Debt Relief with Chinese Characteristics,* Working Paper (China Africa Research Initiative, June 2020).

497 Rachel Savage, "African States' Private Debts Three Times That Owed to China," *Reuters,* July 11, 2022.

498 Brautigam, "A Critical Look at Chinese 'Debt-Trap Diplomacy': The Rise of a Meme."

499 Even years after Western academia had universally rejected it, in fact, the Western press continued to propagate the meme as long as it could; in December 2021, Brautigam described how the *BBC* had quoted her out of context to make it appear as though her interview debunking "debt-trap diplomacy" instead confirmed its existence. (Deborah Brautigam, "BBC Misrepresents My Views on 'Debt Trap Diplomacy,'" *The China-Africa Research Initiative Blog,* December 1, 2021.)

500 Lee Jones and Shahar Hameiri, "Debunking the Myth of 'Debt-Trap Diplomacy': How Recipient Countries Shape China's Belt and Road Initiative," Chatham House Research Event, October 23, 2020 [recording], sec. 6.

501 Agatha Kratz, Allen Feng, and Logan Wright, "New Data on the 'Debt Trap' Question," *Rhodium Group,* April 29, 2019.

unable to pay the debt in 2017, had allegedly used its leverage to secure for a Chinese state-owned enterprise a 99-year lease on this strategically-important piece of real estate. Yet even this example falls apart upon a closer look at the events leading up to the lease agreement. According to a 2020 research paper from Chatham House:

> Sri Lanka's debt distress was unconnected to Chinese lending, arising instead from excessive borrowing on Western-dominated capital markets and from structural problems within the Sri Lankan economy ... there was no debt-for-asset swap. Rather, after bargaining hard for commercial reasons, a Chinese SOE leased the port in exchange for $1.1 billion, which Sri Lanka used to pay down *other debts* and boost foreign reserves. [emphasis added][502]

Sri Lanka's extreme debt crisis had not manifested before the deal to construct the port was made, and the deal was not a significant factor in causing the crisis. According to Sri Lankan economists at Monash University and the Institute of Policy Studies in Sri Lanka in 2019, Chinese loans were made at very low-interest rates and had made up only about 10% of Sri Lanka's foreign debt during the crisis.[503] The payments owed on the loans from China Eximbank to finance the construction of the port itself, in fact, were less than 5% of Sri Lanka's total debt service in 2017—even including interest.[504] Chatham House further notes that the agreement forbade the Chinese navy from using the port, more or less obviating its supposed strategic value to the PRC.[505]

Even if the worst, most sinister motive could be plausibly attributed to the PRC over the Hambantota Port, and the allegations of its "debt trap" to assume control over it were completely accurate, it would stand as an extreme outlier to the general practice of Chinese finance. Hundreds, and now thousands, of such deals to construct needed infrastructure all across the periphery have been conducted with Chinese companies; if the seizure of assets were the PRC's true goal, how could *none* of these

---

502 Lee Jones and Shahar Hameiri, "Debunking the Myth of 'Debt-Trap Diplomacy,'" sec. 4.

503 Dushni Weerakoon and Sisira Jayasuriya, "Sri Lanka's Debt Problem Isn't Made in China," *East Asia Forum,* February 28, 2019.

504 Umesh Moramudali, "The Hambantota Port Deal: Myths and Realities," *The Diplomat,* January 1, 2020.

505 Lee Jones and Shahar Hameiri, "Debunking the Myth of 'Debt-Trap Diplomacy,'" sec. 4.

exhibit the same characteristics as Hambantota? A single incident is not a pattern; the idea that the PRC has acted with deceit in only one instance out of thousands suggests instead that such deceit is in fact either a misinterpretation or outright fabrication.

Nor is Chinese finance motivated by securing raw materials for exclusive use. Brautigam writes that "China does not seem to give more official development aid to countries with more resources"[506] and in fact has investments in nearly every country in Africa, not solely those with an abundance of mineral reserves. Though oil-rich Angola, for example, is the largest recipient of Chinese loans in Africa, Ethiopia is the second-largest, and has no significant oil or mineral resources. (As well, most Chinese construction projects in Angola take place in the interior— roads, hospitals, agriculture—rather than near the largest offshore oil deposits.)[507,508]

---

506 Brautigam, *The Dragon's Gift*, 279.

507 T. L. Deych, "China in Africa: A Case of Neo-Colonialism or a Win-Win Strategy?"

508 Chinese companies that *are* harvesting resources in Africa, when compared to Western corporations in the same line of business, seem to be held to markedly different standards by their respective governments. For example, the oil giant Shell, which has been active in Nigeria for three-quarters of a century, has been repeatedly sued in both Nigeria and the United Kingdom over its liability for numerous oil spills, to only very occasional success. One such case concerning spills in the early 1970s was still being fought in Nigeria's courts in 2019 as Shell's subsidiary endlessly appealed judgments against it (Ignatius Chukwu, "N134bn Supreme Court Verdict: Shell Denies Liability, Ready to Go Ahead with Appeal," *Business Day,* January 14, 2019); in 2017, the UK's high court dismissed claims made by tens of thousands of Nigerians who alleged that Shell was responsible for the pollution of their land (Adam Vaughan, "Nigerian Oil Pollution Claims against Shell Cannot Be Heard in UK, Court Rules," *The Guardian,* January 26, 2017). One successful such case in the UK was settled by Shell for 55 million pounds before reaching the high court in 2015—nearly six years after the spills in question (John Vidal, "Shell Announces £55m Payout for Nigeria Oil Spills," *The Guardian,* January 26, 2015). Around the same time, rather than punish Shell for its activities in Nigeria, ministers from the Foreign Office agreed to lobby the Nigerian government on behalf of Shell for weaker taxes and favorable regulations, according to a report based on UK government documents by the Western environmentalist group DeSmog in 2017 (Chloe Farand, "Revealed: UK Ministers Lobbied Nigeria's Government to Protect Oil Giant Shell," *DeSmog,* January 24, 2017). When Switzerland-based multinational mining conglomerate Glencore—as of 2022 the largest mining corporation in the world with an annual revenue of over $100 billion—was accused as early as 2012 of using child labor in its cobalt mines in the Democratic Republic of the Congo (John Sweeney, "Mining Giant Glencore Accused in Child Labour and Acid Dumping Row," *The Guardian,* April 14, 2012), it faced no consequences from Western governments for a full decade, until finally agreeing to pay a $180 million cash settlement to the DRC in December 2022 (Glencore,

As seen above, Chatham House was unable to determine any pattern of coherent geopolitical aims behind Chinese development finance. The only discernible pattern, in fact, is the remarkable scrupulousness of Chinese financiers in refraining from extortion, coercion, or interference in their African partners' political and economic affairs—or even from insisting that they get all their money back.

China and the International Monetary Fund

According to statistics tracked by the World Bank's World Integrated Trade Solution, between 2015 and 2020, the value of exports classified as "metals" from the Democratic Republic of the Congo to China increased more than eightfold, to a total greater than the DRC's next five largest export destinations combined. In 2020, total reported metals exports were valued at over $9.4 billion, $4.4 billion of which were to China. The Sicomines joint venture in the infrastructure-for-resources deal mentioned earlier in this chapter had begun operations—and would appear to have become quite profitable.[509]

Just how profitable? According to the DRC's Ministry of Mines, mining at Sicomines started in earnest in November of 2015, and had produced 31,000 metric tonnes of copper by the end of June of the following year, nearly 8,000 of which had been produced that month.[510] Using mining activity reports through 2020, estimates for total production and market rate value are as follows:

"Glencore Reaches Agreement with the Democratic Republic of Congo over Past Conduct," December 5, 2022). In September of 2021, however, when the local government of South Kivu province suspended six Chinese-owned mining companies from operating, alleging that they had been operating illegally, the director-general of the Chinese Foreign Ministry's Department of African Affairs not only supported the suspension, but immediately announced that the companies would also be punished and sanctioned by the Chinese government for violating Congolese law, before any type of trial had even begun (Reuters Staff, "China Backs Congo's Ban on 6 Small Chinese Mining Companies," *Reuters,* September 14, 2021).

509 World Integrated Trade Solution, "Congo, Dem. Rep. Metals Exports By Country and Region in US$ Thousand 2015-2020."

510 David Landry, "The Risks and Rewards of Resource-for-Infrastructure Deals: Lessons from the Congo's Sicomines Agreement," *Resources Policy* 58 (October 2018): 165–174.

Estimated Sicomines copper production, 2016–2022

Year	Market price of refined copper* (USD per tonne)	Reported total copper produced by Sicomines** (tonnes)	Market value of copper produced (thousand USD)
2016	4868	110010	535529
2017	6170	133448	823374
2018	6530	140770	919228
2019	6010	143608	863084
2020	6174	155630	960860
2021	9317	200000	1863400
2022	8822	247696	2185174
Total	n/a	1131162	8150649

*From annual averages recorded by the World Bank in 2019,[511] 2022,[512] and 2023.[513]

**From Sicomines' activity reports between 2015 and 2020.[514] In 2022, according to the local *Copperbelt Katanga Mining* magazine, Sicomines had become the single most productive copper mining company, accounting for 247,696 tonnes of copper exports.[515] Production for 2021 is a rough estimate assuming linear growth.

Sicomines very likely did not receive revenue equal to the market value of the metals produced, and despite its generous tax-free profit margin, was still repaying the initial loans from China Eximbank at least a decade on. In 2019, Sicomines reported a revenue of only a little more than $800 million and an outstanding debt balance of $2.1 billion.[516] The same year, political winds shifted; President Joseph Kabila, who had negotiated the contract, was succeeded by opposition candidate Félix Tshisekedi—who was much less favorable to the agreement, and ordered an audit of Sicomines soon after taking office. In 2023, the DRC state auditor's report accused Sicomines of undervaluing its exports and

---

511 World Bank, "World Bank Commodities Price Data (The Pink Sheet)," October 2019, 2.

512 World Bank, "World Bank Commodities Price Data (The Pink Sheet)," August 2022, 2.

513 World Bank, "World Bank Commodities Price Data (The Pink Sheet)," January 2023, 2.

514 Léonide Mupepele, "Etude d'évaluation de la mise en œuvre de la convention de collaboration relative au développement d'un projet minier et d'un projet d'infrastructures en RD Congo Projet SICOMINES" [Evaluation study of the implementation of the collaboration agreement relating to the development of a mining project and an infrastructure project in the DR Congo SICOMINES Project], 65.

515 Constance, "Leading Copper Cathode Exporters in DRC: SICOMINES, KCC, and TFM in 2022," *Copperbelt Katanga*, February 10, 2023.

516 Léonide Mupepele, 66–67.

various other misdeeds.[517] This audit has been disputed by Sicomines, but even if it were only partially accurate, the frustration of the Congolese government with Sicomines is quite understandable; fifteen years after the initial agreement, the DRC had still received virtually no taxes or income from its share in the project. Meanwhile, China had received about 14% of the total resources originally estimated in the contract.

The auditor's report, however, also estimated that over 18% of the infrastructure promised in the deal had been built.[518] Though various disputes, including one in which China Eximbank withheld funding between 2012 and 2014, set the project back several years, the DRC received this share far sooner; five years after the initial agreement was signed, a study by Dr. Johanna Jansson of Denmark's Roskilde University found that nine infrastructure projects totaling nearly half a billion dollars—including a large hospital and hundreds of kilometers of roads—had been completed, and others were in progress, before the mining operation in Katanga Province had even begun.[519] In 2015, eight years into the contract, the DRC government estimated that $800 million of infrastructure had been built—while according to Jansson, the mining had endured delay after delay, "from crippling power shortages to asphyxiating bureaucracy and corruption."[520] Ten years in, Sicomines' partner, Sinohydro, separately began construction of the Busanga Hydropower Station, a $660 million dam in Katanga expected to both solve the power problem and supply 10% of the DRC's electricity, with one-third of its capacity fed into the national power grid.[521]

As of 2023, the Sicomines deal was therefore likely equitable according to the contract, in a negative sense—both parties had received about equally low proportions of what they signed up for. To determine whether the contract *itself* is unequal is less straightforward. If only the relative

517 Inspection Generale des Finances, "Conclusions de l'Inspection Generale des Finances sur la Convention de Collaboration d'Avril 2008 entre la RDC et le Groupement d'Enterprises Chinoises (Contrat Chinois)" [Conclusions of the General Inspection of Finance on the Collaboration Agreement of April 2008 between the DRC and the Group of Chinese Companies], 6.

518 Inspection Generale des Finances, 2.

519 Johanna Jansson, "The Sicomines Agreement Revisited: Prudent Chinese Banks and Risk-Taking Chinese Companies." Review of African Political Economy 40, no. 135 (2013): 152–162.

520 Aaron Ross, "China's 'infrastructure for Minerals' Deal Gets Reality-Check in Congo," *Reuters,* July 8, 2015.

521 Jevans Nyabiage, "China's DR Congo Hydropower Projects: A Win-Win Deal or Short Circuit?," *South China Morning Post,* June 12, 2021.

prices of the goods exported are considered, the PRC was the clear winner; even if the Busanga dam were included, the infrastructure totaled only $1.5 billion, while the copper extracted had been worth $8 billion. It is less clear, however, how much the Chinese side has profited from the arrangement. The $1.5 billion it had spent to build the infrastructure must be accounted for; Sicomines' reported operating expenses from 2015 to 2019 were also about $1.5 billion;[522] the initial investment in the mining operation had been estimated to be at least $3 billion, and was likely more than that due to the extraordinary delays; exactly how much money was lost due to corruption is unknown. A 2018 study from the Johns Hopkins University School for Advanced International Studies, based on "net present value" investment modeling, concluded that "because of the volatile nature of commodity prices, the Sicomines agreement's winner could change multiple times until it reaches its conclusion in about 30 years."[523]

Nevertheless, in 2022, commodity prices remained high, and with the electricity from the Busanga dam, Sicomines had finally begun producing rapidly and would soon break even. Any systemic problems with the arrangement—corruption, export undervaluation, &c.—would begin to have their most severe impact on the DRC's tax revenue very soon. The remedy demanded by the DRC's state auditor included an additional $17 billion of infrastructure, and *Reuters* reported that the DRC's finance minister expected a renegotiation to be completed by the end of the year.[524] This would not be the first time that the contract was renegotiated, nor the first time such a renegotiation sought to change the infrastructure commitment. There had been an unofficial third party to the contract, who does not consistently appear in press coverage of the arrangement yet was responsible for its renegotiation in 2009—the International Monetary Fund.

Western governments had reacted badly to the Sicomines deal. According to Jansson:

Discussions were held between the IMF and China both in Beijing and in Washington. The Belgian government was the first of the

---

522 Léonide Mupepele, 66.
523 Landry, "The Risks and Rewards of Resource-for-Infrastructure Deals: Lessons from the Congo's Sicomines Agreement."
524 "Congo Demands $17 Bln More in Infrastructure Investments from China Deal," *Reuters,* February 17, 2023.

DRC's bilateral donors to react publically [sic] to the agreement, and representatives for the Belgian government even held discussions in China to push for an amendment of the contract. All the DRC's traditional donors united behind the agenda to reduce the size of the loans to finance infrastructure construction and to remove the Congolese state's guarantee on the mining component.[525]

Belgium and other such "traditional donors"—who were, predictably, in the "Paris Club" of Western financiers—ostensibly objected to an increase to the country's debt burden. In 2009, the DRC already had a total external debt of over $13 billion[526]—very little of which, if any, was to the PRC.[527] The unity of the traditional donors on the debt issue at first would seem natural—in theory, the more debts the DRC needed to service, the less each donor would receive, and if the DRC defaulted, their investments would be lost. But at the time of the agreement with China Eximbank, this debt was *already* effectively lost. The DRC had not serviced its loans to Western and international creditors for many years,[528] and had been struggling to meet the HIPC requirements (mentioned earlier in this chapter) for debt forgiveness.[529] Why then were Belgium et al.,

---

525 Johanna Jansson, "The Sicomines Agreement: Change and Continuity in the Democratic Republic of Congo's International Relations," *SAIIA Occasional Paper No 97* (South African Institute of International Affairs, November 1, 2011): 15.

526 International Monetary Fund, "Press Release: IMF Executive Board Approves US$551 Million PRGF Arrangement for the Democratic Republic of the Congo and US$73 Million in Interim HIPC Assistance," December 11, 2009.

527 Jansson notes that PRC-DRC relations were marginal before 2007, with the Chinese presence in the DRC limited to donations, modest credit lines, scholarships to Congolese students, and so forth. (Johanna Jansson, "The Sicomines Agreement," 6.)

528 Johanna Jansson, "The Sicomines Agreement Revisited: Prudent Chinese Banks and Risk-Taking Chinese Companies," *Review of African Political Economy* 40, no. 135 (2013): 152-162.

529 Even were the DRC ever to have intended to pay off the $13 billion, these countries would still likely not have received any payments on their bilateral debts. By convention of the Paris Club—of which the PRC is not a member—the World Bank and the IMF are "privileged creditors" who are to be paid before all others. Referring to the Sicomines deal, Brautigam writes:

"There is no international rule or law on the privileged creditor status. It appears nowhere in the Articles of Agreement establishing these institutions; it is merely a convention. Resource-backed loans complicate this arrangement. It is much simpler (at least as viewed from Washington) if all revenues go into the budget, and then are used to repay debts in order of priority. If a significant share of revenues is held outside the budget and used to repay the very large Chinese debt *first*, this could shake the foundations of the system of privileged creditors." (*The Dragon's Gift*, 147.)

so concerned, if they knew their own loans to the DRC would never be repaid? Perhaps Belgium had been worried for the sake of its former colony, out of pure selflessness or remorse, trying to prevent it from taking a bad deal, thinking only of the welfare of the Congolese—but if that were the case, then strangely, despite such altruism, the idea of simply forgiving the DRC's bilateral debt somehow failed to occur to it.

Rather, in the final analysis, as shown in Chapter Two, debt is only a minor mechanism of exploitation, and is far more important and useful as a mechanism of control. What the Paris Club feared was not a loss of debt, but of *leverage*.

According to Jansson, the IMF's priority in 2009 was to reduce the size of the infrastructure commitment.[530] At first, the Congolese government refused to back down; then in May of 2009, the Managing Director of the IMF himself visited Kinshasa for a private meeting with Kabila. Afterward, Jansson observed,

> On 2 June 2009, less than two weeks after Strauss-Kahn's visit, the Congolese government sent an official letter to CREC requesting that the Congolese state guarantee on the mining investment be removed. On 29 June 2009, CREC responded that '*nous pensons que l'investissement du Projet Minier ... n'a pas besoin de la garantie de la RDC*' (we believe that the investment in the Mining Project ... does not need the guarantee of the DRC). The second tranche (estimated to be worth $3 billion) of the infrastructure investments was subsequently cancelled by the third and final contract amendment, signed in October 2009. In its current form, the agreement is worth a total of $6 billion, with the DRC's debt burden reduced to a maximum of $3 billion, in lieu of the original $9 billion of debt.[531]

Belgium and the other traditional donors soon received their money's worth. The DRC reentered the HIPC process at the end of the year, following the IMF's "structural reform" program designed to weaken the Congolese state. The program focused on "restoring the independence of the Banque Centrale du Congo," "[s]trengthening public financial management," and "[d]eveloping the private sector, including the reform of public enterprises." Government regulations were to be "streamlined" and

---

530 Johanna Jansson, "The Sicomines Agreement," 14.
531 Johanna Jansson, 15.

foreign investment was to be further protected.[532] Only after six months of these "reforms" was the debt finally written off.

In 2009, this result suited the super-empire perfectly. The DRC's government would be even less able to control its own economy, and Western multinational mining corporations then active in the DRC would be further shielded from consequences of their abuses. In the future they would need to share access to the DRC's minerals with Chinese companies, but so what? The metals would end up in the same place anyway—cheap electronics made in China and sold in the West. Most importantly, Sicomines would only build half the infrastructure in the original agreement, infrastructure that over time could have interfered with the underdevelopment of the DRC—and that no Western company or government would find profitable to take the risk of building anyway. (In 2012, the World Bank rated the DRC as the sixth-most difficult country in the world to do business in.)[533]

By 2023, however, although many peripheral countries around the world were again suffering from a fresh cycle of debt crises, the IMF was finding this trick more and more difficult to perform—*due to its victim countries' growing bilateral debt to the PRC.*

In April, U.S. Treasury Secretary Janet Yellen gave a speech accusing the PRC of being a "roadblock" to global debt restructuring. *Reuters* reported that more than half of all low-income countries were unable or nearly unable to service their debts according to IMF estimates; the PRC, the "world's largest official bilateral creditor," was portrayed as "unwilling to accept losses on loans"—but crucially, the article concluded this sentence with "unless private-sector creditors and multilateral development banks shoulder their share of the burden."[534] Quoting a former IMF official, the *New York Times* called the PRC "increasingly isolated" and under "pressure" to participate in debt restructuring.[535] The PRC's Ministry of Foreign Affairs, however, seemed unconcerned, announcing that debt relief should require "joint participation of multilateral, bilateral

---

532 International Monetary Fund, "Press Release: IMF Executive Board Approves US$551 Million PRGF Arrangement for the Democratic Republic of the Congo and US$73 Million in Interim HIPC Assistance."

533 Johanna Jansson, "The Sicomines Agreement Revisited."

534 Andrea Shalal, "Yellen Raps China for Serving as 'roadblock' in Debt Restructuring Process," *Reuters,* April 20, 2023.

535 Alan Rappeport, "Pressure Mounts on China to Offer Debt Relief to Poor Countries Facing Default," *New York Times,* April 14, 2023.

and commercial creditors under the principles of joint actions and fair burden-sharing."[536]

What a conundrum! Both the PRC and the United States, it appears, were happy to restructure the large debts they are owed—but somehow, they were both unable to. They were falling over each other in an attempt to selflessly escape the prisoners' dilemma, yet seemed to still be prisoners when all was said and done. Only with a clear understanding of how the IMF works and what its goals are can this puzzle be solved.

In essence, the United States says loudly, "the world's poorest countries are about to default—we must restructure their debts!" while whispering to itself, *"in exchange for more structural adjustments, which will drain ever more of their wealth into our private banks."* The PRC replies: "very well, let's *all* restructure the debts equally, even private creditors and the World Bank, so that each lender absorbs the same loss." The United States (and its Paris Club partners) can then throw up their hands and complain, "China isn't cooperating!"

At this point, there are three possible scenarios:

1. If the PRC restructures debt first, the IMF will then have no difficulty requiring structural adjustments—victim countries will be in the same position as the DRC in 2009, and the debt trap-IMF-austerity cycle continues. More wealth will be squeezed out of the people of victim countries, and the remaining debts to private Western banks will be serviced. The West remains an exploiter.

2. If the Western governments restructure debt first, and the IMF requires structural adjustments anyway, its victims will be similarly plundered, but the remaining debts to both private Western banks *and* Chinese banks will be serviced. Both the West and the PRC are exploiters in this scenario—though if the PRC also later restructures debt, it simply becomes scenario A.

3. If the Western governments restructure debt first, and the IMF requires no conditions, the debtor countries' remaining debts become manageable, or more so. If the PRC also later restructures debt, this scenario almost becomes the outcome the PRC

---

536 Spokesperson 发言人办公室 (@MFA_China), "To Effectively Resolve the Debt Issue, the Key Lies in Joint Participation of Multilateral, Bilateral and Commercial Creditors under the Principles of Joint Actions and Fair Burden-Sharing."

advocated originally (though the debtor countries must still keep servicing debts to private Western banks).

Absolutely nothing is preventing the U.S. and the Paris Club from pursuing either B or C immediately. These paths would reveal whether the PRC truly means what it says; the PRC would then face *real* pressure to follow the Western governments in restructuring debt, or else become a singular villain in the eyes of the world. Only in scenario A, however, would the Western capitalist class increase its profit *without* having to share. The U.S. and the IMF will therefore attempt to browbeat the PRC into restructuring *first*, and only reluctantly choose option B if the PRC holds out. Meanwhile, the Western press has been working overtime to blame the PRC for the West's own recalcitrance. In May 2023, for example, an article in *Fortune* claimed that a dozen poor countries were "facing economic instability and even collapse" due to large debts, mentioning only the PRC's lending in the headline; yet in analyzing the case study of Zambia, admitted not only that Zambia's debt to the PRC was just one-third of its total external debt, but that the PRC had already begun negotiating separately with Zambia on debt relief before "a group of non-Chinese lenders refused desperate pleas from Zambia to suspend interest payments, even for a few months" in 2020, which created the conditions for Zambia's default later that year.[537]

After Sri Lanka entered a fresh crisis in 2022, the Western press of course found fault with the PRC for not cooperating with the IMF process—*despite the PRC no longer contributing to the problem*. China Eximbank had *already* postponed Sri Lanka's debt service, suspending all payments during 2022 and 2023. For months, the PRC insisted that private creditors and the World Bank do the same, but to no avail.[538] Instead, Sri Lanka began economic "reforms" to meet the IMF's preconditions; income taxes and the price of electricity were increased, further immiserating the population. This was a perfect example of scenario B— which became scenario A in early 2023, when the PRC agreed to the debt restructuring.[539]

---

537 Bernard Condon and Associated Press, "'In a Lot of the World, the Clock Has Hit Midnight': China Is Calling in Loans to Dozens of Countries from Pakistan to Kenya," *Fortune,* May 18, 2023.

538 Anusha Ondaatjie, Philip Glamann, and Tom Hancock, "Sri Lanka IMF Deal Stalls Amid China-World Bank Relief Split," Bloomberg, February 3, 2023.

539 Krishan Francis, "Sri Lanka Leader Says IMF Deal Imminent after China's Pledge," *AP News,* March 7, 2023.

However, the PRC still has another card to play. If a victim of the IMF could somehow lay its hands on enough cash to service its debts, it would not be obliged to accept a structural adjustment; therefore in its own response to these crises, the PRC has simply been lending its partners more and more lately, in the form of *unconditional* "bailout" loans. A 2023 study by researchers from the Harvard Kennedy School and the World Bank tracked a total of $240 billion in such "rescue financing" to more than twenty countries through 2021—nearly all of which was provided since 2016.[540] In 2022, the *Financial Times* called the PRC an "IMF competitor" for "postpon[ing] the day of reckoning" by issuing tens of billions in these secretive emergency loans to struggling countries; one former senior IMF economist complained that such loans were "a major impediment" to the "painful reform" that poor countries supposedly deserved to face at the hands of the IMF.[541]

We do not yet have enough information to deduce the PRC's ultimate intentions in this matter. But thus far, the PRC has shown no sign of imitating the playbook of Western financial institutions (only cooperating with the IMF when its partners do) and has signaled a commitment to fairness and multilateral cooperation in global development and investment. The New Development Bank, in partnership between the PRC and the other BRICS countries,[542] was created with all five founding members having equal equity, and with voting rules preventing the PRC (or any other BRICS member) from commanding a unilateral veto.[543] In a speech at the G20 Leaders Summit of 2013, Xi Jinping spoke of the need to reform the IMF along similar lines:

> We should continue the reform of international financial institutions. The relevant countries should further push forward the implementation of the plan for reforming the management of the International Monetary Fund and for making a new sharing formula that reflects the weight of the economic aggregate of the different countries in the world economy, and continue to strengthen oversight concerning the international financial market, so that the

---

540 Horn et al., "China as an International Lender of Last Resort," NBER Working Paper 124, National Bureau of Economic Research (March 28, 2023), 3.

541 James Kynge and Jonathan Wheatley, "China Emerges as IMF Competitor with Emergency Loans to At-Risk Nations," *Financial Times,* September 10, 2022.

542 Brazil, Russia, India, China, and South Africa.

543 Federative Republic of Brazil et al., "Agreement on the New Development Bank."

financial system will depend on, serve and promote the development of the real economy in a sound way.[544]

The PRC was the first country outside Africa to support the inclusion of the African Union in the G20,[545] as well as greater representation of African countries on the UN Security Council.[546] A commitment and desire for reform have been consistently expressed by the PRC, and in recent years, all the more loudly.

China and the Capitalist World-System

To summarize the investigation of Chinese external finance and trade relations thus far: China has benefited from its integration into the international supply chain as a manufacturing superpower, yet is still by far more exploited than exploiter; the PRC exports its construction capacity to assist in the development of the periphery, yet does not do so for free; and the terms of these contracts involve significant debt to the PRC, yet Chinese investors do not take any special advantage when their clients experience debt distress, instead responding with forbearance or absorbing losses themselves. In contrast with the Russian Federation, which, as described in Chapter Four, lacks the power to become an empire, whatever its intentions might be, it appears that the PRC has the power, yet lacks the will.

Even before having a glimpse of the status of class society within China, it is clear that the dialectic identified by Wallerstein—in which the social transformation of class society *within* a socialist country is in contradiction with that state's participation in the capitalist world-system—has taken on a new dimension. By trading with the neocolonies, the PRC maintains world imperialism; but by developing them, it undermines world imperialism. The unequal exchange described by Emmanuel and his contemporaries is slowly beginning to equalize, not by raising *prices* along the supply chain, but by the PRC's investments in the supply chain's infrastructure and other constant capital. The $2 billion Belt and Road deal signed with Ghana in 2019 to construct roads, railways, and

---

544 Xi Jinping, *The Governance of China*, 2014, vol. 1, sec. Jointly Maintain and Develop an Open World Economy.

545 The AU was later made a permanent member of the G20 in September 2023.

546 Jevans Nyabiage, "China Gives Support to Africa Push for Seat at G20, UN Security Council," *South China Morning Post*, January 28, 2023.

other transport infrastructure,[547] for example, will not directly result in a higher export price of gold or a wage increase for the Ghanaian gold miner referred to in Appendix A. However, it *will* foster more and better-paying employment in the country at large (the Ghanaian economy presently being almost exclusively oriented around the export of gold, oil, and cash crops; in 2020, unwrought gold made up 45% all exports),[548] relaxing the constraints on workers' freedom and mobility that Emmanuel identified as a key factor in maintaining unequal exchange.

China has become a beneficiary, if only a very minor one, of the super-empire's mechanisms of exploitation. Yet the PRC does not exercise—and is increasingly resistant toward participating in—the super-empire's mechanisms of control. The PRC has no preconditions on its loans to other countries and demands no structural adjustments of its clients—in fact, its practice of providing emergency debt relief has begun to *disrupt*, or at least delay, the IMF's role of enforcing global austerity. As of this writing, the People's Liberation Army has not fought a war for well over forty years, and has no significant presence abroad, save for a single base in Djibouti. The PRC has nothing like the multitude of Western soft-power NGOs; it does not meddle in the elections or revolutions of other countries, and does not seek to undermine their sovereignty. In short, though China benefits marginally from world imperialism, the PRC makes no attempt to enforce it. This curious contradiction therefore can only exist as long as the super-empire does. Were the super-imperialist stage to end, the PRC would be unable to maintain such an orientation to the periphery.

Furthermore, while over the last few decades China and the United States have become so integrated through trade that any major disruption would cause severe economic turmoil or collapse, the PRC has also begun to invest even more heavily in the super-empire's greatest national-bourgeois rivals, the Islamic Republic of Iran and the Russian Federation. In just the first months of 2022, trade between the PRC and the Russian Federation increased by nearly 30%, as the PRC offered new markets for Russian exports in the face of the super-empire's new sanctions regime.[549] In 2021, the PRC pledged to invest $400 billion in the Iranian economy

547 Jevans Nyabiage, "Ghana Goes Ahead with US$2 Billion Chinese Bauxite Barter Deal That Has Conservationists up in Arms," *South ChinaMorning Post,* November 17, 2019.

548 Observatory of Economic Complexity, "Ghana."

549 Evelyn Cheng, "China's Xi Says Trade with Russia Expected to Hit New Records in the Coming Months," *CNBC,* June 17, 2022.

over the next 25 years—twice its current investment position in the United States[550]—and allowed the Islamic Republic to join the Shanghai Cooperation Organization and later the BRICS group. Ansarallah, which has made repeated overtures to the PRC,[551,552] praised the agreement, calling it a "non-colonizing and balanced" alternative to predatory Western finance.[553] Hezbollah has repeatedly urged the Lebanese government to accept Chinese investment offers, such as one from the China Machinery Engineering Corporation in 2020, which proposed to build new power plants in Lebanon.[554] [555] The forces of national liberation are increasingly betting on the PRC as the key, directly or indirectly, to advancing their struggle. In November of 2004, Fidel Castro declared in a speech that "China has objectively become the most promising hope and the best example for all Third World countries."[556] Fanon, who concluded in the early 1960s that "the bourgeois phase in the history of underdeveloped countries is a completely useless phase,"[557] nevertheless did so predicated on those countries' lack of capital. He wrote:

> The theoretical question that for the last fifty years has been raised whenever the history of underdeveloped countries is under discussion—whether or not the bourgeois phase can be skipped—ought to be answered in the field of revolutionary action, and not by logic.

550 Farnaz Fassihi and Steven Lee Myers, "China, With $400 Billion Iran Deal, Could Deepen Influence in Mideast," *New York Times,* March 29, 2021.

551 Hakim Almasmari and Asa Fitch, "Yemen's Houthis Seek Iran, Russia and China Ties," *Wall Street Journal,* March 6, 2015.

552 Saba News Agency, "FM Announces Yemen's Solidarity with China."

553 "Houthis Of Yemen Welcome 25-Year Deal Between Iran And China," *Iran International,* March 28, 2021.

554 Fatima Salama, "باالثوائقى: لئاسر لئاصين صينية للحكومة اللبنانية وعروضات.. "راللود رايلم 50لـا دح ىلا لصت عيراشمب نواعتلل دادعتسا [Chinese letters to the Lebanese government and offers to cooperate in projects amounting to $50 billion].

555 This infrastructure would have taken two years to complete; in 2022, Lebanon was still plagued with widespread electricity shortages and frequent blackouts after seeking IMF loans instead.

556 Fidel Castro Ruz, "Discurso pronunciado por Fidel Castro Ruz, Presidente de la República de Cuba, en la ceremonia de condecoración con la Orden 'José Martí', a Hu Jintao, Secretario General del Partido Comunista de China y Presidente de la República Popular China, en el Palacio de la Revolución, el 23 de noviembre de 2004." [Speech given by Fidel Castro Ruz, President of the Republic of Cuba, at the award ceremony of the Order of José Martí to Hu Jintao, Secretary General of the Communist Party of China and President of the People's Republic of China, at the Palace of the Revolution, on November 23, 2004].

557 Fanon, *The Wretched of the Earth,* 176.

The bourgeois phase in underdeveloped countries can only justify itself in so far as the national bourgeoisie has sufficient economic and technical strength to build up a bourgeois society, to create the conditions necessary for the development of a large-scale proletariat, to mechanize agriculture, and finally to make possible the existence of an authentic national culture. [emphasis added][558]

If the PRC, which in Fanon's time attempted and largely failed to export revolution to the periphery, can now supply this economic and technical strength, a path toward the eventual victory of the world's oppressed classes over neocolonialism may finally become clear. The development of the periphery can only be a destabilizing force to the super-empire, and the seriousness of Chinese investors in pursuing this development, even sometimes at a loss, suggests that at the very least, the positions of a great many countries within the capitalist world-system may change in the near future. As described in Appendix B, most countries in Africa have increased exports more to *each other* than to any other region in the past decade. In March 2023, the Western media was stunned when Iran and Saudi Arabia, who had been bitter rivals for decades in a conflict heavily influenced by U.S. strategic interests, reestablished diplomatic ties in talks brokered by the PRC. The U.S., according to the *New York Times*, had been "left on the sidelines."[559] If a great realignment is on the horizon, how then will the PRC react to the results of its own enterprises? Will it seek to create a socialist world-system, or will it attempt to replace the United States as the hegemon of a new super-empire? A proper answer must undertake an examination of the PRC itself and determine the intent behind its relations with the rest of the world.

The discipline of Chinese investment is neither accident nor coincidence. A study published by the Australian National University Press in 2015 found that 89% of the PRC's overseas direct investment were linked to its state-owned enterprises, indicating that it is overwhelmingly not private investors choosing which projects to fund, but the government.[560] China Eximbank, which by 2007 had become by far the world's largest

---

558 Fanon, 175.

559 Peter Baker, "Chinese-Brokered Deal Upends Mideast Diplomacy and Challenges U.S.," *New York Times*, March 11, 2023.

560 Mei (Lisa) Wang, Zhen Qi, and Jijing Zhang, "China Becomes a Capital Exporter: Trends and Issues," in Ligang Song et al. (eds.), *China's Domestic Transformation in a Global Context* (Australian National University Press, 2015), 322.

export credit agency, operates primarily as a tool of the state, and is expected not to turn a profit.[561] Considering that not only China Eximbank, but the four largest banks in China—which are also the four largest in the world by total reported asset value—are all state-owned,[562] there is a real question of whether the PRC may also fail another of Lenin's criteria of imperialism—that of being directed by a financial oligarchy.

Amin, who like many other twentieth-century economists accepted the principle of World-Systems Theory, was particularly notable for also synthesizing from it a coherent mechanism of change, a crucial step that Wallerstein and other contemporaries struggled to make. Amin's theory—which he referred to as "delinking"—prescribed for peripheral countries a type of separation from the capitalist world economy that did not preclude trading relations, but instead involved a "refusal to subject national development strategy to the imperatives of 'worldwide expansion' [of the world capitalist system]."[563] Amin's view by 2016 was that out of every government in the world, China's alone was strong enough to pursue this strategy,[564] and that an essential ingredient was its control over its financial system:

> China is walking on two legs: following the traditions and participating [in] globalization. They accept foreign investments, but keep independence of their financial system. *The Chinese bank system is exclusively state-controlled. The Yuan is convertible only to a certain extent, but under the control of the bank of China. That is the best model that we have today to respond to the challenge of globalists imperialism* [sic]. [emphasis added][565]

561 Brautigam, *The Dragon's Gift*, 111–13.

562 Zarmina Ali, "The World's 100 Largest Banks, 2020," *S&P Global*, April 13, 2020.

563 Samir Amin, *Delinking: Towards a Polycentric World* (Zed Books, 1990), 62.

564 Amin estimated that according to his model, half of China's development was driven by its own sovereign project, while the other half was driven by globalization. This ratio of conflicting forces, however, was stronger than anywhere else outside the super-empire; for Brazil and India, for example, he estimated only twenty percent control by their sovereign projects, while South Africa's had none at all. [Ingrid Harvold Kvangraven, "A Dependency Pioneer - Samir Amin," in Ushehwedu Kufakurinani et al. (eds.), *Dialogues on Development Volume 1: On Dependency* (Institute for New Economic Thinking, 2017), 16.]

565 "Samir Amin: How to defeat the Collective Imperialism of the Triad" (exclusive interview), *Katehon*, September 1, 2016.

Does the unusual behavior of Chinese finance, which appears to consistently be at odds with the interests of the typical Western finance capitalist, imply that it is controlled by a class other than the Chinese bourgeoisie? This question, and the question of which class now holds state power in China, are one and the same.

CHAPTER SEVEN

Who Holds State Power in China?

> *"If foreign economies are to achieve financial*
> *independence, they must create their own regulatory*
> *mechanisms. Whether they will do so depends on*
> *how thoroughly America has succeeded in making*
> *irreversible the super imperialism implicit in the*
> *Washington Consensus and its ideology."*
>
> —Michael Hudson, *Super-Imperialism: The Origin and*
> *Fundamentals of U.S. World Dominance*, 2003[566]

It would be a severe understatement to say that China has had a troubled history. After thousands of years of feudal despotism,[567] it was invaded, subjugated, and plundered by the European colonial powers and the Empire of Japan in an even grimmer period that lasted over 100 years. The civil war that finally ended the Century of Humiliation and established the People's Republic began years before the Second World War, lasted years after the defeat of the Axis Powers, and was won at the cost of millions of lives. The new People's Republic of China had then scarcely come into existence before it was beset by another war against it by the United States and its allies, mass starvation from natural disasters, and the calamitous Cultural Revolution, which the Chinese central government later declared had been "wrongly launched by the leaders" and "brought serious disaster to the Party, the country and the people of all ethnic groups."[568] In light of this long progression of tragedy, perhaps the most surprising outcome of the Reform and Opening Up period that began in 1978 was not the destructive consequences it brought upon the Chinese proletariat and peasantry—which were real and often severe—but rather

---

566 Michael Hudson, *Super Imperialism: The Origin and Fundamentals of U.S. World Dominance* (Pluto Press, 2003), 33.

567 While this term is the best descriptor, it is slightly inaccurate. Pre-revolution China, while ruled by dynastic monarchs, did not exhibit precisely the same features throughout its social and economic structure as the European phenomenon that is traditionally considered "feudalism."

568 人民日报 (*People's Daily*), "关于建国以来党的若干历史问题的决议" [Resolution on Several Historical Issues of the Party Since the Founding of the People's Republic of China], 3.

how muted these hardships were by comparison with the horrors of capitalist restoration in Russia and the rest of the former socialist bloc.

The Capitalist Road and the Socialist High-Speed Railway

Though the PRC pursued an economic program that most certainly resembled structural adjustment during the neoliberal era, privatizing a large part of the public sector and courting foreign investment, it did so on its own terms, and not those of the Western financial oligarchy. The IMF's financial data notes only a single loan to the PRC in its entire history—just over half a billion SDRs in 1986—that was repaid in full by 1991, while the Russian Federation borrowed over 18 billion SDRs throughout its comprador phase in the 1990s, carrying preconditions with devastating effects on the Russian people.[569] Average life expectancy in China, which had never exceeded 35 years before the socialist era, has advanced rapidly ever since, even during the Reform period; according to World Bank statistics, life expectancy increased from nearly 65 years to over 70 years by the end of the 1990s,[570] in sharp contrast to the historic six-year drop suffered by Russia in the Yeltsin era. During the twenty-first century, Russia's suicide rate has never been less than triple China's.[571] While GDP severely declined in the former Eastern Bloc, in China it has only increased; while inflation surged out of control in Russia, in China it remained low. The sudden homelessness epidemic that plagued Russia and the other former socialist countries was mostly avoided by China, where the transition from public to private housing was carefully managed by the government. According to *Forbes*:

> It wasn't until the mid-90s that a series of reforms allowed urban residents to own and sell real estate. People were then given the option to purchase their previously government-owned homes at extremely favorable rates, and most of them made the transition to being property owners. . . .[572]

---

569 International Monetary Fund, "IMF Financial Data Query Tool."

570 World Bank, "Life Expectancy at Birth, Total (Years) - China."

571 World Bank, "Suicide Mortality Rate (per 100,000 Population) - Russian Federation, China."

572 Wade Shepard, "How People In China Afford Their Outrageously Expensive Homes," *Forbes*, March 30, 2016.

This policy resulted in China's 90% homeownership rate in the mid-90s, which outstripped nearly every other country in the world. The PRC's *hukou* system, which regulates internal migration from the countryside to the cities, has often been criticized for its role in producing China's current massive wealth inequality, but it also has mostly prevented urban slums, almost entirely prevented rough sleeping, and allowed the government to guarantee adequate housing for the vast majority of its 1.4 billion people.[573]

In 2021, despite turmoil in the Chinese housing market, the average default rate of residential mortgage-backed securities was just 0.38%,[574] and according to *Foreign Policy* magazine, only 18% of Chinese households even had a mortgage.[575] Though the "crisis" of falling housing prices in China in the early 2020s bears a superficial resemblance to the U.S. phenomenon in the late 2000s, the relationship between banks and homeowners in China is not parasitic, and therefore will not result in the type of mass foreclosures homeowners in the U.S. experienced during the Great Recession. Adjustable-rate mortgages were infamously used by U.S. lenders with low initial "teaser" payments to entice home buyers to enter into the market but these were followed by higher, predatory rates that borrowers were powerless to renegotiate. In China, however, such mortgages are pegged to the "loan prime rate" which the People's Bank carefully *lowered* on multiple occasions throughout the Chinese "crisis."[576] By 2023, instead of undertaking foreclosures, China's central bank was encouraging the renegotiation or refinancing of existing mortgages

---

573 Due to housing subsidies being tied to *hukou* registration, China's small vagrant population consists almost entirely of rural poor who typically have residences in the countryside but have migrated to the cities in the hope of attaining higher-paying urban jobs. A true comparison with homelessness in a capitalist country is therefore not straightforward, Chinese vagrancy being on average qualitatively less desperate and quantitatively more scarce. According to the *Economist*, a Chinese charity estimated the homeless population of central Beijing (a city of over twenty million inhabitants) at "several hundred" in 2019 ("Homelessness Has Become a Problem in China's Cities," November 14, 2019); in contrast, the mid-sized U.S. city of Portland (population of less than one million) was estimated to have well over five thousand homeless during the same year (David Mann, "Tri-Counties Release 1st Count of Portland Area's Homeless Population since 2019," *KGW8*, 2022).

574 John Wu, "China Mortgage Boycott Unlikely to Cause Serious Distress to Banking Sector," *S&P Global,* August 23, 2022.

575 James Palmer, "Chinese Mortgage Boycott Gains Steam," *Foreign Policy,* July 20, 2022.

576 Peter Hoskins, "China Cuts Key Interest Rate as Recovery Falters," BBC, August 21, 2023.

at the expense of bank profits.[577] Thus while over-leveraged developers suffered, mortgage rates fell to historic lows, leading to homeowners finding no difficulty in refinancing.[578]

According to German political economist Isabella M. Weber, on no fewer than two occasions during the early Reform period, amid a debate between Chinese economists on how best to shift towards a market-based economy, the PRC had prepared a "big bang" of shock therapy-style "price reform," but ultimately abstained in favor of a gradual marketization approach.[579] Weber contrasts actual shock therapy with the PRC's Reform strategy by comparing the latter to a game of Jenga, in which only the "blocks" of the welfare state were removed "that could be flexibly rearranged without endangering the stability of the building as a whole."[580] According to Weber, when World Bank economist Adrian Wood visited China during the 1980s, he discovered that the government was still extremely reluctant to relax price controls on essential goods. In his notes, Wood marveled that despite producers consistently recording losses, the "communist dictatorship" would not even "raise the price of matches by 2 cents."[581]

To Deng Xiaoping is famously attributed the quote "To get rich is glorious." Less famous, perhaps, are his words in a 1986 interview with *60 Minutes* correspondent Mike Wallace:

During the "Cultural Revolution" there was a view that poor communism was preferable to rich capitalism. . . . According to Marxism, communist society is based on material abundance. Only when there is material abundance can the principle of a communist society—that is, "from each according to his ability, to each according to his needs"—be applied. Socialism is the first stage of communism. Of course, it covers a very long historical period. The main task in the socialist stage is to develop the productive forces, keep increasing the material wealth of society, steadily improve the

---

577 Fitch Wire, "Chinese Banks and RMBS Could See Minor Impact from Push to Lower Mortgage Rates," *Fitch Ratings,* August 1, 2023.

578 Zongyuan Zoe Liu and Daniel Stemp, "The PBoC Props Up China's Housing Market," Council on Foreign Relations, May 21, 2023.

579 Isabella M. Weber, *How China Escaped Shock Therapy: The Market Reform Debate* (Routledge, 2021), 1.

580 Weber, 10.

581 Weber, 168.

life of the people and create material conditions for the advent of a communist society.

There can be no communism with pauperism, or socialism with pauperism. So to get rich is no sin. *However, what we mean by getting rich is different from what you mean. Wealth in a socialist society belongs to the people. To get rich in a socialist society means prosperity for the entire people. The principles of social- ism are: first, development of production and second, common prosperity. We permit some people and some regions to become prosperous first, for the purpose of achieving common prosperity faster.* [emphasis added] That is why our policy will not lead to polarization, to a situation where the rich get richer while the poor get poorer. To be frank, we shall not permit the emergence of a new bourgeoisie.[582]

The Communist Party under Deng's leadership therefore pursued free-market reforms as a stage it believed was necessary before socialism could be fully established. Far from being a Chinese Yeltsin or even a Gorbachev, Deng himself was in fact a committed and farsighted Marxist, qualities that Mao Zedong himself once recognized.[583]

During the initial Reform period, the Chinese welfare state was grad- ually dismantled. The huge rural peasant population was steadily prole- tarianized, and the proletariat were in turn largely stripped of their pro- tections and pushed into an unforgiving new private sector. Collectively, the masses were made to work under worse conditions for much longer hours, though not for less pay. According to a 2017 paper by Thomas Piketty and other Western economists comparing income inequality in China with that in the United States, the real incomes of the poorest half of the Chinese population had increased by more than four hundred percent since the beginning of the Reform and Opening Up era in 1978,

---

582 Deng Xiaoping, Deng Xiaoping, "Interview With Mike Wallace Of 60 Minutes," Sept. 2, 1986.

583 "In November 1957, Mao took Deng along with him to Moscow for the celebration of the fortieth anniversary of the October revolution. He introduced him to Khrushchev with these words: 'See that little fellow over there? He's a very wise man, sees far into the future.' Then he pulled out all the stops, praising Deng as 'the future leader of China and its Communist Party.' 'This is the future leader,' he said, "he is the best of my comrades in arms. A great growing force.... This is a man who is both principled and flexible, a rare talent.'" [Alexsander V. Pantsov and Steven I. Levine, *Deng Xiaoping: A Revolutionary Life* (Oxford University Press, 2015), 186.]

while the real incomes of the poorest half of the U.S. population had actually declined during the same time period.[584] The closest analogue to the PRC's Reform phase can in fact be found in the Islamic Republic of Iran, in terms of how their transitions toward free-market capitalist economies in the neoliberal era have been carefully moderated, relatively smooth, and did not involve the IMF and its more brutal program; yet in the case of Iran, the national bourgeoisie at the helm of the state are now reaping the benefits of capital accumulation for themselves as poverty increases.[585] The rich have gotten richer in China—much richer—but the very poorest have gotten richer as well, exactly as the Party had planned and predicted.

According to statistics tracked by the World Bank, between 2013 and 2019,[586] the income share held by the highest 20% of the population increased in Iran and decreased in China, while the share held by the lowest 20% decreased in Iran and increased in China.[587] [588] Income being *the rate* at which wealth increases, larger increases in income for those with the least wealth—combined with smaller increases in income for those with the most—will, if sustained, gradually reduce income inequality, which will in turn gradually reduce wealth inequality. For China, at some point in or before 2013 lay an inflection point. Amin, in his writing around this time, distinguished inequality in China from inequality in the neoliberal world in the following way:

> Certainly the growth of inequality is obvious everywhere, including China; but this observation remains superficial and deceptive. Inequality in the distribution of benefits from a model of growth that nevertheless excludes no one (and is even accompanied with a reduction in pockets of poverty—this is the case in China) is one thing; the inequality connected with a growth that benefits only a minority (from 5 percent to 30 percent of the population, depending on the case) while the fate of the others remains desperate is

---

584 Facundo Alvaredo et al., "Global Inequality Dynamics: New Findings from WID.world," *American Economic Review* 107, no. 5 (May 2017): 404-409, 6.

585 See Chapter Four.

586 The most recent uninterrupted period for which data is available for both countries, as of early 2023.

587 World Bank, "Income Share Held by Lowest 20% - Iran, Islamic Rep., China."

588 World Bank, "Income Share Held by Highest 20% - Iran, Islamic Rep., China."

another thing. The practitioners of China bashing are unaware—or pretend to be unaware—of this decisive difference.[589]

Neoliberalism, when practiced in the West, was and is a weapon of class warfare, existing only to steal from the working class and give to the capitalists. The myth of "trickle-down economics" was always a lie intended to fool workers into letting themselves be robbed—yet through the careful intervention of the state, the Communist Party of China had alone found a way to blunt this weapon and force some wealth to actually trickle down. In just the first phase of Reform and Opening Up, from 1978 to 2000—considered the harshest era of neoliberalism worldwide—China experienced a massive reduction in poverty unprecedented in history. According to World Bank estimates, the number of people in China living on less than $1 per day fell by 300 million during this time period, reversing the global trend of increasing poverty that had lasted for half a century. (In other words, if China were excluded, the world's poverty population, i.e. the total number of people in poverty in the world, would have *increased*, rather than declined, throughout the 1980s and 1990s.)[590] Thus Chinese workers were surrendered to the cruelties of the free market for a time, but in a slower and much gentler manner than in the West and its neocolonial subjects, and to an entirely different purpose.

We cannot easily second-guess history. It may be that the PRC could have rejected the "capitalist road" and survived; it may also have remained on the path preferred by the Gang of Four, and then fallen along with the other socialist states in 1989. It may have endured the Cultural Revolution, escaped counterrevolution, and continued on in a severely underdeveloped form, with the great masses of its rural poor still suffering under the super-empire's sanctions and embargoes, as has happened in the DPRK. But mere survival cannot suffice to accomplish the world-historical task of socialism, and it is scarcely conceivable that the PRC could have done other than it has and still by now be in a position to overtake the United States economically. While China did see continued development and economic growth throughout the pre-Reform period—the three decades between the Communist victory in 1949 and

---

589 Samir Amin, "China 2013," *Monthly Review* 64, no. 10 (March 2013).

590 Hu Angang, Hu Linlin, and Chang Zhixiao, "China's Economic Growth and Poverty Reduction (1978–2002)," in Wanda Tseng and David Cowen (eds.), *India's and China's Recent Experience with Reform and Growth* (Palgrave Macmillan London, 2005), 60-61.

the beginning of Reform in 1978, during which time China's GDP more than tripled—its share of *global* GDP had remained stagnant.[591]

In *The German Ideology*, Karl Marx and Friedrich Engels wrote:

> ... it is only possible to achieve real liberation in the real world and by employing real means ... slavery cannot be abolished without the steam-engine and the mule and spinning-jenny, serfdom cannot be abolished without improved agriculture ... in general, people cannot be liberated as long as they are unable to obtain food and drink, housing and clothing in adequate quality and quantity. "Liberation" is an historical and not a mental act, and it is brought about by historical conditions, the development of industry, commerce, agriculture, the conditions of intercourse ...[592]

The steam engine and the spinning jenny, also generally called constant capital, the means or instruments of labor, or even more generally, a part of *the forces of production*, were clearly necessary tools. The question that must be entertained is not whether China could have thrived without them, but how the PRC has used them, for their introduction alone does not bring liberation. A much less speculative and much more useful historical analysis, therefore, lies not in comparing what China has become with a hypothetical China that took another path, but in comparing China with India, another formerly-colonized country in the Global South with an equivalent population that exists today and took an actual capitalist road. Both countries gained their independence in the late 1940s, and from then until even the 1980s they had equivalent GDPs.[593] By 2021, China's GDP was more than five times higher than India's, while India had five times China's infant mortality rate,[594] and trailed China in literacy, life expectancy, and public infrastructure. Though the progress India has made in reducing extreme poverty in the twenty-first century is not insignificant—second only to the PRC's, in fact—the reduction in China has been far more rapid and thoroughgoing. For every threshold measured by the World Bank—the percentage of a population living on less than $2.15, $3.65, and $6.85 (adjusted for purchasing power parity)

---

591 Weber, *How China Escaped Shock Therapy*, 90.

592 Karl Marx and Friedrich Engels, *The German Ideology*, part I.

593 Until the early 1990s, in fact, despite their differences in political leadership, India's economy was quite similar to China's, also being dominated by a large public sector.

594 World Bank, "Mortality Rate, Infant (per 1,000 Live Births) - China, India."

per day—poverty had in fact been slightly *worse* in China than in India during the early 1990s. By 2019, however, poverty in India was still well above the global average for all three thresholds, while poverty in China had fallen far below it. The World Bank showed the largest gap for the $6.85 threshold, with 84% of India's population earning less to only 25% of China's.[595] [596] [597] Moreover, these income statistics may not adequately capture the true prevalence of poverty—according to data from the UN Food and Agriculture Organization, for example, the percentage of the Chinese population that is undernourished has consistently fallen throughout the twenty-first century, to a low of 3% in 2020; but despite a reduction between 2004 and 2017, the percentage of undernourished Indians then began *increasing*, from a low of 13% back to 16% in 2020.[598]

Deng, of course, was not infallible. Though he declared that "we shall not permit the emergence of a new bourgeoisie," it is obvious that such a class now exists in China, and with it the class struggle and corruption was revived. The PRC's economic success and reemergence on the world's stage is undeniable—since 1978, its GDP has increased a hundredfold, and by 2021 it had become the wealthiest country by net worth[599]—but the danger of its Devil's bargain is obvious. Which class will ultimately enjoy the fruits of this success?

As shown in Chapters One through Five, the reemergence of the PRC as a military and economic superpower will be a progressive development for the international working class regardless of whether the PRC becomes a socialist leader or a fully-developed capitalist empire, because either will signal an end to the stage of super-imperialism and thus recreate favorable conditions for the victory of proletarian revolution. Fortunately, however, the (much more desirable) former possibility is more likely, and a close examination of the Chinese economy and its trajectory will show that Chinese workers and peasants are regaining the upper hand, if indeed they ever lost it.

---

595 World Bank, "Poverty Headcount Ratio at $2.15 a Day (2017 PPP) (% of Population) - China, World, India."

596 World Bank, "Poverty Headcount Ratio at $3.65 a Day (2017 PPP) (% of Population) - China, World, India."

597 World Bank, "Poverty Headcount Ratio at $6.85 a Day (2017 PPP) (% of Population) - China, World, India."

598 World Bank, "Prevalence of Undernourishment (% of Population) - China, World, India."

599 Rich Miller, "Global Wealth Surges as China Overtakes U.S. to Grab Top Spot," *Bloomberg,* November 14, 2021.

The pendulum began to swing in the opposite direction during the tenure of General Secretary Hu Jintao, a man whose name a great many in the West never learned. The second phase of Reform and Opening Up that Hu presided over focused on addressing some of the problems the meteoric rise of the Chinese economy had created, namely corruption, wealth inequality, and the environmental consequences of rapid industrialization, though many of these policies did not yield significant results until well after Hu had retired in 2012.

While the Western press exists to serve the bourgeois establishment and is therefore notoriously unreliable, it can usually be counted on to properly identify their enemies. In 2007 the *Economist* reported that in spite of the mass migration of workers to China's eastern urban centers, pay for factory workers was rising at double digit rates in the Pearl River delta near Hong Kong. "Everyone should be aware that China has changed," said a member of the Hong Kong legislature.[600] "Reform has stopped," complained a paper published in 2009 by the Council on Foreign Relations and the Heritage Foundation, citing new laws in the PRC that enhanced workers' rights and restricted private firms from buying or selling goods and services at unreasonable prices. It reserved particular ire for the All-China Federation of Trade Unions, calling it a "xenophobic organ" of the Communist Party that "[assailed] foreign firms" for "minor violations."[601] During Hu's tenure, universal healthcare was readopted.[602] Privatization was halted, then reversed. Bourgeois Western economists, who at first had happily believed their own propaganda and convinced themselves that private capital would ultimately destroy socialism in China on its own, no matter what Deng said, finally noticed an extremely worrying—to them—aspect to the PRC's entire reform program: the vast majority of state-owned companies that had been "privatized" actually hadn't been. Despite being publicly traded on domestic and foreign stock exchanges, China's new private enterprises were quite often still controlled by the government through byzantine ownership structures involving state-run holding companies or domestic financial institutions (which are also state-owned). In 2009, two-thirds of state-owned enterprises had been officially privatized, yet three-quarters of these remained

---

600 Brautigam, *The Dragon's Gift*, 90.

601 Derek Scissors, "Deng Undone: The Costs of Halting Market Reform in China," *Foreign Affairs* 88, no. 3 (May/June 2009): 24-39.

602 Austin Ramzy, "China's New Healthcare Could Cover Millions More," *TIME*, April 9, 2009.

indirectly state-owned—meaning that only about 15% of the public sector had truly entered private control.[603] Between 1998 and 2007, closures and privatizations of state-owned firms were limited to smaller entities while more new large state-owned firms had been created.[604] China's actual private sector did continue to grow and prosper, but not at the expense of the state-run economy. Of the 98 Chinese companies listed on the *Fortune Global 500* list in 2015, only 22 were private, and the largest 12 were state-owned;[605] by 2021, the number of Chinese companies on the list had increased to 130—the most of any country in the world—yet over two-thirds of this increase had come from the public sector, which added 22 companies to the list, while the private sector added only ten.[606]

During the recovery from the 2008 global financial crisis, Chinese banks, under the ownership and the direction of the central government, began a massive economic stimulus that disproportionately redirected capital to the public sector.[607] The amount of money loaned domestically doubled, an enormous part of which was directed into public infrastructure. A phenomenon emerged in China that the Western press named "ghost cities"—huge development projects, including roads, skyscrapers, metro stations, and high-rise apartments—that were rapidly built some distance from existing urban areas and almost entirely unoccupied. In 2010, the *Daily Mail* breathlessly shared satellite photos of quiet streets and unused buildings in what it named "China's biggest ghost city" (a new district of Zhengzhou in Henan Province).[608] In 2011, *Business Insider* gave the same treatment to other new developments in Changsha in Hunan Province, and the new Chenggong district of Kunming, which purportedly had "100,000 new apartments with no occupants" and was

---

603 Derek Scissors, "Deng Undone."

604 Chang-Tai Hsieh and Zheng (Michael) Song, *Grasp the Large, Let Goof the Small: The Transformation of the State Sector in China,* Brookings Papers on Economic Activity (Brookings, Spring 2015).

605 Scott Cendrowski, "China's Global 500 Companies Are Bigger than Ever—and Mostly State-Owned," *Fortune,* July 22, 2015.

606 Tianlei Huang, Nicolas Véron, and David Xu, *The Private Sector Advances in China: The Evolving Ownership Structures of the Largest Companies in the Xi Jinping Era,* Peterson Institute for International Economics Working Papers 22-3 (March 2022), 31.

607 Lin William Cong et al., *Credit Allocation Under Economic Stimulus: Evidence from China,* Chicago Booth Research Paper No. 17-19 (posted November 1, 2016; last revised September 10, 2021).

608 Daily Mail Reporter, "The Ghost Towns of China: Amazing Satellite Images Show Cities Meant to Be Home to Millions Lying Deserted," *Teak Door,* December 17, 2010.

"building skyscrapers by the hundreds."[609] Today, all these new areas each are home to several hundred thousand people, with densities of hundreds or thousands per square kilometer. There was nothing fake or mysterious about them—they were simply built in advance of China's urbanizing and modernizing population. The government was spending so much money that infrastructure was *preceding* development all across the country.[610]

Since the dawn of the twenty-first century, the PRC has turned neo-liberal orthodoxy on its head. Instead of practicing the crushing austerity that private financial institutions in the West currently enforce upon the rest of the world, Chinese public financial institutions have done nothing but build and spend, and build and spend, and build and spend some more. The most dramatic symbol of the success of this philosophy is China's new high-speed railway network, which began construction in the late 2000s and within a single decade grew to become the world's largest— larger, in fact, than all high-speed rail systems in all other countries, which had been much more slowly built in Europe and Japan over half a century, put together. Ürümqi and Lhasa, the capital cities of China's remotest provinces, were connected to the east with high-speed lines at galactic expense. If the full length of the Chinese high-speed rail sys-tem—40,000 kilometers and still increasing—were laid in a single track, it would wrap around the Earth's entire circumference. Over three billion passenger trips are now made by rail in China per year,[611] and even for moderate distances are often quicker than airplanes. While neoliberalism destroyed Argentina's railways, its ideological opposite brought China's into existence from nothing.

There is no way to make high-speed rail construction profitable. Trains traveling at speeds of 300 kilometers per hour must have a straight electrified track, necessitating the careful excavations of hillsides to bore tunnels, the costly construction of massive bridges to span rivers and can-yons, and the placement of hundreds of thousands of elevated concrete columns across countrysides. The China-Laos high-speed railway, which opened in 2021 and spans hundreds of kilometers of mountainous terrain, is nearly two-thirds tunnels and bridges by length.[612] No business model

---

609 Gus Lubin, "New Satellite Pictures of China's Ghost Cities," *Business Insider,* June 16, 2011.

610 "China's Ghost Cities Are Finally Stirring to Life After Years of Empty Streets," *Bloomberg News,* September 1, 2021.

611 Luo Wangshu, "Railways Set Service Goals for New Year," *China Daily,* January 5, 2021.

612 Latsamy Phonevilay, "Construction of Vientiane Station Commences on

can sustain such an expense and still deliver a profit through the sales of tickets and concessions. Instead, the PRC has embraced the construction of mass transit and other infrastructure as a *public good*.

Neoliberal economists have recoiled in horror at China's high-speed rail miracle. The libertarian Cato Institute bemoaned the massive expense and unprofitability,[613] and the India-based Observer Research Foundation warned that the China Railway Corporation (a state-owned enterprise) owed an unsustainable amount of debt to Chinese banks (which are also state-owned).[614] However, if the mindless pursuit of profit is set aside, the economic benefits of high-speed rail nonetheless emerge in stark relief. One such analysis from found that far from being "unprofitable," China's high-speed railways had in fact earned an annual 6.5% return on investment. According to the Paulson Institute in Chicago, the total cost of the network (around $2 trillion) was offset not just by the revenue, but by the difference in operation costs from airline trips that were saved by taking the train, and the time savings that riders would not have accrued otherwise, totaling around $2.4 trillion[615]—a calculation that did not even include the environmental benefits and the vast quantities of jet fuel that has not been expended.

In the bigger picture, it is clear that even before Xi Jinping's tenure as General Secretary of the Communist Party, China's trajectory had shifted away from privatization and profiteering and back toward the state-managed economy and the redistribution of gains. This did not mean, however, that the private sector itself was or is on the verge of being destroyed or reabsorbed by the state. At the Third Plenary Session of the Central Committee in 2013, the Party reaffirmed its ideological commitment to the principles of Reform and announced that it would "[improve] the basic economic system" by "vigorously developing a mixed economy."[616] As the capital accumulation engine of China's unparalleled economic growth, and as a tool to attract needed foreign

Laos-China Railway," *Laotian Times,* July 4, 2020.

613 Randal O'Toole, *The High-Speed Rail Money Sink: Why the United States Should Not Spend Trillions on Obsolete Technology,* Cato Institute Policy Analysis No. 915 (April 20, 2021).

614 Dhaval Desai, "China's High-Speed Railways Plunge from High Profits into a Debt Trap," Observer Research Foundation, June 23, 2021.

615 "Boon or Boondoggle? The Cost and Benefit of China's Bullet Trains," *MacroPolo,* 2021.

616 18th Central Committee of the Communist Party of China, "Decision Of The Central Committee Of The Communist Party Of China On Some Major Issues Concerning Comprehensively Deepening The Reform," November 12, 2013.

investment, private enterprise could not yet be discarded, only directed, with all the risk that implied.

The Great Struggle for Common Prosperity

On June 17, 2019, local Party secretary Huang Wenxiu died in a flash flood in the mountains of the Guangxi Zhuang Autonomous Region. She was 30 years old. Just three years before, Huang had graduated with a master's degree from Beijing Normal University, one of the most prestigious universities in China. But rather than pursue a career in the capital, she chose to return to her home prefecture in Guangxi and volunteered to serve a remote, impoverished village in Leye County, helping its people grow and sell fruit, install streetlamps, and secure funding for a concrete road. The Party honored her as one of 1,800 cadres who had lost their lives in the targeted poverty alleviation campaign, through natural disasters, accidents, or health issues during their service in rural China.[617]

Their sacrifice was not in vain. By the end of 2020, extreme poverty—defined as living on under a threshold of around two dollars a day—had been eliminated in China. The Western press, which was by then critical of any positive news from China, spun rather than denied the achievement. The *New York Times* both printed the World Bank's admission of the PRC's success, and also highlighted the "costly" nature of the government's poverty alleviation campaign[618] that "Beijing may struggle to sustain," citing not the lives lost but the $700 billion spent by the government since Xi Jinping's administration announced it in 2014.[619] However, when evaluated honestly, the details of Chinese poverty alleviation's implementation show that it is not only sustainable, but developmental, consisting more of infrastructural improvements than actual cash payments.

The previous year, every rural village in China had been connected to the country's network of paved roads (either asphalt or cement), with over 99% of rural communities receiving regular bus service.[620] A massive

---

617 International Department of the CPC Central Committee, Beijing Review, "China Honors Role Models in Poverty Eradication Campaign," *China Insight,* Special Issue on China's Complete Victory of Poverty Alleviation (2021), 52–53.

618 As the following chapter will show, this is quite typical of Western newspapers' coverage of Chinese government policy.

619 Keith Bradsher, "Jobs, Houses and Cows: China's Costly Drive to Erase Extreme Poverty," *New York Times,* December 31, 2020.

620 Xinhua, "China to Connect All Townships, Villages with Paved Roads by

effort had been mobilized to modernize the countryside, installing basic sanitation where it was lacking, and constructing modern homes for the poorest villagers. Some of the remotest, most underdeveloped communities saw technological improvements leapfrogging several decades; often a village would be wired for broadband internet access within a year of being connected to running water for the first time in history. The *New York Times* observed that "Though many villages are still reachable only by single-lane roads, they are lined with streetlights powered by solar panels." The unemployed rural population were generally given jobs or job training in addition to or in place of welfare subsidies; small farmers were often given cattle—cows or sheep, which in the undeveloped countryside are some of most lucrative forms of capital—by the government for free.[621] Though a great wealth gap still exists between China's rural poor and its city-dwellers, the progress so far is remarkable, increasing, and permanent.

"But who will pay for it?" is a common reactionary refrain in the West, employed by the bourgeois media to stifle any type of redistributive political program such as universal healthcare or environmental initiatives. In China, this question is not rhetorical, and a clear answer has emerged.

In 2020, China's bloated private sector abruptly became the target of an aggressive expansion of regulations on private business. In November, a $34 billion initial public offering by the Ant Group, the Alibaba corporation's financial affiliate, was predicted to be the largest in history.[622] Regulators intervened, canceling the IPO and instituting strict new antimonopoly rules.[623] The following month, both Alibaba and Tencent, two of China's largest tech companies, were censured for failing to seek government approval for mergers and acquisitions,[624] and Xi declared in a Politburo meeting that the Communist Party would act to "prevent the disorderly expansion of capital."[625] In 2021, Alibaba was ordered to pay a $2.8 billion antitrust fine.[626] In July, in what the *Financial Times* called

End of 2019," *China Daily,* December 19, 2019.

621 Keith Bradsher, "Jobs, Houses and Cows."

622 Arjun Kharpal, "Ant Group to Raise $34.5 Billion, Valuing It at over $313 Billion, in Biggest IPO of All Time," *CNBC,* October 26, 2020.

623 Liza Lin, "China Targets Alibaba, Other Homegrown Tech Giants With Antimonopoly Rules," *Wall Street Journal,* November 10, 2020.

624 Coco Liu and Shiyin Chen, "China Fines Alibaba, Tencent Unit Under Anti-Monopoly Laws," *Bloomberg,* December 13, 2020.

625 "What Xi Means by 'Disorderly Capital' Is $1.5 Trillion Question," *Bloomberg News,* September 9, 2021.

626 Keith Zhai, "Alibaba Hit With Record $2.8 Billion Antitrust Fine in China,"

a "death penalty" for the industry, the government "[cracked] down" on private education companies, "[asserting] Communist party supremacy." The new regulations did not outright ban the $100 billion industry, but instead simply forbade private educators from operating on a for-profit business model.[627] Around the same time, regulators canceled another massive IPO from the ride-hailing corporation Didi, which the *New York Times* said had operated in "legal gray areas" for years, and ordered it removed from app stores.[628] In August, the Supreme People's Court ruled that the Chinese tech industry's practice of pressuring employees into working overtime was illegal.[629] In September, the People's Bank of China officially banned all transactions and digital mining of cryptocurrencies.[630]

The state's expansion was not limited to new legislation, financial maneuvers, and rhetoric, however. The new regulatory regime had teeth. In January of 2022, a former Communist Party secretary of Hangzhou—a second-tier financial center with a population of over 10 million people—was expelled and arrested for accepting bribes and "supporting the disorderly expansion of capital,"[631] the result of a five-month investigation in which the local Party branch of over 25,000 members had been ordered perform "self-examinations" to find any potential conflicts of interest involving the business community.[632] In March of 2021, four major steel mills in Hebei Province were caught falsifying production records to evade carbon emission limits;[633] the following year, dozens of executives responsible for the crime were sentenced to prison.[634] The government's

Wall Street Journal, April 10, 2021.

627 Tom Mitchell, Sun Yu, and Ryan McMorrow, "Xi Cracks down on China's Education Sector to Assert Communist Party Supremacy," *Financial Times*, July 27, 2021.

628 Raymond Zhong and Li Yuan, "The Rise and Fall of the World's Ride-Hailing Giant," *New York Times*, August 27, 2021.

629 Grady McGregor, "The End of '996'? China's Government Takes on Its Brutal Tech Working Culture," *Fortune*, August 27, 2021.

630 People's Bank of China, "关于进一步防范和处置虚拟货币交易炒作风险的通知" [Notice on Further Preventing and Dealing with the Risk of Speculation in Virtual Currency Transactions].

631 "China's Communist Party Expels Former Boss of Hangzhou for Graft," *Reuters*, January 25, 2022.

632 Brenda Goh, "China Orders Communist Party Members to Resolve Conflicts of Interest as Top Hangzhou Official Probed," *Reuters*, August 22, 2021.

633 "China Pollution Crackdown Exposes Rule Breakers in Top Steel Hub," *Bloomberg News*, March 12, 2021.

634 "China Jails Almost 50 Steel Executives for Faking Emissions Data," *Bloomberg News*, January 28, 2022.

anti-corruption campaign also continued, making dramatic public examples of white-collar criminal cases; in January of 2021, Lai Xiaomin,
a Party secretary and senior executive of a state-owned company, was
executed for taking bribes and embezzling millions from public funds.

In general, regulations on business in the PRC are real and carry real
consequences, often in stark contrast with the West. For its role in the
Deepwater Horizon catastrophe of 2010 in the Gulf of Mexico—which
killed nearly a dozen workers and is considered the largest marine oil spill
in history—the British multinational oil corporation BP was compelled
only to pay a fine; no criminal charges against company officials stuck and
no one associated with the disaster spent even a single day behind bars.
However, after the 2015 Tianjin port explosions, which were caused by
the Ruihai Logistics company's avoidance of safety regulations in storing
flammable chemicals, Chinese courts sent dozens of company staff and
complicit government officials to prison, and sentenced the Chairman of
Ruihai Logistics to death.[635]

Sometimes, private corporations were neither banned nor censured,
but simply bought out. The *Wall Street Journal* described how in 2019
two large corporations which had incurred significant debt, Beijing
OriginWater and Zhejiang Great Southeast Company, had been taken
over by state-owned entities through stock purchases, in the case of the
former effectively nationalizing it. Even more commonly, large private
companies were compelled by the government to accept direct supervision by Communist Party committees, which were to play a role in
corporate decision-making.[636] "We Can't Tell if Chinese Firms Work
for the Party" declared a headline in *Foreign Policy* magazine in 2019,
the article complaining that though private Chinese companies still had
nominal autonomy, "when the party comes calling, they have almost no
power to resist direct requests."[637] In his notes made to the Third Plenary
Session of the 18th CPC Central Committee in 2013, Xi Jinping affirmed
the government's commitment to the principle of the "two unswerving-
lys": "to unswervingly consolidate and develop the public sector of the
economy, and at the same time unswervingly encourage, support and

---

635 Merrit Kennedy, "China Jails 49 Over Deadly Tianjin Warehouse
Explosions." *PBS,* November 9, 2016.

636 Lingling Wei, "China's Xi Ramps Up Control of Private Sector. 'We Have
No Choice but to Follow the Party,'" *Wall Street Journal,* December 10, 2020.

637 Ashley Feng, "We Can't Tell If Chinese Firms Work for the Party," *Foreign
Policy,* February 7, 2019.

guide the development of the non-public sector of the economy."[638] The government had not set out to destroy private business, but to control it.

By the summer of 2021, China's private sector had gotten the message. An outpouring of sudden philanthropy ensued as the largest corporations and their billionaire owners announced massive donations to charities and social programs. Tencent and Alibaba each pledged $15 billion; according to *Forbes*, to "avoid Beijing's wrath," founders of other private tech corporations such as Xiaomi, Pinduoduo, and Meituan each donated billions in their companies' stock to philanthropic foundations that participated in poverty alleviation and education programs.[639] "[T]he ability to use [the government's Common Prosperity policy] to grab money from the large capitalist firms is the key," said the founder and director of Orient Capital Research, quoted in a 2023 Australian Broadcasting Corporation article lamenting Chinese property development giant Country Garden's billionaire heiress losing half her fortune. "[T]he government may simply say, 'Well, you know, we want that money' and they'll just take it."[640]

In this light, two important observations can be made which are fundamental to determining the nature of the Chinese political economy. First, it is clear that China now displays many of the economic and social features of an advanced social democracy in a rapidly developing country. Real wages and social benefits are increasing, poverty is decreasing, the public sector is expanding, and public infrastructure is being built on a massive scale. China has surpassed the United States in healthy life expectancy,[641] and compared with the rest of the developed world, Chinese citizens retire earlier[642] and are far more likely to own their own home. Overall, the people of China have without question more prosperity, better health, and greater freedom now than they have ever had in history—things that they themselves have demanded and received.

---

638 Xi Jinping, *The Governance of China*, 2014, vol. 1, sec. Explanatory Notes to the "Decision of the Central Committee of the Communist Party of China on Some Major Issues Concerning Comprehensively Continuing the Reform."

639 Yue Wang, "China's Tech Giants Are Giving Away Their Money To Avoid Beijing's Wrath," *Forbes,* August 26, 2021.

640 Kathleen Calderwood, "Yang Huiyan Is Country Garden's Billionaire Heiress, but Her Fortune Was Just Cut in Half," *ABC News,* August 24, 2023.

641 Kieran Corcoran, "State Media in China Boasted That Their Healthy Life Expectancy Is Now Better than in the US—and They're Right." *Business Insider,* June 3, 2018.

642 "At 54, China's Average Retirement Age Is Too Low," *The Economist,* June 26, 2021.

At every turn, the government's initiatives to bring private business to heel have been supported and demanded by the Chinese working class. According to a survey by the *Washington Post*, the percentage of Chinese citizens who expressed trust in the central government increased to 98% in 2020.[643] "This is a great struggle," said an article from January 2022 on the popular left-leaning internet forum Utopia. "People have gradually understood that those super-rich who have become monopoly compradors are no longer our fellow travelers. What they want to do is to fully implement privatization in socialist China, so as to disintegrate and destroy our socialist system."[644]

That summer, in the wake of the Evergrande Group's default and ensuing real estate crisis, the *Guardian* reported that tens of thousands of new homebuyers across dozens of cities in China were engaging in a coordinated mortgage payment strike, demanding the timely completion of stalled development.[645] *Reuters* considered it a "rare act of public disobedience"—ignoring the fact that if mortgage strikes were rare in China, they were virtually unheard of in the West, despite its history of even worse crises. China's rebellion went unpunished; two months later, the strike had not diminished, but *expanded*.[646] According to *Reuters*, even before the strike, the Chinese real estate sector was effectively being slowly nationalized; months earlier, bankers had been instructed to "steer clear of private real estate firms" and capital had begun flowing primarily to state-owned developers, such as Poly Developments and China Merchants Shekou.[647] Rather than foreclose upon homeowners in arrears, as U.S. banks infamously did en masse in 2008, at every level, the Chinese banks and government hastened to placate the protestors. Regulators vowed to see the strikers' demands met, and according to *Bloomberg*, to "appease angry homebuyers" the government began formulating a new policy of forbearance that would prevent missed mortgage payments from

---

643 Cary Wu, "Did the Pandemic Shake Chinese Citizens' Trust in Their Government? We Surveyed Nearly 20,000 People to Find Out," *Washington Post*, May 5, 2021.

644 Chen Xianyi and Sun Feiyang, "This Is a Great Struggle," *Qiao Collective*, January 27, 2021.

645 Martin Farrer and Vincent Ni, "Mortgage Strikes Threaten China's Economic and Political Stability," *The Guardian*, July 19, 2022.

646 "Analysis: China's Mortgage Boycott Quietly Regroups as Construction Idles," *Reuters*, September 18, 2022.

647 Yawen Chen, "China Property Market Faces More Nationalisation," *Reuters*, December 5, 2021.

negatively impacting credit scores.[648] Increasingly, the PRC's efforts to rein in private capital, often labeled as "crackdowns" and "authoritarian" in the Western press, are being driven not from the top down, but from the bottom up.

As China developed during the twenty-first century, the rhetoric of Westerners ostensibly critical of the PRC from the left has correspondingly changed. In the first phase of the Reform era, such critics conflated the PRC's policy and contemporary Western neoliberalism;[649] during the current phase, their view of the Chinese system now acknowledges its incredible technological progress and achievements in poverty reduction, but dismisses them as "mere social democracy" similar to the mid-twentieth century phenomenon in Western countries that is described at length in Chapter Five. An essay published by the *Los Angeles Review of Books* in August 2023, for example, determined to find no distinction between Chinese and Western political economy, asserted that despite raising millions from poverty, the PRC was now merely "catching up."[650]

Upon a closer look, however, such comparisons quickly collapse. Today, unlike the West in the mid-twentieth century, China does not face the conditions that threatened the Western capitalist class into making its social-democratic compromises.[651] The PRC currently faces only *internal* pressure for wealth redistribution—and the *recent* failures of political movements based on programs of social-democratic reform within Western countries, such as Bernie Sanders' presidential campaigns or Jeremy Corbyn's leadership of the British Labour Party,[652] throw the PRC's success into even starker contrast. Campaigns by Sanders and Corbyn were sunk largely by an overwhelmingly hostile bourgeois media establishment;[653] yet real success is being enjoyed in the PRC, where

---

648 "China Weighs Mortgage Grace Period to Appease Angry Homebuyers," *Bloomberg News,* July 18, 2022.

649 Even Parenti, for example, when eulogizing the Soviet Union in 1997, considered China's reforms to be similar to the concurrent neoliberal disasters in Eastern Europe. (Michael Parenti, *Blackshirts and Reds,* 109.)

650 William I. Robinson, "The Unbearable Manicheanism of the 'Anti-Imperialist' left," *The Philosophical Salon,* August 7, 2023.

651 See Chapter Five.

652 Described earlier in Chapter Five.

653 While the policies advocated by Sanders and Corbyn undeniably held widespread appeal, their reputations as individuals were continually eroded by spurious accusations of misogyny (toward Sanders, whose competition with female candidates was held under unprecedented scrutiny) and antisemitism (toward Corbyn, whose support for the Palestinian liberation movement was presumed to stem from

the government and the government-controlled media have been at the very least nominally friendly to the proletariat throughout its history. The "Common Prosperity" slogan, though only widely publicized after Xi Jinping invoked it in 2021 to characterize the fundamental shift in the PRC's domestic politics, was not his own invention. The phrase, in fact, dates as far back as 1954, when a publication by the *People's Daily* used it to speak of the goal and aspiration to eradicate rural poverty.[654] Deng, quoted earlier in this chapter, repeated the phrase to describe his vision of capitalist accumulation ultimately being made to serve the people. Xi's domestic policy, therefore, represents not a departure from, but a step toward the fulfillment of the Communist Party's four-decade strategy for development.

Moreover, supporters of Sanders and Corbyn themselves displayed considerable animus toward the Western political establishment, while according to survey data, frequent protests in China, interpreted by the Western press as proof of the population's dissatisfaction with the government, are in fact more likely to be attended by those who *support* the central government.[655] The Asian Barometer Survey has found that mainland China had the highest percentage of people who believed their government was responsive to their needs out of nearly a dozen countries surveyed in the region. An article published in *American Affairs* in 2018 admitted that "the Chinese authoritarian government is actually more responsive to the public than a democratically elected government such as in Taiwan" and that the Party actually "spends a large amount of time and resources to calm and compensate protestors and petitioners."[656]

The second important observation is that the state and the economic direction of the PRC are firmly under the control of the Communist Party. The capitalists that thrived and gained obscene fortunes during the Reform and Opening Up period are being prevented from independently organizing for political power and, even according to studies and surveys conducted by Western researchers, the central government has the

---

anti-Jewish bigotry) by the mainstream media, contributing immensely toward their electoral defeats.

654 Central Committee of the Communist Party of China, 中国共产党中央委员会关于发展农业生产合作社的决议 [Resolution of the Central Committee of the Communist Party of China on the Development of Agricultural Production Cooperatives].

655 Wenfang Tang, "The 'Surprise' of Authoritarian Resilience in China," *American Affairs* II, no. 1 (Spring 2018): 109.

656 Wenfang Tang, 111–12.

unswerving and thoroughgoing support and trust of an overwhelming majority of the people. Even prior to the *Washington Post* survey, according to a 13-year study from the Harvard Kennedy School's Ash Center for Democratic Governance and Innovation, overall satisfaction with the central government never fell below 80%, and by 2016 rested at over 93%. While the survey subjects registered greater dissatisfaction with local governments, provincial governments retained a satisfaction rate of 75% or greater, and at no level did the government receive less than majority approval since the beginning of the study in 2003. The study also noted that even before the latest major poverty alleviation campaign had gained its current momentum and levels of success, "more marginalized groups in poorer, inland regions are actually comparatively more likely to report increases in satisfaction."[657] To the extent to which it can be reasonably measured, the will of the poorest in China is currently being expressed through the actions of the Party.

While these observations are in themselves not *sufficient* to adequately judge the present character of the Party, they reflect absolutely *necessary* conditions for the development of socialism. A thorough examination of the Party's composition and how it operates is therefore required to make an accurate estimation of China's political future.

Is the Red Flag Flying?

"China has billionaires" is a common refrain heard in circles of the political left in the West—so common, in fact, that it has become a thought-terminating cliché. There is no doubt that they exist and are significant; at their height in 2021, *Forbes* estimated there were a total of 700 billionaires in China, constituting slightly more a quarter of the world's total. Yet the unique circumstances of their appearance warrant an examination. China and Vietnam, thus far, are the only countries to ever produce private fortunes of billions of dollars while retaining a nominal Marxist-Leninist government structure. The unique features of the new big bourgeoisie in China and their relationship to state power must be thoroughly explored, to determine if they do in fact enjoy the same position and privileges as their Western counterparts.

---

657 Edward Cunningham, Tony Saich, and Jessie Turiel, *Understanding CCP Resilience: Surveying Chinese Public Opinion Through Time* (Ash Center for Democratic Governance and Innovation, July 2020).

First, how does the big bourgeoisie in China compare with this class in a similarly advanced country that is unquestionably ruled by capitalists? Only the United States, with 724 billionaires, was ranked above China on *Forbes'* list in that year—roughly an equivalent number.[658] China and the U.S. have the two highest GDPs in the world, the highest totals of net wealth, and are most similar to each other than any other country in nearly all categories of measuring economic power. Despite being greater overall,[659] however, the riches of China are far less concentrated; collectively, in 2021 the United States' billionaires were nearly twice as wealthy ($4.5 trillion)[660] as China's ($2.5 trillion).[661] In terms of billionaires *per capita*, China is below the world average, and trailed Russia, Greece, Thailand, Malaysia, Eswatini, and dozens of other countries as of 2021. In a more crucial difference, only ten of China's billionaires—scarcely more than 1%—were listed by *Forbes* as belonging to the "finance and investments" category, compared with 189 in the U.S., or 26%. Of these ten, few seem credible as members of a Chinese financial oligarchy; the two most closely associated with financial institutions, Neil Shen[662] and Zhang Lei,[663] have stronger ties to the U.S. financial system (through Sequoia Capital and Hillhouse Capital Management, respectively) than to China's. A few are successful but relatively small-time investors; Yu Yong,[664] another billionaire in this category, derives his wealth from a minority share in a large state-owned enterprise. Despite his inclusion, Changpeng Zhao,[665] the founder and CEO of Binance, the world's largest cryptocurrency exchange, is now something of an exile; he avoided the government's ban on cryptocurrency trading by relocating his company to the Cayman Islands. China's super-rich, it seems, include very few if any bankers, hedge fund managers, venture capitalists, or owners of private equity firms.

China's finance industry is quite advanced—as mentioned in Chapter Six, the four largest banks in the world by total reported asset value are all

658 Forbes, "World's Billionaires List: The Richest in 2021."

659 Rich Miller, "Global Wealth Surges as China Overtakes U.S. to Grab Top Spot," *Bloomberg,* November 14, 2021.

660 Kerry A. Dolan, "Forbes' 35th Annual World's Billionaires List: Facts And Figures 2021," *Forbes,* April 6, 2021.

661 Jennifer Wang, "The 10 Richest Chinese Billionaires In 2021," *Forbes,* April 6, 2021.

662 Forbes, "Profile: Neil Shen."

663 Forbes, "Profile: Zhang Lei."

664 Forbes, "Profile: Yu Yong."

665 Forbes, "Profile: Changpeng Zhao."

state-owned Chinese banks,[666] and a significant number of smaller private banks now exist as well. Yet few individuals have made fortunes through their operation; private banking in China, like much of the private sector, is tightly regulated and often private in name only, controlled by state-owned holding companies, as shown earlier in this chapter. Even the wealthiest of the bourgeoisie lack full control over these institutions and thus are unable to form a financial oligarchy in the same sense as the West has. The Party's grip on the central bank, and the central bank's influence upon lesser state banks, have only strengthened in recent years. In 2021, the *Wall Street Journal* reported that Party discipline inspectors brought the "unusually stern" message that "Beijing has little tolerance for any talk of central-bank independence" to the People's Bank, a sign that its already-limited autonomy was being further stripped away.[667] In 2023, Xi announced the formation of the Central Financial Commission, a new "super-regulator" designed to bring the entire financial sector under more direct Party control.[668]

There are some communists—usually from outside of China—who look upon the Reform and Opening Up period as a betrayal of principles no matter its positive effects on development, compounded ever since by the Party's apparent tolerance of these individuals accumulating vast personal fortunes. To them, these features of the Chinese economy alone are proof positive that the Party has, deliberately or not, achieved full capitalist restoration *de facto*; that the PRC has transformed from proletarian to bourgeois dictatorship; and that instead of the capitalist class being an instrument of the Party, the Party is an instrument of the capitalists. However, if this hypothesis is to be proved correct, the bourgeoisie must at some point acquire the privileges demonstrating their mastery. They must enjoy the protection of the state, and they must reap the benefits of production; else they cannot be called masters. The Chinese banking system represents the single largest engine for capital accumulation, not just in China, but in the entire world; *if* the PRC has become a dictatorship of the bourgeoisie, then *why* does this bourgeoisie not benefit from this potential greatest source of profit?

---

666 Zarmina Ali, "The World's 100 Largest Banks, 2020," *S&P Global,* April 13, 2020.

667 Lingling Wei, "Beijing Reins In China's Central Bank," *Wall Street Journal,* December 8, 2021.

668 Cheng Leng and Edward White, "Xi Jinping Tightens Financial Sector Control as New Super-Regulator Takes Shape," *Financial Times,* October 25, 2023.

Again it is useful to draw a comparison, this time not with the United States, but with the Russian Federation, the country that most closely parallels the PRC with respect to its history of socialism and economic planning, yet differs in that it has since undergone an unquestionably *complete* restoration of bourgeois dictatorship. According to *Forbes*, Russia, with only a small fraction of China's population, had twice as many billionaires in finance in 2021—approximately 17% of its 117 billionaires—despite its own banking system being still largely state-owned.

In fact, the wealthiest of the Chinese bourgeoisie, far from enjoying the sort of political power and freedom from social responsibility that owning large amounts of capital usually buys in the West, actually more often seem to be in some kind of danger—especially if you ask their class allies in the Western press. In 2016, a CNBC article declared "China's disappearing billionaires" to be an "alarming trend," citing the cases of Zhou Chengjian and Guo Guangchang, two billionaire chairmen of private corporations who had reportedly gone missing in the previous months (in fact, they had been detained by the police and later released).[669] The *New York Times* reported how in 2017, billionaire Xiao Jianhua was "snatched" from a luxury hotel in Hong Kong and taken into police custody, after which, according to their sources, he was placed under house arrest and was made to "[cooperate] with the government as it restructured [his] conglomerate." (Xiao had allegedly used connections with political leaders to build his corporate empire, and had been targeted in the government's anticorruption campaign;[670] he was eventually sentenced to thirteen years in prison.)[671] Guo Wengui, also known as Miles Guo, a billionaire who has appeared even more prominently in the Western press due to his connections with President Donald Trump's former counselor Steve Bannon, fled China in 2017 after he was accused of bribery and a warrant was issued for his arrest.[672] When *Forbes'* list was updated in 2022, the year after the campaign for Common Prosperity had begun in earnest, the number of Chinese billionaires had fallen from

---

669 Michael Posner, "China's Disappearing Billionaires - an Alarming Trend," *CNBC*, February 1, 2016.

670 Alexandra Stevenson, "China Is Dismantling the Empire of a Vanished Tycoon," *New York Times*, July 18, 2020.

671 Alexandra Stevenson, "Chinese Canadian Billionaire Sentenced to 13 Years for Financial Crimes," *The Spokesman-Review*, August 19, 2022.

672 "China Says Interpol Seeks Arrest of Tycoon Guo Wengui," *BBC*, April 20, 2017.

700 to 539;[673] *Vice* calculated their collective net loss to be more than half a trillion dollars, attributed to government "crackdowns."[674] *Bloomberg* also blamed Common Prosperity, reporting that summer that China's richest real estate barons had lost $65 billion that year due to the government's interventions.[675] During both years, China's GDP continued to grow; unlike Russia, where the wealthy had suffered in proportion with the economic hardship that affected the entire country, much of the riches lost by the Chinese bourgeoisie had been redistributed to the other classes of their society.

Though the Western press often exaggerates out of class solidarity, legal punishments for Chinese billionaires found guilty of crimes can be quite severe—even for the type of white-collar offenses and financial double-dealing that is practically legal for the wealthy in the United States and other bourgeois dictatorships. Huang Guangyu, a retail magnate who according to *Time* was once the richest man in China,[676] was sentenced to fourteen years in prison in 2010 for bribery and insider trading, ten of which he served before being paroled.[677] In 2020, real estate billionaire Ren Zhiqiang was sentenced to eighteen years in prison for embezzling millions in public funds.[678] In July of 2021, Sun Dawu, billionaire owner of a private agricultural corporation, was also sentenced to eighteen years for a variety of crimes including "conducting coercive trade, illegal mining, illegal occupation of agricultural land [and] illegal absorption of public deposits."[679] Later that year, Alvin Chau, a billionaire casino owner from Macao, was arrested for violating the PRC's gambling regulations.[680] Occasionally, rich white-collar criminals are publicly shamed or even executed, as in the case of Lai Xiaomin; of Zeng Chengjie, who was found guilty of defrauding thousands of victims through a ponzi

673 Forbes, "World's Billionaires List: The Richest in 2022."

674 Alastair McCready, "Why Are Chinese Billionaires $500 Billion Poorer Than Last Year?," *VICE*, April 6, 2022.

675 Venus Feng, "Property Tycoons Lose $65 Billion After China Curbs Excesses," *Bloomberg*, June 6, 2022.

676 James McGregor, "Huang Guangyu," TIME, May 8, 2006.

677 Jason Dean and Jeffrey Ng, "Ex-Gome Chairman Sentenced to 14 Years in Prison," *Wall Street Journal*, May 18, 2010.

678 Steven Jiang, "Chinese Tycoon Who Criticized Xi Jinping's Handling of Coronavirus Jailed for 18 Years," *CNN Business*, September 22, 2020.

679 Ben Westcott, "Outspoken Chinese Billionaire Sun Dawu Sentenced to 18 Years in Prison," *CNN Business*, July 29, 2021.

680 Eduardo Baptista, "Arrest of Macau's 'junket Mogul' Rattles the World's Largest Gambling Hub," *Reuters*, November 30, 2021.

scheme that netted him billions of yuan (and eventually a lethal injec-
tion);[681] and of Jiang Xiyun, the chairman of Hengfeng Bank, who was
sentenced to death in 2019 for taking bribes and embezzling over $100
million.[682] "Why Do Chinese Billionaires Keep Ending Up in Prison?"
wondered a 2013 headline in the *Atlantic*.[683] They didn't always; the first
anticorruption campaign during the second phase of Reform and Opening
Up led to the execution of fourteen billionaires over a period of eight
years.[684]

A study published in 2012 by academics from the China Europe
International Business School and the Shanghai University of Finance
and Economics found that an entrepreneur's inclusion on the Hurun Rich
List (a domestic Chinese equivalent of the *Forbes* list) made them much
more likely to experience serious negative social, legal, and economic
consequences—from both the government and the people at large.
(Indeed, the list is colloquially better known in China as the "kill pigs
list" according to the *Atlantic*.[685]) Referenced in the study was a poll of
the Chinese population carried out by the *People's Daily*, which found
that 69% viewed the rich either "badly" or "really badly." According to
the authors in their conclusion:

> We find that when the Rich List is announced, investors react
> negatively to the companies controlled by the listed entrepreneurs
> and their market values drop significantly in the following three
> years and the government is reluctant to assist listed entrepre-
> neurs and their companies, and even monitors them more closely.
> Furthermore, listed entrepreneurs are far more likely to be investi-
> gated, arrested and charged than other entrepreneurs. In addition,
> they tend to conceal profits through negative earnings management
> to avoid public attention. Finally, we observe that the foregoing

---

681 Mamta Badkar, "22 Chinese People Who Were Handed The Death Sentence
For White Collar Crime," Business Insider, July 15, 2013.

682 "China Sentences Ex-Chairman of Hengfeng Bank to Death," *Bloomberg
News,* December 26, 2019.

683 Rebecca Chao, "Why Do Chinese Billionaires Keep Ending Up in Prison?,"
The Atlantic, January 29, 2013.

684 "China Executes 14 Billionaires in 8 Years, Culture News Reports,"
Bloomberg News, July 22, 2011.

685 Rebecca Chao.

negative reactions are more pronounced for firms involved in rent-seeking industries and with lower charitable donations.[686]

This is of course the polar opposite of the United States (both of its government and of its cultural superstructure) and elsewhere in the capitalist world, where wealth is more often all but worshiped and the state exists to do the bidding of the imperialist bourgeoisie. But again, how do these circumstances compare to those in national-bourgeois anti-imperialist states?

With the horror of the Yeltsin era and its contrast with their socialist past still well within living memory, there can be no doubt that today Russians generally dislike the rich. According to a poll by the Russian Public Opinion Research Center, only 9% of Russians believe that their ultra-wealthy oligarchs do more good than harm.[687] Yet at the same time, as of this writing, Vladimir Putin's government is more solidly in power than ever, with Putin himself consistently enjoying approval ratings in excess of 60%;[688] citing an independent poll, the *New York Times* reported that it had increased to 83% following the military intervention in Ukraine.[689] As shown in Chapter Four, Putin, as the agent of the Russian national bourgeoisie, occasionally had reason to punish the more rebellious compradors; but apart from this small handful of exceptions, and his occasional rhetoric condemning capital flight, over the course of his decades-long presidency the government has taken few actions aligning with the people's wishes regarding Russia's billionaire elite. Despite polls showing that a majority of Russians favor a return to the Soviet system,[690] Putin himself makes no pretense of being a communist at all. If political power can today be so easily maintained without intervening

686 Xianjie He, Oliver M. Rui, and Tusheng Xiao, *The Price of Being a Billionaire in China: Evidence Based on Hurun Rich List* (July 10, 2012). Available at SSRN: https://ssrn.com/abstract=2102998

687 The Russian Public Opinion Research Center (VCIOM), "Are There Oligarchs in Russia? Who Are They?" VCIOM, April 12, 2018.

688 Ilya Arkhipov, "Putin's Approval Rating Slips Amid Covid Surge, Ukraine Tensions," *Bloomberg,* December 2, 2021.

689 Ivan Nechepurenko, "Faced with Foreign Pressure, Russians Rally around Putin, Poll Shows," *New York Times,* March 31, 2022.

690 Левада-Центр (Levada Center), "СТРУКТУРА И ВОСПРОИЗВОДСТВО ПАМЯТИ О СОВЕТСКОМ СОЮЗЕ" [Structure and Reproduction of the Memory of the Soviet Union.].

in the domestic class struggle on workers' behalf,[691] the hypothesis of the Communist Party of China being an instrument of a dictatorship by the national bourgeoisie cannot be reconciled with its frequent persecution of that very class. Indeed, if it were true, there would seem to be little sense in the Chinese bourgeoisie keeping the Communist Party around at all.

During the Cold War, there was of course a benefit and strong incentive for a country or political organization to self-apply the label Marxist-Leninist. Doing so usually meant Soviet (or sometimes Chinese, East German, &c.) aid, cheap loans, military support, and favorable trade relations, whether the recipients truly believed in the possibility of a continuing global revolution or not. Today, there is no significant institution of any kind coming to the PRC's aid for ideological reasons, nor any country that would discontinue trade or diplomatic relations should the PRC declare it has abandoned its trajectory towards communism for good. Since the Communist Party of China still openly professes Marxism-Leninism in a world that has grown so hostile to the ideology, the most coherent interpretation of the Party's actions is that they reflect its word.

Since it has been shown that political power in China is exercised solely by the Communist Party, an examination must be undertaken of the Party itself, its structure, its composition, and the present status of the bourgeoisie's attempts to subvert it. The danger of such attempts is serious, and in a speech at the Party's National Conference on Organizational Work in 2013 Xi expressed deep concerns:

> To be firm in their ideals and convictions means that Party officials must cherish the lofty ideal of communism, sincerely believe in Marxism, strive ceaselessly for socialism with Chinese characteristics, and unswervingly uphold the basic theories, guideline, program, experience and requirements of the Party ...

691 Accordingly, there is the question of why the KPRF, as the successor to the Communist Party of the Soviet Union and the largest opposition party to United Russia, does not command all the votes of those who favor the old system. The stability of Putin's position is likely due to a number of factors, among them his personal popularity, his management of a controlled opposition as described in Chapter Four, and a general perception that the KPRF lacks the full legitimacy and credibility of the old CPSU. The KPRF is also in more or less full agreement with Putin's foreign policy, which obviously eclipsed domestic issues in the public consciousness in 2014 and especially in 2022. Thus as of this writing there is little pressure for Russians to vote KPRF unless or until Russia enters a severe domestic crisis or conditions otherwise change.

It should be fully admitted that most of our officials are firm in their ideals and convictions, and are politically reliable. Nevertheless, there are some Party officials who fail to meet these qualifications. Some are skeptical about communism, considering it a fantasy that will never come true; some do not believe in Marxism-Leninism but in ghosts and gods, and seek spiritual solace in feudal superstitions, showing intense interest in fortune-telling, worship of Buddha and "god's advice" for solving their problems; some have little sense of principle, justice, and right and wrong, and perform their duties in a muddle-headed manner; some even yearn for Western social systems and values, losing their confidence in the future of socialism; and others adopt an equivocal attitude towards political provocations against the leadership of the CPC, the path of socialism with Chinese characteristics and other matters of principle, passively avoid relevant arguments without the courage to express their opinions, or even deliberately deliver ambiguous messages. Isn't it a monstrous absurdity that Party officials, especially high-ranking ones, take no position in the face of major issues of principle, political incidents and sensitive issues?[692]

Many of China's billionaires have shown considerable eagerness to become part of the Communist Party; and after their membership was permitted in 2002, a few have joined quite openly. In 2012, on the eve of the 18th Party Congress (the highest body within the Communist Party) *Forbes* reported that 34 private entrepreneurs, including a few billionaires and several multi-millionaires, had been selected as delegates to the 2,270-member convention. *Forbes* claimed that one of them, Liang Wengen, the billionaire founder of the Sany Heavy Industry Company, "[stood] out as a rising political star" and was considered a "front runner" to become the first private businessman to be elected to the Central Committee, the Party's governing body chosen by the Congress every five years.[693] The same month, *China Daily* had quoted Liang saying, "My property, even my life, belongs to the Party."[694] The *South China Morning Post* reported that internet entrepreneur and billionaire Liu

---

692 Xi Jinping, *The Governance of China*, vol. 1 (2014), sec. Train and Select Good Officials.

693 Laura He, "The Super Rich Rises As China Begins Leadership Transition," *Forbes,* November 7, 2012.

694 Xinhua, "Entrepreneurs' Presence Grows at CPC Congress," November 12, 2012.

Qiangdong had publicly opined that "communism would be realised in his generation," and that Xu Jiayin, billionaire chairman of China's largest real estate developer Evergrande Group, had declared himself a proud member of the Communist Party.[695] The *People's Daily* revealed in 2018 that Alibaba founder and chairman Jack Ma, then the wealthiest man in China, was a Party member.[696]

Such unabashed toadying to power is the most quintessential expression of why the Chinese big bourgeoisie see value in joining the Communist Party: the thinly-veiled hope that membership will bring with it special privileges and perhaps even the opportunity to subvert and steer the Party further toward their class interests. Yet the fortunes of these so-called "red billionaires" have so far shown both agendas to have borne very little fruit. Contrary to *Forbes'* expectations (or hopes), Liang was not elected to the Central Committee, which as of this writing remains capitalist-free. Jack Ma, who in October of 2020 had given a speech denigrating the (state-owned) banks and the government's financial regulations, soon found that his connection to the Party did not prevent himself from becoming a target. Regulators intervened to stop his Ant Group (a private financial services corporation) from making its IPO the following month. In December, the government launched an antitrust investigation of Alibaba, and its market capitalization sank by over $200 billion.[697] The Western press speculated wildly after Ma made no public appearances for the next several weeks (an article in *Newsweek* even suggested that he may have been executed).[698] Ma eventually signaled that he would cede his control over Ant Group in 2022 to appease regulators,[699] and in 2023, in a move *Bloomberg* called "appeasing . . . a government distrustful of Big Tech," Alibaba also announced that it would split into six separate entities.[700] When the Evergrande Group went into default in 2021 following the government's new financial regulations that lowered

---

695 Zhang Lin, "Chinese Communist Party Needs to Curtail Its Presence in Private Businesses," *South China Morning Post,* November 25, 2018.

696 Huang Jingjing, "Beijing to Honor Founders of Three Internet Giants," *People's Daily,* November 26, 2018.

697 Laura He, "China Launches Antitrust Investigation into Alibaba," *CNN Business,* December 24, 2020.

698 Ewan Palmer, "As Jack Ma Goes Missing, Video Predicting He Will Either Die or Go to Jail Resurfaces," *Newsweek,* January 4, 2021.

699 Lulu Yilun Chen, "Jack Ma Plans to Give Up Control of Ant, Dow Jones Says," *BNN Bloomberg,* July 28, 2022.

700 Jane Zhang, Zheping Huang, Henry Ren, and Alice Huang, "Alibaba's $32 Billion Day Signals Breakups for China Tech," *Bloomberg,* March 28, 2023.

corporate debt limits, Xu Jiayin found that his Party membership did not help him one iota. The Chinese government did intervene—but not to provide a multi-billion-dollar bailout as the United States Federal Reserve had given AIG and other corporations during the 2008 financial crisis. Instead, according to the *Wall Street Journal*, the government began to dismantle his real estate giant in a "controlled implosion," compelling it to sell assets to other companies while keeping the market stable.[701] Xu Jiayin himself, who ultimately lost 98% of his own personal fortune (ceasing to be a billionaire) after the government also insisted he use it to help pay Evergrande's debts,[702] was later arrested in 2023.[703]

Even though wealthy capitalists are now allowed in government, the evidence suggests that their role is mostly if not entirely to be carefully managed token participants or observers who are not allowed access to any actual power. Their invitations to the 18th Party Congress probably did not launch any political careers for Liang Wengen or his fellow capitalists; in fact, careers in the Congress and the Central Committee are quite short, with the latter's turnover rate usually exceeding 60% for the last several decades.[704] (Liang was not invited to the 19th Party Congress in 2017; with somewhat comic naïveté, in the same breath as their prediction of Liang's appointment to the Central Committee, *Forbes* also remarked that "to many people's surprise" real estate billionaire Wang Jianlin, who had served as a delegate to the 17th Congress, had not been invited back to the 18th.[705]) Though the Hurun Report has listed around 100 Chinese billionaires who are members of the National Political Congress,[706] Western news coverage of this factoid seldom mentions that the NPC is in reality entirely subordinate to the Communist Party, which

---

701 Keith Zhai, Elaine Yu, and Anniek Bao, "China's Plan to Manage Evergrande: Take It Apart, Slowly," *Wall Street Journal,* November 10, 2021.

702 Chloe Taylor, "Embattled China Evergrande's Founder Is No Longer a Billionaire after the Man Once Worth $42 Billion Loses 98% of His Wealth," *Yahoo! Finance,* October 25, 2023.

703 "Evergrande Founder Joins List of Chinese Tycoons Investigated, Arrested," *Reuters,* September 29, 2023.

704 Cheng Li, "Preparing For the 18th Party Congress: Procedures and Mechanisms," *China Leadership Monitor,* no. 36 (January 6, 2012): 8.

705 Laura He, "The Super Rich Rises As China Begins Leadership Transition," *Forbes,* November 7, 2012.

706 Sophia Yan, "China's Parliament Has about 100 Billionaires, According to Data from the Hurun Report," *CNBC,* March 2, 2017.

controls the selection of all delegates, and has never diverged from the Party's agenda in any meaningful way.[707]

As of 2021, the Communist Party had over 95 million members. When broken down by occupation, peasants and industrial workers formed a plurality of 34%. Another 8% were Party and government employees, and a further 27% were white-collar professional workers or managerial staff. The remainder were mostly college students and retirees; fewer than 7.6% were categorized as "other" which presumably includes capitalists as well as the petit bourgeoisie, athletes,[708] performers, and various less common occupations.[709] This percentage has not increased during Xi's tenure as General Secretary, and in fact has declined a fraction of a point since Party membership statistics were published in 2010 by the *People's Daily*.[710] Ultra-wealthy members are a drop in a vast ocean, unable to subvert anything and are constrained against deviating from the will of the proletariat by the Party's philosophy of democratic centralism, which is designed both to make the organization resilient to infiltration and to bend bad actors to its will despite their intentions.[711] Corruption of existing Party officials, rather than entryism, is the Chinese bourgeoisie's best hope of restoring their dictatorship.

Furthermore, the question must be asked: if the Party is currently the instrument of the bourgeoisie, why have they chosen Xi Jinping as its General Secretary?

Throughout his tenure, Xi has waged an unceasing struggle against corruption in the Party. In 2023, a record number of senior officials

---

707 The NPC consists of nearly 3,000 members from multiple different political parties, who are elected by local constituents only after their nominations are approved by the Communist Party.

708 Many famous athletes are members of the Party, such as table tennis world champion Fan Zhendong [Xinhua, 国乒男队重温入党誓词 ("National Table Tennis Men's Team Renews Party Oath")] and speed-skating Olympic gold medalist Wu Dajing, who was a delegate to the 20th Party Congress in 2022 ("A Look at How Delegates to Upcoming 20th CPC National Congress Were Elected," *Xinhua*, September 29, 2022).

709 "Strength in Organization," *Global Times*, June 30, 2021.

710 "The Communist Party of China (CPC, CCP)," *China Today*, October 22, 2022.

711 Communist parties throughout the world, in fact, have always expected infiltration. A legendary anecdote, supposedly originating from the British Socialist Workers Party, illustrates the effectiveness of the democratic centralist model: when a cadre was exposed as a police spy and forced to leave the organization, rather than express dismay over the betrayal, an organizer instead bemoaned the fact that he had lost his best newspaper salesman.

were investigated or punished by Xi's signature policy.[712] Though many high-profile Party officials have lost their positions, their freedom, and sometimes even their lives as a result of the anticorruption campaign, the success of these efforts can also be found in statistical evidence. A 2018 study published in the Oxford University Press's *Quarterly Journal of Economics* attempted to measure corruption in the Party through an analysis of land transactions by private firms connected to Party officials, analyzing how much more likely these firms were to obtain a discount on leasing land from the government. The authors conclude:

> To curb corruption, President Xi Jinping stepped up investigations and strengthened personnel control at the province level. Using a spatially matched sample (e.g., within a 500-meter radius), we find a reduction in corruption of between 42.6% and 31.5% in the provinces either targeted by the central inspection teams or whose party secretary was replaced by one appointed by Xi. Accordingly, this crackdown on corruption has also significantly reduced the promotional prospects of those local officials who rely on supplying a discount to get ahead.[713]

Nor are such anticorruption efforts merely excuses to persecute Xi's own personal rivals. "[T]he officials being neutralized," *Politico* observed of the spike in investigations in 2023, "are not members of hostile political factions but loyalists from the inner ring of Xi's own clique. . . ."[714] Whatever its shortcomings or inadequacies may have been in the past, anticorruption in China has now become institutionalized and does not play favorites.

Ideologically, Xi has consistently sounded like the very last person the Chinese capitalists would prefer to be running the Party. Marxism featured prominently in his speech to the 20th Party Congress in October 2022, in which he called it the Party's "fundamental guiding ideology";[715] but this focus on ideology has scarcely been less strong at any time during

---

712 "Xi's Corruption Crackdown Nets Record Number of Top Officials," *Bloomberg News,* November 16, 2023.

713 Ting Chen and James Kai-sing Kung, "Busting the 'Princelings': The Campaign Against Corruption in China's Primary Land Market," *The Quarterly Journal of Economics* 134, no. 1 (February 2019): 185–226.

714 "China's Xi Goes Full Stalin with Purge," *Politico,* December 6, 2023.

715 Xinhua Live Record, 二十大报告（实录全文）[Report of the 20th National Congress of the Communist Party of China].

Xi's tenure as General Secretary. In his collected speeches and writings, Xi has repeatedly stressed not only the need to fight corruption, but the need for greater Marxist education. "We should not abandon Marxism-Leninism and Mao Zedong Thought; otherwise, we would be deprived of our foundation. . ."[716] he said in a speech at a group study session of the Political Bureau of the 18th Central Committee. In a 2013 speech, Xi said, "Our publicity and theoretical work aims to consolidate Marxism as the guiding ideology in China"[717] and outlined plans for expanding political education not just within the Party, but throughout Chinese society:

> Marxism must be a required course in Party schools, executive leadership academies, academies of social sciences, institutes of higher learning and groups for theoretical studies. These places should serve as the centers for studying, researching and disseminating Marxism.
>
> New and young officials in particular should work hard to study Marxist theory, learn to observe and solve problems from the Marxist stand, viewpoint and method, and become firm in their ideals and convictions.[718]

By 2016, over 1 million undergraduates were enrolled in the Communist Youth League's Marxist training programs in 1,000 colleges across the country.[719] "Cheers greeted [President Xi Jinping] as he toured Beijing's Renmin University of China in April" as he told students and teachers that they must "continue to promote the modernization of Marxism," *Bloomberg* reported in 2022. The visit, said *Bloomberg*, "highlighted China's pivot to funding and supporting researchers who are suspicious of the power of private business, with some advocating barring private capital from entire sectors. The message was clear: In today's China, Marxism is back, and investors had better take note."[720]

Xi frequently speaks of the Party's goal of building a modern socialist country by the PRC's centenary in 2049, and has reiterated the "long-term

---

716 Xi Jinping, *The Governance of China*, vol. 1 (2014), sec. Study, Disseminate and Implement the Guiding Principles of the 18th CPC National Congress.

717 Xi Jinping, vol. 1, sec. Enhance Publicity and Theoretical Work.

718 Xi Jinping, vol. 1, sec. Enhance Publicity and Theoretical Work.

719 Zhang Yu, "China Pushes Forward Marxist Training on Campus, Attracts 1 Million Students," *Global Times,* June 16, 2016.

720 Tom Hancock, "Marxism Makes a Comeback in China's Crackdown on 'Disorderly Capital,'" *Bloomberg,* June 6, 2022.

goal of realizing communism" and the need to "stand firm against various erroneous views aimed at abandoning socialism, and rectify all erroneous and unrealistic mindsets, policies and measures that go beyond the current primary stage of socialism."[721] Of the Party itself, Xi remarked in another speech in 2013:

> First, we must make sure that the working class is our main force. The working class is China's leading class; it represents China's advanced productive forces and relations of production; it is our Party's most steadfast and reliable class foundation; and it is the main force for realizing a moderately prosperous society in all respects, and upholding and building socialism with Chinese characteristics.[722]

Though the bourgeoisie may usually be taken at their word when they identify their enemies publicly through their newspapers and media institutions, they are at their *most* trustworthy when they confer amongst themselves and feel a confidence that their words will not be exposed to the eyes of the people. What information about Xi do the managers of the super-empire privately consider relevant and reliable? A leaked U.S. diplomatic cable from 2009 said of the Communist Party's future General Secretary:

> According to a well connected Embassy contact, Politburo Standing Committee Member and Vice President Xi Jinping is "exceptionally ambitious," confident and focused, and has had his "eye on the prize" from early adulthood. Unlike many youth who "made up for lost time by having fun" after the Cultural Revolution, *Xi "chose to survive by becoming redder than the red."* [emphasis added][723]

The cable further related the view of the embassy's contact, who had had a long association with Xi during his formative years, that "Xi also does not care at all about money and is not corrupt." Of Xi's attitude toward corruption itself, the cable reported:

---

721 Xi Jinping, *The Governance of China*, vol. 1 (2014), sec. Study, Disseminate and Implement the Guiding Principles of the 18th CPC National Congress.

722 Xi Jinping, vol. 1, sec. Hard Work Makes Dreams Come True.

723 "Portrait of Vice President Xi Jinping: 'Ambitious Survivor' of the Cultural Revolution" [leaked cable], *Wikileaks,* November 16, 2009.

Xi knows how very corrupt China is and is repulsed by the all-en-compassing commercialization of Chinese society, with its atten-dant nouveau riche, official corruption, loss of values, dignity, and self-respect, and such "moral evils" as drugs and prostitution, the professor stated. *The professor speculated that if Xi were to become the Party General Secretary, he would likely aggressively attempt to address these evils, perhaps at the expense of the new moneyed class.* [emphasis added][724]

To summarize: in the latter phase of Reform and Opening Up, the Party's control and popularity have both increased, while the influence of the big bourgeoisie upon the Party has declined. The bourgeoisie, both inside and outside the Party, has waged a continuous class struggle against the proletarian character of the Party through graft and corruption, striving to twist the Party to its own ends; yet the Party's response, expressed most dramatically through their selection of Xi Jinping as General Secretary, has thus far been much stronger, and indicates that in general, the left wing of the Party is dominant. China's economy remains in transition, but it has some time ago ceased to transition toward capitalism and is now transitioning toward socialism, though the time scale remains long.

In his *Critique of the Gotha Programme*, Karl Marx wrote:

Between capitalist and communist society there lies the period of the revolutionary transformation of the one into the other. Corresponding to this is also a political transition period in which the state can be nothing but the *revolutionary dictatorship of the proletariat.*[725]

In the autumn of 1917, just weeks after the Bolsheviks had taken power in Petrograd, Lenin wrote:

For socialism is merely the next step forward from state-capitalist monopoly. Or, in other words, socialism is merely state-capitalist monopoly *which is made to serve the interests of the whole people* and has to that extent *ceased* to be capitalist monopoly.[726]

---

724 "Portrait of Vice President Xi Jinping" [leaked cable].
725 Karl Marx, *Critique of the Gotha Programme* (1875), chap. IV.
726 V. I. Lenin, *The Impending Catastrophe and How to Combat It* (1917), sec. Can We Go Forward If We Fear To Advance Towards Socialism?

In 1922, to rebuild after the destructive civil war, the Soviet Union adopted the New Economic Policy, which according to Lenin allowed the creation of "a form of capitalism that is deliberately permitted and restricted by the working class."[727] Writing in 1999, Marxist academic Domenico Losurdo drew an explicit parallel between Reform and Opening Up and Lenin's New Economic Policy, evaluating the PRC's program as "quite conscious of the necessity to connect continually socialism, democracy, and the market with one another."[728]

In light of this analysis, the question of whether China is presently "capitalist" or "socialist"—a question that is frequently debated within circles of the political left the world over—can be answered. In the words of Xi himself in 2014:

> We have set the goals of completing the building of a moderately prosperous society in all respects by the centenary of the CPC in 2021 and building China into a modern socialist country that is prosperous, strong, democratic, culturally advanced, and harmonious by the centenary of the PRC in 2049 so as to realize the Chinese Dream of the rejuvenation of the Chinese nation.[729]

Thus *even the Communist Party* does not apply the label "socialist" to the PRC without qualification,[730] but instead has the *goal* of transforming it into a modern socialist country by the year 2049. On the question of whether the USSR (the Union of Soviet Socialist Republics) could properly be called "socialist," Lenin had this to say in 1921:

> No one, I think, in studying the question of the economic system of Russia, has denied its transitional character. Nor, I think, has any Communist denied that the term Soviet Socialist Republic implies the determination of the Soviet power to achieve the transition to

---

727 V. I. Lenin, "To the Russian Colony in North America," January 10, 1923.

728 Domenico Losurdo, "Flight from History? The Communist Movement between Self-Criticism and Self-Contempt (1999)," sec. VI. The People's Republic of China and the historical analysis of socialism, *Nature, Society, and Thought* 13, no. 4 (October 2000): 494–501.

729 Xi Jinping, *The Governance of China*, vol. 1 (2014), sec. Hard Work Makes Dreams Come True.

730 Typically, Xi and other officials speaking on behalf of the PRC have referred to China's current economic system as the "primary stage" of socialism.

socialism, and not that the existing economic system is recognised as a socialist order.[731]

Therefore, the question of whether China is "still" socialist or not is entirely a matter of semantics. In every country that has existed that has ever been called socialist, this label has had at best an aspirational, rather than material, significance. Neither communism nor socialism, as economic systems by the Marxist definition, have yet been established; the question of the character of the Chinese economic system that is so often posed is therefore in reality the question of whether the PRC can *politically* still be considered a revolutionary dictatorship of the proletariat or not. The increasingly clear qualitative difference between Western social democracy, which is in terminal decline, and Chinese social democracy, which is healthy and ascendant, is nothing more than two different answers to the question of which class (or alliance of classes) is in control of the government. While foreign (especially Western) communists may increasingly dismiss the PRC's accomplishments as "mere social democracy," it is also increasingly clear that social democracy can expand nowhere but in a proletarian state as long as world imperialism remains in the super-imperialist stage.

One final question is useful to ask: if the bourgeoisie have not already prevailed in China, then what further consequences would ensue if they were to do so?

According to Losurdo:

> To speak of a restoration of capitalism in China would be looking at the problem too superficially. A solid bourgeoisie has undoubtedly emerged there, although it currently has no possibility of transforming its economic power into political power. We need to understand the difficult situation in which the Chinese leaders find themselves. On the one hand, they have to push forward with the democratization process. This is an essential element of socialist modernization as it is also a means of consolidating power (today the only principle of legitimation is that of investiture from below). On the other hand, they must avoid having the democratization process lead to a conquest of power by the bourgeoisie, which, by the way, is the goal sought in an entirely unremitting fashion by

---

731 V. I. Lenin, *The Tax in Kind (The Significance Of The New Policy And Its Conditions)* (1921).

the United States. It is resolved to undermine the hegemony of the Communist Party by any means necessary. . . .[732]

The ground that was surrendered to the capitalist mode of production during the first phase of Reform and Opening Up does not by any means represent the whole or even the commanding heights of the Chinese economy. State-owned enterprises still have a monopoly on key industries such as energy, telecommunications, aviation, and other transportation,[733] and occupy a significant portion of most other sectors, heavily subsidized by the government with cheap credit. The financial industry, as shown earlier, is almost entirely controlled by the state. If proletarian power was at last to be broken, these industries would face a terrible reckoning with the bourgeoisie. Mass privatizations could follow, causing increases in unemployment, poverty, and mortality, perhaps even to the degree that Russia experienced during its capitalist restoration in the 1990s. A national bourgeoisie, fully in control of the state, could unwind the social-democratic redistribution that the latter Reform period has steadily institutionalized; real incomes would likely decline, especially in rural areas, as they have under national-bourgeois governments in Iran and Russia since the end of commodities boom of the 2000s,[734] while the billionaire class would reap galactic profits. Land, which is still collectively owned by the state and currently leased, rather than sold, to private entities, would be entirely privatized; housing prices and homelessness would then increase, and bourgeois families would consolidate generational wealth through the inheritance of estates.

Though these are already sufficiently grim examples, we should not deceive ourselves that they would be the worst that may befall China should it face a complete capitalist restoration. If a *comprador* bourgeoisie were to gain supremacy even for a short time, it is all but guaranteed that China's large territory and multi-ethnic population would undergo a process of balkanization. Just as the Soviet Union dissolved into over a dozen individual countries along largely ethnic lines, China's landlocked

---

732 Domenico Losurdo, "Flight from History?"

733 State-owned Assets Supervision and Administration Commission of the State Council (SASAC), "Name List of Central SOEs."

734 Iran's declining real wages are described in Chapter Four; according to a study from Novosibirsk State University, per capita real income was stagnant in Russia between 2016 and 2020, and in many regions declined overall since the early 2010s. [Konstantin Gluschenko, *Costs of Living and Real Incomes in the Russian Regions* (Department of Economics, Novosibirsk State University, February 16, 2022), 13.]

minority-majority autonomous regions such as Tibet and Xinjiang, as well as other highly diverse regions such as Yunnan and Guangxi, would most likely be transformed into separate neocolonies. The super-empire is already poised to effect this transition, should the PRC fall; the National Endowment for Democracy spends millions of dollars per year to foment unrest in Tibet[735] and Xinjiang[736] through NGOs composed of exiles and expatriates, whose reactionary leaders are expected to form new comprador governments that will open these regions fully to the iron fist of neoliberalism and the tyranny of exploitation by international finance.

The world will not soon forget what happened after socialism was destroyed in Yugoslavia, which out of all the socialist countries had a multi-ethnic character most closely resembling China's minority autonomous regions. Throughout the 1990s, as the IMF ruthlessly strangled the Yugoslavian economy and the super-empire exploited worsening conditions to goad the people further and further toward ethnic nationalism, the country dissolved in a series of wars and genocidal massacres. Given that this Western-authored catastrophe still lingers within living memory, is it any wonder that the Harvard Kennedy School researchers found that minorities in the inland regions of China were more likely to express support for the central government, which under the guidance of the Communist Party currently forms the strongest bulwark against such a fate?[737]

In the summer of 2021, after a severe typhoon season brought unprecedented rainfall in central China, floods devastated Henan and several other provinces along China's major rivers. Hundreds were killed and many thousands more were displaced. The government immediately launched a massive rescue effort, mobilizing tens of thousands of workers to save those stranded by flood waters.[738] A viral post on Weibo that day described a popular sentiment among the people:

735 National Endowment for Democracy, "Tibet (China) 2020."

736 National Endowment for Democracy, "Xinjiang / East Turkestan (China) 2020."

737 Edward Cunningham, Tony Saich, and Jessie Turiel, *Understanding CCP Resilience: Surveying Chinese Public Opinion Through Time* (Ash Center for Democratic Governance and Innovation, July 2020).

738 Xu Ruiqing, Liu Jinhui, Sun Qingqing, Feng Dapeng, and Niu Shaojie, "China Launches Massive Rescue Efforts after Henan Rainstorms," *Xinhua,* July 21, 2021.

Us common folk, why do we defend the government? Is it because we're stupid plebians who don't know any better? No, it's because we have a conscience. As the storms rage and the rivers overflow, they went to clear the drainage shafts, dig ditches, stack sandbags, doing door to door inspections, sending doctors and medicine, food and water. And aren't those government workers also people like us? "They're supposed to!" some say. Don't give me that, where do things ever just happen because they're "supposed to" in this world?

In America at the feet of their beachside condos, the maggots on the corpses have already bred for four generations[739]—who was "supposed to" take care of those souls? When the pandemic came, their government was clear they did not care who lived or died, they even gave it a name, "herd immunity," forcing people to admit that they were "supposed" to die, and who could they petition otherwise?

As a student of history, I have one main takeaway: common folk like you and I, our lives are like the morning dew on the grass. When Heaven shows its power with intention of taking human lives, surviving is good fortune, and dying is expected—what rhyme or reason is there to speak of?

In those times, when some people stand up, take responsibility, and put your welfare on their heart, sacrificing themselves to come wrestle with Heaven, then that's you and I's undeserved fortune—to say nothing of their top tier competence in doing so too. [emphasis added]

Others treat us with the heart of a Bodhisattva, thus I repay them with a righteous heart—neither of us failing each other—this is the world the Buddhists spoke of. Who am I to play high and mighty at this critical hour? When the waves come crashing down at me, what good is it to have felt sanctimonious and rebellious as I take my last breath in the sewer?[740]

---

739 Refers to the condominium building collapse in Surfside, Florida, on June 24, 2021. The bodies of those killed in the disaster were not all found until weeks afterward, and at the time of this post (nearly a full month later), recovery efforts were still ongoing.

740 No-zhuangbility, "我们这些平头小百姓，为什么替政府说话?" [Why do we ordinary people speak for the government?].

CHAPTER EIGHT

The Propaganda Siege

"The crown prince was being sent as a hostage to Handan.
Pang Cong, who was to accompany him, asked the king of Wei:
'If today one man said there is a tiger in the marketplace,
would Your Majesty believe it?'

"The king said: 'No.'

"Pang Cong said: 'If two men said there is a tiger
in the marketplace, would Your Majesty believe it?'

"The king said: 'I would doubt it.'

"Pang Cong said: 'If three men said there is a tiger
in the marketplace, would Your Majesty believe it?'

"The king said: 'I would believe it.'

"Pang Cong said: 'It is clear there is no tiger in the
marketplace, but the words of three men can still make a tiger.
Now Handan is farther from Daliang[741] than the marketplace,
and more than three men here would speak ill of your servant.
I hope Your Majesty will not take them at face value.'"

—战国策 [*Strategies of the Warring States*], compiled circa 20 B.C.[742]

The Russian bourgeoisie, as shown in Chapter Four, are indisputably real and in control of their government. Western news media seem to agree universally on this point and waste no opportunity to refer to them as "oligarchs" or an "oligarchy"—not even when in the very next breath they portray this purported oligarchy's representative, Vladimir Putin, as an absolute dictator. On the other hand, though Xi Jinping is named a "dictator" nearly as often as Putin, and though the Chinese bourgeoisie are vastly more wealthy and nearly an order of magnitude more numerous than Russia's, the phrase "Chinese oligarchs" is quite seldom if ever printed. In China there are no oligarchs; instead, there are "entrepreneurs," "tycoons," "billionaires," and perhaps a "mogul" or two.

---

741 The capital of Wei, now known as Kaifeng, Henan.

742 Liu Xiang (compiler), "Strategies of the Warring States," a collection of stories, speeches, and historical records from the Warring States period (490–221 BC)

The owners of the Western media—the *Western* oligarchy—have clearly done much the same class analysis as this book and arrived at the same conclusions. The Russian capitalists have been designated enemies while the Chinese capitalists remain potential allies and perhaps future compradors; the Communist Party, as the oppressor of the Chinese capitalists and the highest expression of peasant and proletarian power in China, is of course the Western bourgeoisie's greatest enemy.

By its very existence, the Party presents by far the greatest threat to the Western capitalists' dominance of class society. The task of the Western press is therefore twofold: first, to lionize and evoke sympathy for the Chinese capitalist, and second—far more importantly—at all costs to vilify and incite hatred for the Party. As shown in Chapter Seven, the Party has unchallenged control over the government; therefore, it too must receive the same treatment, as must Xi himself, as its chosen representative. The Western bourgeoisie had of course always been hostile to the Chinese government, but far less so until the turning point during the late 2000s, when they at last began to realize that proletarian power in China was not diminishing but increasing.

Nothing positive regarding China may therefore be printed. Any overture of friendship the Chinese government makes toward another country can only be a nefarious ruse, certain to bring the other country harm, either then and there or at some later date. The PRC's great infrastructure projects, when they are begun, can only be doomed to failure; and when they are completed, they can only have been a colossal waste of money. Initiatives to help the poor can only be a sham; if they do have undeniably positive effects, those effects must have come at too great a cost. Every member of the Party can only be irredeemably corrupt, except for those who are actually arrested for corruption. If any Chinese people speak positively of the Party, this can only be the result of the government's brainwashing. Those who speak critically of the Party, however, are always brave and clear-thinking truth-tellers, soon to be "disappeared" by the government; when they are seen in public thereafter, their reappearance must somehow be "staged" by the government. There can be no criminals in China, only political prisoners who have been falsely accused; neither are these political prisoners kept in prisons, for there can be no prisons in China, only prison *camps*.

In fact, every policy adopted by the government can only be the latest expression of its brutal totalitarianism. The Party can be the author only of evil, for the sake only of evil. Any and all reporting on China must presume the guilt, rather than the innocence, of the Party. If no evidence can be found of the Party's sinister abuses of human rights, this can only indicate the government's terrifyingly efficient censorship. No story casting the Chinese government in an unflattering light is too outlandish for publication, and no acknowledgement of its successes may be printed without heavy qualification. Any and all research into Chinese government policy that has a suitably critical conclusion is fit to be published, whether it is credible, peer-reviewed, and methodologically rigorous or not; any such research with positive findings is not to be trusted—especially if it is conducted by Chinese academics, even when their research is done independently of the government.

Through the hegemony of the super-empire, anti-China propaganda has become ubiquitous. The market dominance of Western information technology over the internet ensures that it is the first, and often only, narrative read by the average user. English-language news has become completely saturated with stories demonizing China, each careful to include a multitude of references to other such stories, so that the weakness of any one claim in particular cannot be evaluated without being overwhelmed by the collective. The most spurious or unverified details are typically hidden behind paywalls or multiple layers of citations, deterring skeptics by adding barriers to the formulation of any specific criticisms.

The audience is of course not just the Western public, but the entire world. The NED and other soft-power NGOs transform anti-China propaganda into pro-Western political power in regions throughout the periphery, seeking constantly to redirect toward China any existing anger over unrelated grievances. An even greater expansion of this system is being sought. In early 2022, the U.S. House of Representatives voted to spend $500 million dollars to produce journalism for overseas audiences that was critical of China, the majority of which was to be allocated through the U.S. Agency for Global Media. The Senate, in their version of the legislation, went even further, seeking a total of $1.5 billion that should be spent in order to "raise awareness of and increase transparency regarding the negative impact of activities related to the Belt and Road Initiative."[743] To maintain its control over the poor and working classes in the periphery and at home, the super-empire must at all costs keep them divided. Any local or international organization premised upon class solidarity with the Chinese worker cannot be allowed to flourish, and the Communist Party's

---

743 Lee Harris, "Congress Proposes $500 Million for Negative News Coverage of China," *The American Prospect,* February 9, 2022.

class character and its relationship to the people must be obscured; it may be portrayed—all 95 million members—only as a vague instrument of "authoritarianism" or "dictatorship," a wicked and hostile antagonist to the masses, and never as a champion of their interests.

It then follows that it is of greatest importance to publish any and all information that might draw attention to the Party or the government's shortcomings with respect to ethnic minorities, the rural poor, women's rights, religious freedom, the treatment of those with non-conforming gender identities and sexual orientations, and other categories of marginalization. If any such shortcomings are real, they must be broadcasted again and again, even long after they have later been addressed or ameliorated by the government's actions; if such shortcomings are mild, unforthcoming, or unverifiable, new ones must be invented or inferred.

Media Decoupling

> *"[T]he amount of energy needed to refute bullshit is*
> *an order of magnitude bigger than to produce it."*
> —Alberto Brandolini[744]

The 1980s saw a period of unrest in the Tibet Autonomous Region which was quickly seized upon by the Western press. In 1989 the *Washington Post* published an op-ed that related accounts from Tibetan exiles living in India, who described harrowing oppression by the Chinese authorities allegedly enforcing coercive and draconian family planning policies, including nightmarish "birth-control teams" that roamed from village to village, performing forced abortions and sterilizations of native Tibetan women. The infanticide of healthy newborns was supposedly commonplace. A pair of "refugee Buddhist monks" described a lurid picture of a "growing pile of fetuses" outside one such team's tent next to their monastery as they proceeded to mass-sterilize the entire village.[745] A report published in 1987 by the U.S. Tibet Committee (an NGO) claimed that the PRC had adopted a "final solution" designed to "within ten to twenty years" cause "the demise of the Tibetan race itself."[746]

---

744 Alberto Brandolini (@ziobrando), Twitter post, January 1, 2013: "The Bullshit Asimmetry: The Amount of Energy Needed to Refute Bullshit Is an Order of Magnitude Bigger than to Produce It."

745 Blake Kerr, "Witness to China's Shame," *Washington Post,* February 25, 1989.

746 John F. Avedon, *Tibet Today: Current Conditions and Prospects* (Wisdom

Academics at Beijing's Population Research Institute disputed these accusations, citing actual policy that largely exempted rural Tibetans from the government's family planning initiatives. Professors Melvyn Goldstein and Cynthia Beall of Case Western Reserve University in Ohio noted that "The gulf between these very different accounts of birth control policy in Tibet is so enormous and the reliability of the respective data sources (Tibetan refugees versus published data from China) so uncertain that there has been no way to make an informed judgment on this issue." In an attempt to resolve this contradiction, they traveled to Tibet to conduct an extensive study of ethnic Tibetan rural communities in China.[747]

Goldstein and Beall spent 16 months performing fieldwork in the Tibet Autonomous Region, employing traditional anthropological methods involving formal and informal interviews. All conversations were conducted in the Tibetan language, and according to their report they were neither accompanied by government officials nor were there any restrictions placed upon such meetings.[748] According to the data collected, they concluded:

> ... the Tibetan Autonomous Region is actually experiencing high population growth rates rather than suffering a policy of coercive and restrictive birth control that is causing population decline and threatening the continued existence of Tibetans. At current growth rates, over half a million Tibetans will be added to the TAR's population in the last decade of this century.[749]

They in fact remarked upon the excessive burden the increase in population would likely have upon limited resources and farmland in Tibet—exactly the harmful scenario that it was the purpose of actual reasonable family planning interventions to prevent. Only in the cities were any family planning policies enforced, and then only the standard (at that time) one-child limit upon the Han residents (who comprise the vast majority of the Chinese population overall), and a two-child limit upon Tibetans who were themselves government officials or members of the Communist Party. They directly observed many large families and

---

Publications, 1988), 2.

747 Melvyn C. Goldstein and Cynthia M. Beall, "China's Birth Control Policy in the Tibet Autonomous Region: Myths and Realities," *Asian Survey* 31, no. 3 (March 1991): 290–91.

748 Goldstein and Beall, 293.

749 Goldstein and Beall, 300.

found no evidence of "roving sterilization teams" or of forced abortions or infanticide anywhere.[750]

A likely factor in the stark discrepancy between their findings and the dominant Western media narrative, suggested Goldstein and Beall, were exaggerations or fabrications by the other reports' refugee interviewees, who by the conditions of their exile (either forced or elective) to India may have harbored deep-seated anger and hostility toward the Chinese government. They also criticized the methodological flaws of the reports, particularly their authors' reliance on selectively choosing to interview only refugees who had a lurid story to tell, rather than comparing and contrasting refugee experiences in any systematic way. The reports that the Western press had been so eager to publish, they determined, were "an illustration of how easily strong political emotions can misinform objectivity."[751] Barry Sautman, a Professor of Social Science at Hong Kong University of Science and Technology, in a detailed analysis published in the *Texas International Law Journal*, offered the explanation that such exaggerations might be a deliberate media strategy adopted by the Tibetan émigré community: "[w]ith many causes competing for the attention of those from whom the Tibetan émigrés seek support, it may appear to them that the most extreme, rather than the most accurate, language best serves their cause."[752]

A decade later, Goldstein, Beall, and their research partners returned to Tibet, this time to evaluate similarly conflicting claims regarding the welfare of rural Tibetans. A report submitted to the United Nations by a group of Western NGOs in 1998 again accused the PRC of imposing forced abortions and sterilizations upon Tibetan women, and levying heavy fines including the dispossession of land as penalties for any deviations from the family planning restrictions. A *Washington Post* headline declared "Genocide in Tibet,"[753] referencing a 370-page report by the International Commission of Jurists that accused the Chinese government of forced abortions, infanticide, and numerous other abuses against Tibetans.[754] Again these reports were based upon selective interviews with

---

750 Goldstein and Beall, 300–301.

751 Goldstein and Beall, 301–303.

752 Barry Sautman, "'Cultural Genocide' and Tibet," *Texas International Law Journal* 38 (2003): 241–42.

753 Maura Moynihan, "Genocide in Tibet," *Washington Post,* January 24, 1998.

754 International Commission of Jurists, *Tibet: Human Rights and the Rule of Law* (January 1, 1997), 312.

exiles and speculative interpretations of public documents,[755] a pattern it is useful to describe with the phrase "anecdote-speculation" since it has been repeated so many times in Western media coverage of China that it is necessary to refer to it by a shorthand.[756] Again, Chinese researchers disputed the findings.

Goldstein et al. took an even more rigorous approach, involving focus groups, a household survey, interviews, and observation; research sites were chosen by the authors and "[n]o information was censored by the Chinese government and no provincial or local government officials accompanied the researchers while they did their fieldwork." No prior arrangements needed to be made to conduct interviews, nor were inter-viewees subject to questioning by local officials afterward.[757] The results were again similar. While a three-child limit had indeed been officially placed upon Tibetan families in the countryside, Goldstein et al. found that this limit was not being effectively enforced, local authorities having considerable autonomy regarding the policy. Despite some complaints about government rules, "no formal or informal discussions with villagers about family planning, birth limits or local problems revealed even a hint of forced abortions," and when the women surveyed were asked about what happens when someone became pregnant with a child who would be above the limit, "not one said that they would have to undergo an abortion or be sterilized."[758] Families that had had four or more children were not even fined. The study, they concluded, "highlights the dangers of using refugee reports and anecdotal evidence to interpret highly politicized situations."[759]

---

755 International Commission of Jurists, 9.

756 The Western press is well-aware of this phenomenon, and in the time before the propaganda machine was fully focused on China, would sometimes freely admit it. For example, in early 2014, when cultivating anti-immigrant xenophobia was still considered a greater priority, an article in the *New York Times* headlined "Asylum Fraud in Chinatown: Industry of Lies" deplored a plethora of applicants for asylum in the United States, writing that most asylum applications "were at least partly false, from fabricated narratives of persecution to counterfeit supporting documents and invented witness testimony." (Kirk Semple, Joseph Goldstein, and Jeffrey E. Singer, "Asylum Fraud in Chinatown: An Industry of Lies," *New York Times*, February 22, 2014.)

757 Melvyn C. Goldstein et al., "Fertility and Family Planning in Rural Tibet," *The China Journal* 47, no. 47 (January 2002): 19–21.

758 Goldstein et al., "Fertility and Family Planning in Rural Tibet," 31–32.

759 Goldstein et al., 39.

Obviously, the "final solution" that was supposedly to have been implemented in Tibet during the 1990s was never anything but a complete fabrication. According to *Voice of America* (the United States government's own media mouthpiece), the staunchly anti-communist "Tibetan government in exile" and the PRC have agreed on the total number of Tibetans living in China since 2010—over six million, a significant increase since Goldstein et al.'s research.[760] In a further paper published in 2005, Goldstein, Beall, and their colleagues Ben Jiao and Geoff Childs (a sociocultural anthropologist from Washington University in St. Louis) compared the fertility rates between Tibetans in the TAR and the Tibetan exile community, finding that since the mid-1980s—when the rate for both had been approximately *six births per woman*[761]—it had declined in both communities at nearly the same rate due to the increased availability of contraceptives, even despite the "leaders in the exile community advocat[ing] pronatalism as a nationalistic responsibility."[762]

While Goldstein and Beall's meticulous fieldwork appears to have had little effect on the propaganda machine at the time, their research represents an important first-hand perspective on government policy in Tibet that was not only qualified and external, but studiously independent. (Not all of their findings painted the PRC in the best light; for example, in another paper published in 1989, Goldstein and Beall remarked upon the "trade exploitation" of the Tibetan nomads. In 1981 the central government in Beijing had ordered the Tibet Autonomous Region to be exempted from all taxes and trade quotas—a type of tax-in-kind in which the nomads had been compelled to sell a portion of their goods to the government at below-market prices. However, Goldstein and Beall found that due to corruption on the county and district level, the quota system remained discreetly in place.)[763] Thirty years ago, or perhaps even ten,

---

760 "Beijing: Tibetan Population Actually over 7 Million," *Voice of America*, June 20, 2014.

761 Geoff Childs et al., "Tibetan Fertility Transitions in China and South Asia," *Population and Development Review* 31, no. 2 (June 2005): 346.

762 Geoff Childs et al., 347.

763 According to their study published in 1989:

"Nomads are presently compelled to sell butter and sheep to district officials for those officials' own consumption needs. Here too, the system works not by an open market economy but by establishing a contract (quota) at prices below the market. The district officials decide how much butter and meat they need and then establish a per animal quota to yield that amount, which is then passed on to the nomads based on the number of head of livestock they hold. On the other hand, because these officials want the 'contracts' to appear voluntarily entered into, they cannot pay the nomads too

such research by outside observers was possible; today, the super-empire's policy of decoupling largely precludes independent Western investigations, and limits the primary source material of any such research to anecdote-speculation.

"Decoupling," or sometimes "de-risking"—the terms used explicitly by the U.S. security state and Western media—is best understood as an imperialist mirror to Amin's theory of "delinking." The periphery, according to Amin, may be able to delink itself from its harmful near-total political integration with the core without sacrificing trade, and thus without jeopardizing its economic survival—a feat that the PRC has to a great degree already accomplished. This has also rendered the super-empire unable to subject China to the mechanisms of control detailed in Chapter Two: the nuclear deterrent precludes direct military intervention, China's new wealth is proof against the leveraging of debt for structural adjustment, and China's manufacturing and export dominance prevents the super-empire from employing significant sanctions against it without also bringing economic ruin to itself. The United States, Europe, Australia, &c. must first "decouple" from their integration with China by gradually reducing their trade dependency on it.

The West's fourth mechanism of control—soft power—is currently the only weapon the super-empire can bring to bear against China, but when in the late 2000s the success of the PRC's delinking became fully apparent, the use of this weapon was not fully unconstrained either. Multilateral diplomatic agreements between the PRC and Western countries, as well as a recent history of cooperation on global issues such as climate change, could not be undone overnight. Though the Western bourgeoisie must destroy the Communist Party to retain their dominance over class society, their tremendous capital exports to China—according to UNCTAD, foreign direct investment in China totaled $2 trillion in 2021[764]—and their revenues from the Chinese market cannot be easily discarded, and give many individual Western corporations a contradictory incentive to avoid confrontation. Since the 1990s, many avenues for the exchange of culture, education, and information between China and the United States

---

little and thus provoke them to protest to Lhasa." [Melvyn C. Goldstein and Cynthia M. Beall, "The Impact of China's Reform Policy on the Nomads of Western Tibet," *Asian Survey* 29, no. 6 (June 1989): 634.]

764 United Nations Conference on Trade and Development, "UNCTAD/WIR/2022," 215.

had been opened. These also needed to be decoupled in order to clear the path for greater hostility.

A more thorough assessment of the current decoupling strategy will be presented in Chapter Twelve; this chapter is concerned with its effects on journalism and the media. It is now a common thought-terminating cliché that China's "freedom of the press" is considered among the lowest of any country in the world. Yet this was not always the case. According to a special report by the New York-based NGO Committee to Protect Journalists, press rights in China in 2010 were in fact stronger than ever before.[765] This has certainly changed, and foreign journalists are indeed treated very poorly in China today, but seldom (if ever) does the Western press honestly address the question of *why* this has changed.

Chinese public opinion of the United States, once positive, or at least ambivalent, during the latter twentieth century, had worsened by the 2000s due to the perception of persistent anti-China bias in the Western media.[766] A report published in the *Cornell International Law Journal* found that China had in fact been subjected to a serious double standard; Western NGOs, ostensibly concerned with human rights, disproportionately focused on alleged violations in China despite much worse abuses occurring elsewhere in the world; the U.S. government continually attempted to censure the PRC before the United Nations Commission on Human Rights, while ignoring other countries' egregious abuses;[767] and the Western press exclusively covered negative news in China, selectively focusing only on individual cases that were not representative of actual conditions.[768] Meanwhile, though it did have shortcomings, China's actual human rights situation was far *better* than the average country in its income class in nearly every category.[769]

In 2005, the PRC played a role in mediating peace in Sudan's decades-long, exceptionally bloody civil war.[770] As early as 2006, the PRC was

---

765 According to the report: "many journalists, even those who have suffered directly as a result of their work, said press rights are stronger than they once were." (Madeline Earp, "In China, a Debate on Press Rights," Committee to Protect Journalists, October 19, 2010.)

766 Randall Peerenboom, "Assessing Human Rights in China: Why the Double Standard," Cornell International Law Journal 38, no. 1 (2005): 71–172.

767 Randall Peerenboom, 150–51.

768 Randall Peerenboom, 76–77.

769 Randall Peerenboom, 75.

770 Hend ElMahly Mahhoud Sultan and Degang Sun, "China's Participation in the Conflict Resolution in Sudan and South Sudan: A Case of 'Creative Mediation,'" *BRIQ* 1, no. 2 (2020): 8.

funding the African Union peacekeeping force and actively negotiating to end the humanitarian crisis in Darfur.[771] In 2007 its efforts had major success, the government in Khartoum agreeing to host a stronger joint United Nations-African Union peacekeeping operation—UNAMID— which though not 100% successful in ending the conflict, became the largest UN mission in the world to date and for the duration of its mandate almost certainly prevented hundreds of thousands of further deaths.[772] Chinese diplomacy alone had produced results where the West's airstrikes and economic sanctions had failed—an unsurprising observation, given that the true purpose of these sanctions (see Chapter Two) was not to end war but to maintain Sudan's underdevelopment.[773] The PRC had not participated in the sanctions; for this reason, rather than acknowledge the PRC's role in ending the bloodshed, or admit the West's own culpability in crimes against humanity in Sudan,[774] Western newspapers spat in its face. In 2007, the *Wall Street Journal* published an op-ed labelling the upcoming Summer Olympics in Beijing the "Genocide Olympics."[775] In 2008, the *New York Times* ran its own column titled "China's Genocide Olympics,"[776] and Steven Spielberg withdrew from his role as artistic

---

771 Hend ElMahly Mahhoud Sultan and Degang Sun, 13.

772 Hend ElMahly Mahhoud Sultan and Degang Sun, 15.

773 The Western press was remarkably candid in admitting, several years after the fact, that the sanctions on Sudan had done absolutely nothing to stop the bloodshed in Darfur. In 2018, *Foreign Policy* called the sanctions a "global face-saving exercise after evidence of war crimes in Darfur began to emerge" that had done nothing to hinder the Sudanese government or help the people of Darfur. (Nesrine Malik, "Sanctions Against Sudan Didn't Harm an Oppressive Government—They Helped It," *Foreign Policy,* July 3, 2018.) Predictably, the sanctions themselves had done them even *more* harm, by effectively preventing even basic medical supplies from reaching Sudan. (Amy Maxmen, "Sudan Sanctions Deprive 'Whole Nation' of Health Care," *Foreign Policy,* January 14, 2016.)

774 The cruelty of the super-empire's policy toward Sudan has already been briefly mentioned in Chapters Two and Six. To take another particularly horrific example, less than a decade earlier, in 1998, an airstrike by the U.S. military had destroyed the Al-Shifa pharmaceutical factory that had produced the majority of the country's basic medicines, resulting in a three-month disruption of all medical supplies during the bloody civil war. [Werner Daum, "Universalism and the West: An Agenda for Understanding," *Harvard International Review* 23, no. 2 (Summer 2001):19–23.]

775 Ronan Farrow and Mia Farrow, "The 'Genocide Olympics'," *Wall Street Journal,* March 28, 2007.

776 Nicholas Kristof, "China's Genocide Olympics," *New York Times,* January 24, 2008.

advisor to the event, explicitly citing PRC-Sudan relations in his public explanation.[777]

"Now, when a journalist from the West asks us questions," Fanon wrote in 1961, "it is seldom in order to help us."[778] This lesson was re-learned in China. 2008 proved to be an inflection point in receptivity to foreign press; later, in April, CNN became the target of a wave of outrage and multiple lawsuits in both China and the United States after one of their news commentators remarked about China that "they" were a "bunch of goons and thugs" on air. The Western establishment, however, closed ranks; the CNN commentator kept his job[779] and the New York-based Hai Ming law firm soon dropped its case, citing pressure from other clients.[780] The *Los Angeles Times* dismissed subsequent Chinese demonstrations against Western media bias as "xenophobic."[781]

Western news media thus soon faced an increasingly hostile public reaction in China, and one largely of their own making. Over the next decade, things steadily worsened. Increasingly, reporters fell afoul of police, but more often they were accosted by men in plainclothes whom they could not identify, and sometimes simply by crowds of angry locals. In 2011, NPR noted a "crackdown" on foreign journalists, in which Chinese authorities threatened to revoke visas;[782] in December of 2014, the *New York Times* reported on a pattern of harassment of Western reporters, citing an incident in Beijing in which an Associated Press camera crew was "attacked by a crowd of thugs who damaged their equipment, splashed them with water and snatched one of the correspondents' phones."[783]

As the super-empire began to pursue decoupling in earnest, Western governments took any opportunity to escalate these tensions. In February 2020, the U.S. State Department revoked protections for all journalists of China's five largest news agencies, who would henceforth be treated

777 Helene Cooper, "Spielberg Drops Out as Adviser to Beijing Olympics in Dispute Over Darfur Conflict," *New York Times,* February 13, 2008.

778 Fanon, *The Wretched of the Earth*, 77.

779 "China Joins Furor Over Fox News Host's 'Chinaman' Comments," *Wall Street Journal,* July 15, 2014.

780 Klaudia Lee, "Legal Action against CNN Dropped," South China Morning Post, May 12, 2008.

781 Mark Magnier, "Dialing Back Chinese Anger," *Los Angeles Times,* April 19, 2008.

782 "China Cracks Down On Reporters, Potential Protesters," *NPR,* March 4, 2011.

783 Andrew Jacobs, "China Gets Even Colder for Reporters," *New York Times,* December 17, 2014.

as foreign government operatives.[784] In retaliation, the Chinese Ministry of Foreign Affairs revoked visas for three *Wall Street Journal* reporters the next day, accusing the paper of racism for its publication of an article headlined—at the height of the COVID-19 pandemic—"China Is the Real Sick Man of Asia."[785] The State Department again punished Chinese news agencies, restricting their staff and effectively forcing dozens of Chinese citizens to leave the country.[786] The next month, the Ministry of Foreign Affairs further retaliated, requiring journalists of major American newspapers whose press credentials expired at the end of the year to surrender them within ten days.[787] In May, the U.S. Department of Homeland Security further restricted Chinese journalists' visas.[788] In June, the homes of four Xinhua News Agency correspondents in Australia were raided and their property was confiscated by the authorities; later that year, when Chinese police deemed two Australian journalists "persons of interest" in a criminal investigation, the Australian government advised the Australian Broadcasting Corporation to withdraw them from the country, leaving Australian media with no accredited foreign correspondents in China for the first time in nearly 50 years.[789] By October, the *New York Times* had only one foreign correspondent left in all of China, and the *Washington Post* had zero.[790]

On May 11, the documentary *Voices from the Frontline: China's War on Poverty*, written and produced by China expert Robert Lawrence Kuhn, debuted on PBS member station PBS SoCal; the film, made possible by the unprecedented access to the Chinese countryside that Kuhn had cultivated throughout his career, was a mostly-positive depiction of the PRC's targeted poverty alleviation program. Within weeks, PBS mysteriously removed the film from their platform for "not meet[ing] its

---

784 Lara Jakes and Steven Lee Myers, "U.S. Designates China's Official Media as Operatives of the Communist State," *New York Times,* February 18, 2020.

785 Alexandra Stevenson, "China Expels 3 Wall Street Journal Reporters as Media Relations Sour," *New York Times,* February 19, 2020.

786 Lara Jakes and Marc Tracy, "U.S. Limits Chinese Staff at News Agencies Controlled by Beijing," *New York Times,* March 2, 2020.

787 Marc Tracy, "China Announces That It Will Expel American Journalists," *New York Times,* March 18, 2020.

788 Sha Hua, "U.S. Puts New Limits on Visas for Chinese Journalists," *Wall Street Journal,* May 9, 2020.

789 James Mayger and Jason Scott, "Australia Raided Homes of Chinese Reporters, Seized Electronics," *Bloomberg,* September 9, 2020.

790 Keith B. Richburg, "China Feels It No Longer Needs the Foreign Media. But It Still Can't Hide," The University of Melbourne *Asialink,* October 14, 2020.

editorial standards"; in a statement to the press, PBS SoCal confirmed that the film had passed their editorial standards, yet followed suit, suspending any future re-airing.[791] That summer, the U.S. Peace Corps ended operations in China,[792] and President Trump issued an executive order terminating the Fulbright Program, which had previously provided opportunities for the exchange of students and a wide array of academic research and cooperation between the PRC and the United States.[793] The Biden Administration and the 117th Congress upheld the termination;[794] as of the summer of 2023, despite repeated objections from many U.S. scholars, neither program had been restored.[795] There were to be no more Professor Goldsteins in this new generation of U.S.-PRC relations; no first-hand reporting, no fieldwork, and no independent investigations. There was to be only anecdote-speculation and propaganda.

Nowhere is this clearer than in the present controversy over the Xinjiang Uyghur Autonomous Region. Since 2018, Western press and NGOs have accused the government of a litany of human rights abuses, many of them quite similar to the accusations regarding Chinese Tibetans decades earlier. The Hoover Institution, a conservative U.S. policy think tank attached to Stanford University, published an article in 2018 titled "China's Final Solution In Xinjiang."[796] An op-ed headline in the *Washington Post* declared that "In China, every day is Kristallnacht" in 2019.[797] The East Turkistan National Awakening Movement, a

---

791 Julian Wyllie, "After PBS Drops Film, PBS SoCal Reviews Documentary Produced in Association with a Chinese State TV Network," *Current*, May 27, 2020.

792 Simone McCarthy, "US Peace Corps' Exit from China Cuts Valued Channel of Sino-American Dialogue," *South China Morning Post*, July 4, 2020.

793 Executive Office of President Donald J. Trump, "The President's Executive Order on Hong Kong Normalization," Executive Order 13936 of July 14, 2020, *Federal Register*, July 17, 2020.

794 The Fulbright Program in China was briefly included in a general push by the Democratic Party to roll back many Trump-era policies; the America COMPETES Act, approved by House of Representatives in 2022, included a reversal of the termination. [NAFSA: Association of International Educators, *The America COMPETES Act (H.R. 4251)*, 3.] However, a bipartisan consensus was quickly reached to avoid any rapprochement with the PRC. A few months later the language was quietly dropped from bill, which later became law as the CHIPS and Science Act.

795 Bochen Han, "Want to Improve US-China Relations? Bring Back Fulbright Programme, Advocates Say," *South China Morning Post*, April 28, 2023.

796 Miles Maochun Yu, "China's Final Solution In Xinjiang," *The Caravan*, Hoover Institution, October 9, 2018.

797 Fred Hiatt, "In China, Every Day Is Kristallnacht," *Washington Post*, November 3, 2019.

Washington-based NGO created in 2017, alleged that the Party had killed millions of people in Xinjiang, imprisoned 8 million Uyghurs and other minorities in concentration camps, and forcibly aborted nearly 4 million Turkic babies.[798] In 2020, a Washington-based defense policy think tank issued a report accusing the Communist Party of perpetrating a massive campaign of forced sterilization specifically targeting the Uyghur ethnic minority, sourced entirely from anecdote-speculation, i.e. a handful of accounts from refugees or expatriates and extrapolations of local population statistics.[799] In 2021, the State Department officially declared that a genocide consisting of a "systematic attempt to destroy Uighurs by the Chinese party-state" was ongoing in Xinjiang.[800] In all such analyses, of course, the testimony of at most a few dozen selectively-chosen émigrés was treated as unquestionably factual. No independent studies of Uyghur communities in China were undertaken and no Western researchers even traveled to Xinjiang to attempt to confirm the accusations. Indeed, they largely could not; a decade of mistrust deliberately sown by Western governments and the Western press had led to the severing of academic ties, making the organization of any fieldwork prohibitively difficult.

Neither are these the only, or even sufficient, obstacles to independent confirmation. The noncompliance of any government into investigations of their alleged crimes does not excuse the lack of investigation; Goldstein and Beall, as mentioned above, conducted their study despite the Chinese government's refusal to allow Western NGOs such as the International Commission of Jurists access to Tibet at around the same time. In a more contemporary example, the United Nations Human Rights Council's fact-finding mission to investigate the mass murder of the Rohingya people in Myanmar in 2018 "[regretted] the lack of cooperation from the Government of Myanmar"[801] but proceeded anyway, conducting numerous field missions between September 2017 and July 2018,[802] nearly a thousand in-depth interviews with victims and eyewitnesses that were both targeted and randomly selected, and relying only on verified and

---

798 East Turkistan National Awakening Movement, "Genocide."

799 Adrian Zenz, *Sterilizations, IUDs, and Mandatory Birth Control: The CCP's Campaign to Suppress Uyghur Birthrates in Xinjiang* (Washington, DC: The Jamestown Foundation, June 2020).

800 Edward Wong and Chris Buckley, "U.S. Says China's Repression of Uighurs Is 'Genocide,'" *New York Times,* January 20, 2021.

801 United Nations Human Rights Council, *Report of the Independent International Fact-finding Mission on Myanmar* - A/HRC/39/64, August 27, 2018, 3.

802 United Nations Human Rights Council, 4.

corroborated information.[803] Not long afterward, however, the Western press and soft-power NGO network itself moved to prevent the Human Rights Council from conducting any similar investigation in Xinjiang.

In 2021, after Michelle Bachelet, the United Nations High Commissioner for Human Rights, publicly announced that such an investigation into the allegations regarding Xinjiang was needed, the Chinese government invited her to visit the region, not for an investigation, but as a diplomatic step toward trust and future cooperation. A month later, the United States government and its soft-power appendages began to pressure Bachelet, urging her to make a statement condemning the PRC over Xinjiang with no investigation at all.[804] In March of 2022, after she agreed to the visit, Western NGOs published an open letter, signed by a multitude of groups such as Amnesty International and the NED-funded Chinese Human Rights Defenders, insisting that she publish a condemnation of the Chinese government immediately.[805] "Ms. Bachelet—Don't Go To Xinjiang" demanded the Heritage Foundation that April.[806]

Bachelet, in fact, never intended her visit to be a thorough investigation of the allegations, which her initial statement made explicitly clear:

This visit was not an investigation—official visits by a High Commissioner are by their nature high-profile and simply not conducive to the kind of detailed, methodical, discreet work of an investigative nature.

Instead, she said she hoped to "raise concerns" and "pave the way for more regular, meaningful interactions in the future"; at no point did she declare the question of genocide or of other human rights violations had been settled, and according to her statement she had pressed the government on those topics during her visit.[807] Nevertheless, this positive step toward gaining the PRC's cooperation with future investigations would

---

803 United Nations Human Rights Council, 3.

804 Nuriman and Joshua Lipes (translator), "'Letters of Hope' for Uyghurs Urge Rights Czar Bachelet to Break UN 'Silence' on Xinjiang," *Radio Free Asia,* April 6, 2021.

805 Stephanie Nebehay, "U.N. Rights Boss to Visit China in May, Including Xinjiang, but Activists Demand Report," *Reuters,* March 8, 2022.

806 Olivia Enos, "Ms. Bachelet—Don't Go To Xinjiang," *Forbes,* April 4, 2022.

807 Michelle Bachelet, "Statement by UN High Commissioner for Human Rights Michelle Bachelet after Official Visit to China," *United Nations Human Rights Office of the High Commissioner,* May 28, 2022.

not lead anywhere. The Western media firestorm grew even more intense; numerous Washington-based think tanks, NGOs, and media figures universally demanded Bachelet's resignation and condemned the UN itself as an institution.[808] Two weeks later, Bachelet announced (unexpectedly, according to her colleagues) that she would not seek another term as High Commissioner for "personal reasons."[809]

This proved insufficient to satisfy the Western press, which continued to demand a summary report unequivocally condemning the PRC. Bachelet pledged to release one before the end of her term, stating that she was under "tremendous pressure";[810] as her final day approached, this even began to come from her colleagues at the UN itself. In August, the UN's Special Rapporteur on contemporary slavery issued his own report announcing that allegations of Uyghurs being employed in "forced labor" were credible. His report, however, cited as evidence a handful of other reports by Western defense industry think tanks and academics which themselves relied entirely upon anecdote-speculation;[811] one such academic was quoted by *Bloomberg* as saying that it would be "awkward" if Bachelet's report disagreed.[812]

The Human Rights Council's report on Xinjiang, when it did appear, was published only minutes before Bachelet had officially ended her position on the last day of August. Her name was not on it and she did not promote it; the *Financial Times* reported that Bachelet's own office staff "had to overcome resistance to publishing the report from Bachelet herself."[813] An independent analysis by Australian legal expert Jaq James called the report "Willing to Wound, but Afraid to Strike," due to its self-contradictory reliance on an inordinate amount of cautious language qualifying its claims, such as the statement that there "may" have been "crimes against

---

808 Bethany Allen-Ebrahimian, "Advocates Denounce UN Official's China Visit as 'Ultimate Betrayal,'" *Axios,* May 31, 2022.

809 Emma Farge and Wendell Roelf, "Michelle Bachelet, U.N. Rights Chief, Says No to Second Term amid China Trip Backlash," *Reuters,* June 13, 2022.

810 Emma Farge, "UN Rights Chief 'under Tremendous Pressure' over Report on China's Uyghurs," *Reuters,* August 25, 2022.

811 Tomoya Obokata, *A/HRC/51/26: Contemporary Forms of Slavery Affecting Persons Belonging to Ethnic, Religious and Linguistic Minority Communities,* United National Human Rights Office of the High Commissioner, July 19, 2022, 8.

812 "UN Expert Finds Forced Labor Claims in China's Xinjiang Credible," *Bloomberg News,* August 16, 2022.

813 Yuan Yang and Henry Foy, "'Under Tremendous Pressure': The Battle behind the UN Report on China's Xinjiang Abuses," *Financial Times,* September 13, 2022.

humanity," the purpose of which, according to James, was to allow "grave imputations to hang in the air without the burden of committing to them."[814] Nor did the report mention Bachelet's visit to China in May; nor did it contain any data obtained through any independent investigation whatsoever, relying instead upon the selectively-chosen testimony of a handful of Uyghur exiles, subjective interpretations of Chinese law, and prior "research" by defense think tanks and U.S. government-linked organizations—such as the Australian Strategic Policy Institute (ASPI) and the Victims of Communism Memorial Foundation—that were universally based upon the same anecdote-speculation and other unverified information.[815]

Nor, however, did any of these remarkable concessions to the pressure upon Bachelet entirely please those who had applied it; immediately after the report was published, *The Diplomat* responded with an op-ed focusing entirely upon her "permanently damage[d]" reputation and "fall from grace";[816] other organizations said she had "failed spectacularly"[817] and that her performance was a "tragedy for the UN."[818] Bachelet's history of having been tortured by the Pinochet regime and her legacy of subsequently rising to become the new president of Chile was easily brushed aside. The message was quite clear: anyone who took the slightest step toward even attempting to meaningfully corroborate the propaganda machine's new speculative horror stories would face relentless attacks on their character and exile from the public arena.

In September of 2020, the U.S. Congress began to craft legislation to sanction all products from the XUAR, which included 20% of the world's cotton supply, with the rationale that "forced labor" might have been used to craft them.[819] Under pressure, the Better Cotton Initiative, an interna-

---

814 Jaq James, *The Assessment on Human Rights in Xinjiang by the United Nations Office of the High Commissioner for Human Rights: A Critical Analysis,* Working Paper, CO-WEST-PRO Consultancy (April 2023): 9–10.

815 Office of the High Commissioner for Human Rights, "OHCHR Assessment of Human Rights Concerns in the Xinjiang Uyghur Autonomous Region, People's Republic of China," United National Human Rights, August 31, 2022.

816 Mark S. Cogan, "Michelle Bachelet's Spectacular Fall From Grace," *The Diplomat,* August 31, 2022.

817 Abdulhakim Idris, "Goodbye, Ms. Bachelet: The Uyghurs Will Not Miss You," *Bitter Winter,* August 31, 2022.

818 Mercedes Page, "A Tragedy in Xinjiang, a Tragedy for the UN," *The Interpreter,* September 2, 2022.

819 Evan Clark, "Xinjiang's Cotton Ban Debated in House Hearing," *Yahoo! Finance,* September 17, 2020.

tional sustainability NGO funded by USAID,[820] declared the following month that it was withdrawing its operations from the region. The BCI had not found any evidence that forced labor was being used to harvest cotton; in fact, for the previous eight years, it had trained both Uyghur and Han cotton farmers in sustainable cotton practices without ever finding any such evidence. If forced labor were being used, or had suddenly begun to be used, of any Western or international organization the BCI would have been the best placed to discover the extent and evidence of such abuses; yet instead the group announced that it would "cease all field-level activities in the region effective immediately, including capacity building and data monitoring and reporting" in the XUAR.[821] It joined a growing group of international labor rights auditors that had stopped operating in Xinjiang. In September, the *Wall Street Journal* reported on five such auditing organizations that had withdrawn from the region—not because the Chinese government had forbidden their activities, but because Washington-based NGOs and defense industry specialists had urged them to.[822] In 2019, Paris-based auditor Bureau Veritas certified a factory in Xinjiang operated by the Yili Zhuowan Garment Manufacturing Company as free of forced labor—but the United States Customs and Border Protection agency disagreed, including it in sanctions due to "[i]nformation reasonably indicat[ing] that these entities use prison and forced labor." The CBP did not disclose the nature or the source of this "information"[823] but Bureau Veritas swiftly agreed to stop operating in Xinjiang by the following week. The PRC had always been guilty until proven innocent, but now not even an *attempt* to prove its innocence would be permitted. The Party's guilt had become an unfalsifiable hypothesis.

The Western propaganda machine's grip is naturally weaker outside the anglophone media and internet. For example, in 2021, Professor Tomoo Marukawa of the University of Tokyo's Institute of Social Science, who specialized in the Chinese economy and had conducted research in Xinjiang in the past, wrote multiple articles in his column for *Newsweek Japan* with detailed analysis casting doubt on several allegations against the Chinese government that had been taken for granted by the Western

---

820 Better Cotton Initiative, *2020 Annual Report,* 24.

821 Evan Clark, "Better Cotton Initiative Stops Xinjiang Field Activity," *Women's Wear Daily,* October 21, 2020.

822 Eva Xiao, "Auditors to Stop Inspecting Factories in China's Xinjiang Despite Forced-Labor Concerns," *Wall Street Journal,* September 21, 2020.

823 U.S. Department of Homeland Security, "DHS Cracks Down on Goods Produced by China's State-Sponsored Forced Labor," September 14, 2020.

press.[824][825] Professor Hiroshi Onishi, an economist at Keio University who had performed fieldwork in Xinjiang nearly a dozen times throughout the 2000s and 2010s,[826] also disagreed, and published a paper discrediting—through on-the-ground observation—specific claims made by a NED-funded Uyghur exile group. Onishi also referenced recent interviews with Uyghur residents of Konasheher County in Kashgar Prefecture that he had conducted through his research partners in the area without the government's knowledge; the responses, he concluded, indicated that the community widely considered the government jobs programs denounced by Western "experts" as "forced labor" to in fact be voluntary.[827] Yet this information was still easily prevented from entering the Western public consciousness; none of Marukawa's and Onishi's work on Xinjiang, or other such analyses, were ever translated into English or reported on by the Western press. Information separation had become total; in the era of media decoupling, no news whatsoever regarding Xinjiang was permitted to be discovered or published except that which had been approved—or invented—by Washington and its network of soft-power organizations.

Propaganda as a Weapon

Xinjiang was no exception—indeed the opposite—to China's historical trend of suffering identified at the beginning of Chapter Seven. Before the Western media's recent focus there (which began in earnest only in early 2018), it was little disputed that the history of the region involved great tragedy, and that even in recent years, ethnic minorities there and throughout China endured lives of great difficulty.

Until the establishment of the PRC, the Uyghur people inhabiting their heartland of southern Xinjiang[828] had virtually never done so except

---

824 丸川知雄 (Tomoo Marukawa), "新疆の綿花畑では本当に「強制労働」が行われているのか?" [Is "forced labor" really being practiced in Xinjiang's cotton fields?].

825 丸川知雄 (Tomoo Marukawa), "新疆における「強制不妊手術」疑惑の真相" [The Truth About the Suspicion of Forced Sterilization in Xinjiang].

826 Record China, "事実を確かめずにウイグル会議情報を流布－現地11回調査の大西慶大教授が西側キャンペーンに反論" [Dissemination of Uyghur Congress information without confirming the facts: Professor Onishi of Keio University, who conducted 11 local surveys, refutes Western campaigns].

827 大西 広 (Hiroshi Onishi), "「ウイグル問題」に関する西側キャンペーンを検証する" [Examining Western Campaign on "Uyghur Issue"], 13–14.

828 "Southern Xinjiang" here refers to the geographical region south of the Tianshan mountain range, also called the Tarim Basin, Nanjiang, or Altishahr (the

as subjects or vassals, either to the old Mongolian khanates or to successive Chinese feudal dynasties. The khanate in northern Xinjiang,[829] which conquered the south in the seventeenth century, and attempted to conquer Tibet, suffered even worse when the majority of its population was annihilated in the eighteenth during the Ten Great Campaigns of the Qing Empire. Though the Qing's feudal ruling class which had ordered the massacre were Manchu, many of the soldiers who carried it out were Han—assisted by the Uyghurs in the south, who had rebelled against the khanate, and became subjects of the Qing thereafter. The tale of ethnic minorities suffering at the hands of the Han majority—or even simply the story of one Chinese ethnic group oppressing another—is therefore an easy one for the Western press to report, due to the virtue of having already been largely true for centuries.

Neither is the Communist Party beyond reproach regarding its policies toward minorities—a fact that the Party itself has admitted in its public condemnation of the former leaders who had mistakenly pursued the so-called Great Proletarian Cultural Revolution, which had suppressed the cultural and religious practices of minority groups during the late 1960s and early 1970s. Not even Mao Zedong was exempt from criticism; of Mao's role in the GPCR, Deng Xiaoping said in an interview with Italian journalist Oriana Fallaci in 1980:

> . . . it's imperative for me to make a clear distinction between the nature of Chairman Mao's mistakes and the crimes committed by Lin Piao and the Gang of Four. I must remind you that Chairman Mao devoted most of his life to China and saved the party and the revolution in the most critical moments. In other words, he gave such a contribution that, without him, in the least the Chinese would have spent much more time in groping their way in the darkness. Then let's not forget that it was Chairman Mao who combined the principles of Marxism and Leninism with the realities of China, it was Chairman Mao who creatively applied those principles not only to politics but also to philosophy, art, literature, military affairs. Yes, until the Sixties, or to be exact before the later part of the Fifties, some ideas of Chairman Mao were very correct, and many of the principles through which we achieved victory. *Then,*

---

historical Uyghur name).

829 The neighboring area to the north of the mountains, also called Beijiang or Dzungaria (the historical Mongolian name).

unfortunately, in the last part of his life, he committed mistakes.
Particularly the Cultural Revolution mistake. And as a result many
misfortunes were brought upon the party, the country, the people.
[emphasis added][830]

Generally, however, Western journalists and historians take little note
of Deng's careful handling of Mao's legacy, preferring to exaggerate—
often cartoonishly—the errors Deng identified, to blame Mao for even
more mistakes committed by others, and sometimes to invent new ones
from rumor or speculation. The nature of the errors made by Mao and the
Party were in fact fundamentally distinct from the cycles of oppression
that characterized the centuries of feudal dynasties, and Mao's actual
attitudes toward China's ethnic minorities, as well as the policies that he
led the Party to implement in the early years of the PRC, substantially
belie their reputation in the West.

In 1956, Mao met with a delegation from Mongolia to discuss the
Chinese contribution to Mongolia's industrial development, which that
year had included the loan of thousands of workers and technicians and a
grant of 160 million rubles. When his Mongolian counterpart expressed
their gratitude for the PRC's aid, Mao responded:

We should do our duty, because our ancestors exploited you for
three hundred years, oppressed you, they ran up quite a debt; therefore, today we want to repay these debts. In the past our national
minorities were also oppressed this way, and we also want to repay
our debts to them—this is our duty ...
   ... In the past, we oppressed you, therefore now we want
to admit our mistake. *We not only do it so with you but with all*
national minorities inside the country. In the past, we oppressed
them; therefore, if we now do not admit our mistakes, we cannot
root out Great Han nationalist thinking and implement [principles
of] equality of nationalities. [emphasis added] This is [our] basis,
not pretty words. Isn't that so? In the past we oppressed you, but
now you do not even have a word of complaint. The aid we are
giving you is small. It is repayment of debt and not aid.[831]

---

830 Oriana Fallaci, "Deng: Cleaning Up Mao's 'Feudal Mistakes,'" *Washington Post,* August 31, 1980.
   831 Mao Zedong and Khutukhtu, "Memorandum of Conversation between Mao Zedong and the Delegation of the Mongolian People's Revolutionary Party and

Mao's words on the subject were not only diplomatic pleasantries; they were also echoed in internal decision-making processes at the Party's highest levels. The following year in Beijing, in a private meeting between members of the Politburo and the Tibet Work Committee on the possibility of reforming the oppressive feudal system in Tibet, Deng remarked:

> According to the Chairman [Mao] no reforms in the twentieth century ... No reforms for several decades or for fifty to one hundred years ... This is based on [the model of] the Far East Republic... Even if the 1.2 million serfs remain [in Tibet], this will not affect our socialist construction [in the rest of China]. Leave the Tibetan currency and the Tibetan army alone. We should make an agreement with them—we give them some money and let them do the work. Even if they embezzle all the money, leave them alone... In Tibet, it [reforms] will take decades.[832]

Such was the commitment by Mao and the Central Committee to the Seventeen Point Agreement with the Dalai Lama (which ensured Tibet's self-governance in exchange for Chinese sovereignty over it) that they were willing to wait generations before pressing for reform and modernization, out of respect for the cultural traditions and religious hierarchy of Tibet. "Reform is necessary ... for without it the minority nationalities cannot eliminate poverty,"[833] Deng had said in a speech several years earlier, "but reform must not be carried out until conditions within the minority nationalities are ripe for it."[834] Nor was his policy only driven by the political consideration of keeping good relations with the Dalai Lama and the Tibetan aristocracy; even after the Seventeen Point Agreement was abolished following the unsuccessful revolt and flight of the Dalai

---

Comments on the Distribution of the Memorandum of Conversation," September 24, 1956.

832 Melvyn C. Goldstein, *A History of Modern Tibet*, chap. 4, "In the Eye of the Storm: 1957–1959," 67–68.

833 Tibet in 1950 had no inter-city roads or railways, and the capitalist mode of production scarcely existed. The vast majority of the population were rural, often nomadic; the existence of Lhasa—a city of at most a few tens of thousands—was more due to the profusion of monasteries than of a true petit bourgeoisie.

834 Deng Xiaoping, "The Question of Minority Nationalities in the Southwest" [speech], 1950.

Lama in 1959, reforms proceeded glacially for the nomads. Goldstein, et al. write of the areas they surveyed:

> ... households newly classified as "wealthy" or "representatives of the lord" (*ngatsab*) were not expropriated with the exception of one former leader who had actively supported the Dalai Lama's revolt. All households kept the animals and pastures they then held and managed their herds as they had in the past. Debts dating from before 1959 were rescinded and those contracted in 1959 were recalculated with reduced interest.

Though in 1961 a relatively mild policy of mutual aid (*rogre*) was implemented in the countryside, in which the wealthiest nomads were not allowed to join pasture co-ops and required to pay higher wages to employees, rural Tibetan social and economic life was not fundamentally altered until the GPCR.[835]

Did the Cultural Revolution show Mao and his cadre to at last be hypocrites on the national question? The accounts Goldstein and Beall collected certainly suggest that it did. Wanam, the pseudonymous head of one of the wealthiest families in Phala, told them the story of his abrupt and radical change in fortune:

> One morning in 1970, Wanam recalled, the local Tibetan leaders of the Cultural Revolution appeared before his tent and ordered him outside.
>
> "They called me a reactionary and a class enemy," he said. "They told me, 'From today on, your animals and goods are confiscated, and you will live under the guidance of the people, just as the poorest of the poor lived in the old society.'
>
> "They ripped off my earring, my rings, my necklace, and took my silver flint striker and my bullet holder," Wanam continued. "They also confiscated my sheepskin robe, saying it was too good for the likes of a class enemy such as me. In its place they gave me an old worn-out robe."
>
> "What happened to the rest of your family's possessions?" we asked.

---

835 Goldstein and Beall, "The Impact of China's Reform Policy on the Nomads of Western Tibet," 622.

"We lost them all," Wanam answered. "At the time my family owned about 1,200 sheep and goats and 100 yaks. The new leaders took everything except 40 goats. They left us only one pot, some barley grain, and a little tsamba. And then they took away our fine yak-hair tent, giving us an old, tattered canvas tent in its place." He shook his head.

"We were stunned. Our whole life's wealth was eliminated in minutes. We didn't know how we would survive, since the leaders also said we could not join the people's commune but had to fend for ourselves."

In fact, Wanam and his family survived only on the meager yield from their milk goats and by doing odd jobs for the commune that they were not allowed to join. Finally, two years later, the leaders relented, and Wanam's family joined the commune.

At 50 Wanam is once again one of the wealthiest nomads in Phala. His recovery typifies the economic and cultural rebirth of the Tibetan nomads after the disastrous decade of enforced communes.[836]

Despite its associated violent upheaval and slow economic growth, the GPCR was not entirely without merit and still has a few defenders today (though most of these are from outside China); unlike the old feudal tyrants, the intent of the Party—though premature and (self-admittedly) misguided—had not been to extract wealth from minorities through dispossessive accumulation, but to eliminate the inequality among them. What Deng later referred to as "poor communism"[837] did improve the welfare of the poor by redistributing what wealth did exist; average life expectancy in China saw its biggest increase during this period, and average caloric intake and literacy increased dramatically as well. Yet it was widely rejected by China's communities of ethnic minorities, who had seen less of these benefits than the Han and had experienced overall economic stagnation during this decade. They typically swiftly restored their religious and cultural traditions after the GPCR ended in the 1970s.

What happened next? Goldstein and Beall remarked upon a substantial rise in rural Tibetan prosperity during the 1980s, and the construction of new roads, storerooms, and houses, which were built from imported

---

836 Melvyn C. Goldstein and Cynthia M. Beall, "The Remote World of Tibet's Nomads," *National Geographic* 175 (January-June 1989): 759–64.

837 See Chapter Seven.

wood, since no trees grew in Tibet's highest and most inhospitable regions. The Tibetans strongly embraced house-dwelling, which made the harsh winters of the plateau far more bearable, and incorporated it into their nomadic lifestyle.[838] Without any coercion by the government, more and more nomads were making use of the new "truckable" roads to transport livestock products, which they expected to yield much greater profits.[839] The entire TAR was exempted from taxes.[840] Pastureland was not expropriated and there was no inducement for nomads to resettle.[841] Health care was also made free for all residents.[842] The divisions between rich and poor did reappear, yet the poor now received decent wages and contracts for their work, and fared far better than they had under the feudal system.[843] By any objective assessment, the new policies of the Reform period were a vast improvement from the GPCR and greatly increased ethnic minorities' quality of life, yet objective assessments such as Goldstein and Beall's were a tiny minority in the West.

Through the lens of the Western press, any change in the PRC's policies could only be harmful. Development in the countryside could only be an unwelcome imposition of Han values. Roads and modern houses could only destroy minorities' traditional culture, and Han engineers who came to build them could only be conniving land-grabbers, certain to remain despite their lack of residency permits. No distinction could be drawn between rural poverty and this traditional culture, and no distinction could be drawn between the GPCR and the new Reform era; in fact the Reform policies needed to be *more harmful*. If no evidence for a negative change existed, it needed to be invented, ergo the conflation of the PRC's family planning initiatives that were announced in the late 1970s (which in reality *discriminated against the Han*, limiting them to one or two children per family, and exempted rural minorities, who were permitted three) with genocide, as shown in examples cited earlier in this chapter.

---

838 Goldstein and Beall, "The Remote World of Tibet's Nomads," 777–79.

839 Goldstein and Beall, "The Impact of China's Reform Policy on the Nomads of Western Tibet," 636.

840 However, as explained earlier in this chapter, this exemption was not fully implemented on the local level.

841 Goldstein and Beall, "Change and Continuity in Nomadic Pastoralism on the Western Tibetan Plateau," 17.

842 Goldstein and Beall, "The Impact of China's Reform Policy on the Nomads of Western Tibet," 630.

843 Goldstein and Beall, "The Impact of China's Reform Policy on the Nomads of Western Tibet," 637–40.

While the Communist Party had demonstrated its ability to adapt and to learn from its mistakes, the Western propaganda machine would never demonstrate the slightest inclination to do so. Only when the PRC's policy toward ethnic minorities changed once again was the early Reform period at all rehabilitated in the Western media; it was safe to admit the benefits minorities had received only when they could be used to attack and discredit the newest policy.

By the early 2010s, Chinese ethnic minority regions had reaped considerable gains from China's rapid economic rise. In 2011, prominent Chinese academics Hu Lianhe and Hu Angang calculated that throughout the entire Reform era (i.e. at the time, 1978 to 2008) average yearly regional GDP growth had been 9.79% in Tibet, 11.69% in Inner Mongolia, and 10.35% in Xinjiang, exceeding the growth rates of all other high-growth countries in the world (except China overall). Similarly, the increase in China's minority autonomous regions' Human Development Index had been the highest in the world; at the beginning of Reform, the Inner Mongolia Autonomous Region's HDI had been lower than Mongolia's, and the TAR's lower than India's, yet by 2008 both exceeded those of their neighboring countries.[844] Despite its own gains, however, Xinjiang still lagged behind several of its many neighbors. Its HDI was still average for the region, behind not only Russia but Kazakhstan, barely equaling Mongolia's, and only ahead of the other Central Asian republics to the west and south—several of which would likely have had more favorable comparisons to the even-less-prosperous Uyghur heartland of southern Xinjiang alone.[845] Moreover, though Hu and Hu noted that the relative gap between the inland minority autonomous regions and the Han-majority coastal areas was currently narrowing, it remained significant, and during the 1990s—when neoliberal influence in China had reached its peak—this gap had increased.[846] The Party's strategy, described by Deng as "permit[ting] some people and some regions to

---

844 胡鞍钢 and 胡联合, "第二代民族政策：促进民族交融一体和繁荣一体" [The Second Generation Ethnic Policy: Promoting National Integration and Prosperity], 2–3.

845 Jeroen Smits and Iñaki Permanyer, "The Subnational Human Development Database," *Scientific Data* 6, no. 190038 (2019).

846 胡鞍钢 and 胡联合, "第二代民族政策：促进民族交融一体和繁荣一体" [The Second Generation Ethnic Policy: Promoting National Integration and Prosperity], 3.

become prosperous first, for the purpose of achieving common prosperity faster"[847] had focused on developing the Han-majority areas first.

There were good geographical reasons for this. Xinjiang contains the "Eurasian Pole of Inaccessibility" giving it the unfortunate distinction of being the most landlocked region on Earth. The geography of the province is commonly summarized by the phrase "two basins between three mountains"—i.e. two deserts surrounded by the Altai, Tianshan, and Kunlun mountain ranges, the latter two in southern Xinjiang being among the highest in the world. Between these mountains, southern Xinjiang consists mostly of the vast and inhospitable Taklamakan Desert (interpreted ominously through folk etymology as "the place of no return"); its historical Uyghur name Altishahr referred to the "six cities" around its only oases that could support communities of any significant size. Tibet is even more remote, containing some of the highest elevations of continuous human habitation in the world. The development of these regions was a tremendous logistical task that could not be reasonably prioritized at China's Reform-era stage of prosperity. Yet southern Xinjiang's development also faced the unintended consequences and inadequacies of the central government's own ethnic minority policy.

Ethnic minorities in China have the constitutional right to be educated in their native language but in practice during the Reform era, such education often became exclusive, resulting in widespread monolingual education in separate school systems, which by the 2000s had produced a new generation in minority communities that could speak little Standard Chinese in a country where well over 90% of the population relied upon it as a common language.[848] Since relatively few jobs were available within the XUAR, this severely limited the scope of their employment opportunities. Many Uyghurs, traveling to the eastern provinces to find jobs in the new factories, found themselves estranged from and sometimes looked down upon by their Han coworkers, with whom they could not communicate; others remained chronically unemployed. According to Hu and Hu, the PRC's Reform-era "affirmative action" policies sometimes actually reinforced inter-ethnic resentment or segregation; the practice of automatically giving minorities higher scores on college entrance exams

---

847 Deng Xiaoping, "Interview With Mike Wallace Of 60 Minutes," September 2, 1986.

848 During the 1990s, in some areas it was very difficult to learn Standard Chinese even for Uyghurs who wished to, according to a 2014 interview (republished in *Foreign Policy*) with a bilingual Chinese Uyghur from Hotan who had managed to do so. (Chi Zhang, "One Uighur Man's Journey Goes Viral," May 14, 2014.)

had in some areas resulted in *de facto* discrimination against the children of interracial couples.[849] Regardless of whether such effects were significant or somehow outweighed the benefits of affirmative action overall, it was nonetheless true that those benefits had been severely hindered by the decades of privatization; local government officials had become either increasingly corrupt or simply less able to enforce preferential employment for minorities in the private sector.[850] [851]

The Western press and Western soft-power organizations of course happily publicized these deficiencies throughout the early twenty-first century. "Unemployment among Uyghurs is very high" said *Radio Free Asia* in 2009,[852] criticizing in multiple articles the XUAR's high rate of joblessness, including by interviewing a Uyghur academic who claimed it was "among the highest in the world";[853] London-based NGO Minority Rights Group International claimed in 2008 that the Uyghur unemployment rate in Xinjiang was "a staggering 70 per cent."[854] In 2013, the *Atlantic* highlighted the high unemployment rate among the Uyghur population in a profile on Xinjiang,[855] as did the *New York Times*, remarking that "Uighurs are largely frozen out of the region's booming gas and oil industry" as well as several forms of transport labor.[856] "In southern Xinjiang, it is hard for Uighurs to find jobs" a Uyghur employee of the PRC's state-run television broadcaster told Hong Kong magazine *Phoenix Weekly* in 2014;[857] the same month, a senior researcher at Western NGO Human Rights Watch praised a suicide bombing on Ürümqi South railway station that killed one bystander and injured dozens of

---

849 胡鞍钢 and 胡联合, "第二代民族政策：促进民族交融一体和繁荣一体" [The Second Generation Ethnic Policy: Promoting National Integration and Prosperity], 6.

850 Barry Sautman, "Scaling Back Minority Rights?: The Debate about China's Ethnic Policies," *Stanford Journal of International Law* 46 (June 1, 2010): 51–120.

851 刘仲康, 韩中义, and "古丽夏, 关于正确认识和处理新形势下新疆宗教问题的调查报告" [Investigation Report on Correct Understanding and Handling of Religious Issues in Xinjiang under the New Situation].

852 "Who Are the Uyghurs," *Radio Free Asia,* July 9, 2009.

853 Sarah Jackson-Han, "Uyghur Scholar Calls for Jobs," *Radio Free Asia,* March 6, 2009.

854 Minority Rights Group International, *World Directory of Minorities: Uyghurs,* 3.

855 James Palmer, "The Uighurs, China's Embattled Muslim Minority, Are Still Seeking an Identity," *The Atlantic,* September 27, 2013.

856 Andrew Jacobs, "Uighurs in China Say Bias Is Growing," *New York Times,* October 7, 2013.

857 Chi Zhang, "One Uighur Man's Journey Goes Viral."

commuters, attributing it to "people amongst the colonized who are ready to use violence against the colonizer," or the alleged retribution against Han migrant workers who had stolen jobs from local Uyghurs.[858] The government in Xinjiang, in fact, did publicly agree that a change in policy was needed, admitting to *Xinhua* in 2009, that "the employment picture in Xinjiang, especially for the ethnic minorities, is still bleak" and ordered businesses to employ more local residents.[859] By 2014, these efforts had still seen very little success, especially in the countryside. (Estimates of the XUAR's rural joblessness in 2013 and a comparison with the present are given in Appendix D.)

Hu and Hu had prescribed greater ethnic integration, the enforcement of equal rights, the end of affirmative action policies, and more government spending in minority regions.[860] Xi Jinping began to emphasize in his speeches the need for bilingual education and ethnic unity; during a visit to Xinjiang in 2014, *Xinhua* reported him saying what became a common government slogan:

All ethnic groups should understand each other, respect each other, tolerate each other, appreciate each other, learn from each other, help each other, and hold each other tightly like pomegranate seeds.[861]

The government began new education and jobs programs in Xinjiang on a massive scale. In 2017, the 19th National Congress of the Communist Party declared that "socialism with Chinese characteristics has entered a new era, and that the principal contradiction of the Chinese society has evolved into the one between unbalanced and inadequate development and the people's ever-growing needs for a better life."[862] The strategy of developing the productive forces of China by letting some get rich before

---

858 Michael Martina, "In China's Xinjiang, Economic Divide Seen Fuelling Ethnic Unrest," Reuters, May 6, 2014.

859 Xinhua, "China's Xinjiang Orders Businesses to Recruit More Locals," September 24, 2009.

860 胡鞍钢 and 胡联合, "第二代民族政策：促进民族交融一体和繁荣一体" [The Second Generation Ethnic Policy: Promoting National Integration and Prosperity], 4.

861 新华网, "习近平:扩大新疆少数民族到内地居住规模" [Xi Jinping: Expand the scale of ethnic minorities in Xinjiang living in the interior].

862 Embassy of the People's Republic of China in the Republic of South Africa, *Q&A on the 19th National Congress of the Communist Party of China.*

others was completed; the era of Common Prosperity and of redistributing those riches had begun.

The Western propaganda machine swiftly responded. Headlines proclaimed a genocide in Xinjiang; lurid stories of torture and brutality from Uyghur émigrés were splashed uncritically throughout the press and social media. Numerous academic reports on human rights, based upon little but zoomed-in satellite photography and anecdote-speculation, were published by defense industry think tanks such as the Jamestown Foundation and ASPI; these reports were then cited or imitated by a host of Western newspapers and other NGOs. Though the extent of Hu and Hu's actual influence on the Party was unclear, the government appeared to have adopted at least some of their recommendations, leading Western soft-power organizations to seize upon their work as the supposed foundation of the changes to the PRC's ethnic minority policy. The Tibetan government-in-exile considered their suggestions to be synonymous with the "eradication" of Tibetan culture.[863] The *Wall Street Journal*, citing both the Jamestown Foundation and ASPI, blamed Hu and Hu for the PRC's alleged new policy of "ethnic assimilation";[864] The Jamestown Foundation breathlessly reported that minority rights in China—and the very existence of the ethnic autonomous regions—were hanging by a thread, claiming that minorities' bonus points on college entrance exams[865] had been "significantly reduced," and repeating a litany of dubious rumors of religious oppression, such as an anonymously-sourced account of Chinese Muslims being forced to eat pork.[866] In addition to their position on ending affirmative action, Hu and Hu had advised "downplaying" (淡化) ethnic consciousness,[867] and taking such actions as removing ethnic

863 西藏新闻社记，"消灭西藏文化是所謂第二代民族政策的最終" [The elimination of Tibetan culture is the ultimate goal of the so-called second-generation ethnic policy].

864 Eva Xiao, Jonathan Cheng, and Liza Lin, "Beijing Accelerates Campaign of Ethnic Assimilation," *Wall Street Journal,* December 31, 2020.

865 College entrance exams in China have paramount importance, given the intense competition for university places. A single point can sometimes determine a young student's entire future. According to Sautman, affirmative action in the Chinese university system had on the whole been a positive experience for ethnic minorities. [Barry Sautman, "Affirmative Action, Ethnic Minorities and China's Universities," *Washington International Law Journal* 7, no. 1 (Jan. 1, 1998): 109].

866 James Leibold, "Planting the Seed: Ethnic Policy in Xi Jinping's New Era of Cultural Nationalism," *China Brief* 19, no. 22 (The Jamestown Foundation, December 31, 2019).

867 胡鞍钢 and 胡联合，第二代民族政策：促进民族交融一体和繁荣一体 ("The Second Generation Ethnic Policy: Promoting National Integration and

identity from identification documents[868] and ending recognition of the PRC's 56 officially-recognized ethnic groups,[869] advice which Western academics both interpreted as genocidal and assumed had been fully accepted by the Party. An article in the *China Journal*, drawing on the work of a frequent Jamestown contributor, crudely mistranslated the title of another of Hu and Hu's works, claiming it meant they advocated for "...the Integration of the Peoples of China into a Single Nation-Race," inserting for its Western audience a dark eugenicist overtone.[870]

Criticism of Hu and Hu's perspective is surely warranted, yet the disingenuous conflation of their political beliefs and government policy is anything but. A closer—and more honest—examination of the PRC's policy toward minorities cannot help but show that the Party has taken an approach that is quite distinct from their vision. The policy did indeed change—but, according to Sautman, this change was "not the shift that proponents of curbing minority rights have sought."[871] Contrary to their desires—and to most Western reporting—affirmative action policies were not weakened in the PRC, but *strengthened*. While it was technically true that several regional governments had begun reducing the number of bonus points given to ethnic minorities on college entrance exams, these were the governments of the eastern provinces, the wealthiest in China, where even minorities were considerably better off than elsewhere. In 2017, Beijing canceled the 5 extra points it had previously given minorities—but only minorities from Beijing.[872] Transfer students from "the frontiers, mountainous areas, pastoral areas, and areas inhabited by ethnic minorities" now received the bonus instead. Hunan, a southeastern-central province with scarcely more than half a typical coastal province's GDP per capita, gave minorities from ethnic minority autonomous regions,

---

Prosperity"), 6.

868 胡鞍钢 and 胡联合, "中国梦的基石是中华民族的国族一体化," 111.

869 胡鞍钢 and 胡联合, 115.

870 Mark Elliott, "The Case of the Missing Indigene: Debate Over a 'Second-Generation' Ethnic Policy," *The China Journal* 73 (January 1, 2015): 194–95.

871 Barry Sautman, "Paved with Good Intentions: Proposals to Curb Minority Rights and Their Consequences for China," *Modern China* 38, no. 1 (January 1, 2012): 10.

872 As early as 2000, in fact, the census indicated that Beijing's ethnic minority population had higher university enrollment rates than the Han by four percent, indicating that the bonus points policy had been a success, and was therefore less needed for *Beijing's* minorities. [Reza Hasmath and Jennifer Hsu, *China in an Era of Transition: Understanding Contemporary State and Society Actors* (New York: Palgrave Macmillan, 2009), 53.]

counties, and townships 20 extra points; minorities from minority-majority counties received an extra 10 points, and minorities from other areas received an extra 5 points.[873]

Similarly, it is technically true that the total amount of bonus points granted declined overall, yet the bonuses that remained were increased and targeted to where wealth disparities were the greatest (the entire point, after all, of affirmative action).[874] A representative from the National Education Advisory Committee summarized the new distribution with the phrase "less icing on the cake and more charcoal in the snow"; in the interest of fairness to the less-developed rural areas, fewer bonuses would be allocated for programs in which they lagged behind, such as athletics and the arts, while *more* would be given to disadvantaged groups.[875] As of 2019, a majority of all provinces had reformed their bonus point system, and all continued to provide help to minorities with new policies specifically tailored to regional ethnic conditions, giving the same or more to the poor and less to those who had prospered.

Rather than de-recognize or even "downplay" the 56 ethnic groups, the government doubled down, mentioning the policy even *more* in official communications. In a choreographed symbolic display at the opening ceremony to the 2022 Winter Olympics in Beijing, representatives from each of the 56 groups stood together to pass the Chinese flag across the stadium in front of all of China and the entire world.[876] The policy of ethnic autonomous regions was likewise unchanged. The constitution of the PRC had contained numerous extra rights for ethnic minorities, as well as explicit commitments by the government to combat Han chauvinism[877]

---

873 中国民族报 (China National News), "中国民族报：今年高考少数民族加分政策进一步'瘦身'、完善" [China Ethnic Daily: This year's college entrance examination bonus points policy for ethnic minorities will be further "downsized" and improved].

874 Affirmative action may obviously be done away with once society has developed to the point where people of all ethnicities enjoy equal opportunities and equal outcomes in all aspects of social and economic life, and China's rapid rise in prosperity meant that conditions had greatly changed, necessitating some reforms; but the Party had correctly understood that overall this point was still far away.

875 中国民族报 (China National News), "中国民族报：今年高考少数民族加分政策进一步'瘦身'、完善" [China Ethnic Daily: This year's college entrance examination bonus points policy for ethnic minorities will be further "downsized" and improved].

876 Chad de Guzman, "China Knew It Couldn't Escape Politics at the Olympics Opening Ceremony. It Didn't Try," *TIME*, February 4, 2022.

877 People's Republic of China, *Constitution of the People's Republic of China*, sec. Preamble.

and to assist ethnic minority areas in accelerating their development;[878] though the constitution was changed several times after 2017, none of these clauses were removed. A 2019 amendment updated a few, not to remove any language, but simply to add that the state would *also* uphold harmony between all ethnic groups.[879]

Naturally, none of this made the slightest impression upon the Western press, which mentioned such policies only in order to misrepresent them, or to say their existence only proved that a secret genocide was indeed underway. The new policy of ethnic harmony was smeared as "assimilation" by media organizations such as *Bloomberg*,[880] and the *Guardian* published an op-ed claiming that the Party wished to "shepherd" ethnic minorities "into extinction."[881] A platform was given to any and all Chinese émigrés willing to state this as fact. The corroboration of victim or witness accounts of alleged torture or discrimination was either not attempted, or not possible, as Western institutions decoupled from Xinjiang en masse. Just as it had during the 1980s, the premise that any change to Chinese government policy could only be more harmful went unquestioned. Under this premise, any new jobs in the XUAR became "forced labor" and any new schools became "concentration camps."

Thus, the West watched with skillfully manufactured horror as the masses of impoverished Uyghur peasants were rapidly proletarianized and given paid work. The propaganda machine's pre-2017 litany of complaints about Uyghur unemployment in Xinjiang vanished quickly as the Party intervened to solve it, never to be spoken of again; instead—without an ounce of shame—this machine devoted all of its efforts toward trying to make the very same Uyghurs unemployed again.

By 2020, it had become clear to Western propagandists that the narrative published by every major newspaper throughout 2018 and 2019 regarding the PRC's alleged campaign of "concentration camps" or "internment camps" for increasingly-large numbers of Uyghur detainees[882] would

---

878 People's Republic of China, *Constitution of the People's Republic of China*, art. 4.

879 Thirteenth National People's Congress of the People's Republic of China, *Amendment to the Constitution of the People's Republic of China*.

880 "Xi Warns Missteps on Ethnic Issues Would 'Destabilize' China," *Bloomberg News*, March 7, 2022.

881 Thomas S Mullaney, "How China Went from Celebrating Ethnic Diversity to Suppressing It," *The Guardian*, June 11, 2021.

882 Initially estimated at "tens of thousands" by Human Rights Watch ("China: Big Data Fuels Crackdown in Minority Region," February 26, 2018), then 2 million in a statistical extrapolation of anecdote-speculation published by the NED-funded

soon lose its grip on the public consciousness as news involving them became more and more scarce. The "camps," allegedly opened in 2017, were described by the Chinese government as post-secondary schools which taught the Standard Chinese language, basic civics, and vocational skills;[883] though Western media instantly dismissed this claim, Western journalists struggled to uncover direct evidence to contradict it. In July of 2019, two years after the alleged mass incarceration had begun—a period strangely similar to the length of a typical trade school education—the Chinese government had announced that most students of these facilities had graduated.[884] Western newspapers grew increasingly desperate; at one point in September of 2020 a *Washington Post* journalist recounted a visit to Kashgar in which she noted no conspicuous absence of young Uyghur men (supposedly the "prime targets for the detention campaign") from its busy streets; she carefully refrained from talking to anyone, and instead invented an entirely subjective "blankness in people's eyes" and a "palpable heaviness in the air" to perpetuate the "concentration camp" myth.[885] By 2021, most had given up; an article in the Associated Press reluctantly confirmed the "camps" closure with the headline "Xinjiang eases its grip, but fear remains," commenting on the reduction of police security in Kashgar, and described seeing Uyghur teenage boys "flirt with girls over pounding dance music at rollerblading rinks."[886] In 2022, the *Washington Post* admitted the "camps" had been closed since 2019, and that "scattered checks by journalists" had since found the alleged "camp sites" abandoned or converted to other purposes.[887] But the propaganda machine had also pivoted to keep up; as large numbers of graduates

---

Chinese Human Rights Defenders ("China: Massive Numbers of Uyghurs & Other Ethnic Minorities Forced into Re-Education Programs," August 3, 2018), and ranging as high as 8 million, or the vast majority of the entire Uyghur population (East Turkistan National Awakening Movement, "Genocide").

883 The State Council of the People's Republic of China, *The Fight Against Terrorism and Extremism and Human Rights Protection in Xinjiang* [white paper], March 2019.

884 Chris Buckley and Steven Lee Myers, "China Said It Closed Muslim Detention Camps. There's Reason to Doubt That," *New York Times,* August 9, 2019.

885 Anna Fifield, "As Repression Mounts, China under Xi Jinping Feels Increasingly like North Korea," *Washington Post,* September 28, 2020.

886 Dake Kang, "Terror & Tourism: Xinjiang Eases Its Grip, but Fear Remains," *AP News,* October 10, 2021.

887 Eva Dou and Cate Cadell, "As Crackdown Eases, China's Xinjiang Faces Long Road to Rehabilitation," *Washington Post,* September 23, 2022.

entered the workforce, Western media quickly labeled their employment "forced labor."

The Australian Strategic Policy Institute, together with the *Washington Post*, began a coordinated push in March of 2020 with a 52-page report provocatively-titled "Uyghurs for sale," consisting of a handful of case studies which allegedly indicated that Uyghur factory workers were employed against their will. The *Washington Post* decided the involuntary nature of Uyghur workers' employment at Taekwang Shoes, a company operating a factory in Qingdao, solely by hearsay from a pair of anonymous local street vendors. The article described how Uyghur workers had patronized their stalls by "[using] hand gestures and rudimentary Mandarin to buy dried fruit, socks and sanitary pads"—only to rely, in the following paragraphs, on the two vendors' speculation that the very workers with whom they had been unable to communicate were not there by choice:

"Everyone knows they didn't come here of their own free will. They were brought here," said one fruit-seller as she set up her stall. "The Uighurs had to come because they didn't have an option. The government sent them here," another vendor told the Washington Post.

No other evidence of forced labor at Taekwang Shoes beyond descriptions of the security system at the factory—which housed Han as well as Uyghur workers—was provided; the article cited the ASPI report to further support its claim,[888] which in turn circularly cited the same *Washington Post* article.[889] Other case studies in the report were similarly vague.[890] Sketchers USA, whose supplier in Guangdong Province was also named in the report, conducted multiple unannounced audits of the factory in an attempt to confirm the allegations, none of which "revealed

888 Anna Fifield, "China Compels Uighurs to Work in Shoe Factory That Supplies Nike," *Washington Post,* February 29, 2020.

889 Vicky Xiuzhong Xu et al., "Uyghurs for Sale: 'Re-Education', Forced Labour and Surveillance beyond Xinjiang," 10.

890 According to ASPI's job advertisements, their data analysts are in fact recruited specifically for their "flair for using data to tell stories" and their "Enthusiasm and comfort with ambiguity and drawing sound inferences from incomplete information" rather than any specific degrees, certifications, or any other academic qualifications. (Australian Strategic Policy Institute, "Jobs at ASPI: ICPC Data Analyst.")

any indications of the use of forced labor, either of Uyghurs or any other ethnic or religious group, nor did the audits raise any other concerns about general labor conditions" according to their statement.[891] James' analysis of the report concluded that "not one" of the accusations made by ASPI regarding forced labor in China "survive[d] close scrutiny" and that the report "was not a work of scholarly analysis, but rather a piece of strategic disinformation to exact harm"[892]—yet the report would be used as the foundation for Western foreign policy toward Xinjiang, not in spite of this fact, but because of it.

Others soon followed ASPI's example. In July, Washington-based policy think tank Center for Strategic and International Studies (CSIS) published its own report characterizing the PRC's poverty reduction campaign in Xinjiang as "forced labor," citing the ASPI report and publications by a Jamestown Foundation researcher.[893] As mentioned earlier in this chapter, by September major international auditors were pressured to "decouple" from Xinjiang, and U.S. Customs and Border Protection issued unilateral sanctions on multiple companies in the XUAR. In another coordinated effort in December, the BBC commissioned a report alleging that Uyghur "forced labor" was being used to harvest cotton in Xinjiang.[894] *Bloomberg*[895] and various Western NGOs such as Amnesty International published similar reports throughout 2021, citing it and ASPI numerous times,[896] and relying on uncorroborated testimonies.[897] In June of that year, the *Washington Post* again published an article alleging that a Chinese manufacturing company used forced Uyghur labor—this time Hoshine Silicon, the world's largest producer of metallurgical-grade silicon needed to construct solar panels.[898]

---

891 Skechers, "Statement of Skechers USA, Inc. on Uyghurs," March 2021, 2.

892 Jaq James, *The Australian Strategic Policy Institute's Uyghurs for Sale Report: Scholarly Analysis or Strategic Disinformation?*, CO-WEST-PRO Consultancy Working Paper 1 (2022): 87.

893 Amy K. Lehr, "Addressing Forced Labor in the Xinjiang Uyghur Autonomous Region," Center for Strategic and Inernational Studies, *CSIS Brief*, July 30, 2020.

894 John Sudworth, "China's 'Tainted' Cotton," *BBC*, December 2020.

895 Dan Murtaugh et al., "Secrecy and Abuse Claims Haunt China's Solar Factories in Xinjiang," *Bloomberg*, April 13, 2021.

896 Amnesty International, "'Like We Were Enemies in a War': China's Mass Internment, Torture, and Persecution of Muslims in Xinjiang," June 10, 2021.

897 Jaq James, *Amnesty International & Human Rights Watch's Forced Xinjiang Labour Claims: Junk Research or Noble Cause Corruption?*, CO-WEST-PRO Consultancy Working Paper 2 (2022): 81.

898 While hypocrisy does not *in itself* disprove any particular claim, the

All of these reports struggled tremendously to find some way to distinguish Uyghur workers' experiences from ordinary free employment. The *Washington Post* bizarrely began its exposé of Hoshine by admitting in the first paragraph that Uyghur workers who were supposedly forced to work in the factories earned $600 a month—over 4,000 yuan, a rather high income in Xinjiang—to operate electric furnaces. The *Post* quoted a Uyghur émigré who lived overseas to support their claim that the jobs were compulsory, then even more bizarrely included an interview with a Uyghur worker at the factory who told the *Post* that he had come to work there voluntarily.[899] The report commissioned by the BBC attempted to show that two below-average monthly incomes reported by cotton field-workers were below the minimum wage in Xinjiang—either mistakenly or deliberately omitting county-level minimum wage differences in the XUAR, which indicated that for the year in question these incomes would only have been below minimum wage in a county where no cotton was cultivated.[900] Yet the details or factual accuracy of this report were of

---

shamelessness of the *Washington Post* cannot be passed over with no remark. When the news broke in 2015 that United States-based solar corporation Suniva used U.S. federal prison labor to manufacture solar panels, it was reported by *Reuters* (Nichola Groom, "Prison Labor Helps U.S. Solar Company Manufacture at Home," June 9, 2015), but apparently was not considered important enough to be covered by *Washington Post* reporters! As of this writing, the only *Post* articles available online that even mention Suniva were published two years later—one of them an op-ed written by Suniva's own executive vice president, who praised the new tariffs on China and expressed the hope that President Trump would further protect the U.S. solar industry. Neither the Suniva VP nor the *Post's* editors made any mention of his company's history of profiting from the labor of actual prisoners (Matt Card, "Trump Is Right to Protect U.S. Manufacturers. Here's How He Could Help Us," November 24, 2017).

899 Lily Kuo, Pei Lin Wu, and Jeanne Whalen, "Solar Industry's Ties to China's Xinjiang Region Raise Specter of Forced Labor," *Washington Post,* June 24, 2021.

900 A brief explanation is called for. The report claims that to remain above China's absolute rural poverty line in 2019, "a household of five would need to earn a total of 20,000 RMB or 1,667 RMB per month. To compare, Xinjiang's minimum wage in 2018 amounted to 1,820 RMB per month." (Adrian Zenz, "Coercive Labor in Xinjiang: Labor Transfer and the Mobilization of Ethnic Minorities to Pick Cotton," New Lines Institute, December 14, 2020, 18.) This is extraordinarily misleading, given that the minimum wage in Xinjiang was set at the county level in 2018, and in fact ranged from 1,460 to 1,820 RMB according to a public release by the People's Government of the XUAR, which assigned the highest minimum wage of 1,820 RMB to only two areas: Taxkorgan Tajik Autonomous County and Karamay City. (新疆维吾尔自治区人民政府, "新政发[2018]19号 新疆维吾尔自治区人民政府关于调整新疆维吾尔自治区最低工资标准的通知 [Notice of the People's Government of Xinjiang Uygur Autonomous Region on Adjusting the Minimum Wage Standards of

little concern to the Western press, and even less to its true audience, the United States Congress, which voted overwhelmingly to pass the "Uyghur Forced Labor Prevention Act" in the following months. By the end of 2021, it became law. The act presumed that any and all goods from the entire region of Xinjiang—or even containing materials that had originated in Xinjiang—were made by "forced labor"; such goods were consequently banned from the United States unless the importer could establish "with clear and convincing evidence" for the Customs and Border Protection agency that no forced labor had been used to produce them.[901] The PRC had again become guilty until proven innocent; the Western media now not only marshaled public opinion against the targets of the super-empire, but fulfilled the even more sinister purpose of building support for legislation actually designed to destroy the economic progress of the Uyghur people.

Such was the life cycle of the "forced labor" narrative. First the governments of the super-empire (the United States, the United Kingdom, Australia) paid their NGO appendages (ASPI, Jamestown, the NED) to produce "academic" reports from dubious and unverified primary sources. Then the Western press (the *BBC*, the *Washington Post*) credulously covered these reports, building a consensus and public pressure to act. With this mandate, those very same governments happily legislated economic warfare against Xinjiang. Propaganda had been weaponized.

Much like the United States' own New Deal of the 1930s, the jobs programs initiated by the government in Xinjiang often directly employed workers in the public sector, yet many were hired by private companies

---

Xinjiang Uygur Autonomous Region].)

The report continues, claiming "One account of transferred cotton pickers claimed an average monthly income of 4,800 RMB. Two other accounts, however, give average income figures of only 1,670 and 1,805 RMB per month" (Adrian Zenz, "Coercive Labor in Xinjiang: Labor Transfer and the Mobilization of Ethnic Minorities to Pick Cotton," 18.)—supposedly indicating that fieldworkers were not properly compensated according to the minimum wage.

Therefore, in order to actually have been compensated below the minimum wage, these workers would need to have picked cotton in either Karamay City or Taxkorgan. This is quite unlikely; according to the map of cotton farmland in Xinjiang provided in the report, Taxkorgan did not contain a single cotton field (Adrian Zenz, 6), and Karamay City is in *northern* Xinjiang where both relatively few Uyghurs live and most cotton harvesting is mechanized.

901 Rep. James P. McGovern [D-MA-2], H.R.6256 - 117th Congress (2021–2022): To ensure that goods made with forced labor in the Xinjiang Uyghur Autonomous Region of the People's Republic of China do not enter the United States market, and for other purposes.

as well. These were the weakest links and became prime targets of the propaganda machine. Hoshine was immediately sanctioned by the U.S. CBP.[902] Lens Technology, one of Apple's major suppliers of smartphone touch screens, hastily laid off over 400 Uyghur workers following ASPI's initial report and froze hiring of any new Uyghur employees.[903] Taekwang Shoes, under pressure from its major customer Nike, also terminated its entire Uyghur workforce.[904] A media analysis published by Pakistan's Islamabad Policy Research Institute found that the *New York Times'* coverage of Uyghur human rights issues between 2019 and 2021 clearly diverged from news organizations in the Islamic world by urging for increased sanctions against Chinese companies.[905]

As such sanctions loomed, private companies began once again to discriminate against racial minorities, either unofficially or by proxy. In 2021, American smart home technology company Universal Electronics ended its relationship with a staffing agency that had hired Uyghur employees to work in its Chinese suppliers' factories.[906] The Hong Kong-based Esquel Group, the world's largest woven shirt maker, had the resources to sue the U.S. Commerce Department over its inclusion in a sanctions list, and won due to lack of evidence of forced labor[907]—but not before lost business had led to the closure of several factories in China, which laid off thousands of workers.[908] The Western propaganda machine's cynical criticisms of Xinjiang's high minority unemployment rate during the 2000s were shown to be hollow a decade later as it cruelly deprived thousands of Uyghurs of their jobs and did its best to push them back into the hell of

902 Lily Kuo and Jeanne Whalen, "Biden Administration Bars Imports of Solar Panels Linked to Forced Labor in China's Xinjiang Region," *Washington Post,* June 24, 2021.

903 Liza Lin, Eva Xiao, and Yoko Kubota, "Chinese Suppliers to Apple, Nike Shun Xinjiang Workers as U.S. Forced-Labor Ban Looms," *Wall Street Journal,* July 20, 2021.

904 Joshua Lipes, "Nike Says China-Based Supplier Sent All Uyghur Workers Home Amid Forced Labor Allegations," *Radio Free Asia,* July 21, 2020.

905 "How the Uyghur Issue Has Been Framed Across Global Media - A Snapshot," *G5iO,* September 20, 2021, 3.

906 "Universal Electronics <UEIC.O> Ended Relationship with Agency Linked to Uyghur Workers," *Reuters,* October 20, 2021.

907 Chad Bray, "Nike's Former Supplier Esquel Group Scores a Rare Win in a Bid to Remove Xinjiang Unit from US Forced-Labour Sanctions List," *South China Morning Post,* August 4, 2021.

908 Owen Churchill, "Esquel Group Sues US over Unit's Inclusion on 'Entity List', as Company's Chief Says It Faces 'Devastating Harm,'" *South China Morning Post,* July 7, 2021.

rural poverty. Just as the United States' embargo on Cuba was designed to bring about hunger and desperation, its sanctions on Xinjiang were carefully crafted to undermine the Party's efforts to lift the people up to better lives.

Comparing Chinese to Western Propaganda

The use of propaganda by the Western press and NGOs to build support for imperial policy is hardly a novel phenomenon;[909] throughout the stage of super-imperialism, fictional or heavily manipulated "atrocity propaganda" has quite often been used to justify military interventions by the United States and NATO. Often, all that Western governments require from a newspaper or NGO is merely for it to republish or rubber-stamp stories they themselves had already fabricated. In 1990, Amnesty International claimed it had "verified" a fictional account of Iraqi troops murdering over 300 premature babies in Kuwait, putting an imprimatur on the hoax that was likely essential to bringing about the subsequent U.S. invasion of Iraq. President H.W. Bush personally publicized the story to build support for the war over the next few months, eventually convincing a divided U.S. Senate to authorize the use of military force against Iraq in January of 1991 by a margin of only five votes.[910] In 2003, anecdote-speculation derived from the testimony of Iraqi émigrés was used to justify a second invasion, this time through bogus claims that the Iraqi government possessed weapons of mass destruction and had ties to Al Qaeda.[911] Being so ubiquitous in the West, modern atrocity propaganda

---

909 Nor, crucially, is its use to demonize governments controlled by communist parties. During the Cold War, for example, Reuters and AFP were infiltrated and manipulated into republishing stories of fictional atrocities by Cuban soldiers in the Angolan Civil War that the CIA had planted in local African newspapers. According to the former chief of the CIA's Angolan task force that was responsible for manufacturing these tall tales, his covert actions team "didn't know of one single atrocity" actually committed by the Cubans. (*John Stockwell, Former CIA Agent John Stockwell Talks about How the CIA Worked in Vietnam and Elsewhere,* Witness to War YouTube video [15:12], posted on September 29, 2017.)

910 According to a CBC documentary about the hoax, the incubator baby story was brought up a total of seven times in the Senate's debate over the vote. [Neil Docherty (director), *To Sell a War* (1992).]

911 After the invasion had succeeded, when no such weapons could be found, newspapers that had spread the story were eventually forced to acknowledge that they had been fooled; the *Guardian*, for example, admitted in 2004 that "Iraqi defectors tricked us with WMD lies." (David Rose, "Iraqi Defectors Tricked Us with WMD Lies, but We Must Not Be Fooled Again," May 29, 2004.)

is no longer remarkable; what *is* remarkable is that despite the negative (in the West, and to an extent internationally) reputation of modern China's infamously Party-controlled news media, it does not operate in an even remotely similar fashion.

Nowhere is this distinction clearer than in the response to the July 5 incident. In June of 2009, at a toy factory in the city of Shaoguan near China's eastern coast, a brawl between Uyghur and Han co-workers—set off by false rumors and a tragic misunderstanding surrounding a young Han woman who had accidentally entered the Uyghur workers' dormitory—left two Uyghur men dead. The perpetrators were eventually caught, tried, and convicted; a Han man identified as the "principal instigator" was given the death penalty and the rest lengthy prison sentences.[912] However, in the confusion after the melee, the instigators had fled the scene and were initially not apprehended, fueling wild speculation on the internet. The *Guardian* reported that Uyghur exile groups quickly circulated video and pictures of the fighting, along with unverified claims that many more deaths had occurred, throughout the following week.[913] On the 5th of July, tensions finally boiled over on the other side of China, where a demonstration in the XUAR's Ürümqi organized around the rumors devolved into a bloody anti-Han pogrom. Hundreds of buses and buildings were set on fire, and almost 200 people, nearly all of them Han, were stabbed or beaten to death by the mob in a single night. Well over a thousand more were injured. In an interview with Hong Kong news magazine *Yazhou Zhoukan*, Uyghur journalist Hailette Niyaz, who had witnessed some of the destruction, reported hearing rioters shout slogans such as "Kill the Han!" and "We want to establish an Islamic country and strictly implement Islamic law"—signs he believed indicated the mob had been organized by Hizb-ut-Tahrir al-Islami, or the Islamic Liberation Party, a fundamentalist organization active throughout Central Asia that aimed to establish a global caliphate.[914]

---

912 According to *Xinhua*, a total of seven other Han who participated in the deadly brawl were sentenced to prison, one with a life sentence; three Uyghurs involved in the brawl were also given relatively shorter terms of five to six years. (David Barboza, "China Sets Sentences in Brawl Tied to Riot," *New York Times*, October 11, 2009.)

913 Jonathan Watts, "Old Suspicions Magnified Mistrust into Ethnic Riots in Urumqi," *The Guardian*, July 10, 2009.

914 海莱特·尼亚孜 (Hailette Niyaz), 專訪: 維族NGO工作者、前新疆法制報總編室主任海莱特 他在七五事件前就預警. 李永峰 [Interview: Uyghur NGO worker Hailette, former director of the editorial office of Xinjiang Legal News who gave early warning before the July 5 incident. Li Yongfeng].

An observer unable to distinguish between the class that controls the United States' government and the class that controls China's might have expected the July 5 incident to become China's "9/11 moment." The world today still feels the aftershocks of the United States' horrific retaliation to the September 11 attacks; a report published by scholars at Brown University found that two decades after 2001, the Global "War on Terror" (GWOT) had caused the deaths of a total of nearly one million people through invasion, bombing, and disease,[915] and displaced over 38 million more.[916] The ruling class of the super-empire and its propaganda machine had gleefully used the specter of "radical Islamic terrorists" who "hated freedom" as a justification for military interventions throughout the periphery, which destabilized vast regions of Africa, the Middle East, and Central Asia in order to quell organized resistance to the dispossessive accumulation process.[917] The U.S. media, while paying lip service to President George W. Bush's official public announcement that not all Muslims were violent and that Al Qaeda had only "hijacked" a peaceful religion,[918] nevertheless took every opportunity to demonize Muslims and particularly Arabs to a global audience. Almost overnight, "radical Islamic terrorists" became the villains of innumerable films, television shows, first-person shooter video games, and other mass media. According to FBI statistics, between 2000 and 2001, hate crimes against Muslims in the U.S. increased by sixteen hundred percent.[919] The Western press happily fanned the flames, platforming commentators and media personalities

---

915 Neta C. Crawford and Catherine Lutz, "Human Cost of Post-9/11 Wars: Direct War Deaths in Major War Zones: Afghanistan & Pakistan (Oct. 2001–Aug. 2021); Iraq (March 2003–Aug. 2021); Syria (Sept. 2014–May 2021); Yemen (Oct. 2002–Aug. 2021) and Other Post-9/11 War Zones" [paper], *Costs of War,* Watson Institute of International and Public Affairs at Boston University, 2021.

916 David Vine et al., "Creating Refugees: Displacement Caused by the United States' Post-9/11 Wars," *Costs of War,* Watson Institute of International and Public Affairs at Boston University, September 21, 2020.

917 This objective was made explicit in a book by the chairman of U.S. geopolitical think tank STRATFOR, who was quoted at greater length in Chapter Two: "The third series of interventions was in the Islamic world, designed to block al Qaeda's (or anyone else's) desire to create a secure Islamic empire. The interventions in Afghanistan and Iraq were both a part of this effort." (George Friedman, *The Next 100 Years,* 63–64.)

918 In one of Bush's first speeches after the attacks, he told Congress that "The terrorists are traitors to their own faith, trying, in effect, to hijack Islam itself." (George W. Bush, "Text: President Bush Addresses the Nation," *Washington Post,* September 20, 2001.)

919 Federal Bureau of Investigation, "Uniform Crime Report."

who openly opined that Islam (and by implication all Muslims) was an inherently violent faith.[920] September 11 itself is still perpetually memorialized as the United States' officially-proclaimed "Patriot Day" holiday.

Nothing like any of this occurred in China.

Even the Washington-based Uyghur émigré organizations were shocked when the Chinese government arrested Hailette Niyaz for giving his interview to *Yazhou Zhoukan*.[921] After all, Niyaz had been a *supporter* of the government, in the very same interview speaking contemptuously of the émigré World Uyghur Congress and condemning the idea of Uyghur separatism, calling it a concept "built up by the Turks and forcibly thrust upon us."[922] He was later sentenced to *fifteen years* in prison for endangering state security[923]—one of the harshest punishments the PRC has ever given a journalist, according to the Committee to Protect Journalists.[924] The true reason for making an example of Niyaz was twofold: first, he had drawn attention to racially-motivated violence *against* the Han *by* ethnic minorities, and second, he had done so on a Chinese-language foreign website.[925] During the United States' GWOT the Western propa-

---

920 In 2016, the *International Communication Gazette* published a comprehensive meta-analysis of 345 studies of the media's portrayal of Muslims and Islam, which found that through the catalyst of 9/11, "most of the Western mainstream media" had "constructed negative images of Muslims and Islam," consistently presenting Muslims as threatening. (Ahmed and Matthes, "Media Representation of Muslims and Islam from 2000 to 2015: A Meta-Analysis.")

921 Reuters Staff, "China to Try Uighur Journalist on 'Security' – Report," *Reuters,* July 22, 2010

922 海莱特·尼亚孜 (Hailette Niyaz), 專訪：維族NGO工作者、前新疆法制報總編室主任海莱特 他在七五事件前就預警. 李永峰 [Interview: Uyghur NGO worker Hailette, former director of the editorial office of Xinjiang Legal News who gave early warning before the July 5 incident. Li Yongfeng]

923 Tania Branigan, "China Jails Writer for 15 Years for 'Endangering State Security,'" *The Guardian,* July 25, 2010.

924 As of 2021, the CPJ recorded only two receiving longer prison sentences in China (for any reason) ever since. (Committee to Protect Journalists, "Journalists Imprisoned," loc. China.)

925 Western media has speculated that Niyaz's punishment was *solely* for giving an interview to foreign media, but this is clearly not the case. Kurbanjan Samat, a Uyghur photographer who in 2014 had given an interview to *Phoenix Weekly* (another Hong Kong magazine) about his own experiences, in which he repeatedly mentioned July 5, was not similarly arrested or incarcerated, despite his own dim view of Islamic fundamentalism. Samat's story included some frank descriptions of *Han* chauvinism that he had faced as a minority in eastern China yet did not describe Uyghur racial chauvinism or violence against the Han. (张弛 (Zhang Chi), "一个维族家庭的生活：不去讲经班遭亲戚排斥" [Life of a Uyghur family: Relatives ostracize them for not going to lectures].)

ganda machine publicized any criticism or disrespect of Islam itself by its prized pro-Western apostates; but when the Chinese government had the similar option of using vocally anti-separatist Uyghurs to manufacture public support for repression in Xinjiang, it silenced them instead, out of fear that they might incite retaliatory violence from the Han majority.

Indeed, in the aftermath of July 5, the PRC's state-owned media was reluctant to disclose the ethnicity of the victims.[926] The Western press capitalized on this hesitation, seizing the opportunity to immediately propagate the falsehood that there had in fact been a massacre of Uyghurs by a Han mob instead. The *Telegraph*'s foreign correspondent in Shanghai hastily kept ahead of the facts by announcing that the deaths reported by the Chinese government—156 was the initial count—were of Uyghurs, and only issued a correction after his on-the-ground colleagues in Ürümqi admitted otherwise.[927] A Han mob did in fact assemble to take revenge, armed with wooden clubs and other improvised weapons, less than forty-eight hours later;[928] however, the authorities were prepared. The local government declared a curfew, and the police came out in force, teargassing the mob to prevent it from entering a Uyghur neighborhood.[929] The *Telegraph* noted how the local Party secretary "risked his dignity by standing on the roof of a police car with a megaphone beseeching the crowd to go home." Most did so by early evening, and no deaths were reported connected to the demonstration.[930] While the Chinese state-owned press officially blamed the World Uyghur Congress for fomenting the riot, the government at every level seemed far more concerned with protecting Uyghur innocents than making accusations.

---

926 Anthony Kuhn and Melissa Block, "China Ethnic Unrest Kills 156," NPR, July 6, 2009.

927 Perversely, the NED-funded World Uyghur Congress, which most likely played a significant role in organizing the initial demonstration that transformed into a pogrom, continued to claim that several hundred Uyghurs had been secretly killed by police on the 5th, which even the *Telegraph* (Malcolm Moore, "Urumqi Riots Signal Dark Days Ahead," July 8, 2009) *Reuters*, and other Western newspapers have universally contradicted (Yu Le and Lucy Hornby, "China Sentences Four More to Death for Urumqi Riot," January 26, 2010). On the 6th, the *Guardian* reported that at a local hospital, doctors were still treating nearly 300 injured victims from the previous night, of whom only about 40 were Uyghur (Jonathan Watts, "Old Suspicions Magnified Mistrust into Ethnic Riots in Urumqi," July 10, 2009).

928 Ürümqi, in northern Xinjiang, is three-quarters Han by population.

929 Tania Branigan, "Han Chinese Launch Revenge Attacks on Uighur Property," *The Guardian*, July 7, 2009.

930 Peter Foster, "Eyewitness: Tensions High on the Streets of Urumqi," *The Telegraph*, July 7, 2009.

President George W. Bush had given a public address on the morning of September 11, and a subsequent prime time speech to the country that evening; neither President Hu Jintao nor any member of the Politburo had so much as mentioned the Ürümqi riot for days after the event.[931] The Western press had identified the 9/11 hijackers as Arab Muslims almost immediately, within hours of the attacks, and news broadcasters rushed to heighten their audiences' panic by reporting additional fictional attacks[932] throughout the day;[933,934] but after the riot in Ürümqi, the spread of news in China was tightly controlled. July 5 had been a Sunday; by early Monday morning the internet was shut down in Xinjiang and foreign social media websites had been blocked entirely throughout the country. *Reuters* reported that comments and photographs of the violence were quickly scrubbed from domestic social media within a few hours of being posted, and that keywords such as "Uighur" and even "Ürümqi" returned no search results.[935] Rather than deliberately fan the flames of anti-Muslim outrage, the Party and its censors did whatever they could to extinguish them.

However well-intentioned, this policy of course had serious drawbacks, notably an erosion of trust in the reliability of news reported by state-owned media, which amid malicious rumors such as those regarding the incident in Shaoguan could instead result in even further violence. The *Financial Times* reported how several Han chauvinist blogs accused the central government of having "no clear position" and demanded it send troops to Xinjiang; such blogs, the *Times* said, "unrepresentative as they might be, are the sole outlets for opinions untainted by the government line."[936,937]

---

931 Richard McGregor, "Beijing Handles Political Management of Riot," *Financial Times,* July 7, 2009.

932 Associated Press, "A Stunning 48 Hours of News" (archived on the Wayback Machine).

933 "A Number Of Men Arrested With Explosives On Jersey Turnpike," *CNN* Live Event/Special aired September 11, 2001.

934 Jim Naureckas, "As if Reality Wasn't Bad Enough: Dan Rather Spread Alarmist Rumors on September 11," FAIR, *Extra!* (Nov.-Dec. 2001).

935 Ben Blanchard, "China Tightens Web Screws after Xinjiang Riot." *Reuters,* July 6, 2009.

936 Richard McGregor, "Beijing Handles Political Management of Riots." *Financial Times,* July 7, 2009.

937 According to Sautman, such "internet outpourings" of chauvinism are not representative of Han in general, and "there is no firm indication that Han resentment of minority rights is a deeply felt sentiment, unlike the pervasive resentment of the rich in China." (Sautman, "Scaling Back Minority Rights?")

Yet while the government did arrest many of those involved in the violence, its line did not bend to the chauvinists' desires. The People's Liberation Army neither instituted martial law in Xinjiang nor significantly increased the troops at its bases there after July 5, and by December of 2009, though it had arrested what suspects it could identify, the government's only serious policy changes had been to restrain the Han inhabitants of the region. Many Han residents of Ürümqi had attempted to self-segregate in the months after the riots, but the local government intervened, forbidding Han who lived in mixed-ethnic or predominantly-Uyghur neighborhoods to sell their homes. Local business were also strongly encouraged to hire more minorities.[938] Where identifiable, discrimination and boycotts of Uyghur goods and services were punished; Han taxi drivers who refused service to a minority were fined 1000 RMB (about one week's income).[939] The July 5 incident is not memorialized in China and is rarely mentioned today.[940] The entries for Ürümqi on Baidu[941] and Baike.com,[942] the two largest online Chinese encyclopedias, do not even mention the event.[943]

While the United States' ultimatum to Afghanistan came nine days after September 11,[944] and by December its invasion force had driven the Taliban from every major city in the country, the so-called "people's war on terrorism" was not declared until 2014. Where the U.S. government had taken only hours, the PRC waited a full five *years* after the July 5 incident, its best and greatest opportunity. If the Party's intentions were the same, what accounts for this delay?

---

938 Sautman, "Scaling Back Minority Rights?"

939 SCMP Reporter, "Urumqi Remains Divided by Fear and Mistrust," *South China Morning Post,* December 22, 2009.

940 In a discussion with the author in 2023, a native Xinjianger who had traveled outside the province in later years related that almost none of his acquaintances outside Xinjiang were even aware of the July 5 incident, and of those who had heard of it, almost none knew any details.

941 Baidu Baike, "乌鲁木齐" (Ürümqi).

942 快懂百科 (Baike.com), "乌鲁木齐" [Ürümqi].

943 Riots and terrorism do not feature prominently on either website, other than in articles about specific incidents. As of this writing, the Gongyuan North Street suicide bombings in Ürümqi, the deadliest terrorist attack in China in modern history, was also not mentioned on either page; Baidu's entry for the Kunming Railway Station (Baidu Baike, "昆明站" [Kunming Railway Station]) contained one sentence referencing the coordinated mass stabbing attack earlier that year that killed over 30 passengers, while Baike.com did not mention it at all. (快懂百科 (Baike.com), "昆明站" [Kunming Railway Station].)

944 "Bush Delivers Ultimatum," *CNN,* September 21, 2001.

According to publicly available information aggregated by Chinese diaspora media organization, the Qiao Collective, between 1990 and 2014 there were no less than 52 significant terrorist attacks in China. 11 of these occurred in 2014, making it stand out as the worst such year, yet the total number of victims killed that year was just more than a hundred, considerably less than the death toll of July 5.[945] For decades, the Party had considered terrorism to be a manageable problem[946]—and one that a serious attempt to solve was not yet within the Party's capabilities.

It is not a coincidence that the "people's war on terrorism" was announced only two months after the beginning of the government's targeted poverty alleviation campaign,[947] which as mentioned in the previous chapter involved spending $700 billion to develop the countryside over the next six years. As the Common Prosperity era of social-democratic wealth redistribution dawned, the Party looked for places to spend the new wealth that decades of Reform had accumulated—and saw southern Xinjiang, where such alleviation was needed more than nearly anywhere else in China.

As a materialist, Marxist organization, it is the ideological belief of the Communist Party that the only way to permanently end terrorism is to make not just the strategy but its *goal* undesirable. For the East Turkestan separatists to no longer wish for independence in the first place, there was a great unfulfilled prerequisite: development. It was the Party's view that any organization that employs terrorism as a strategy thrives upon repression but evaporates upon prosperity; suicide bombers willing to kill innocent strangers cannot be easily recruited among people who feel they have a future in *this* world, and economic concerns—having adequate

---

945 Qiao Collective, *Attacks on Xinjiang and Beyond.*

946 Indeed, even *Western* academics have long considered separatism in Xinjiang to be a hopeless cause. In 2003, for example, Professor Marika Vicziany of Monash Asia Institute wrote that "Uygur terrorism has no hope of achieving its ends of establishing a separate state of East Turkestan" [Marika Vicziany, "State Responses to Islamic Terrorism in Western China and Their Impact on South Asia," Contemporary South Asia 12, no. 2 (2003): 259]. Even after July 5, Sautman concluded that separatism could only succeed in the extreme case of the collapse of China's central government. (Sautman, "Scaling Back Minority Rights?")

947 In March of 2014, the report from the Second Session of the Twelfth National People's Congress announced a fundamental acceleration of anti-poverty efforts (Li Keqiang, *Report on the Work of the Government* delivered at the Second Session of the Twelfth National People's Congress on March 5, 2014); on May 23, *Xinhua* reported that the government had approved the anti-terrorism campaign. (Michael Martina, "China Launches Crackdown on 'terrorist Activities' after Attack," May 23, 2014).

food and shelter, an income, and a promise of growth—are the most fundamental conditions of life.

Since nearly every government in the world had its own domestic anti-terrorism program during the early twenty-first century,[948] it is illustrative to compare the PRC's with those of other countries, particularly the United States, but also of China's own neighbors. It is a relatively simple mental procedure to classify the PRC's anti-terrorism policy in the same category as the United States', and one that is now strongly encouraged by the Western press; indeed, today the Western press has accused the PRC and the Communist Party of adopting its own more recent counter-terrorism policies for very same purpose—i.e. as a justification to harvest raw materials and extract super-profits from ethnic minorities. Yet as this chapter will show, the similarities in form necessarily concealed vast differences in content.

The deception underlying the United States' GWOT is easiest to apprehend. From the beginning, the Bush Administration publicly recognized the distinction between Islam and terrorism; the President proclaimed Islam a religion of peace on September 11 itself, met with Islamic leaders within days afterward,[949] and organized numerous public relations events with the Muslim community in the U.S., including the first Iftar ceremony at the White House.[950] These practices largely continued under President Obama; in 2010 he even expressed qualified support for plans to build a mosque two blocks from the World Trade Center "Ground Zero."[951] Neither administration, however, was particularly secretive in ruthlessly persecuting Muslims at home and abroad, nonetheless. Under Bush, the White House made no attempt to rein in a bigoted media establishment, and openly pursued a campaign to smear the country's largest Muslim civil rights organization with accusations that it harbored terrorist "co-conspirators."[952] Their public relations campaigns did little to mask

---

948 For many countries this was not optional, considering the enormous political pressure the United States placed upon the entire world to support its GWOT; with the bloody examples of Afghanistan and Iraq on display, quite often, peripheral countries with large Muslim populations (restive or not) needed to demonstrate their compliance, in order to avoid being invaded and subjugated themselves.

949 Aymann Ismail, "'There Was a Betrayal,'" *Slate,* September 10, 2021.

950 U.S. Department of State, "The Global War on Terrorism: The First 100 Days." https://2001-2009.state.gov/s/ct/rls/wh/6947.htm

951 Ryan Creed, "President Obama Supports Building of Mosque Near Ground Zero," *ABC News,* August 14, 2011.

952 Neil MacFarquhar, "Muslim Groups Oppose a List of 'Co-Conspirators.'" *New York Times,* August 16, 2007.

their brutal foreign policy, which included not only the direct military invasions described multiple times in this book, but the "targeted killing" drone program codified under Obama that with a 90% civilian casualty rate overall amounted to little more than the indiscriminate shelling of Arab homes and public gatherings throughout the Middle East.[953]

Similarly, Prime Minister Narendra Modi of India's nationalist Bharatiya Janata Party has always publicly stated his admiration of Islam and its message of peace, and throughout his administration strongly emphasized the distinction between the religion and the practice of terrorism;[954] Modi's address at Aligarh Muslim University in 2019, for instance, was interpreted by the *Print* as a direct appeal to international students from countries with significant Muslim populations to help improve India's reputation in their home countries.[955] Within India, however, the BJP is widely believed to have an unofficial electoral strategy of inciting anti-Muslim hatred, which has resulted in pogroms against India's Muslim minority. In its assessment of one such pogrom in Delhi in 2020, the Delhi Minorities Commission called the violence "one-sided [and] well-planned," targeting Muslim homes and businesses.[956] Rashtriya Swayamsevak Sangh, a paramilitary organization associated with the BJP, is often considered a recurring perpetrator. In 2016, scarcely two years after Modi became prime minister, another brigade of the Indian Army was deployed in the restive, predominantly-Muslim region of Jammu and Kashmir[957] (though the Indian military presence there had been considerable even before the BJP's coalition government).[958]

---

953 Jeremy Scahill, *The Assassination Complex: Inside the Government's Secret Drone Warfare Program* (Simon & Schuster, 2017).

954 "Narendra Modi Praises Islam for Its Message of Peace, Harmony," *The Economic Times,* March 17, 2016.

955 Shekhar Gupta, "In Modi's AMU Pitch to Muslims, Retreat from Party Politics Hurting Foreign Policy Interests," *ThePrint,* December 26, 2020.

956 Shinjini Ghosh, "Delhi Violence 'One-Sided, Well-Planned', Says Minorities Panel," *The Hindu,* March 4, 2020.

957 Sumir Kaul, "Army Quietly Launches Operation Calm Down in South Kashmir," *India Today,* September 13, 2016.

958 Indian governments typically do not speak officially on troop deployments in Kashmir. Estimates of Indian military strength in Kashmir have therefore varied considerably. In 2014, *Reuters* reported that more than 700,000 police and soldiers had been deployed to the region (Douglas Busvine and Fayaz Bukhari, "Kashmiris Wary as Modi Challenges for Power," April 23, 2014). In 2019, the Indian press published lower estimates. An op-ed on the far-right tabloid website *OpIndia* claimed only about 230,000 security forces were in Kashmir (Rohit Vats, "Half a Million or 1 Million? While Media Peddles Fantastical Claims, Here Are the Actual Number

Any analysis of how a government—China's or any other's—contending with terrorism *publicly presents* its policy to the rest of the world is therefore useless. The most vocally "pro-Islam" administrations may in fact be among the most oppressive toward Muslims. With the well having so thoroughly been poisoned by the United States government's public relations deceit, the Chinese press was completely unprepared to "sell" its alternative response to terrorism, the New Deal in Xinjiang, to the world. Indeed, it may not even have anticipated the need to do so; in 2014, the Western propaganda machine was not yet fully oriented toward the demonization of China and was still far more heavily focused on the demonization of Islam.

The so-called Islamic State in Iraq and Syria (ISIS), before then a complete unknown in the West, swiftly rose to dominate the front pages of Western newspapers that year after it seized control of Fallujah in December 2013 and launched its military campaign to conquer Iraq. The PRC subsequently faced greater scrutiny—not for allegedly repressing Islam, but for its apparent failure to do so, as it became known that many in the ranks of ISIS had come to Iraq and Syria from China.

In May, *Foreign Policy* published an account by Uyghur photographer Kurbanjan Samat, who warned of rising extremism in Xinjiang, where in some areas most people had "turned toward a darker side" and wanted Xinjiang "to become another Afghanistan."[959] That summer, a *Wall Street Journal* headline proclaimed a "conservative shift" among Uyghur women, who were increasingly wearing the veil, which had been rarely seen in Xinjiang the previous decade.[960] *Reuters*, reporting on Uyghur émigrés in Türkiye the next year, displayed photos of Uyghur women cloaked entirely in black chadors and niqabs.[961] A journalist for a Dubai

---

of Troops Deployed in Jammu and Kashmir," *OpIndia*, August 28, 2019); the *Print*, citing unspecified documents, reported a total of about 340,000 (Snehesh Alex Philip, "What Imran Khan Says Is 9 Lakh Soldiers in Kashmir Is Actually 3.43 Lakh Only," November 12, 2019). Even if the lowest such estimate is correct, it would be several times larger than the People's Liberation Army's presence in Xinjiang (a region of twice Jammu and Kashmir's population and many times its geographical area). According to the *Hindustan Times*, the PLA had only 50,000–70,000 troops stationed in Xinjiang as of 2021 ("PLA Modernises Xinjiang's Military Units in 'reaction' to India-China LAC Row," *Hindustan Times*, May 17, 2021).

959 Chi Zhang, "One Uighur Man's Journey Goes Viral."

960 Jeremy Page, "In Xinjiang, Veils Signal Conservative Shift Among Uighur," *Wall Street Journal*, July 31, 2014.

961 Humeyra Pamuk, "Turkish Help for Uighur Refugees Looms over Erdogan Visit to Beijing," *Reuters*, July 27, 2015.

TV station, reporting undercover from Idlib, later claimed that ten to twenty thousand "Chinese jihadists" had joined the Al Qaeda-affiliated Al-Nusra Front in Syria.[962] [963] In a segment praising the trend of more female imams among China's Muslim communities in 2010, NPR had taken note of resistance to the practice from "harder-line Wahhabi and Salafi influences" in Xinjiang.[964] *The Diplomat* further dissected the spread of Islamic fundamentalism in China under the headline "Chinese Salafism and the Saudi Connection," alleging then what has now become taboo to mention: that rather than being an authentic foundation of any Chinese ethnic group's long Islamic cultural heritage, fundamentalism was largely a new, modern, and foreign phenomenon, imported from Saudi Arabia in the twentieth century. The "salafisation" of Islamic culture in China, said *The Diplomat*, had primarily occurred since only the mid-1980s, when "a growing number of Saudi private organizations and individuals (mainly preachers and missionaries bringing in religious literature)" began to "increasingly work outside established [Islamic Association of China] channels."[965] In the face of such coverage from the Western media, the PRC not only had a strong incentive to conceal or downplay any of its policies that encouraged or defended the practice of Islam,[966] but was under considerable external pressure to show that it was taking action against extremism.

The Chinese press therefore began taking every opportunity to promote the PRC's anti-terrorism efforts—in English. On April 30 of 2014, news of the suicide bombing at the Ürümqi South railway station was first broken by *Xinhua*'s English-language account on social media, and was covered by both *CGTN America*[967] and the *Global Times*' English

---

962 Christina Lin, "Chinese Uyghur Colonies in Syria a Challenge for Beijing," *Asia Times*.

963 Around the same time, the Syrian government estimated that between four and five thousand "Xinjiang jihadists" were operating within its borders. (Ben Blanchard, "Syria Says up to 5,000 Chinese Uighurs Fighting in Militant Groups," *Reuters*, May 11, 2017.)

964 Robert Seigel and Michele Norris (hosts), "Female Imams Blaze Trail Amid China's Muslims," Louisa Lim interview with Imam Yao Baoxia, *NPR*, July 21, 2010.

965 Mohammed Al-Sudairi, "Chinese Salafism and the Saudi Connection," *The Diplomat*, October 23, 2014.

966 In a leaked cable to the U.S. State Department in 2006, for instance, the American embassy described how the local government was quietly intervening to discourage the spread of Christianity among Muslim communities in southern Xinjiang (American Embassy in Beijing, "Christianity Gaining Popularity in Xinjiang, Even").

967 "China Points to Suicide Blast in Urumqi Attack," *CGTN America*, April 30, 2014, updated May 2, 2014).

service.[968] Domestic publicity of the incident, however, seemed little different from 2009—initial reports of the bombing were heavily censored, social media posts about it were swiftly removed, and search terms including the word "Ürümqi" were restricted on Weibo.[969] On the night of the bombing, *CGTN* had posted photos on Twitter of injured victims being rushed to the hospital;[970] the front page of the *People's Daily* (the largest Chinese-language newspaper), however, displayed none of them, and reprinted *Xinhua*'s official Chinese-language report on the bombing—which, the *New York Times* observed, was "uniformly reproduced" by *Chinese* media outlets[971]—below a photograph of Xi shaking hands with a group of Uyghurs described as "model workers and progressives" instead.[972] The paper's editorial on the bombing made no mention of Islam, religion, Uyghurs, Han, or any specific ethnic groups, and instead tepidly focused on promoting social harmony and development.[973]

On September 9 of 2015, the *South China Morning Post* reported that mainland journalists had been instructed to suppress news relating to the August bombing of the Erawan Shrine in Bangkok for nearly a month due to the possibility that the alleged perpetrators were Chinese Uyghurs[974]—and later remarked that a *Global Times* article speculating on the bombers' identity had been "swiftly deleted."[975] On the same day, ISIS took Chinese national Fan Jinghui—a journalist and former middle-school teacher who was visiting Iraq—hostage for ransom, perversely announcing "Chinese prisoner for sale" underneath photos of Fan in its

968 Bai Tiantian, "Xinjiang Bombing 'More Characteristic of Intl Terror.'"

969 Heng Shao, "Explosion Hits Urumqi Right After President Xi Jinping's Visit," Forbes, April 30, 2014.

970 CGTN (@CGTNOfficial), "Picture: Injured Passengers Sent for Medical Treatment after #terror Attack at a Railway Station in #Xinjiang on Wed."

971 Didi Kirsten Tatlow, "Online, a Censored Reaction to Urumqi Bombing," *New York Times*, May 1, 2014.

972 新华社 (Xinhua News Agency), "深刻认识新疆分裂和反分裂斗争长期性复杂性尖锐性坚决把暴力恐怖分子的嚣张气焰打下去" [Deeply understand Xinjiang's separatism and the long-term complexity of the anti-separation struggle].

973 人民日报 [*People's Daily*], "人民日报评论员：坚决把暴恐分子嚣张气焰打下去" [People's Daily commentator: resolutely suppress the arrogance of violent terrorists].

974 Andrea Chen, "Bangkok Bomb Linked to East Turkestan Islamic Movement, as Chinese Media Stops Downplaying Issue Due to Sensitivities over Uygurs," *South China Morning Post*, September 9, 2015.

975 AFP, "Is Beijing Bullying Thai Police? Bangkok Blast Investigation Has Veered Sharply Away from Uygur Link," *South China Morning Post*, September 15, 2015.

online magazine *Dabiq*.[976] As the first Chinese hostage taken by ISIS, Fan and his kidnapping were significant news internationally—but not in the *People's Daily*, which considered its lead stories covering the World Economic Forum and the opening ceremony for a new highway to Lhasa to be more newsworthy the next day instead.[977] Rather than use Fan as propaganda fodder to build domestic support for repressive policies or military actions—as the Western media had done on the many occasions when ISIS had kidnapped or murdered Westerners—the PRC instead began quietly arranging to pay his ransom. In a rather stark contrast, Norwegian captive Ole Johan Grimsgaard-Ofstad, whose ransom ISIS had demanded at the same time, was headline news in *Aftenposten*,[978] which printed Prime Minister Erna Solberg's swift public refusal to pay.[979] ISIS murdered both Fan and Grimsgaard-Ofstad in November— though in Fan's case despite his government's attempts to negotiate for his release, which ultimately failed due to a disruption of communications caused by renewed French and Russian air strikes in Syria.[980] The PRC's Ministry of Foreign Affairs loudly condemned Fan's murder, yet once again, domestic news and social media topics relating to Fan and ISIS were strictly censored until after the government had issued its official response.[981] Only 48 hours later, three China Railway Construction exec- utives were murdered by Al Qaeda-affiliated gunmen in Bamako, Mali; and even as the Western press quoted President Xi's response in which he vowed to "resolutely fight violent terrorist activities," Chinese social media outrage over the attack was similarly erased.[982]

The Communist Party's press strategy had become the exact inverse of the BJP's—publicizing the necessity of anti-terrorism to a *global* audi- ence, while attempting to *de*-escalate tensions and advocating for ethnic

976 "ISIS Tries to 'Sell' Chinese, Norwegian Hostages in Online Magazine," *RT International*, September 10, 2015.

977 彭波，"俞正声率中央代表团出席拉林公路建成段开通仪式" [Yu Zhengsheng led the central delegation to attend the opening ceremony of the completed section of Lalin Highway].

978 The Norwegian-language paper of record.

979 Aftenposten, "Aftenposten (September 10, 2015)."

980 Cameron Stewart, Debra Killalea, and wires, "ISIS: Chinese Hostage Rescue 'Thwarted' by France, Russia Air Strikes in Syria," *Herald Sun*, November 24, 2015.

981 Beimeng Fu, "China Wiped The Name Of A Man Killed By ISIS From The Internet." *BuzzFeed.News*, November 18, 2015.

982 Hannah Beech, "As More Chinese Fall Victim to Terrorism, Beijing Fumbles for a Response," *TIME*, November 26, 2015.

harmony at home. In internal communications, where the need to please public or foreign audiences did not exist, the Party made its actual position on Islam explicit. In a speech at a session of the Politburo in April of 2014, Xi announced that terrorism was "not an issue of ethnicity, nor an issue of religion";[983] the next month, he gave a secret speech to Party leaders in Beijing in which he proclaimed that the view that "Islam should be restricted" was "biased" and "wrong." Top-level government officials responsible for implementing anti-terrorism policy were instructed by Xi himself not to discriminate against Uyghurs and to respect their right to worship. His speech remained a state secret for more than five years, until it was leaked in 2019.[984]

Any success this strategy may have had in shielding China from Western hostility was short-lived, and it soon became a tremendous liability instead. By the end of the 2010s, the word "salafisation" had been erased from the Western media's vocabulary and replaced with "sinicization," an apparently even more sinister concept. Though the "sinicization" of Islam that became the target of the Western media's fresh fearmongering campaign amounted to little more in reality than the reversal of salafization, the Western propaganda machine devoted every effort to conflate it with the suppression of Islam itself. Many such efforts failed to fully conceal what had previously been highlighted—an early report by *Radio Free Asia* in May 2015, for example, published a notice issued by the authorities in a village in Hotan that required shops and restauranteurs to sell alcohol, yet included a quote by a Party official explaining that these establishments had faced pressure by fundamentalists to *stop* selling alcohol as recently as 2012.[985] Numerous reports and articles based on anecdote-speculation claimed that Muslims in Xinjiang were being forced to drink; in 2021 the *Associated Press* asserted that consuming alcohol was "once unimaginable" in the "pious rural areas of southern Xinjiang."[986] (The Uyghur people, in fact, have had a continuous tradition of drinking alcohol—including the culturally-Uyghur museles

---

983 Xi Jinping, *The Governance of China*, vol. 1 (2014), sec. Safeguard National Security and Social Stability.

984 Austin Ramzy and Chris Buckley, "'Absolutely No Mercy': Leaked Files Expose How China Organized Mass Detentions of Muslim," *New York Times,* November 16, 2019.

985 Joshua Lipes and Shohret Hoshur, "Chinese Authorities Order Muslim Uyghur Shop Owners to Stock Alcohol, Cigarettes," *Radio Free Asia,* May 4, 2015.

986 Dake Kang, "Terror & Tourism: Xinjiang Eases Its Grip, but Fear Remains," *AP News,* October 10, 2021.

wine—predating the adoption of Islam by centuries; a study conducted between 2007 and 2010 and published in the *European Journal of Preventive Cardiology* found that Uyghur and Kazakh men from northern, eastern, and southern Xinjiang—including Hotan—were in fact *less* likely to forswear alcohol than the Han, and a majority described themselves as "current drinkers.")[987]

An ASPI report titled "Cultural erasure: Tracing the destruction of Uyghur and Islamic spaces in Xinjiang" purported to show through an analysis of satellite photos that a majority of mosques in Xinjiang had been destroyed or "damaged" through the removal of "Islamic-style" domes and minarets,[988] yet struggled to produce examples;[989] its principal case study covered four mosques with domes and minarets that had been *added* to each structure in the early 2010s.[990] [991] "[F]or almost 20 years there was a lot of pressure on [Chinese Muslims] from outside and themselves to build 'authentic' mosques, as if because it's Arab it's authentic," Professor Jacqueline Armijo of Qatar University's department of international affairs told UAE-based newspaper the *National* in 2012, flatly contradicting the common Western misconception, later perpetuated by ASPI, that Arab architecture and "Islamic" architecture are one and the same. "Foreign organizations, including those from Saudi Arabia" had also been heavily involved in financing this new generation of mosques, the *National* observed.[992] The ASPI report calculated through a mathematical extrapolation—based on ASPI researchers' comparison of their "systematic visual search of mosques using pre-2017 satellite imagery"

---

987 Xie et al., "Alcohol Consumption and Carotid Atherosclerosis in China: The Cardiovascular Risk Survey," *European Journal of Preventive Cardiology* 19, no. 3 (June 2012): 315–16.

988 Nathan Ruser et al., "Cultural Erasure: Tracing the Destruction of Uyghur and Islamic Spaces in Xinjiang," *ASPI Policy Brief Report* No. 38 (2020): 5.

989 Though they are extremely common in Saudi Arabia and the neighboring Gulf states, of the millions of mosques throughout the world, a great many—particularly in Indonesia, the largest country in the world with a Muslim demographic majority—lack a domed roof, minarets, or both. In Xinjiang, there are mosques that display these features, such as the famous (and un-"damaged") Id Kah Mosque in Kashgar, but many do not.

990 Or else, buildings that had been converted into mosques during that time—the inherent lack of context around a photograph taken by satellite and not verified from the ground makes such a distinction impossible to determine.

991 Nathan Ruser et al., 10–13.

992 Daniel Bardsley, "China Shifts to More 'authentic' Arabian-Style Mosques," *The National News*, July 17, 2012.

with the official number of mosques in the 2004 census[993]—that thousands of mosques were missing, despite not conducting any on-the-ground verification and failing to publish even *one* satellite image of a "destroyed or damaged" mosque that had *not* first been modified or converted after 2010. In the space of only a few years, the Western propaganda machine had pivoted from fearmongering about creeping salafist influence in China to cynically portraying the renovation of buildings that were less than a decade old as the tragic destruction of ancient cultural heritage.

After two decades of instilling fear of Islamic fundamentalism, the Western media instead became its champion. ASPI aligned itself with the most extreme version of salafist doctrine, which regarded traditional Uyghur cultural practices such as the meshrep (a fraternal harvest festival gathering) and the twelve muqams (ancient Uyghur music), as haram (forbidden in Islam); the PRC's efforts at protecting Uyghur culture by registering them with the United Nations Educational, Scientific and Cultural Organization (UNESCO) were painted as evidence that the practices themselves were the Party's own insidious machinations.[994] [995] Perspectives from the global Muslim community, which overwhelmingly rejected fundamentalism, needed to be shut out of the Western press entirely. Western journalists incoherently grappled with the uncomfortable reality that outside of Europe, no countries with a Muslim majority (or even a significant minority) would co-sign attempts to condemn the PRC at the United Nations,[996] and that dozens of them instead co-signed statements in *support* of the PRC's policy in Xinjiang.[997] In 2020, *Newsweek* admitted that a joint statement of condemnation by the United States and its subordinate exploiter countries was "swiftly overwhelmed by a series of rebuttals" by nearly double the amount of signatories of

---

993 Nathan Ruser et al., "Cultural Erasure," 37–40.

994 Nathan Ruser et al., 35.

995 This was in fact the only way to perpetuate the fiction that the Party was suppressing Islam—the enormous weight of photographic and video evidence produced by tourists and visitors to Xinjiang that showed nothing but people living ordinary lives, going to mosque, or participating in public celebrations of Islamic holidays such as Eid al-Adha could only be explained by denialists at ASPI and other Western think tanks as all being part of a continuous performance orchestrated by some elaborate government conspiracy.

996 In fact, with the exceptions of Japan and Western settler-colonies Australia and New Zealand, such attempts very rarely garnered support from *any* country outside Europe and North America.

997 "Chinese Actions in Xinjiang Become a Matter of International Dispute," *The Economist*, July 27, 2019.

the initial statement.[998] No attempts were made to ask representatives from these countries why they might support the PRC, and accounts by journalists from the periphery who visited Xinjiang were carefully kept out of Western newspapers, only appearing in either Chinese media or their own domestic press.[999]

Correspondingly, the super-empire's policy undertook a dramatic about-face, presaged by the media souring on President Trump's "radical Islamic terror" rhetoric. Shortly after taking office, President Biden reversed Trump's restrictions on immigration from Muslim-majority countries,[1000] reduced (though did not end entirely) Obama's signature "targeted killings," and finally withdrew US forces from Afghanistan after George W. Bush had sent them there twenty years before, reorienting the super-empire's military establishment away from counter-insurgency and back toward preparation for great-power confrontations. The U.S. occupation of Syria and military operations in Somalia were both still ongoing as of 2023, yet both countries had almost entirely vanished from Western

---

998 John Feng, "Nearly Twice As Many Countries Support China's Human Rights Policies Than Are Against It."

999 A 2019 article in Ugandan newspaper *New Vision*, for example, detailed the experience of one such Muslim journalist who observed Ramadan in China and remarked that Muslims in China were both free to worship and in fact fasted longer than those in Uganda; (Mubarak Mugabo, "There's Freedom of Worship and Fasting in China.") his writings of course have been universally ignored by Western media. Sultan M Hali, a journalist writing for Pakistan's *Daily Times*, had this to say in 2021:

"This scribe has toured every inch of Xinjiang and personally witnessed how the once underprivileged community is now enjoying perks of a higher quality of life ensured by President Xi Jinping's mega development projects like the Belt and Road Initiative of which Xinjiang in general and the Uighurs in particular are the prime beneficiary.

"Interestingly, since 2018, more than 1,200 people from over 100 countries have visited Xinjiang including this scribe. The visitors comprised UN officials, foreign diplomats posted in China, some countries' permanent representatives to Geneva, journalists and religious groups. We personally observed a region thriving with stability and prosperity and commended its exemplary counter-terrorism [sic] and deradicalization efforts. Critics are oblivious to a reality that we Muslims, especially Pakistanis are quick to jump to the support of oppressed Muslims, be they Indian Muslims, Kashmiris, Rohingya or Palestinians. If we have not taken up the cudgel on behalf of the allegedly oppressed Uighurs, it is not because of our love for China but because we are privy to the truth that the accusations of suppressing the Uighurs are totally baseless." (S M Hali, "Exposing the Occident's Baseless Lies about Xinjiang," *Daily Times*, February 13, 2021.)

1000 Scott Simon (host) and Iman Awad (guest), "Biden Has Overturned Trump's 'Muslim Travel Ban.' Activists Say That's Not Enough," *NPR*, March 6, 2021.

headlines. According to the *Atlantic*, Biden's National Security Council had been tasked with "keeping the Middle East off the president's desk"; there were to be "[n]o new projects" in the region as his administration "focus[ed] the nation's gaze on China."[1001] The Western press quieted its "terrorism" rhetoric and began to downplay news of terrorist attacks, particularly when their victims were Chinese; when on April 26 of 2022 a suicide bombing orchestrated by the Balochistan Liberation Army outside the University of Karachi's Confucius Institute killed three Chinese academics and a Pakistani worker, the *New York Times* made no mention of it the following day,[1002] and waited a full week before publishing an article—which sympathized with the suicide bomber, giving full voice to her perspective that Chinese teachers deserved death for being "on the side of the [Pakistani] exploiters and oppressors."[1003] Until October 7, 2023 and Israel's subsequent bombing campaign against Gaza, the GWOT had ceased to be the super-empire's priority—in large part an ironic consequence of the PRC pretending to join it.

1001 Franklin Foer, "Biden Will Be Guided by His Zionism," *The Atlantic*, October 10, 2023.

1002 *New York Times*, "The Times in Print For April 27, 2022."

1003 Zia ur-Rehman, "Rising Violence by Separatists Adds to Pakistan's Lethal Instability," *New York Times*, May 4, 2022.

CHAPTER NINE

Settler-Colonialism? A Comparative Analysis

Proportional to the population of the Democratic People's Republic of Korea, the war of 1950-1953 was among the most destructive ever fought in the history of the world. According to the Soviet Union's military archives, an estimated 20% of the DPRK's population, including well over one million civilians, were killed by the U.S. and its proxies during those three years.[1004] Even before open hostilities erupted, the Republic of Korea under the government of Syngman Rhee, formed with the authorization of its predecessor the U.S. Army Military Government in Korea, had by some modern estimates already killed over half a million Koreans in a brutal reign of terror against anyone suspected of communist sympathies.[1005] Such a rapid, severe, and deliberate depopulation of a country has only been matched by a few very extreme tragedies such as the Holocaust in Belarus or An Gorta Mór[1006] in Ireland. The newly-christened United States Air Force made no distinction between civilian and military infrastructure, destroying dams, schools, hospitals, and leveling every city and more than three-quarters of all structures in northern Korea. By the end of the war, targets for U.S. bombers were so scarce they often jettisoned their ordnance into the sea in order to land safely.[1007]

This horrific crime against the Korean people—and against humanity—is made even more astonishing by the fact that its perpetrators have offered no apology nor made any real attempt to conceal their guilt.[1008]

1004 The Cold War International History Project, "New Evidence on North Korean War Losses," Wilson Center, August 1, 2001.

1005 A. B. Abrams, *Immovable Object: North Korea's 70 Years at War with American Power* (Clarity Press, 2020), 23.

1006 The Great Hunger of 1847.

1007 Michael E. Robinson, *Korea's Twentieth-Century Odyssey: A Short History* (University of Hawaii Press, 2007), 119.

1008 To date, the only apology the U.S. government has offered for its actions during the war has been specifically for the Nogeun-ri Massacre, in which U.S. forces gunned down hundreds of south Korean civilians, most of them women and children. (Andrew Salmon, "Belated American Apology for Korean War Massacre," *Asia Times,* November 16, 2020.)

Top U.S. military officials have blithely confirmed Soviet casualty estimates,[1009] and the reality of the war can plainly be read by anyone in the U.S. or the world with an internet connection. Unlike the DPRK or the PRC, the super-empire (with a few exceptions) does not employ the tools of outright censorship in this instance; yet vanishingly few Westerners condemn the U.S. government for these crimes, or grant the Korean people any recognition as victims.

In fact, in the West, the DPRK is widely ridiculed. Kim Jong-Un and his family are seen as larger-than-life caricatures, and all 25 million north Korean people as desperate inmates of one enormous gulag, utterly subject to Kim's bizarre and arbitrary whims. Just as with China, Western journalists need not confirm testimony from north Korean émigrés, and no fairy tale is too outlandish to be published. Some of the stories printed in Western media are merely odd, for example reports of compulsory haircuts in Kim's style,[1010] or headlines proclaiming such absurdities as "North Korea bans sarcasm,"[1011] "North Koreans banned from laughing,"[1012] or "There's no word for love in North Korea"[1013] yet more often the Western press revels in accounts of Kim's alleged sadism. Tales of elaborate executions ordered by Kim saturate the English-language internet; Western audiences have heard that Kim has supposedly fed one of his generals to a tank of piranhas, fed his uncle to a pack of hungry dogs,[1014] and ordered other officials executed with an anti-aircraft gun. Whenever an individual "executed" by Kim later inconveniently turns up alive—which has happened on multiple occasions[1015] [1016]—it only barely

---

1009 Blaine Harden, "The U.S. War Crime North Korea Won't Forget," *Washington Post,* March 24, 2015.

1010 Australian Broadcasting Corporation, "Kim Jong-Un Haircut Now Compulsory for North Korean Students, Reports Claim," *Australia Network News,* March 28, 2014.

1011 Harriet Agerholm, "North Korea Bans Sarcasm Because Kim Jong-Un Fears People Only Agree with Him 'Ironically,'" *The Independent,* September 9, 2016.

1012 Yaron Steinbuch, "North Koreans Banned from Laughing as Country Mourns Kim Jong Il's Death," *New York Post,* December 17, 2021.

1013 Yeonmi Park, *There's No Word for Love in North Korea,* Google Zeitgeist video segment [16:11].

1014 Felicity Morse, "Kim Jong-Un's Executed Uncle Jang Song Thaek 'Stripped Naked, Fed to 120 Dogs as Officials Watched,'" *The Independent,* January 3, 2014.

1015 Michael Pearson, "North Korean General, Reported Executed, Turns up at Party Congress," *CNN,* May 10, 2016.

1016 Ben Mathis-Lilley, "North Korean Singer Thought to Have Been Killed by Firing Squad After Sex-Tape Scandal Turns Up Alive," *Slate,* May 19, 2014.

registers, and evokes little awareness that the standards of reporting for the DPRK are nonexistent.[1017]

Thus does the Western ruling class obscure its own crimes and divert attention from its ongoing plunder of the world. Drenched head to toe in blood, the super-empire can only hope to exculpate itself by inventing or exaggerating crimes by its victims or enemies, manufacturing monsters even more grotesque than itself. The propaganda machine in fact functions best as a mirror to the West's own dispossessive accumulation, amplifying the super-empire's worst qualities and projecting them onto others. The preferred way to distract conscientious Westerners who are moved by observing the suffering caused by their governments' excesses is not to conceal such excesses, but to convince them that the very same yet worse suffering, suffering more urgent and more deserving of their energies, is currently being endured elsewhere.

Such is the basis of this propaganda machine's present attempts to portray Xinjiang and Tibet as "internal colonies" or "settler-colonies" of the PRC, and therefore cloak the super-empire's murderous intent in the mantle of "decolonization." Fantasies of a "decolonized" China proliferate in the West, either as dreams of independent "East Turkestan" or the circulation on social media of maps showing some hypothetical balkanization of China achieved by carving away most or all of its provinces. The "Uyghur genocide" is frequently deployed in Western rhetoric to marshal left-wing dissent into anti-China xenophobia. It has become a thought-terminating cliché, a moral cudgel to silence any who would speak favorably of the PRC's accomplishments, and thus restrains the Western proletariat from recognizing anything positive about their Chinese class allies.

The use of propaganda as a distraction from human rights abuses in the West has become increasingly blatant. In early May of 2021, the Israeli Supreme Court was expected to deliver a ruling on the eviction of Palestinian families from the Sheikh Jarrah neighborhood of Jerusalem, precipitating protests by the Palestinian inhabitants that were brutally suppressed; Israeli riot police fought with protestors throughout the night of May 9, injuring hundreds and by dawn storming the al-Aqsa Mosque,

---

1017 Western journalists themselves occasionally acknowledge their industry's remarkable lack of standards. In 2014, an article in the *Washington Post* remarked that with respect to the DPRK, in major US media outlets "almost any story is treated as broadly credible, no matter how outlandish or thinly sourced" (Max Fisher, "No, Kim Jong Un Probably Didn't Feed His Uncle to 120 Hungry Dogs," January 3, 2014).

one of the holiest sites in Islamic tradition.[1018] Global audiences were stunned the next day to see videos of a crowd of ultranationalist Israeli settlers cheering and waving flags as fires burned near the mosque.[1019] The violence then escalated even more rapidly; Hamas began rocket attacks that evening after their demand for the immediate withdrawal of Israeli security forces went unmet, and the Israeli Defense Force responded with airstrikes on Gaza, killing dozens, including several children.[1020] Within 48 hours, the U.S. State Department sprang into action—to publish a report on the PRC's alleged persecution of religious minorities. In a move calculated to obfuscate and divert attention from Palestine, the report was shared with a statement specifically describing *Xinjiang* as an "open-air prison"—a phrase that is most commonly used to describe the Gaza Strip by the Palestinian liberation movement.[1021]

While the phenomenon of settler-colonialism—a form of dispossessive accumulation distinct both from traditional direct colonialism and from modern neocolonialism—is most clearly practiced today in Israel, Australia, and the Americas, China's minority regions do appear to bear a considerable resemblance to them. Though the incorporation of Xinjiang, Tibet, and Inner Mongolia into the PRC followed a long history of their subsummation in prior feudal relationships, some of the present disparities between the Han and minority ethnic groups in western China are broadly similar to the inequalities introduced by European-descended settlers in their encounter with indigenous peoples in the Western Hemisphere. Much of China's natural resources lie within its minority autonomous regions and are increasingly being extracted to fuel its economic growth—with the concomitant accusations by the Western press, as noted in the previous chapter.

In providing basic education on a massive scale, the New Deal in Xinjiang might be compared with the "civilizing" missions of Western colonists, which certainly did amount to forced assimilation and genocide, and whose tragic legacy is today still being brought to light. But only superficially. There is no Chinese counterpart to Canada's system of

---

1018 Oliver Holmes and Peter Beaumont, "Israeli Police Storm Al-Aqsa Mosque Ahead of Jerusalem Day March," *The Guardian,* May 10, 2021.

1019 Robert Mackey, "This Is Not Fine: Why Video of an Ultranationalist Frenzy in Jerusalem Is So Unsettling," *The Intercept,* May 11, 2021.

1020 Elizabeth Palmer, "Israel Strikes Gaza, Hamas Fires Rockets after Hundreds of Palestinians Wounded in Clashe," *CBS News,* May 10, 2021.

1021 "U.S. Calls Xinjiang an 'open-Air Prison,' Decries Religious Persecution by China," *Reuters,* May 12, 2021.

"residential schools," for example, which purported to "educate" indigenous children by isolating them from their native culture, and in practice severely abused and underfed these children, who died "at rates that were far higher than those experienced by the general school-aged population" according to the Truth and Reconciliation Report that concluded only as recently as 2015, and were buried by the thousands in unmarked and unrecorded graves.[1022] Nonetheless, the propaganda machine's strategy is first of all to construct a mental connection between China's minority regions and Western settler-colonies by continually publicizing any similarities between them that do exist. Once this link is established, even the worst atrocities committed by the United States and other governments of the super-empire can only damn the PRC further. Consumers of Western media are invited make the supposition: if *we're* doing *this*, just imagine what *China* must be up to!

This strategy of course can succeed only if audiences are never exposed to, or never attempt, a comparative analysis between southern Xinjiang and various other regions which are presently unambiguous internal colonies of other countries. Thus, while the similarities mentioned above are given great attention, any *differences* are omitted; and if a difference is too significant to be ignored, it must be dismissed as somehow fabricated by the Party. If the propaganda machine adequately fulfills its task, its audience will not only be unable to make the slightest distinction between Xinjiang and a Western colony, but will even refuse to entertain the possibility that significant differences could exist. The ideal consumer of Western media's anti-China propaganda is entirely passive, never learning anything substantial about Chinese society, and never having a motivation to seek out such knowledge.

The largest such omission concerns China's history. The propaganda machine may of course amplify any ancient ethnic animosities between the Han and minorities,[1023] yet China has no *post-feudal* colonial legacy beyond its own painful subjugation by Japan and the Western empires during its Century of Humiliation, which coincided with the greatest wave of colonization in North America. Only a few years after the United States government began enforcing the Indian Removal Act, the feudal Qing Empire was defeated in the First Opium War. The remainder of the nineteenth century saw both the forced relocation of the vast majority of all

---

1022 Joanna Smith, "Truth and Reconciliation Commission's Report Details Deaths of 3,201 Children in Residential Schools," *Toronto Star,* December 15, 2015.

1023 Several of these were mentioned in Chapter Eight.

indigenous American tribes and the gradual decline and neocolonization
by the West of the ancient Chinese state. Both targeted populations were
made to face debilitating addictions to drugs imported by the colonists, to
sign unequal treaties surrendering their homelands, and to endure "civilizing" missions. The Qing, who had been forced to become compradors,
were replaced by the weak and short-lived[1024] Republic of China in 1912,
which was never able to exert its control over the vast majority of the
Qing's former territory.[1025] Only after the establishment of the People's
Republic in 1949 did a central state become powerful enough to unite
the most distant provinces under one government. Chinese colonialism
of the western minority regions, if it exists, can therefore only be a *recent*
phenomenon.

How recent? Sautman, in papers directly posing the question of whether
Xinjiang and Tibet were internal colonies of the PRC, concluded through
extensive analysis that the descriptor was highly inaccurate in both cases
as late as 2000 and 2001 respectively. The entire XUAR, Sautman noted,
ranked above average for 18 out of 25 per capita economic metrics from
1997 statistical data, and on key indicators such as rural net income and
life expectancy—both highly correlated to the impoverished Uyghur
heartland of southern Xinjiang—still outperformed a few of the poorest
Han-majority provinces elsewhere in China.[1026] More crucially, all available information indicated that even though considerable extraction of
raw materials such as cotton and oil was taking place, much more wealth
flowed *into* Xinjiang from the central government than vice versa. The
majority of credit provided to Xinjiang by the PRC's state-owned central banks, for example, was received by local state-owned enterprises,
which at the time were recording record losses and not expected to repay
loans.[1027] According to Sautman:

> Xinjiang is economically dependent on the subsidies provided by
> Beijing. Economists have measured the rate of "state extraction"
> from Chinese provinces, i.e. the amount of surplus or deficit of each

---

1024 Though the ROC still technically exists as of this writing, it has not had
any control or influence over the mainland since 1949.

1025 Indeed, the first fifteen years of the ROC's existence is known as China's
"Warlord Era" due to the civil war and widespread chaos that reigned in the outlying
provinces in the face of its government's impotence.

1026 Sautman, "Is Xinjiang an Internal Colony?," *Inner Asia* 2, no. 2 (2000):
249.

1027 Sautman, "Is Xinjiang an Internal Colony?," 255.

province as compared with its expenditure which was remitted to or subsidised by the central government. Xinjiang's negative rate of extraction is high even among western region provinces (Chai 1996: 53)...

In 1993, regional government revenue was 2.83 billion yuan and expenditures were 6.63 billion yuan. The PRC requires provinces to balance their budgets. The centre thus had to provide Xinjiang with some four billion yuan, over 57 percent of regional spending. In 1994, Xinjiang revenue was 2.49 billion yuan; expenditures were 7.65 billion yuan (*XJRB* 1994, 1995). The centre provided more than 5 billion yuan, over two-thirds of the budget. Yet even the centre's Xinjiang oil ventures—the most frequently cited indicator of internal colonialism—seem to be loss-makers thus far and are unlikely to have generated taxes and profits exceeding the centre's subsidies.[1028]

Similarly, he considered the allegations of colonialism in Tibet to be "polemical hyperbole writ large"[1029] and concluded that "[n]one of the main contours of classic colonialism are found in the Tibet case. In some respects—the limited, but significant industrialization in Tibet is an example—an outcome opposed to archetypal colonial practice (de-industrialization) is present."[1030] Despite common Han chauvinist attitudes, Sautman observed that,

> [T]he PRC state does not, however, carry out the systemic discrimination characteristic of colonial systems, whereby subaltern peoples were deprived by law of rights enjoyed by metropolitan citizens. Minority people have the same rights as Han, plus preferential policies that exist side-by-side with ethnic nepotism in non public employment, a situation also common in other countries where internal colonialism is not at issue.[1031]

Even the harshest aspects of the PRC's administration did not indicate any policy bias against ethnic minorities; Han political prisoners such as

---

1028 Sautman, "Is Xinjiang an Internal Colony?," 257–261.

1029 Barry Sautman, "Is Tibet China's Colony?: The Claim of Demographic Catastrophe," sec. VI, *Columbia Journal of Asian Law* 15, no. 1 (September 1, 2001).

1030 Sautman, "Is Tibet China's Colony?," sec. III.

1031 Sautman, "Is Xinjiang an Internal Colony?," 259–60.

adherents of the proscribed Falun Gong sect, for example, were given similar punishments as ethnic separatists and at similar rates.[1032] Within the ethnic autonomous regions, in fact, the justice system had long been directed by the Party's controversial "two restraints and one leniency" (两少一宽)—the policy of intentionally not arresting or not prosecuting minorities suspected of minor offenses, and giving lighter sentences to minorities convicted of serious crimes.[1033] [1034]

A common argument for "Chinese settler-colonialism" that is naturally compelling—and obvious—is the existence of settlers. Han migration into Xinjiang, though inconsistent over the years, is unquestionably real. Though it has frequently been cited by Uyghur émigré organizations as a kind of "smoking gun" proving the existence of colonialism, at the time of Sautman's analysis, this migration was in fact almost entirely confined to northern Xinjiang, which has no history of exclusively-Uyghur habitation. Sautman noted that the vast majority of Han in Xinjiang lived north of the Tianshan, while the vast majority of Uyghurs lived in the south and east, making up over 90% of southern Xinjiang's population.[1035] In a book published around the same time, Justin Rudelson, a board member of Washington's NED-funded Uyghur Human Rights Project, admitted that the Chinese government's policy was to confine Han immigrants in "new lands not occupied by Uyghurs or in new towns adjacent to older Uyghur communities."[1036] [1037] In 2015, *Radio Free Asia* admitted that Han

---

1032 Sautman, "Is Tibet China's Colony?," sec. III.

1033 Sautman, "Scaling Back Minority Rights?"

1034 Many Western countries today have enshrined equal rights for all ethnic groups in their constitutions, yet few go as far as the PRC's, which in its preamble specifically affirms that combatting Han chauvinism is of greatest importance (People's Republic of China, "Constitution of the People's Republic of China," sec. Preamble). (The United States' constitution, in contrast, makes no mention of white supremacy or white chauvinism.) "Negative" affirmative action, or policies that are explicitly harsher toward the Han, have thus been common in the PRC for decades, most notably the family planning policy, which set the most restrictive targets for urban-dwelling Han parents. Han Chinese found guilty of inciting ethnic tensions are often punished quite severely, as in the case of a Han man from Inner Mongolia whose video of himself stepping on a picture of Genghis Khan went viral on social media in 2017. When complaints by ethnic Mongolians brought the incident to the attention of the authorities, the man was sentenced to a year in prison. (Alice Shen, "Chinese Man Jailed for a Year for Insulting Genghis Khan," *South China Morning Post,* December 15, 2017.)

1035 Sautman, "Is Xinjiang an Internal Colony?," 241.

1036 Rudelson, Rudelson, and Ben-Adam, *Oasis Identities: Uyghur Nationalism Along China's Silk Road* (Columbia University Press, 1998), 38.

1037 Restrictions on migration to southern Xinjiang were in place even under

migrants to the south were "largely relocating to the main cities" in the area rather than taking over land in the Uyghur-dominated countryside.[1038] Even since their first arrival in southern Xinjiang over a millennia ago, the Uyghur people have never been subject to any form of the mass displacement that is usually associated with settler-colonialism. Sautman similarly noted in 2001 that "Tibetans have not been deported or forcibly relocated on account of their ethnicity"[1039] and that migration to Tibet was "not sharply different from that to other PRC regions: most migrants enter urban areas, while the countryside remains populated mainly by local people."[1040]

Thus at the turn of the twenty-first century, even the most dramatic characteristic of a settler-colony—the wholesale appropriation of land from its indigenous inhabitants—was not evident in China. This marks a staggering contrast to actual settler-colonies elsewhere in the world, which were notoriously formed through blatant dispossessive accumulation. Prior to the end of the apartheid system in the Republic of South Africa, only 7% of all arable land in the country was allocated to native Africans by law,[1041] the remainder being reserved for white settlers and their descendants, who accounted for only 13% of the population.[1042] Before the arrival of the Europeans, nearly every corner of North America's 10 million square miles had been inhabited; in the United States today, the Bureau of Indian Affairs recognizes only 55 million acres of Native American territory (even this small fraction being held "in trust" by the U.S. federal government), or slightly more than 2% of the United States' total land area of 2.4 billion acres.[1043] In 1948, Zionist militias established the modern state of Israel by seizing over 75% of the land formerly controlled under the British Mandate for Palestine; the remaining Palestinian territories have been gradually reduced over the

---

the Qing Dynasty. After the local Uyghur elites had sworn fealty to the Qing, Han and Hui peasants were forbidden from visiting the region, and Han merchants who traveled there to trade were not permitted to settle. [Clarke, *Xinjiang and China's Rise in Central Asia - A History* (Routledge, 2011), 20.]

1038 Jilil Kashgary and Joshua Lipes, "Loosened 'Hukou' Restrictions in Xinjiang Benefit Hans, Not Uyghurs," June 10, 2015.

1039 Sautman, "Is Tibet China's Colony?," sec. V.

1040 Sautman, "Is Tibet China's Colony?," sec. V.

1041 South African History Online, "The Native Land Act Is Passed, June 19, 1913."

1042 O Chimere-dan, "Apartheid and Demography in South Africa," *Etude de la Population Africaine,* no. 7 (April 1992): 26–36.

1043 Bureau of Indian Affairs, "About Us."

decades by Israeli settlements and military occupation, and according to Jerusalem-based non-profit B'Tselem, currently less than 30% of the West Bank is still even partially administered by the Palestinian Authority ("Area A" and "Area B" as defined by the Oslo Accords), which together with the Gaza Strip constitute less than 15% of the original Mandate for Palestine yet hold 40% of the entire present-day population.[1044]

Of course, even if colonial relationships did not exist in China at this time, it is nevertheless possible that one might finally have emerged within the last two decades. Some also promulgate the view that while the theft of land by Western settlers was a historical tragedy, the dispossessive accumulation process has since ceased in Western settler-colonies, and the remaining indigenous peoples there now enjoy full rights and privileges comparable to the general population. The following comparative analysis of the *present* conditions in southern Xinjiang (where the Uyghur population is and has historically been the greatest) and the Navajo Nation (the largest Native American reservation in the United States) will therefore decide both questions. Note that due to differences in how the data for each country's statistical indicators are collected and calculated, they are not directly comparable to each other. Instead, to the extent that it is possible, this chapter will attempt to examine each group's *relative improvement over time* for each category, specifically during the twenty-year period between 2000 and 2020.

1044　B'Tselem, *Planning Policy in the West Bank.*

Income and Poverty[1045]

According to the United States Census Bureau, annual per capita household income[1046] in the Navajo Nation was $27,303 in 2000[1047] and $42,337 in 2020, an increase of 55%; when accounting for cumulative inflation of the dollar, this amounted to a 3% increase in purchasing power.[1048] Overall per capita household income for the United States increased

---

1045 This section will tabulate the changes in real income in rural southern Xinjiang and the Navajo Nation between 2000 and 2020. Real income means actual purchasing power, i.e. income adjusted for inflation; cumulative inflation of each country's currency is determined by the ratio of its Consumer Price Index in 2020 to its CPI in 2000, as recorded by the World Bank. For the U.S. dollar, this ratio was $\frac{118.7}{79}$ or 1.50, (World Bank, "Consumer Price Index (2010 = 100) - United States.") or equivalent to cumulative inflation of 50%, while for the Chinese yuan, it was $\frac{118.7}{79}$ or 1.58, (World Bank, "Consumer Price Index (2010 = 100) - China.") or 58%. The following formula yields the percent change in purchasing power:

$$\frac{(2020\,currency\,value)}{(2000\,currency\,value) \times (CPI\,ratio)} - 1$$

For example, if a U.S. worker was paid a wage of $10 per hour in 2000, and $20 per hour in 2020 (a gross increase of 100%), the percent increase in that worker's purchasing power can be calculated with the following equation:

$$\frac{\$20}{\$10 \times 1.50} - 1 = 33\%$$

Other key differences between U.S. and Chinese income statistics and the limitations of each must be noted. Chinese statistics organize income data by province, prefecture, and urban/rural, not by ethnic group, so rural per capita disposable household income in southern Xinjiang is used as the best proxy for the Uyghur population. (Note that only *disposable* income, i.e. net income after taxes, is available, meaning that the *gross* per capita income of Chinese rural households may be larger.) Though some areas of the Navajo Nation (such as Tuba City, Arizona or Shiprock, New Mexico) would seem to qualify as "urban" according to the U.S. Census Bureau's definition, data for the Navajo Nation is not clearly organized by urban/rural; therefore U.S. income comparisons will use the overall national average rather than the rural national average.

1046 Per capita household income is defined as the *mean average* income by household, i.e. the income of the entire population divided by the number of households.

1047 Calculated by dividing the total household income of the region ($1,304,041,800) by the total number of households (47,761). (United States Census Bureau, "Navajo Nation Data," 40.)

1048 It must be noted that while these figures are the best data available, they come with considerable margins of error, owing to the chronic undercounting of indigenous people in the U.S. census. (Shondiin Silversmith, "Large Census Undercount of Indigenous People on Tribal Lands Means Fewer Resources, Political Power.")

from \$55,409 in 2000[1049] to \$91,547 in 2020, a 10% increase in purchasing power over the same period. Between 2000 and 2020, the Navajo Nation's per capita income had fallen against the national average, from 49% to 46%.[1050] [1051] The stagnant real incomes of the Navajo and their vast and persistent gap with the national average are symptoms of one of the most significant forms of dispossessive accumulation that still exist *within* the United States, which is the systemic underpayment of indigenous workers. Presently, more than half of all indigenous mothers are the primary breadwinners of their families, a greater proportion than any other ethnic group except Black women in the United States. According to an analysis by the National Women's Law Center, indigenous women are paid sixty cents for every dollar paid to white male workers, resulting in a total of \$1 million in labor extracted from the average indigenous woman over her entire lifetime, in exchange for nothing.[1052] The percentage of all individuals in the Navajo Nation with income below poverty level was 38% in 2020—about three times the national average of 13%.[1053]

Region	Per capita household income, 2000 (USD)	Comparison with national average, 2000 (%*)	Per capita household income, 2020 (USD)	Comparison with national average, 2020 (%*)	Gross increase* (%)	Purchasing power increase* (%)
Navajo Nation	27303	49	42337	46	55	3
United States	55409	100	91547	100	65	10

*All values are rounded to the nearest %.

Between 2000 and 2020, per capita rural household income in Xinjiang rose from 1,618 yuan to 14,056 yuan, an increase of 770%. While this may be considered a very rough approximation for the overwhelmingly-rural southern area of Xinjiang, rural areas in Han-dominated northern Xinjiang might still be wealthier and thus skew this average higher. Therefore a more accurate approximation can be found by averaging the per capita rural household incomes of Aksu, Kashgar, and Hotan—three

1049 Calculated by dividing the total household income of the United States (\$5,807,966,620,638) by the total number of households (104,819,002). [American Community Survey 2000, "Aggregate Household Income in the Past 12 Months (in 2000 Inflation-Adjusted Dollars), Households."]

1050 American Community Survey 2020, "B19025 | Aggregate Household Income in the Past 12 Months (in 2020 Inflation-Adjusted Dollars)."

1051 American Community Survey 2020, "S1101 | Households and Families."

1052 Jasmine Tucker, "Native American Women Need Action That Closes the Wage Gap," 1.

1053 American Community Survey 2020, "B17001 | Poverty Status in the Past 12 Months by Sex by Age."

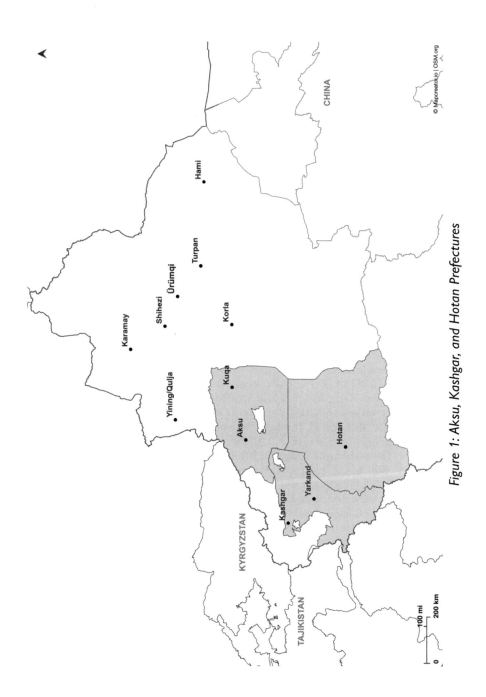

Figure 1: Aksu, Kashgar, and Hotan Prefectures

major prefectures in the south with overwhelming Uyghur demographic majorities—which stood at 1,678 yuan,[1054] 1,010 yuan,[1055] and 794 yuan[1056] in 2000, with an average of only 1,161 yuan. In 2020, these incomes had risen to 14,588 yuan,[1057] 10,276 yuan,[1058] and 9,733 yuan[1059] respectively, with an average of 11,532 yuan, reflecting an increase of 893%. When accounting for cumulative inflation of the yuan, this amounted to an increase in purchasing power of more than five hundred percent.[1060]

Such gains were typical in the Chinese countryside, which saw a tremendous increase in wealth and real income by the end of this period; rural Xinjiang however advanced by comparison with the rest of the country. According to the China Statistical Yearbook, in 2000 per capita rural household income for Xinjiang was 72% of China's national average; by 2020 it had increased to 82%. Xinjiang improved its rural income

---

1054 阿克苏地区统计局 [Aksu Regional Bureau of Statistics], "阿克苏地区2000年国民经济和社会发展统计公报" [Statistical Bulletin of the National Economic and Social Development of Aksu Region in 2000].

1055 喀什地区统计局 [Kashgar Regional Bureau of Statistics], "喀什地区2000年国民经济和社会发展统计公报" [Statistical Bulletin of the National Economic and Social Development of the Kashgar Region in 2000].

1056 和田地区统计局 [Hotan Regional Bureau of Statistics], "和田地区2000年国民经济和社会发展统计公报"" [Statistical Bulletin of the National Economic and Social Development of Hotan Region in 2000].

1057 阿克苏地区统计局 [Aksu Regional Bureau of Statistics], "阿克苏地区2020年国民经济和社会发展统计公报 [Statistical Bulletin on National Economic and Social Development of Aksu Region in 2020].

1058 喀什地区统计局 [Kashgar Regional Bureau of Statistics], "喀什地区2020年国民经济和社会发展统计公报" [Statistical Bulletin on National Economic and Social Development of Kashgar in 2020]."

1059 和田地区统计局 [Hotan Regional Bureau of Statistics), "和田地区2020年国民经济和社会发展统计公报" [Statistical Bulletin of the National Economic and Social Development of the Hotan Region in 2020).

1060 In the Central Asian countries, similarly dramatic jumps in income between 2000 and 2020 were in fact the norm—and also could be observed, for example, in Mongolia, Tajikistan, or Kyrgyzstan. China's comparatively very low inflation rate, however, was unique to the region. The National Statistics Office of Mongolia, for example, reported that the average income per rural household increased from 102,666 tugriks in 2000 to 1,270,289 tugriks in 2020. (National Statistics Office, "Monthly Average Income per Household, by Urban and Rural, /1997-2021/.") However, adjusted for cumulative inflation of the tugrik during this period—388% according to the World Bank (World Bank, "Consumer Price Index (2010 = 100) - Mongolia.")—this was a 153% increase in purchasing power, or less than one-third the rate of real increase in rural household income in southern Xinjiang. Mongolia is not credibly accused of containing "internal colonies" by anyone, yet income growth in the Mongolian countryside has been dramatically outperformed by the Uyghur heartland in the twenty-first century.

ranking from 25th to 24th out of 31 provinces measured, having newly surpassed both Ningxia and Shanxi, and overtaken by only one other province—the Tibet Autonomous Region, where rural per capita income had risen by one thousand percent, or an increase in purchasing power of approximately six hundred percent. The income gap between the poorest minority-majority provinces and the rest of China, which had widened during the 1990s, has begun closing again.[1061] [1062] In the year 2000, there were well over four hundred million people in China living in extreme rural poverty (about half of the entire rural population, millions of which were in Xinjiang), defined as living on less than 11 yuan per day (the poverty standard for a developing country).[1063] By the end of 2020, that number had fallen to zero.[1064]

Region	Per capita rural household income, 2000 (yuan)	Comparison with national average, 2000 (%*)	Per capita rural household income, 2020 (yuan)	Comparison with national average, 2020 (%*)	Gross increase* (%)	Purchasing power increase* (%)
Aksu	1678	74	14588	85	769	450
Kashgar	1010	49	10276	60	917	544
Hotan	794	35	9733	57	1126	676
Average	1161	52	11532	67	893	529
XUAR	1618	72	14056	82	769	450
TAR	1331	59	14598	85	1000	594
China	2253	100	17131	100	660	381

*All values are rounded to the nearest %.

The economic situation in rural southern Xinjiang in 2020 was also favorable compared with nearly all of its closest neighbors. Southern Xinjiang borders Kazakhstan, Kyrgyzstan, Tajikistan, Pakistan, Afghanistan, and the other Chinese provinces of Tibet, Gansu, and Qinghai. The approximate per capita *net* household income of *rural* southern Xinjiang (i.e. the previously-calculated average of Aksu, Kashgar, and Hotan) exceeded the *overall* per capita household income of every

---

1061 China Statistical Yearbook 2005, "10-21 Per Capita Net Income of Rural Households by Region."

1062 China Statistical Yearbook 2021, "6-30 Per Capita Disposable Income of Rural Households by Region."

1063 Joe McDonald, "China Celebrates Official End of Extreme Poverty, Lauds Xi," *AP,* February 25, 2021.

1064 China Statistical Yearbook 2021, "6-36 Poverty Conditions in Rural Areas."

neighboring country but Kazakhstan;[1065] of its neighboring provinces' rural per capita income, Xinjiang's was exceeded only by Tibet's.

When compared to the overall economic situation of regional countries' nearby *minority regions*, that of rural southern Xinjiang was also often quite favorable. In Russia, minorities still enjoyed higher average incomes than in rural southern Xinjiang, yet in rural southern Siberia, the gap between their income and the Russian national average *increased* during the same time period. In 1998, per capita income in the nearby Republic of Tuva, a federal subject of the Russian Federation populated overwhelmingly by its ethnic Tuvan minority, was 61% of Russia's national average[1066]—a considerably smaller gap than existed between rural southern Xinjiang and China's national average in 2000, noted earlier (52%). But by 2020, according to a study from Novosibirsk State University, Tuva's per capita income had declined against Russia's national average, to only 52%, while rural southern Xinjiang's had risen to 67% of China's.[1067]

How did these vast differences come about? The meteoric rise in rural income in the poorest regions of China and disappearance of extreme poverty are best explained by the combination of three trends. The first and most persistent is urbanization. For decades throughout China, the rural population has been steadily shrinking as more and more people move to the cities. Secondly, those who have remained have found relatively well-paying jobs. Rural unemployment in Xinjiang, once the

---

1065 Though not of every region neighboring the *entire* XUAR (both north and south); per capita income in Russia, for example, also remained higher as of 2020.

1066 Tuva's income per capita (314 rubles) was about 61% of the national average (515 rubles), according to figures calculated by United Nations researchers using Goskomstat data from 1998. [Stanislav Kolenikov and Anthony Shorrocks, *A Decomposition Analysis of Regional Poverty in Russia,* WIDER Discussion Paper, No. 2003/74 (Helsinki: The United Nations University World Institute for Development Economics Research, 2003), 26.]

1067 This study tracked data only between 2009 and 2020; however, its figure for Tuva's per capita income in 2009 (61.3% of the national average) was similar to Goskomstat's in 1998. It must be noted that this decline suffered by minorities in Sibera is a regional and *not* a country-wide trend. Ethnic Russians in Siberia have also experienced a decline, while the incomes of other Turkic minorities in the Far Eastern Federal District have in fact relatively improved. Sakha, for example, another minority-majority Russian republic, had a per capita income that was 95.2% of the national average in 2009, and 98% of the national average in 2020. [Konstantin Gluschenko, *Costs of Living and Real Incomes in the Russian Regions* (February 10, 2022). 24–25.]

highest nearly anywhere in China, has all but disappeared.[1068] Finally, beginning in the mid-2010s, the targeted poverty alleviation campaign of the Common Prosperity era has accelerated both the aforementioned trends with large infusions of government spending (described later on in this chapter.)[1069] This combination is not significantly evident anywhere else in Xinjiang's general geographic region. The Uyghur people, though immensely poor at the turn of the twenty-first century—and even if still among the poorest in *Xinjiang*—have nevertheless seen a narrowing income gap, becoming considerably wealthier than the poor nearly everywhere else in Central Asia, and in the near future standing to become even richer if present trends continue.

Water and Electricity

The poor quality of drinking water in the United States is notorious throughout the world, particularly due to high-profile incidents such as the multi-year lead contamination crisis in Flint, Michigan, or the water crisis in Jackson, Mississippi in which long-neglected water treatment infrastructure was overwhelmed by flash floods in 2022. In 2018, CBS reported that lead contamination was a "national problem" and that according to the non-profit American Water Works Association, the United States' vast network of lead water pipes was being replaced at an average rate of 0.5% per year, a pace that would see the problem resolved in approximately two centuries.[1070] Yet some communities in the United States lack even the infrastructure to provide running water at all. Countrywide, the proportion of households that lack indoor plumbing has recently fallen below half a million, or less than 0.4%; yet according to the U.S. Census Bureau, in the Navajo Nation, 9,254 occupied housing units out of a total of 43,398 (21%) still lacked full indoor plumbing

---

1068 For a more detailed analysis of rural unemployment in the XUAR and the neighboring Gansu Province, see Appendix D.

1069 In 2004, the percentage of rural Xinjiang's per capita net household income that came from "Household Operations" (i.e. peasant farming) was 88%, the percentage from wages and salaries was 6%, and the percentage from transfers (i.e. government subsidies) was 2%. [China Statistical Yearbook 2005, "10-22 Per Capita Net Income of Rural Households by Source and by Region (2004)."] By 2020, a majority of their income was from the combination of wages and salaries (nearly 30%) and transfers (24%). [China Statistical Yearbook 2021, "6-31 Per Capita Disposable Income of Rural Households by Source and Region (2020)."]

1070 Rachel Layne, "Lead in America's Water Systems Is a National Problem," *CBS News,* November 21, 2018.

in 2010, and by 2020 this proportion had only declined to 8,642 out of a total of 49,913, or 17%. If this rate of installation remains constant, indoor plumbing will not be universally accessible in the Nation until at least 2035. (Nor even is the Nation the worst-affected community in this regard; in the Yukon–Koyukuk Census Area in Alaska, which according to the 2020 census was over 70% Native American by population, the proportion of households without indoor plumbing was still as high as 35% in 2020.)[1071] [1072] At the end of 2019, the *Washington Post* reported that one-third of the population in the Navajo Nation still did not have access to a flushing toilet.[1073] Outhouses are common, and many residents rely exclusively on showers and bathrooms in community centers, rather than in their homes. Many households must drive considerable distances to haul water from the nearest wells for daily use. In June 2023, the Supreme Court ruled that the U.S. government was not required "to take active steps to secure water access" for the Navajo Nation.[1074]

Similarly, many lack access to the power grid. A 2021 report by the Brookings Institution estimated that 30% of homes in the Navajo Nation did not and have never had electricity.[1075] Only in recent years have significant efforts been made provide power to rural households, but these initiatives are severely limited by available funding; the Navajo Tribal Utility Authority's Light Up Navajo program succeeded in connecting 230 homes to the power grid in 2019, and a further 137 homes in 2022.[1076] At an average rate of 190 homes connected per year, the Navajo Nation will not be fully electrified until the twenty-second century.

In his analysis, Sautman remarked that both rural Xinjiang and rural China in general had a shortage of services overall in 1997, but that services in rural Xinjiang, though increasing, were less abundant.[1077] In

---

1071 American Community Survey 2010, "B25048 | Plumbing Facilities for Occupied Housing Units."

1072 American Community Survey 2020, "B25048 | Plumbing Facilities for Occupied Housing Units."

1073 Frances Stead Sellers, "It's Almost 2020, and 2 Million Americans Still Don't Have Running Water, According to New Report," *Washington Post,* December 11, 2019.

1074 Lawrence Hurley, "Supreme Court Rules against Navajo Nation in Water Rights Dispute," *NBC News,* June 22, 2023.

1075 Heather Tanana and Warigia Bowman, "Energizing Navajo Nation: How Electrification Can Secure a Sustainable Future for Indian Country," *Brookings,* July 14, 2021.

1076 American Public Power Association, *Light Up the Navajo Nation.*

1077 Sautman, "Is Xinjiang an Internal Colony?," 258.

2015, at the beginning of the implementation of the Party's new targeted poverty alleviation program, water and sanitation services were still severely lacking in rural Xinjiang; for example, in February, with considerable glee, *Radio Free Asia* seized upon a report made to the Twelfth People's Congress that more than half the population of Hotan prefecture still lacked access to clean water.[1078]

The PRC's 13th Five-Year Plan, to be executed between 2016 and 2020, called for at least 80% of all rural areas to have access to tap water.[1079] A massive effort was organized in southern Xinjiang, and by the end of 2017, over eight thousand villages in rural Xinjiang were connected to tap water, and basic plumbing and running water was being installed at a rate of four hundred new villages per year.[1080] The 2017 Kashgar Statistical Yearbook reported that 2,286 out of a total of 2,312 villages in the prefecture had access to tap water as of that year, or 99% of the total.[1081] By 2020, the percentage of rural households lacking access to a centralized water supply in China had fallen to 6% in "state poverty counties" including seven counties in Aksu Prefecture;[1082] by 2022, according to Xinjiang regional authorities, the tap water penetration rate had reached 97.5% for the entire province.[1083] Basic sanitation likewise improved considerably; according to statistics from UNICEF and the World Health Organization, the percentage of China's rural population that had access to basic sanitation services had increased from 45% in 2000 to 88% in 2020,[1084] and the percentage that practiced open defecation (i.e. lacking access to any form of toilet) in China was 4% in 2000, and by 2019 had reached zero.[1085]

1078 Jilil Kashgary and Joshua Lipes, "More Than One Million Lack Clean Water in Xinjiang's Hotan Prefecture," *Radio Free Asia,* February 4, 2015.

1079 Communist Party of China, "The 13th Five-year Plan for Economic and Social Development of the People's Republic of China (2016-2020)," 103.

1080 Xinjiang Statistical Factbook 2019, "12-1 Basic Conditions of Rural Areas in Main Years."

1081 Kashgar Statistical Yearbook 2017, "Statistics on the basic situation of rural areas by counties in Kashgar in 2016."

1082 China Statistical Yearbook 2021, "6-37 Realization of Registered Poverty-Stricken Households' 'Two Assurances and Three Guarantees' and Drinking Water Safety (Main Results of National Poverty Relief Census)."

1083 "Wondrous Xinjiang: Access to Potable Water Enhances Quality of Life in Rural Xinjiang." *Xinhua,* May 24, 2022.

1084 World Bank, "People Using at Least Basic Sanitation Services, Rural (% of Rural Population) - China."

1085 World Bank, "People Practicing Open Defecation, Rural (% of Rural Population) - China."

The XUAR as a whole consumed eighteen billion kilowatt-hours of electricity in 2000, more than only four other provinces in China; in 2020 it consumed over three hundred billion kilowatt-hours, more than every other province but six.[1086] The total domestic living consumption of electricity in Xinjiang increased by four hundred percent during the same period.[1087] A 2018 study co-authored by scholars from Rutgers University and the Johns Hopkins-Nanjiang University Center for Chinese and American Studies found that household energy consumption in the north-western provinces (including Xinjiang) was 50% higher than the national average, and higher than every other region of China except the northern municipalities of Beijing and Tianjin.[1088] In 2019, *Xinhua* reported that the State Grid Corporation would invest over two billion yuan to upgrade the power grid for rural areas in Hotan, Kashgar, Aksu and other prefectures in southern Xinjiang.[1089]

Pakistani journalist Sultan M Hali wrote that in touring rural Chinese farms in 2010, he noticed "the dilapidated abodes of farmers had been replaced by modest but concrete apartments and among other facilities, hi-speed internet and electricity was being provided free of cost."[1090] In contrast, the Western press was reduced to mournfully eulogizing the rapidly-disappearing rural poverty in southern Xinjiang, with a 2020 article in *Radio Free Asia* waxing poetic in describing the "distinct way of life" that had been lost in Deraboyi village in Hotan, where once the people had lived in reed houses "free of electricity" and hauled their water from nearby wells. The residents, whom *Radio Free Asia* viewed as once "torchbearers of traditional Uyghur culture," had since been built houses with modern utilities, schools, and a hospital.[1091] While there is still some distance yet to travel, for a rural area in a developing country, southern

---

1086 China Statistical Yearbook 2021, "9-14 Electricity Consumption by Region."

1087 Xinjiang Statistical Factbook 2019, "7-13 Electricity Balance Sheet in Major Years."

1088 Haiyan Zhang and Michael L. Lahr, "Households' Energy Consumption Change in China: A Multi-Regional Perspective," *Sustainability* 10, no. 7 (2018).

1089 "Xinjiang Invests 10 Bln Yuan on Power Grid Upgrades," *Xinhua*, April 9, 2019.

1090 S. M. Hali, "Has China Eliminated Extreme Poverty?" *The News International*, January 4, 2021.

1091 Gulchehra and Joshua Lipes, "Relocation of Ancient Uyghur Village Ruse to Assimilate Residents, Appropriate Resources: Experts," *Radio Free Asia*, December 10, 2020.

Xinjiang has already experienced a miracle of expansion of basic services in the span of only a few years.

Roads, Railways, and Infrastructure

The Chinese phrase "要想富先修路"—"if you want to get rich, first build a road"—has become famous. China's overall economic success has proven the concept of transportation infrastructure being foundational to development, yet the intersection of infrastructure and colonialism is not so easy to analyze. The transportation infrastructure built within a colony by an imperial power is typically solely "extractive" i.e. for the exclusive purpose of moving raw materials from the mine, plantation, or sawmill to the river or seaport. Thus Africa's railways at the time of decolonization largely connected inland areas to the ocean but did not connect neighboring countries with each other. The coastal cities of Brazil had far less contact with each other than they had with Lisbon during the first centuries of Portuguese colonization. Within a *settler*-colony, interconnecting infrastructure is typically developed to a high degree, yet is designed to benefit the settlers rather than the indigenous inhabitants.

The modernization of Brazilian infrastructure in fact began *before* independence from the crown, but only *after* the Portuguese court resettled to Rio de Janeiro to flee Napoleon's invasion of their home country at the beginning of the nineteenth century. Famed Uruguayan journalist Eduardo Galeano writes that to maintain a market for British goods, "Portugal destroyed the seeds of any kind of manufacturing development in Brazil: until 1715 sugar refineries were banned, in 1729 it was made a criminal offense to open new roads in the mining region, and in 1785 local looms and spinning mills were ordered burned."[1092] Yet the underdevelopment of Rio did not suit the Portuguese ruling class once they had to live there; the city was therefore quickly transformed with new sidewalks, street lights, an efficient sewer system, and more roads and bridges to connect suburban neighborhoods to the city center.[1093] These things were intended for them and only them; for Brazil's vast population of enslaved laborers, who had toiled first on the sugar plantations, and then in the gold mines, this ruling class envisioned no future but death.

1092 Eduardo Galeano, *Open Veins of Latin America* (New York: Monthly Review Press, 1997), 56.

1093 Kristen Schultz, *Tropical Versailles: Empire, Monarchy, and the Portuguese Royal Court in Rio De Janeiro, 1808-1821* (New York: Routledge, 2001), chap. 4.

A careful analysis of the nature and distribution of infrastructure must therefore be made before an internal colonial relationship can be properly identified. The United States, for example, has some of the most developed (if now notoriously poorly maintained and crumbling) systems of streets, roads, and highways in the world, yet their distribution is highly unequal. In 1911, within a year of Arizona's official promotion to statehood, the city streets of Phoenix were paved for the first time,[1094] and highways through the state began to be upgraded and expanded with modern surfacing techniques.[1095] Yet now, decades into the twenty-first century, the vast majority of roads within the nearby Navajo Nation remain unpaved. "Drive a few miles off the reservation in any direction," the *Navajo Times* wrote in 2010, "and you'll see a lot more pavement." Instead, millions of dollars are spent yearly to rescue thousands of Navajo drivers who become stuck in the dirt roads during wintertime, when they become muddy from the weather.[1096] A lack of paved roads also means higher infant mortality, lower school attendance, precludes the timely arrival of emergency response vehicles, and makes the trap of rural poverty all but impossible to escape.

In 2019, University of Southern California investigative journalist Amy Linn reported that 80% of the Nation's 11,600 miles of roads were unimproved dirt and sand, and only 16 miles of new roadways are constructed each year. The existing roads, meanwhile, were in extremely poor condition and constantly deteriorating, the Navajo Nation Division of Transportation (NDOT) being chronically underfunded. In a typical year, the U.S. federal government supplies between 5 and 15 percent of the money NDOT requires for maintenance, and in some years denies transportation funding to tribal governments altogether.[1097] The Navajo Nation's only major railroad, which is unconnected to any other U.S. rail system, was unquestionably extractive, only connecting the reservation's coal mine in Kayenta, Arizona with the coal-fired Navajo Generating

1094 Brad Hall, "The Day They Paved the Roads in Phoenix for the First Time, 1911," *History Adventuring,* August 15, 2017.

1095 Melissa Keane and J. Simon Bruder, *Good Roads Everywhere: A History of Road Building in Arizona* (Arizona Department of Transportation Environmental Planning Group, 2003), 62.

1096 Cindy Yurth, "Where's the Tar?," *Navajo Times,* February 11, 2010.

1097 Amy Linn, "The Navajo Nation's Horrendous Roads Keep Killing People and Holding Students Hostage, but Nothing Changes," USC Annenberg Center for Health Journalism, September 4, 2019.

Station on the Nation's border, which supplied electricity not to the reservation but to Phoenix, Las Vegas, and Los Angeles.[1098]

In southern Xinjiang, the general amount and condition of infrastructure have been on a trajectory of continuous and accelerating improvement. During the 1990s, several large infrastructural projects began or were completed, including a 1500-kilometer north-south railway to Kashgar, which as Sautman noted passed through some of southern Xinjiang's most impoverished communities, potentially providing opportunities for economic development.[1099] If southern Xinjiang were a settler-colony, however, such infrastructure would have existed solely to benefit a settler population or to extract resources from the south to the Han-dominated north, while the quality of infrastructure available to the indigenous population would be either stagnant or in decline. A careful analysis of more recent development is therefore warranted.

In terms of rail, it is unlikely that the existing or planned railways serve or were intended to serve an exclusively extractive purpose. Rather than conveying goods or raw materials to the north, or further east towards China's metropolitan centers, the most recent projects are designed for internal development or trade with neighboring countries. In June 2022, the Hotan-Ruoqiang railway was completed, together with existing lines forming a continuous loop around the perimeter of the Taklamakan Desert that lies at the center of southern Xinjiang, connecting the major southern cities of Hotan, Ruoqiang, Kashgar, Aksu, and Korla. If the purpose of such a railroad system was only extractive, there would seem to be little reason to connect Kashgar with both Hotan *and* Aksu; only one route would be sufficient to convey Kashgar's wealth to Ürümqi, or to Beijing by way of Qinghai.[1100] The completed loop will, however, greatly facilitate the flow of economic activity between prefectures *within* southern Xinjiang. Further routes are planned to directly connect southern Xinjiang with its western neighbors; later that year, *Voice of America* admitted that plans for the China-Kyrgyzstan-Uzbekistan railway were in motion and that construction would begin in 2023, despite the considerable expense and logistical challenge of laying rail from Kashgar through the western

---

1098 David Kidd, "The Navajos' Only Railroad Reaches the End of the Line," *Governing,* July 16, 2020.

1099 Sautman, "Is Xinjiang an Internal Colony?," 258.

1100 Kate Zhang, "New Railway Completes 2,700km Loop of Taklamakan Desert in Move to Integrate Xinjiang with Rest of China," *South China Morning Post,* June 17, 2022.

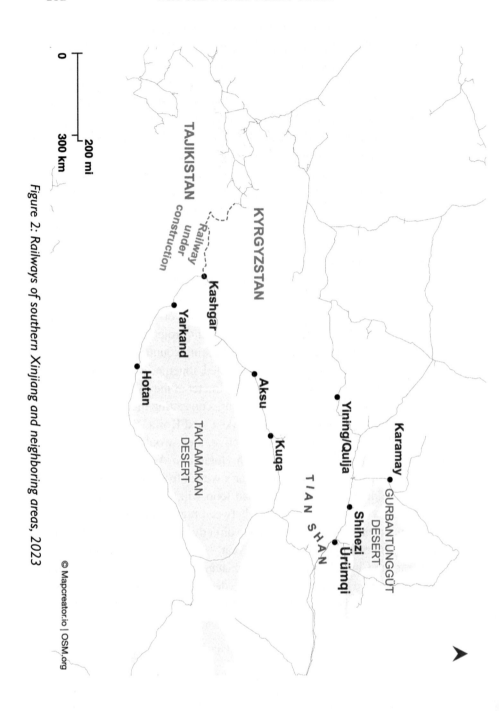

Figure 2: Railways of southern Xinjiang and neighboring areas, 2023

mountains.[1101] In 2020, Washington-based think tank the Middle East Institute had criticized the project, pointing out that the length of the track between Tashkent and Turpan (the transport hub that trains traveling *through* Kashgar to eastern China would need to pass through) would in fact be longer than the length of the existing Ürümqi-Tashkent railway,[1102] thereby (doubtless unintentionally) verifying that such a railway would therefore bring no significant new benefit to China's Han-majority areas, with the PRC instead building a new economic corridor at great expense to benefit *Kashgar* (and Kyrgyzstan, through which the railway will also pass).

The character of the improvements to southern Xinjiang's road network is even more apparent. In 2003, the central government announced that it had invested over 70 billion yuan in the construction of new infrastructure in Xinjiang over the previous three years, including highways, power plants, dams and telecommunication facilities.[1103] Over the next two decades, roads and electrical and communications infrastructure were built to connect rural villages to the rest of the province more and more quickly. A generation ago, villages in Taxkorgan County in western Kashgar Prefecture, one of the remotest regions in China at an average elevation of more than three kilometers above sea level, were accessible only by horse, yak, or camel; by 2018, roads connected several villages to the county seat, cutting travel time in half. Taxkorgan's Pili Village, for example, was accessible only via a human-powered cable ferry across the Yarkand River two decades ago, and the nearest school was days of travel away; in 2014, a bridge was constructed and the village was connected to a road (initially gravel).[1104] In 2020, stable electricity was supplied to the valleys, and construction began on the first airport serving the county.[1105] By the end of 2020, every rural village in China was connected to the rest

---

1101 Navbahor Imamova, "Despite Skepticism, China-Kyrgyzstan-Uzbekistan Railway Deal Chugs Forward," *VOA,* October 4, 2022.

1102 Péter Bucsky and Tristan Kenderdine, "The Ferghana Valley Railway Should Never Be Built," Middle East Institute, March 17, 2020.

1103 "Xinjiang Reports Progress in Infrastructure Construction," *Xinhua, March 15, 2003.*

1104 央视新闻客户端，"重访新疆塔县皮里村 惊险'天路'今安在？" [Revisiting the thrilling 'Heavenly Road' in Pili Village, Taxian County, Xinjiang, where is it today?].

1105 Zhang Zhongkai, Gao Han, and Zhong Qun, "Xinhua Headlines: Flying High: China's Ethnic Tajik People See Life Ascending on Pamir Plateau." *XinhuaNet,* June 16, 2020.

of the country by a paved road.[1106] By the end of 2022, six new highways, most with planned lengths of over 100 kilometers, were under construction, not only further connecting southern Xinjiang to the north and east, but also to Kyrgyzstan, through the Tianshan.[1107]

There can be little doubt, therefore, that the rural population in southern Xinjiang—which consists overwhelmingly of Uyghurs and other ethnic minorities—has reaped tremendous benefits from the massive infrastructure development in the region. Even Western observers have taken note of the highest-profile projects; in 2007, the World Bank published a report praising the PRC's complete restoration of the Tarim River in southern Xinjiang, which resulted in "increased social status and employment opportunities for many women," a seventy percent reduction in poverty within the river restoration area, and significant afforestation and environmental reclamation of the desert region.[1108] In 2020, the World Bank country director for China admitted that the eradication of absolute poverty in rural areas had been successful.[1109] [1110] In the years between Xinjiang's incorporation into the PRC and 2015, desertification in the province has been reversed and forested oasis areas have more than doubled in size due to the PRC's forty-year tree-planting initiative, the largest environmental project in human history.[1111] Some Western environmentalists have praised China for its success in planting more trees than the rest of the world combined over the past five decades, and specifically

---

1106 "Paved Road Links China's 'Last Village' with Outside World," *XinhuaNet,* July 1, 2020.

1107 逯风暴, "新疆：6个重点公路项目集中开工" [Xinjiang: 6 key highway projects started intensively].

1108 World Bank, "Restoring China's Tarim River Basin," May 29, 2007.

1109 Keith Bradsher, "Jobs, Houses and Cows: China's Costly Drive to Erase Extreme Poverty," *New York Times,* December 31, 2020.

1110 Chapter Two is devoted in part to describing the paradoxical nature of the World Bank. Though the World Bank's public mission statement consists entirely of a pledge to end extreme poverty in the world (World Bank, "Who We Are"), its function as an institution is in fact to maintain and increase the super-empire's rate of profit, thus typically *expanding* poverty in the periphery. Though China's financial security has prevented it from becoming another victim, the World Bank can still make *rhetorical* use of China as a convenient means to sustain this deception; by sponsoring the Party's genuine and effective anti-poverty efforts, the Bank is able to claim their success as its own, thus disguising its "failures" elsewhere in the world that result in extreme debt by peripheral countries to Western creditors and the galactic transfer of wealth through interest payments, structural adjustments, and unequal trade.

1111 人民网 (People.cn), "新疆绿洲面积已从1950年的4.3%增至9.7%" [The oasis area of Xinjiang has increased from 4.3% in 1950 to 9.7%].

identify the efficient karez irrigation system in Turpan (eastern Xinjiang) that made growing vegetables possible in the absence of rainfall.[1112]

Subsidies

For two decades beginning in 1996, the Native American Housing Assistance and Self-Determination Act granted a total of $1.6 billion to the Navajo Housing Authority for the construction of new homes. On paper, this was not an inconsiderable sum, amounting to approximately $500 per capita per year, yet it was wholly insufficient for the needs of the Navajo Nation. By 2016, an investigation by the *Arizona Republic* found that only several hundred new homes had been built over the entire period; most of the money had instead been spent on the colossal need for repairing and modernizing existing residences, or on other non-residential projects such as community youth centers.[1113] The NHA, in fact, was also unable to spend all the money; by the early 2010s, the U.S. Department of Housing and Urban Development rescinded the grant and assessed millions of dollars in penalties for misallocation of funds following a private contractor's embezzlement scandal.[1114]

In 2022, the Navajo Nation received another $2 billion as part of the American Recovery Rescue Plan Act; time will tell what effect these funds will have on the quality and availability of services, but it is unlikely that they will be sufficient to do much more than offset the disaster that the COVID-19 pandemic has been for the Nation.[1115] Overall, as seen earlier in this chapter, real income in the Nation is stagnant; to raise it a much more significant and meaningful contribution would be required. In general, the U.S. federal government's subsidies to Native American tribes are woefully inadequate and do little to permanently improve conditions. Reservations are exempted from taxes, but only on income earned within the reservation, where jobs are typically extremely scarce. In 2017, the Navajo Nation applied for a federal subsidy for the Kayenta, Arizona

---

1112 Alessandro Gallo, "China, the Green Wall Which Will Stop the Desert Advancing," *ecobnb,* July 10, 2019.

1113 Such centers are vital to Navajo communities, being for some families their only access to running water or the internet.

1114 Craig Harris and Dennis Wagner, "The Navajo Nation Accepted More than $1 Billion for Houses. So, Where Did It Go?," *The Arizona Republic,* December 14, 2016.

1115 Arlyssa D. Becenti, "With $1B in Recovery Funds, Navajo Nation Will Upgrade Infrastructure and Create New Jobs," *The Arizona Republic,* July 2, 2022.

coal mine;[1116] the application was not granted, and in 2019, the mine was shut down instead. Mining had been the largest source of income for the Nation and the neighboring Hopi Reservation, and the mine's closure resulted in the loss of nearly a thousand jobs and a reduction of over $30 million in annual revenue for the Nation and $12 million in revenue for the Hopi, or around 85% of the general fund budget.[1117] In 2022, federal legislation was passed to compensate the Navajo Nation for the mine's closure with a pittance of $1.6 million annually—or only about 5% of the lost revenue—for a fixed period of 15 years.[1118]

Today, all available evidence indicates that the massive subsidies to Xinjiang by China's central government, which Sautman identified in his analysis in 2000, have continued to the present day. In 2021, Xinjiang received 271 billion yuan in transfer payments from the central government, and ranked fourth out of 31 provinces for the highest amount received per capita, below Qinghai and Ningxia; Tibet ranked first, with more than double any other province.

Central government transfer payments by region in 2021[1119] [1120]

Region	Total population (10,000 persons)	Transfer payments (100 million yuan)	Transfer payments per capita (yuan)
Beijing	2189	959.55	4384
Tianjin	1373	416.23	3032
Hebei	7448	3125.66	4197
Shanxi	3480	1793.97	5155
Inner Mongolia	2400	2321.34	9672
Liaoning	4229	2457.43	5811
Jilin	2375	2016.06	8489
Heilongjiang	3125	2852.41	9128
Shanghai	2489	615.76	2474
Jiangsu	8505	1462.29	1719
Zhejiang	6540	727.28	1112

1116 Peter Maloney, "Navajo Nation Looks to Federal Subsidies to Keep Coal Mine, Plant Open," *Utility Dive,* April 3, 2017.

1117 Shondiin Silversmith and Ryan Randazzo, "Largest Coal Plant in the West Shuts down, Dealing Financial Losses to Native American Tribes," *USA Today,* November 18, 2019.

1118 U.S. Department of the Interior, "Biden Administration Announces Nearly $725 Million to Create Good-Paying Union Jobs, Catalyze Economic Revitalization in Coal Communities" [press release], February 7, 2022.

1119 China Statistical Yearbook 2022, "2-5 Population at Year-End by Region."

1120 中华人民共和国财政部 [Ministry of Finance of the People's Republic of China], "2021年中央对地方一般性转移支付分地区情况汇总表" [Summary Table of General Transfer Payments from the Central Government to Local Governments by Region in 2021].

Region	Total population (10,000 persons)	Transfer payments (100 million yuan)	Transfer payments per capita (yuan)
Anhui	6113	2925.11	4785
Fujian	4187	1251.75	2990
Jiangxi	4517	2382.49	5274
Shandong	10170	2444.83	2404
Henan	9883	4105.79	4154
Hubei	5830	3085.32	5292
Hunan	6622	3307.83	4995
Guangdong	12684	1156.72	912
Guangxi	5037	2836.02	5630
Hainan	1020	919.29	9013
Chongqing	3212	1680.54	5232
Sichuan	8372	4550.14	5435
Guizhou	3852	2554.74	6632
Yunnan	4690	2989.16	6373
Tibet	366	1480.61	40454
Shaanxi	3954	2324.28	5878
Gansu	2490	2302.03	9245
Qinghai	594	1184.54	19942
Ningxia	725	831.89	11474
Xinjiang	2589	2710.3	10469

In 2020, an additional total of 45 billion yuan was spent by China's regional governments in economic assistance to other provinces. Wealthy eastern regions, in particular the urban centers of Guangdong Province and the Shanghai Municipality, paid the most; minority autonomous regions in the west, such as Xinjiang, Tibet, and Inner Mongolia, paid nothing at all.[1121] In 2017, *Reuters* reported that the Chinese government paid higher subsidies to cotton farmers in Xinjiang than in any other province.[1122]

Conclusions

There is no doubt that being a minority in China is difficult. The persistent historical, geographical, and political reasons for this predate the PRC and are not quickly or easily eliminated. Despite the Party's efforts, Han chauvinism remains a problem. Nor can it be imagined that not a single person in Xinjiang has been unjustly incarcerated, punished, or censured by the state. (Indeed, few would argue for example that Hailette Niyaz, mentioned in the previous chapter, deserved his incarceration.) Any policy that seeks to radically transform a society of 25 million people, even to their collective benefit and for the best possible reasons, no

1121 China Statistical Yearbook 2021, "7-6 General Public Expenditure by Region (2020)."

1122 Reuters Staff, "China Rejigs Cotton Policy for Top Grower Xinjiang." *Reuters,* March 16, 2017.

matter how socially and economically necessary, cannot make zero errors and will not adequately serve every individual. Yet the nature of such injustices—that no doubt form a kernel of truth around which the Western media has built a labyrinth of anecdote-speculation and fabrications—is not a systemic one. The idea that Uyghurs are subjected to police brutality or that Uyghur prisoners are tortured or abused is unsupported; a full six years have passed since the Western press began to construct its fantasy of a secret genocide in China, and no verifiable physical evidence of this has yet been discovered. In contrast, it took less than one year after the U.S. military's takeover of the Abu Ghraib prison in Iraq before photographs of U.S. soldiers torturing and humiliating Iraqi prisoners there were leaked to the press;[1123] in an era of ubiquitous cell phone cameras, the narrative that such abuse could take place over several years—and on a scale orders of magnitude greater, allegedly involving *millions* of prisoners—without even a single photograph of it becoming public truly beggars belief.

The dispossessive accumulation attendant to settler-colonialism does not exist in China's minority regions to even the slightest degree. Rather than the theft of land, labor, and resources that presently continues in the West, the relationship between southern Xinjiang and northern Xinjiang—and indeed the relationship between the XUAR and eastern China—is best described as an increasingly favorable exchange. Land is not being appropriated from its inhabitants but developed for their benefit; labor power is not being coerced, but paid for; resources are being extracted, but only with substantial compensation that is transforming millions of lives for the better. Poverty is neither persistent nor increasing but disappearing.

In 2000, Sautman advised that in Xinjiang, "[i]nvestment in physical and cultural infrastructure, especially in education and health care, should be drastically accelerated."[1124] In the time since his analysis, this appears to be exactly what has happened. On virtually every dimension of economic and social development, China's minority regions are advancing dramatically. They have greater access to education, healthcare, and public services; between 2000 and 2020, they saw a tenfold increase in not only household income, GDP, and industrial and agricultural output, but total enrollment in higher education; the total number of hospital beds more than tripled, as did the number of full-time teachers in higher education;

1123 Rebecca Leung, "Abuse of Iraqi POWs by GIs Probed," *CBS News,* April 27, 2004.

1124 Sautman, "Is Xinjiang an Internal Colony?," 262.

the total length of railways and highways tripled; public spending by their provincial governments increased by three thousand percent.[1125] Through November 2022, in the entire Xinjiang Uyghur Autonomous Region, only three people had died from an infection of the COVID-19 virus.[1126]

More and more ethnic minorities are becoming fluent in Standard Chinese, yet literacy in native ethnic languages has actively been preserved as well. An article published in the *Journal of Language, Identity & Education* in 2020, for example, concluded from interviews of Uyghur university students who were "targets of Uyghur language policy in China" that "none of them sought complete inland China assimilation, and all retained their unique identities as Uyghur." One interviewee remarked, "Chinese is our national language. We cannot stay in Xinjiang all the time. Therefore, I have to study the national language . . . [but] I am a member of the Uyghur people and Uyghur is my mother tongue. I don't want to be a guy who can speak Chinese well but forgets my own language."[1127] In another example, a study of Tibetan literacy by a scholar from the University of Wisconsin-Madison conducted from 2013 to 2014 found that Tibetans born and raised in Tibet were considerably more literate in the Tibetan language than Tibetans raised in India.[1128]

The TAR's dramatic rise in prosperity has had a corresponding effect on the Tibetan diaspora. "[I]n their headlong rush for greener pastures," the *Los Angeles Times* admitted in 2010, some Tibetan émigrés "underestimated the hardship of starting anew, and even the benefits of living under Chinese rule." One told the *Times* that in Lhasa in the mid-2000s, she had earned over five times her current income as a shopkeeper in Dharamsala. "After I got here, I kept thinking, 'There must be another India I'm missing,'" another said. "Now I want to go back but can't. I'm stuck."[1129] Even today, to say that Tibetans in India are treated as second-class citizens is inaccurate—they are not considered citizens at all, but as "foreigners"

1125 China Statistical Yearbook 2021, "25-18 Principal Aggregate Indicators on National Economic and Social Development in Ethnic Minority Autonomous Regions."

1126 Ensheng Dong, Hongru Du, and Lauren Gardner, "An Interactive Web-Based Dashboard to Track COVID-19 in Real Time." *Lancet Infectious Disease* 20, no. 5 (May 2020): 533–34.

1127 Yawen Han and Cassels Johnson, "Chinese Language Policy and Uyghur Youth: Examining Language Policies and Language Ideologies," *Journal of Language, Identity and Education* 20, no. 3 (2021): 10–11.

1128 Dirk Schmidt, "Tibetan Language Readability & Literacy" (2017), 2–3.

1129 Mark Magnier, "Tibetan Exiles in Dharamsala, India, Settle in with Disillusionment," *Los Angeles Times,* September 22, 2010.

under the law, forbidden to own land and property, and have much greater difficulty finding employment. Tibetan migration from China to India almost entirely stopped by 2010; the "Tibetan government in exile" itself admitted that the number of Tibetans "fleeing Chinese rule," once thousands per year, had fallen to "about 100" in 2018.[1130] The government of India, which had hosted the vast majority of all Tibetan émigrés, revealed that over the previous seven years, their numbers had fallen from approximately 150,000 to 85,000—a 43% decline. A "large number" of these, according to the government's advisor on Tibetan Affairs, had returned to China.[1131] The Dalai Lama has publicly announced that Tibet no longer seeks independence, and instead wants greater development as part of China.[1132] According to *Voice of America* in 2009, a spokesman of the "Tibetan government in exile" also indicated that a survey of Tibetans living in China found that over 60% did not want independence.[1133]

The Western narrative of Tibetans and Uyghurs—as well as Mongolians and other non-Han ethnic groups—as perpetual victims of state repression cannot be reconciled with the advancement they have seen in the quality of their social and economic life. A more accurate characterization would have been of a minority frustrated by their exclusion from the great fortune the PRC had been building in the east, growing resentful from being made to wait for more than a generation, and now finally receiving their due. But the gap between their level of prosperity and that of the Han majority is steadily shrinking. In its pursuit of Reform and Opening Up, the Party built Shanghai first; it could not have done otherwise, but by doing so incurred a great debt. Now Shanghai is repaying it. Fanon, quoting the National Liberation Front's response to the French government's support of the settlers in Algeria in 1956, wrote that "colonialism only loosens its hold when the knife is at its throat";[1134] if true, the narrative of the Party as a perpetrator of colonialism is decisively contradicted.

Though the differences explored in this chapter between the PRC's ethnic autonomous regions and Western settler-colonies are both dramatic

1130 Kunal Purohit, "After 60 Years in India, Why Are Tibetans Leaving?," *Al Jazeera*, March 21, 2019.

1131 Rahul Tripathi, "'Tibetan Refugees down from 1.5 Lakh to 85,000 in 7 Years,'" The Indian Express, September 11, 2018.

1132 "'Past Is Past': Dalai Lama Says Tibet Wants to Stay with China, Wants Development," *Hindustan Times*, November 23, 2017.

1133 Voice of America, "Tibetan Exiles Discuss Future of Tibet," *VOA*, November 1, 2009.

1134 Fanon, *The Wretched of the Earth*, 61.

and numerous, they all originate from a single distinguishing characteristic, which is *class*. As the instrument of the Western capitalist class, the U.S. federal government must *above any other imperative* facilitate the accumulation of private wealth. While the bourgeois state exists, there is no higher law, and no competing interest that could prevail against it. Whatever concessions or subsidies the indigenous peoples manage to wrest from their oppressors, no matter how hard-won, can only be meaner than the super-profits generated by their continued underdevelopment.

In contrast, as the instrument of Chinese workers and peasants, the PRC must ultimately provide for *their* class interests above those of the Chinese (or foreign) bourgeoisie. Since the wealth accumulated by the capitalists in China represents a theft of the surplus value of workers' labor, whenever prudent and possible, the state must intervene to redistribute it, or face a widespread loss of legitimacy. The victims of wage-labor exploitation in China recognize the state as their ally, and expect it to support them; despite considerable resentment toward and from the Han, ethnic minorities nevertheless view the Party as the best lever of positive change in class society. According to the study by the Harvard Kennedy School,[1135] minorities in western China were more likely to express support for the central government;[1136] only two years before the July 5 incident,[1137] near the height of the bitterest ethnic tensions in Xinjiang, a study of Chinese high school students found that Uyghurs, Mongolians, and other ethnic minorities were more supportive of the state than their Han peers were.[1138] In general, the presence of proletarian rule has been valued and preferred throughout the entire region of Central Asia, and its absence greatly missed; according to Sautman, "[in] the part of the Soviet Union that most closely resembled Tibet and Xinjiang in terms of development levels and high degree of subsidization, local leaders opposed dissolution of the Soviet state, in part because central subsidies had done much to improve living standards in the Central Asian republics."[1139]

In contrast with much of Eastern Europe, former Soviet Central Asian republics still prominently display statues of Lenin in public areas. In

---

1135 First mentioned in Chapter Seven.

1136 Edward Cunningham, Tony Saich, and Jessie Turiel, *Understanding CCP Resilience: Surveying Chinese Public Opinion Through Time* (Harvard Ash Center, July 2020).

1137 See Chapter Eight.

1138 Barry Sautman, "Ethnic Policies: China vs. U.S. and India," *The Adelaide Review*, September 10, 2013.

1139 Sautman, "Scaling Back Minority Rights?"

2011, *Reuters* interviewed retirees in Tajikistan and Kazakhstan who preferred their lives as citizens of the Soviet Union;[1140] in 2022, *The Diplomat* warned of "Rising Soviet Nostalgia" among the youth in Kyrgyzstan;[1141] a 2005 study of attitudes in Kazakhstan, Kyrgyzstan, and Uzbekistan published by the Washington-based National Council for Eurasian and East European Research found that respondents in all three countries believed the Soviet government had been more responsive to the citizens' needs, and in no demographic category did more than one-third of respondents believe their current capitalist government adequately served their interests.[1142]

The winter of 2020–2021 was particularly hard on Uzbekistan; temperatures remained below freezing for over 50 straight days, and the high demand for heat caused power plant failures and periodic blackouts in Tashkent. The government's energy minister admitted that ever since Uzbekistan's independence in 1991, the utility infrastructure had not been maintained, and was running on "inertia [for] 30 years." A particularly irate man from the southern province of Qashqadaryo, whose family had been without power or gas for two months, recorded a video on social media asking President Shavkat Mirziyoyev, "What is a country's independence good for if you cannot provide people with basic help? Might it be better to join Russia or China? You have deprived us of the electricity that Lenin gave us."[1143]

1140 Dmitry Solovyov, "Soviet Nostalgia Binds Divergent CIS States," *Reuters,* December 8, 2011.

1141 Colleen Wood, "Rising Soviet Nostalgia in Central Asia: Kyrgyzstan's Young Pioneers," *The Diplomat,* June 1, 2022.

1142 Kelly M. McMann, *Central Asians and the State: Nostalgia for the Soviet Era* (Case Western Reserve University, February 16, 2005): 10.

1143 "Uzbekistan: Temperatures Plummet, Tempers Soar," *Eurasianet,* January 20, 2021.

CHAPTER TEN

An Ecological Civilization

In terms of economic growth, 2022 was considered China's first "normal" year in decades with an annual GDP increase of 3%—less than half its long-running yearly average, yet still comfortably above the average growth of the U.S. economy.[1144] In 2023, Western financial institutions speculated hopefully that China's days of meteoric, double-digit growth might be behind it for good. (As of the second quarter of 2023, China's GDP growth had rebounded to an impressive but comparatively modest 6.3%, still far higher than the global average.)[1145]

In fact, the "normalcy" of China's economy is underscored by how very far from normal the year was in other respects. The PRC's Zero-Covid policy, which dominated Western headlines for its shortcomings (both real and imagined), was a remarkable success in preventing the hundreds of thousands or even millions of deaths from the COVID-19 pandemic that were suffered by the U.S. and other countries, even though the policy severely curtailed production in China. U.S. sanctions on the Chinese electronics industry dealt it a severe blow,[1146] though one from which it is already springing back. More attention was paid to all of these, however—at least internationally—than the environmental disaster that unfolded during the summer months.

The 2022 heat wave was the most severe ever recorded in China; one weather historian judged it to be the worst ever recorded anywhere in world, when accounting for the combination of extreme intensity, duration, and affected geographic area.[1147] Thousands of factories in Sichuan were shut down due to flagging hydroelectric power generation as China's rivers dried up;[1148] large wildfires broke out in the mountainous Chongqing Municipality; many crops failed, and some areas suffered shortages of drinking water.

1144 Though as this chapter will show, this comparison is likely misleading with respect to the U.S.

1145 NHK World-Japan, "China's Q2 GDP Grows 6.3% Year-on-Year."

1146 See Chapter Twelve.

1147 A record that will surely again be broken in the near future.

1148 Michael Le Page, "Heatwave in China Is the Most Severe Ever Recorded in the World," *New Scientist,* August 23, 2022.

Scattered protests in November after a deadly apartment fire in Ürümqi that was blamed on the local government's poor implementation of the COVID-19 lockdown accomplished what months of haranguing by the Western press had failed to—it convinced the central government to relax the Zero-Covid policy and allow home isolation. To the domestic Chinese population, the new measures seemed to suffice; the protests lasted only a few days, and ceased after the government signaled a change in policy would be forthcoming.[1149] Meanwhile, the government stepped up its campaign to vaccinate at-risk elders in preparation for an anticipated health crisis following even a partial reopening.[1150] More than anything, the government's response to the anti-lockdown protests is further evidence that while the Party prioritizes the public welfare, it is the public themselves who have the final say. It cannot be imagined that after suffering such an extreme *climate* disaster—one that will surely be repeated in the coming years with increasing frequency—the government would risk even greater public anger by failing to act.

In the United States, local and federal governments are notorious both for their minimal disaster relief efforts—such as after hurricanes in New Orleans and Puerto Rico and the wildfire in Maui—and for their generally poor and insufficient environmental legislation, which concentrates mainly on dubious market-based schemes involving opaque carbon trading or providing mild tax incentives to private entities in the hope that they will modernize their energy infrastructure. Such failures are a frequent source of outrage among the U.S. population—while blaming the government for inadequate responses to natural disasters is uncommon in China, for the simple reason that the government's responses are typically adequate. The difference between U.S. and Chinese environmental policy, moreover, could scarcely be more profound.

Carbon Emissions and Clean Energy

The image of urban China having become a polluted industrial wasteland as a consequence of breakneck economic growth has been carefully cultivated by the Western press since the 1990s. Even during the early years of the twenty-first century, it retained some basis in fact. Eventually,

---

1149 Simone McCarthy, "China Signals It Could Soften Its Zero-Covid Policy, but There Are More Questions than Answers," *CNN*, December 2, 2022.

1150 Jack Lau, "China in Push to Boost Covid-19 Vaccination among Elderly," *South China Morning Post*, November 29, 2022.

however, even Western newspapers were forced to quietly admit that the PRC's clean air policies had not only cut air pollution almost in half between 2013 and 2020, but that the reduction had driven a global decline in average air pollution. (Just as with the global poverty population during the latter twentieth century, if China's contribution were tallied separately, the overall pollution rate would have *increased* rather than decreased.)[1151] Much is made of the statistic that China is the world's "biggest carbon emitter"—which is true only in overall terms. As the largest country in the world by population as of 2022, it would seem that China could only by a miracle of green technology or by severe underdevelopment *fail* to rank first in country-level emissions. However, per capita, China emits less than not only the United States—which is responsible for a disproportionately *high* level of emissions, fully twice China's—but also less than most of its own industrialized neighbors: Russia, Japan, and the Republic of Korea.[1152] Yet in the final analysis, *neither measurement* of carbon emissions—gross or per capita—makes sense.

It is *production*, not population, that presently correlates the most to how much carbon a country emits. Most emissions are driven by industry, agriculture, and freight; and as the home of 30% of the world's industrial manufacturing in 2021,[1153] if anything, it is remarkable that China's share of global carbon emissions remains disproportionately low at only 27%.[1154] Climate change is a *globalized* problem, in which *every* country in the world-system—China included—is *forced* to be complicit, regardless of its position in the supply chain insofar as the West consumes products manufactured in China from raw materials harvested from the periphery; all countries *must* participate in this cycle or face the consequences. Therefore the "blame" for carbon rests with China in only the most proximate sense.

Though the problem of climate change is a globalized and compulsory one, the solution is not. If a peripheral country were to suddenly refuse to continue exporting its fuel, minerals, or cash crops, it would be unable to

1151 Kripa Jayaram, Chris Kay, and Dan Murtaugh, "China Reduced Air Pollution in 7 Years as Much as US Did in Three Decades," *Bloomberg*, June 13, 2022.

1152 World Bank, "CO2 Emissions (Metric Tons per Capita) - China, Russian Federation, United States, Japan, Korea, Rep."

1153 The State Council of the People's Republic of China, "China Accounts for 30% of Global Manufacturing Output in 2021," June 15, 2022.

1154 World Bank, "China's Transition to a Low-Carbon Economy and Climate Resilience Needs Shifts in Resources and Technologies," October 12, 2022.

service its debts and find itself subjected to any or all of the super-empire's brutal mechanisms of control to bring it back into production. The same is not true of any country's embrace or rejection of renewable energy; currently, environmentalism is almost entirely opt-in.

As with other recent changes identified throughout the preceding three chapters, China's overall carbon emission rate displays an inflection point[1155] near the end of the twenty-first century's first decade. Before, as China industrialized, an increase in emissions of over 13% was the norm *per year*—for example, from 5.1 million kilotons to 5.8 million kilotons between 2005 and 2006—yet after, a 13% increase was seen only over the 8-year period between 2011 and 2019, or less than a 2% average increase per year.[1156] The PRC's objective—openly declared in front of the entire world in 2020—is to reach peak emissions that decade, and full carbon neutrality by 2060. "Did Xi Just Save the World?" a headline in *Foreign Policy* asked after the announcement;[1157] if the PRC can live up to its promise, climate models predict that the total global temperature increase would be reduced by 0.2 to 0.3 degrees centigrade from its original catastrophic estimate of 2.7 degrees centigrade.[1158] Anyone who seriously doubts that the PRC is both willing and capable of fulfilling this objective is not paying attention.

To describe China as merely the "world leader" in renewable energy is a colossal understatement. The advancement China has already made in renewables is not just greater than *anyone* else, but also greater than *everyone* else. In each year from 2020 to 2022, China accounted for about 140 gigawatts of new renewable electricity generation capacity—according to *Financial Times*, more than the United States, the European Union, and India combined.[1159] A majority of China's total lay in solar farms, yet nearly a third consisted of new wind power; in 2021, China installed more offshore wind generation capacity in one year than the rest of the world

---

1155 In mathematics, an inflection point describes the point where the curvature of a function changes direction, and is precisely defined as the point where the *rate of the rate of increase* becomes negative.

1156 World Bank, "CO2 Emissions (Kt) - China."

1157 Adam Tooze, "Did Xi Just Save the World?," *Foreign Policy,* September 25, 2020.

1158 Climate Action Tracker, "China Going Carbon Neutral before 2060 Would Lower Warming Projections by around 0.2 to 0.3 Degrees C," September 23, 2020.

1159 Martin Wolf, "The Market Can Deliver the Green Transition—Just Not Fast Enough," *Financial Times,* November 22, 2022.

combined had installed in the past five years. As of January 2022, China operated half of all the world's offshore wind turbines.[1160]

The rate and scale of these projects are only accelerating. In December 2022, ground was broken on what *Bloomberg* reported was "the world's largest renewable project in a desert" in Inner Mongolia, to meet a planned total of 1,200 gigawatts just in wind and solar capacity by 2030.[1161] Record growth in solar power capacity was expected in 2023—between 95 and 120 gigawatts, according to projections by the China Photovoltaic Industry Association, or between 8% to 37% *more* than the previous record in 2022.[1162] As of this writing, however, such projections are proving to have been overly modest. By the end of April, nearly three times as much new solar capacity had been installed in 2023 than in the same period in 2022; the chairman of Tongwei Solar predicted that installations of new solar capacity alone might fall between 200 and 300 gigawatts in 2024.[1163] These statistics and estimates in fact still seriously *underestimate* China's role in driving a global transition away from fossil fuels. In 2021, China accounted for over 80% of all stages of solar photovoltaic manufacturing, four times as much as the rest of the world combined—yet accounted for only 36% of global demand, making Chinese industrial production the *sina qua non* of solar power generation worldwide. In other words, a solar panel chosen at random anywhere in the world has only a one in five chance of *not* being made in China.[1164]

Though itself astonishing, the pace of expansion of China's renewable energy capacity is rivaled by pace of expansion of its nuclear energy capacity. China's "nuclear pipeline," or the total capacity of all its new reactors under development, is also larger than that of the rest of the world combined, with 19 reactors under construction, 43 reactors awaiting permits, and another 166 reactors planned, for a total of almost 250 gigawatts of zero-carbon capacity as of 2021.[1165] In April of 2022,

---

1160 David Vetter, "China Built More Offshore Wind In 2021 Than Every Other Country Built In 5 Years," *Forbes,* January 26, 2022.

1161 Luz Ding, "China Starts Work on Huge $11 Billion Desert Renewables Project," *Bloomberg,* December 28, 2022.

1162 Muyu Xu, "China Solar Power Capacity Could Post Record Growth in 2023," *Reuters,* February 15, 2023.

1163 "China's Solar Boom Is Already Accelerating Past Last Year's Record Surge," *Bloomberg News,* May 22, 2023.

1164 International Energy Agency, Special Report: *Solar PV Global Supply Chains* (July 2022), 7.

1165 Nick Ferris, "Weekly Data: China's Nuclear Pipeline as Big as the Rest of the World's Combined," *Energy Monitor,* December 20, 2021.

plans for a further six new reactors were announced,[1166] and according to state-owned China National Nuclear Corp., an estimated 30 additional reactors were expected to be constructed around the world via the Belt and Road Initiative by the end of the decade.[1167] The newest Chinese nuclear reactors are also the most technologically advanced in the world, with greater efficiency and lacking water consumption requirements for cooling. In 2022, for example, *Power* magazine reported the activation of the first "fourth-generation" reactor in Shandong Province;[1168] in the summer of 2023, the world's first modular nuclear reactor, capable of powering over half a million households and designed to eventually be mass-produced, was installed in Hainan.[1169] There is no doubt that China leads the world in any and every type of zero-emissions technology; even China's struggling coal-fired power plants, now a minority of all installed capacity, are considerably cleaner and more efficient than those in the West or indeed anywhere else, with plants approaching 50% efficiency— setting the world record, and a vast improvement compared with a typical Australian plant's efficiency of 30%.[1170] As early as 2017, the Center for American Progress reported that China's coal sector was undergoing a "massive transformation" with stricter emissions standards and superior technology that consumed less coal, emitted less carbon, and produced more power than an equivalent number of the most advanced U.S. coal plants.[1171] [1172]

1166 "China Approves Construction of Six New Reactors," *World Nuclear News,* August 1, 2023.

1167 Reuters Staff, "China Could Build 30 'Belt and Road' Nuclear Reactors by 2030: Official," *Reuters,* June 19, 2019.

1168 Sonal Patel, "China Starts Up First Fourth-Generation Nuclear Reactor," *Power Magazine,* February 1, 2022.

1169 "Core Module Completed for Chinese SMR," *World Nuclear News,* July 14, 2023.

1170 Angus Grigg, "The Thomas Edison of China Gives Donald Trump Ideas on Reviving Coal Sector," *Financial Review,* January 20, 2017.

1171 Melanie Hart, Luke Bassett, and Blaine Johnson, "Everything You Think You Know About Coal in China Is Wrong," *Center for American Progress,* May 15, 2017.

1172 While China's reliance on coal-fired power plants is a common target for criticism in the Western press, the frequently-cited overall figures of total coal generation capacity or the number of coal plants planned are often misleading. According to an analysis by David Fishman, a senior manager of Asia Pacific energy consultancy firm The Lantou Group, a "significant portion" of the new coal capacity allowed by the 14th Five-Year Plan's 150GW limit would likely be abandoned due to poor project economics and a recent trend of early cancellations as of August 2022. Moreover, due to the relative expense of coal power, most such plants increasingly

Electrical power plants, of course, are only one aspect of the elusive climate solution, but in all others, China is also far and away the world leader. In 2022, the *New York Times* admitted that more electric cars would be sold in China than in the rest of the world combined; in 2014, the central government had set what the *Times* called an "aggressive" goal to make electric vehicles account for 20% of all new car sales by 2025, a goal which was met and exceeded three years ahead of schedule.[1173] [1174] Also in 2022, more than twice as many public electric vehicle chargers were installed in China as in the rest of the world combined,[1175] and 98% of all electric buses in the world were deployed in Chinese cities, according to *Sustainable Bus* magazine.[1176] China's electric high-speed rail system is larger by total length than all high-speed railways in the rest of the world combined, and over three billion passenger trips are made on China's railways each year.[1177]

Since 1980, the Three-North Shelter Forest Program (dubbed the "Great Green Wall" initiative by the press) has doubled forest coverage in China, having already planted more new trees than the rest of the world

---

operated as "backup power," ramping up utilization rates only during peak demand hours or at times of day or during weather conditions when sunlight, wind, or hydroelectric power were less available. Fishman's analysis estimated that new coal plants would likely see usage rates of only 30-40% once completed, and that in several provinces, almost no coal-fired power was used during the daytime by 2022 (David Fishman, "China Coal: Nine Questions," The Lantau Group, February 2023). Fishman estimated that China's coal consumption would peak in 2023, and thereafter begin a long decline (David Fishman, "China Is Going to Use Less Coal, despite Reports to the Contrary," *The China Project,* September 21, 2023). Meanwhile, demand for coal in the EU is increasing with no clear plan or strategy for phasing it out (Frédéric Simon, "With Russian Gas Gone, Coal Makes EU Comeback as 'Traditional Fuel,'" *Euractiv,* January 26, 2023), and the U.S. and Canada are ramping up oil and natural gas drilling, despite already producing more than enough oil and gas for domestic needs. A study by U.S.-based NGO Rocky Mountain Institute has recently found that due to methane leakage, natural gas is no more clean than coal—a comparison that was doubtless made to vastly inefficient *Western* coal-fired plants, rather than to cleaner Chinese plants (Deborah Gordon and Shannon Hughes, "Reality Check: Natural Gas's True Climate Risk," *RMI,* July 13, 2023).

1173 Daisuke Wakabayashi and Claire Fu, "For China's Auto Market, Electric Isn't the Future. It's the Present," *New York Times,* September 27, 2022.

1174 The United States, by comparison, only reached the much more modest benchmark of EVs accounting for 5% of total sales in the same year.

1175 Ryan Fisher, "There's No Such Thing as Too Many Electric-Car Chargers in China," *Bloomberg,* June 20, 2023.

1176 "Electric Bus, Main Fleets and Projects around the World," *Sustainable Bus,* September 14, 2023.

1177 See Chapter Seven.

combined.[1178] According to the Global Forest Resources Assessment published by the United Nations' Food and Agriculture Organization, between 2010 and 2020 China had an average annual net gain in forest area of almost two million hectares, over four times as much as Australia's (the country with the second-largest net gain) and nearly twenty times as much as the United States'.[1179] In 2021, the government set a new target rate of afforestation of 36,000 square kilometers per year—or 3.6 million hectares in total, nearly double its previous rate, enough new trees to cover the land area of Belgium.[1180]

As of this writing, it is growing increasingly clear that 2023 will go down in history as the year of China's fossil fuel peak. That summer, Sinopec, the country's largest fuel distributor, reported that gasoline demand would peak that year and decline thereafter—two years earlier than original estimates, due to the electric vehicle boom.[1181] By the end of the year, Western climate experts began predicting that the rapid pace of renewable energy installation in China had reached a tipping point. "A drop in [China's] power-sector emissions in 2024 is essentially locked in," Lauri Myllyvirta, the co-founder and lead analyst of the Finland-based research organization Centre for Research on Energy and Clean Air told the *Telegraph* in November.[1182] The PRC has reached its first major climate milestone seven years ahead of time.

Financing the Future

How is all this possible? There are two principal reasons why the PRC's unprecedented crusade against climate change stands in stark contrast to the rest of the world. The first and most obvious is that the rest of the world is dragging its feet. No other country has both the economic resources and the political independence required to do anything like what the PRC is doing even if it wished to. Many, if not most other countries,

1178 "China's 40-Year, Billion-Tree Project Is a Lesson for the World," *Bloomberg*, September 13, 2020.

1179 Food and Agriculture Organization of the United Nations, *A Fresh Perspective: Global Forest Resources Assessment 2020*, 18.

1180 David Stanway, "China to Step up Tree Planting Campaign to Help Reach Net Zero," *Reuters*, August 20, 2021.

1181 "China's Gasoline Demand to Peak Early on Fast Adoption of EVs," *Bloomberg*, August 3, 2023.

1182 Ambrose Evans-Pritchard, "China's CO2 Emissions May Be Falling Already, in a Watershed Moment for the World," *The Telegraph*, November 21, 2023.

must certainly wish to do more than they are currently doing, but cannot; even their own economic resources are not their own.

Conventional economic wisdom suggests that GDP, debt, income, and the balance of trade are the best, if imperfect, tools available to measure the strength and performance of a country's economy. Indeed, earlier chapters have relied on them, to the extent that they are available, to make the best estimation of trends in development, whether in China, Russia, Europe, or the periphery. Any such estimation and any predictions that follow from it are only as solid as the data. Critics of the PRC sometimes point out that its meteoric rise in GDP during the twenty-first century does not in itself reflect an improvement in health, education, or the standard of living. Many negative examples exist, in the West and in many neo-colonies, of rising GDP combined with increases in poverty and all its associated dimensions of human suffering.

In China's case, such criticism is easily challenged, given the simultaneous development and reductions in poverty that have occurred during the Common Prosperity era and are measurable in other ways. In general, poverty cannot be left behind without a corresponding economic rise, making an increase in GDP a necessary but insufficient condition for an increase in standard of living over the long term, particularly in a peripheral or semi-peripheral country.[1183] But if healthy GDP growth *can* conceal a country's unhealthy shortcomings, it may be that *modest* GDP growth can also conceal a greater strength.

In 2013 and 2022, Starrs offered analyses in direct contrast to the frequent prognostications of the United States' decline following the 2008 financial crisis.[1184] According to Starrs, the global nature of the crisis was in fact indicative of U.S. dominance of the global economy, and the U.S. economy, far from being in absolute or even *relative* decline compared with the rest of the world, had actually grown to even *greater* heights than before the crisis. Country-specific GDP figures, which had seen the United States' share of global GDP decline from nearly 40% in 1960 to

---

1183 There are of course exceptions in the short term. The redistribution of wealth following successful proletarian revolutions, for example, such as in Cuba or in the China of 1949, can temporarily obviate the necessity of overall growth. Yet redistribution alone is zero-sum; if pursued in seriousness, there nevertheless eventually comes a point at which there remains no more wealth held unequally that can be redistributed.

1184 Even the U.S. press often expresses a remarkable insecurity regarding their own supposed decline—an insecurity that conveniently justifies ever-increasing defense spending.

less than one-quarter in 2008 for the first time, belied a gigantic increase in American ownership of foreign and trans-national corporations (TNCs), which, being domiciled abroad, were not properly reflected in country-level statistics.[1185]

As mentioned in Chapter Seven, according to recent estimates, China's *overall net wealth* has overtaken that of the United States, yet these estimates, provided by McKinsey, are measurements of total assets. Assets must be distinguished from *capital*, which is a specific type of asset that is held for the purpose of making money. Neither are all capital assets created equal. Real estate, for example, accounted for a vast amount of such capital—two-thirds of all global net wealth, according to McKinsey, most of which existed as residential real estate[1186]—and the *profit* generated from real estate is proportionally unremarkable compared to other sectors of the economy. Within the capitalist world-system, it is corporations (and not homeowners), above all else, that not only acquire *new* wealth—generated either by extracting raw materials from the Earth, or by combining existing capital with labor—but accumulate that wealth as profit. Control over *corporate capital* is therefore the most determinative measure of economic power.

American investors, Starrs concluded, were not only the predominant owners of American corporations, but of European corporations as well, and enjoyed disproportionate ownership over the world's top TNCs.[1187] Three years after the 2008 stock market crash, Starrs writes, "the top American financial services firms have increased their global dominance to 53% of the total profit of the financial services sector in the *Forbes Global 2000* (2012)."[1188]

The financial oligarchy of the super-empire has therefore not only endured in the twenty-first century, but grown even more powerful and more concentrated. In purely economic terms, they are not declining, but ascending. The only significant accumulation of capital that American capitalists have no control over, in fact, is in China. According to Starrs' most recent research based on data from 2021, the PRC's share of ownership in the global top 500 firms had not significantly increased since 2012; only

1185 Sean Starrs, "American Economic Power Hasn't Declined—It Globalized! Summoning the Data and Taking Globalization Seriously," *International Studies Quarterly* 57, no. 4 (December 2013): 820.

1186 "The Rise and Rise of the Global Balance Sheet: How Productively Are We Using Our Wealth?," McKinsey & Company, November 15, 2021.

1187 Starrs, 818.

1188 Starrs, 820.

6% of the world's most valuable corporate capital was controlled by the PRC, while nearly half was controlled by either U.S.-dominated banking institutions, U.S. corporations, or U.S. investors (collectively) through even more gargantuan multinationals. In fact, though seeing a significant decline in the banking sector and a very slight decline in software and electronics since 2012, the United States' share of ownership in the global top 2000 firms had *even further expanded* in other industries by 2021, particularly financial services, media,[1189] and aerospace and defense, in which U.S. investors enjoyed a *92% profit share.*[1190]

Thus while the PRC heavily invests its relatively modest chunk of the world's resources into the preservation of human civilization, the Western capitalist oligarchy has contributed only pennies relative to its own, much vaster fortune. According to *Bloomberg*, in 2021 the PRC was the largest spender in the global energy transition, in combined public and private investment—as it has been for every year running since 2012. The European Union collectively accounted for less than half of Chinese spending, while the U.S. scarcely spent one-third of China's contribution. Proportional to Starrs' calculations of global corporate capital ownership—and thus to economic power—in which U.S. investors had 46% and the PRC only 6%, the U.S. contribution to the global energy transition was one-twentieth of China's in 2021.[1191] In a June 2023 article headlined "China's Green Revolution is Quietly Succeeding," the *Wall Street Journal* admitted that 62 gigawatts of new wind and solar capacity—over half the *maximum* expectation for the *entire* year—had already been added in China in just the first four months; and in typical Western media fashion, the *Journal* took the opportunity to complain of the "mixed blessing for investors" who were finding it "tougher to make money from Chinese renewable stocks."[1192] The PRC is singular among the institutions of this world in that it both has the power to act and is actually treating the climate emergency like an emergency.

In 2015, *The Diplomat* reported on the Chinese central government's unprecedented new policy of subjecting local government officials to an

---

1189 Notably, according to Starrs' research, percentage of profit from media corporations in the global top 2000 that flowed to China was zero.

1190 *Signs of the Times #3 - On U.S. Decline, with Sean Starrs,* Interview with Sean Starrs, Sage4Age YouTube video [36:41], June 3, 2022.

1191 Aaron Clark, "Even With Biggest-Ever Climate Bill, US Lags China's Green Spending," *Bloomberg,* August 15, 2022.

1192 Jacky Wong, "China's Green Revolution Is Quietly Succeeding," *Wall Street Journal,* June 2, 2023.

environmental audit; according to the officials in charge of the auditing process, its implementation presented great difficulty, not least because even as late as 2015, no other country in the world had any similar policies they could learn from.[1193] Then, as now, China could cross the river only by feeling for the stones.

Can this truly be the reality we all share on this Earth? Even the most avaricious capitalists, the most misanthropic billionaires, are still human beings; they could not wish to see the destruction of the ecosystem that has sustained us through all the tribulations of humankind. Indeed, no matter how remote their mansions or gated their communities, they still inhabit the same planet, and if nothing else would prefer to spend their days above ground beneath a livable atmosphere. Surely, with their enormous fortunes, they have even more to lose than we do, and ought to be willing to spend generously to save our shared future.

If by this point the reader is convinced that the Western oligarchy would, with or without remorse, kill any number of people to increase their profit, then this book has grimly succeeded. But in the final analysis, human beings are not meaningfully motivated by greed, nor by cruelty, nor sadism, nor any such darker impulse. Above any individual's psychology lies the collective calculus of class interest—though rarely is it in fact acknowledged or calculated. Not one billionaire considers him/herself evil, but they may be driven to *any* evil to maintain their position within the hierarchy of class society. Competition rules their world; a conscience—and thus actual philanthropy—penalizes their ability to compete, and thus not only impedes their ability to succeed but even just to endure. Any capitalists who cannot abandon theirs are naturally selected out of the running long before they can wield any real power. Thus, the Western oligarchy may very much like to avert the pending climate catastrophe but would also very much prefer only to spend someone else's money to do so.

By the end of August 2022, after weeks of struggle, the wildfires besieging Chongqing were driven back and extinguished. In the end, the fires were defeated not just by water, sand, chemicals, or controlled burns, but by community. Professional firefighters had been joined by twenty thousand civil servants and volunteers, who climbed or biked up and down the mountain in the sweltering 40-degree-centigrade heat to deliver supplies and construct fire barriers; through their collective action, the

---

1193 Zhang Chun, "China's New Blueprint for an 'Ecological Civilization,'" *The Diplomat*, September 30, 2015.

cities were saved.[1194] With 1.4 billion members, China's is among the largest communities on the planet, and also still the community most capable of acting freely. The solutions to the slow-motion climate apocalypse are mundane—economic planning, technological development, and the redistribution of resources—but the freedom to pursue those solutions is very rare and very dear.

1194 Tan Yingzi and Deng Rui, "Chongqing Residents Unite to Vanquish Wildfires," *China Daily,* August 29, 2022.

CHAPTER ELEVEN

A "Multipolar" World?

As with all world-historical events, the ideological currents of the impending changes and their material underpinnings are interrelated and mutually reinforcing; but just as one must manifest first, that one must be examined first. This chapter will therefore concern itself with the material nature of the impending shifts in the geopolitical landscape—the actual relations between countries, their military and economic strengths and weaknesses, and most importantly their relationship with the existing paradigm of super-imperialism, while the following chapter will address the associated intentions of the major players and the ideologies that seek to describe or influence their actions.

There is no question that cracks are at last appearing in U.S. hegemony. One of the most visible is an incipient de-dollarization. Moves in this direction are frequently publicized; by the end of 2022, even *Bloomberg* published an article headlined "Suddenly Everyone Is Hunting for Alternatives to the U.S. Dollar," calling the emerging new system "a three-tier structure with the dollar still very much on top, but increasing bilateral payment routes and alternative spheres such as the yuan that seek to seize on any potential U.S. overreach."[1195] Regardless of how rapid or gradual this process may be, it is undeniable that dollar hegemony, or the use of the dollar as the world's reserve currency, is encountering unprecedented challenges. In 2023, the American Institute for Economic Research declared that "De-dollarization has begun."[1196] Many countries, especially the Russian Federation, but also the PRC, India, the Gulf states, and some of the periphery are now conducting some trade in their own and other non-dollar currencies, or attempting to. Fueling this shift are the U.S. government's sanctions on the Russian Federation, which attempted to isolate Russia from the global economy by taking the unprecedented step of locking it out of the global SWIFT payment system in 2022. It was far from the first time the U.S. has weaponized its currency, but it

---

1195 Michelle Jamrisko and Ruth Carson, "Suddenly Everyone Is Hunting for Alternatives to the US Dollar," *Bloomberg,* December 21, 2022.

1196 Peter C. Earle, "De-Dollarization Has Begun," American Institute for Economic Research, April 4, 2023.

may be one of the last; if the rest of the world finally drops the dollar, the U.S. may lose a source of tremendous economic leverage, and the super-empire's second mechanism of control identified in Chapter Two— economic isolation—will become virtually useless.

The word seemingly on the lips of everyone who might wish to see an end to super-imperial hegemony is "multipolarity." The term has seen continuous aspirational use by world leaders and other political and academic figures even as far back as the Cold War.[1197] Putin has repeatedly used the word in public speeches,[1198] and even before he became president, the Russian leadership favored such an arrangement. In 1997, the PRC and the Russian Federation issued a "Joint Declaration on a Multipolar World and the Establishment of a New International Order," signed by both Yeltsin and Jiang Zemin, in which they promised to "promote the multipolarization of the world."[1199] Even German Chancellor Olaf Scholz recently referred to his government's desire to peacefully adapt to the "multipolar world" in late 2022.[1200] If the stage of super-imperialism is indeed ending, or nearing an end, what is the nature of this "multipolar world" that would replace it?

In a multipolar world, according to the Joint Declaration in 1997,

Every country has the right independently to choose its path of development in the light of its own specific conditions and without interference from other States. Differences in their social systems, ideologies and value systems must not become an obstacle to the development of normal relations between States.

All countries, large or small, strong or weak, rich or poor, are equal members of the international community. No country should seek hegemony, engage in power politics or monopolize international affairs.[1201]

1197 Elizabeth Dickinson, "New Order," *Foreign Policy,* October 15, 2009.

1198 "Putin Calls for Strengthening Emerging Multipolar World Order in Address to BRICS Summit," *TASS,* September 9, 2021.

1199 Russian Federation and People's Republic of China, "China-Russia: Joint Declaration on a Multipolar World and the Establishment of a New International Order," *International Legal Materials* 36, no. 4 (July 1997): 987.

1200 Olaf Scholz, "We Don't Want to Decouple from China, but Can't Be Overreliant," *Politico,* November 3, 2022.

1201 Russian Federation and People's Republic of China, "China-Russia: Joint Declaration on a Multipolar World and the Establishment of a New International Order," 987.

Putin has called it a more "just [and] democratic" world order.[1202] It seems that according to the biggest proponents of multipolarity, there are, or will be, not a few poles but many, enough to make possible self-determination for all peoples of the world. Is this hopeful rhetoric at last nearing fulfillment? If significant concentrations of power are forming outside of the West, then what specifically are the "poles" of this new configuration?

Amin's vision of "multipolarity," which he offered in 2006, included four distinct conditions:

A genuinely multipolar world will become a reality only when the following four conditions have been satisfied.

1. Real advances towards a different, "social" Europe, and hence a Europe that has begun to disengage from its imperialist past and present and to embark on the long transition to world socialism. Evidently this implies more than a mere exit from Atlanticism and extreme neoliberalism.

2. The prevalence of "market socialism" in China over the strong tendencies to an illusory construction of "national capitalism," which would be impossible to stabilize because it would exclude the majority of workers and peasants.

3. Success of the countries of the South (peoples and states) in rebuilding a "common front." This is also essential to provide the leeway for popular classes to impose "concessions" in their favour and to transform existing systems of rule, replacing the dominant comprador blocs with new "national, popular and democratic" blocs.

4. Advances at the level of national and international legal systems, harmonizing respect for national sovereignty (including moves from state to popular sovereignty) with respect for all individual and collective, political and social rights.[1203]

1202 Danil Bochkov, "Russia and China Are Aligning Their Visions for a Multipolar World, and Eyeing New Supporters," *South China Morning Post,* November 2, 2022.

1203 Samir Amin, *Beyond US Hegemony? Assessing the Prospects for a Multipolar World* (Zed Books, 2006), 157.

Fifteen years on, only the second of these four conditions has been unambiguously met—the shift back to a transition toward socialism within China, which as described in Chapter Seven began only a few years after Amin's words were published.[1204]

Amin's optimism regarding China[1205] was at this stage in his writings more guarded; he regarded the PRC as unable to solve the "peasant question" to which he gave paramount importance; rather than seeing the Party as an extension of proletarian and peasant will, he referred to a "Chinese ruling class" that consisted of a "hegemonic bloc [that] excludes the great majority of workers and peasants."[1206] Amin projected that if current trends continued, there would be "a total of 800 million rural Chinese in the year 2020—the same number as today, but constituting 53 per cent (instead of the present 67 per cent) of the total population."[1207] By 2021, China's rural population had fallen to approximately 530 million—not 67%, or 53%, but 37% of the total.[1208] In the twenty-first century China has exceeded even the expectations of its anti-imperialist supporters. However long the road to multipolarity may ultimately be, the first disruption to the dominance of the unipolar super-empire will undoubtedly only be made possible by the PRC.

The United States' Neocolonization of Europe

> "...we must seek to prevent the emergence of European-only security arrangements which would undermine NATO."
> —Secret draft of U.S. Department of Defense policy document, 1992[1209]

Amin's first condition of multipolarity was an independent European bloc that rejected neoliberalism, leading to a "tripolar" world consisting of a diminished super-empire (the United States, Canada, Australia, Japan, and perhaps the United Kingdom, if it were to remain Atlanticist), a bloc led by the PRC (consisting of Russia, Iran, and their satellites), and a European Union bloc, led by Germany and France. Since the time of

---

1204 This shift largely began as a response to the 2008 global financial crisis—see Chapter Seven for a detailed analysis.
1205 See Chapter Six.
1206 Samir Amin, *Beyond U.S. Hegemony?*, 28.
1207 Samir Amin, 37.
1208 World Bank, "Rural Population (% of Total Population) - China."
1209 Patrick E. Tyler, "U.S. Strategy Plan Calls for Insuring No Rivals Develop," *New York Times,* March 8, 1992.

Amin's writing, the hope that Europe would turn away from neoliberal-ism seems to have faded; as shown in Chapter Five, social democracy has been continuously eroded throughout the continent, in several countries disappearing entirely as political force. As of this writing, neoliberal par-ties and centrist coalitions rule in most countries, while a few pioneers of the nativist far-right have gained power, such as in Hungary and Italy.[1210] However, the EU is rebuilding its military power. According to a stra-tegic document leaked in 2022, the German military planned to greatly increase its strength to ensure deterrence to the Russian Federation;[1211] the same year, the Polish government publicly announced that it would double its defense spending.[1212] Military power is after all needed for real sovereignty; could this be the origin of an independent European bloc?

The economic situation faced by the EU as of the winter of 2022-2023 was not promising. Inflation was on the rise. The steady supply of Russian oil and natural gas, upon which Germany and many of its neighbors had become dependent on, had dried up. As of November 2022, fuel prices in Europe had increased to six times their long-run average.[1213] According to the *Financial Times* in December, the demand for gas had fallen by nearly a quarter across the EU; commodity analytics found that industry was driving the biggest reduction in consumption, due to high prices disincentivizing use.[1214] Though a warmer-than-expected winter in 2022-2023 bought Europe precious time to address the looming problem of how to maintain gas reserves, now it must be solved without Russia; in the meantime, as of this writing, industrial production—primarily in Germany—continues to decline.

Who benefits from Europe's energy austerity and deindustrialization? The Russian Federation is surely not displeased to see its enemies' sup-pliers endure misfortune, yet Europe's misfortune has not yet produced any favorable results for Russia. As of 2023, the NATO alliance, about

---

1210 Chico Harlan and Stefano Pitrelli, "Right-Wing Victory in Italy Expected to Bring Swift Changes to Migration," *Washington Post,* September 26, 2022.

1211 Matthias Gebauer and Marina Kormbaki, "Vorbereitung auf »aufgezwungenen Krieg« – Bundeswehr soll deutlich kampfkräftiger werden" [Preparation for 'forced war' - Bundeswehr should become significantly more powerful], *Spiegel,* November 14, 2022.

1212 Matthew Karnitsching and Wojciech Kość, "Meet Europe's Coming Military Superpower: Poland," *Politico,* November 21, 2022.

1213 "Europe Faces an Enduring Crisis of Energy and Geopolitics," *The Economist,* November 24, 2022.

1214 Shotaro Tani, "Europe Cuts Gas Demand by a Quarter to Shed Reliance on Russia," *Financial Times,* December 4, 2022.

to swell its ranks with the accession of Sweden and Finland, is stronger and more united than ever. European weapons manufacturing has not followed the general industrial trend; in November 2022, *Reuters* reported that the arms industry in Eastern Europe was "booming" as more weapons flowed to Ukraine.[1215] The Federation would no doubt much prefer a neutral Europe that continued to purchase its gas, but there is no going back; the destruction of the Nord Stream pipelines has made the new status quo irrevocable for at least several years even if Europe were to reverse its policies.

Nor have Chinese interests been particularly served by the crisis in Europe. Increased trade with Russia is to the PRC's benefit but has come at a cost. Though trade relations between Europe and the PRC have mostly remained healthy, the United States is placing increasing pressure on the EU to decouple its high-tech industry from China through sanctions and export controls.[1216] By November 2022, Huawei had begun withdrawing from the European market, consolidating all its operations in Germany and abandoning the UK entirely.[1217]

Within Europe, the clear winner is Norway, which has enjoyed a 200% increase in petroleum industry profits between 2021 and 2022 after it replaced Russia as the EU's largest source of gas. The average Norwegian has felt little pain; Norway's Labour Party, still in power through a coalition with the centrists, has weathered the reckoning faced by social democrats better than most, and during the crisis their government moved to heavily subsidize household electricity bills whenever wholesale prices rose above prescribed levels.[1218] The biggest beneficiary of the crisis, however, has been the United States.

Energy imports from the United States, in the form of liquified natural gas, have also increased dramatically in Europe, at prices four times higher than its own domestic fuel prices. EU officials have increasingly complained at the huge profits flowing to the U.S.; President Emmanuel Macron of France publicly remarked that U.S. prices were not friendly.[1219]

1215 Michael Kahn, Anna Koper, and Robert Muller, "Insight: Weapons Industry Booms as Eastern Europe Arms Ukraine," *Reuters,* November 24, 2022.

1216 Kevin Whitelaw, "U.S. Asks Europe to Consider Export Controls on China," *Bloomberg,* October 30, 2022.

1217 Laurens Cerulus and Sarah Wheaton, "How Washington Chased Huawei out of Europe," *Politico,* November 23, 2022.

1218 Charlie Duxbury, "'Selfish' Norway Accused of Ukraine War-Profiteering," *Politico,* September 15, 2022.

1219 Barbara Moens, Jakob Hanke Vela, and Jacopo Barigazzi, "Europe

In the summer of 2022, the United States Congress passed the Inflation Reduction Act, legislation that provided $400 billion in subsidies to domestic manufacturing and energy producers. European companies responded almost immediately, with major manufacturers expanding production in the United States. German multinational BASF, the world's largest producer of chemicals, announced plans to permanently shrink its European operations.[1220]

Europe may slow the offshoring of its industry with subsidies of its own but can do little to stop it. The knife at its throat has not been sharper since 1991; Germany, which will proportionately suffer the most, is currently occupied by forty thousand U.S. troops—two-thirds the size of the German Army—out of a total of one hundred thousand in Europe overall, nearly half of which were deployed in 2022 and as of this writing have no plans to leave.[1221] As European weapons stockpiles are depleted in Ukraine, the U.S. will gain even more control, its arms industry—the world's largest by a significant margin—being the only available source to replenish them quickly.

The Second Cold War will be far more unkind to Europe than the First. The entire continent is on a trajectory toward de-development; instead of an independent pole in a multipolar world, or even the junior partners of imperialism, the countries of Europe appear more likely to become U.S. neocolonies, with all the violence and exploitation this fate entails. Chapter Four described the hostile attitude of the super-empire's ruling class toward any potential new partners; now, in order to wring even more profit from the world—and to deny the PRC further influence—this ruling class has resorted to cannibalizing its own appendages, demoting even *current* partners in the ever-more-exclusive club. As the continent's only nuclear power, with a large economy that does not depend on natural gas, France is the best-positioned to assert its interests, and presumably lead the EU toward independence; in 2023, Macron gave voice to this potential, declaring Europe's need for "strategic autonomy"—during a visit to China.[1222] Though whether it will succeed remains very doubtful,

---

Accuses US of Profiting from War," *Politico,* November 24, 2022.

1220 "Europe Faces an Enduring Crisis of Energy and Geopolitics," *The Economist,* November 24, 2022.

1221 Ellie Kaufman and Barbara Starr, "US Likely to Keep 100,000 Troops in Europe for Foreseeable Future in Face of Russian Threat, US Officials Say," *CNN,* May 20, 2022.

1222 Jamil Anderlini and Clea Caulcutt, "Europe Must Resist Pressure to Become 'America's Followers,' Says Macron," *Politico,* April 9, 2023.

particularly in light of the recent upheavals taking place across the French neocolonies in West Africa, re-expanding diplomatic and trade relations with the PRC is the first step Europe must take to extract itself from its predicament.

The Second Pink Tide

> *"Is everything forbidden us except to fold our arms? Poverty is not written in the stars; under development is not one of God's mysterious designs."*
>
> —Eduardo Galeano, 1971[1223]

Amin's third condition for a multipolar world concerned the periphery, and the potential for diverse peoples and states to overthrow their comprador rulers and form a "common front." The prospects for such a revolutionary outcome may be improving; as seen in Chapter Six, there is considerable evidence that the PRC's investment in the periphery, especially in Asia and Africa, is working to gradually industrialize and develop these regions, which can only make neocolonialism and unequal exchange more difficult to enforce in the long run. Marxist political parties around the world, though still a very marginal force overall, may be starting to recover from their long decline.

Assuming that a new "pole" might eventually arise in the periphery, Latin America and the Caribbean would appear the likeliest candidate. A second "Pink Tide"—echoing the wave of left-wing electoral victories in Latin America that began with the election of Hugo Chávez in 1998—has swept the entire hemisphere. During his campaign, President Luiz Inácio Lula da Silva of Brazil announced his intention to create a new Latin American currency to free the region from U.S. dollar hegemony;[1224] his Peruvian counterpart Pedro Castillo won the presidency in 2021 promising a nationalization of Peru's mining industry.[1225] Later that year, Barbados swore in its first president, officially removing Queen Elizabeth as its head of state. In 2022, President Andrés Manuel López Obrador declared the nationalization of Mexico's lithium reserves, and Gustavo Petro, a

---

1223 Eduardo Galeano, *Open Veins of Latin America*, 7.

1224 "Brazil: Lula Proposes to Create a Latin American Currency," *TeleSUR English,* May 2, 2022.

1225 Shanghai Metals Market, "Pedro Castillo Wins a New Round of Elections in Peru to Recommend Nationalization of Mines." *SMM,* April 15, 2021.

former left-wing guerrilla fighter, was elected president of Colombia. A multitude of policy proposals aimed at loosening neocolonial dominance over the region, many of them quite radical, have been advanced by the new cadre of political leaders. Could this be the beginning of Amin's hypothesized "common front"?

The first step to any analysis must be a comparison between the first and second Pink Tides. At the peak of the first in 2011, members of the São Paulo Forum, the Americas' conference of left-wing political organizations, controlled the governments in every country in South America but Colombia, Chile, Guyana and Suriname—but their victories were short-lived. A ruthless wave of reaction, alternately planned, supported, or enabled by the United States and Europe, followed the Pink Tide even as it spread. Chávez himself, for example, faced a U.S.-orchestrated coup attempt only a few years after he took office.[1226] Economic pressure brought several others to heel, just as it had Venezuela's Pérez and Caldera two decades before;[1227] President Lenín Moreno of Ecuador, for example, signed an agreement with the IMF and introduced severe austerity measures during the late 2010s. Others were "legally" neutralized by the comprador establishment, typically charged—often on scant or manufactured evidence—with corruption and sometimes even imprisoned, as in the case of Lula da Silva before he could run for an earlier term in 2018.[1228] In more extreme cases, left-wing leaders were brought down by force. In 2004, President Jean-Bertrand Aristide of Haiti was removed from power in a coup d'état aided by the U.S. military;[1229] in 2009, the Honduran military overthrew President Manuel Zelaya, and the United States quickly pushed the Organization of American States to legitimize the interim coup government that brutally quelled a popular uprising

---

1226 See Chapter Three.

1227 See Chapter Two.

1228 According to leaked correspondence between Brazilian prosecutors, they had deliberately targeted Lula despite a lack of conclusive evidence against him, for the political purpose of spoiling his party's performance in the upcoming election (Glenn Greenwald and Victor Pougy, "Hidden Plot: Exclusive: Brazil's Top Prosecutors Who Indicted Lula Schemed in Secret Messages to Prevent His Party From Winning 2018 Election," *The Intercept,* July 3, 2019). The Supreme Court of Brazil later annulled the conviction against him ("Brazil High Court Confirms Annulment of Lula Graft Convictions," *Agence France-Presse,* April 16, 2021).

1229 Mentioned in Chapter Two. According to the *Washington Post,* multiple witnesses confirmed Aristide's account of being taken from his home by U.S. military and private security forces and threatened into boarding a plane leaving the country (Peter Eisner, "Aristide Back in Caribbean Heat," *Washington Post,* March 15, 2004.).

demanding his return.[1230] In November of 2019, President Evo Morales of Bolivia's Movement to Socialism (MAS) was also deposed and fled the country in a coup d'état spurred by the U.S. media's coordinated effort to spread manufactured claims of election fraud; the Bolivian military opened fire on demonstrations by his supporters, killing dozens.[1231] By the end of the decade, the Pink Tide had receded back to Venezuela's borders; nearly every other such anti-neoliberal government in Latin America had fallen one way or another.

The coup in Bolivia, however, did not quite go according to plan. Militant protests, driven by a powerful indigenous movement, forced the new comprador regime to hold new elections the following year; a resurgent MAS won easily, then arrested the coup leaders, reversed their policies, and returned the IMF money they had accepted.[1232] Another attempt to overthrow the government of Venezuela in 2019 ended in humiliation, as U.S.-supported "Interim President" Juan Guaidó failed utterly to gain popular support.[1233]

These failures proved to be a turning point. In 2022, rumors and threats to assassinate President Petro abounded during his campaign, and many in Colombia expected the military to move against him even before he was sworn in;[1234] but—as of this writing—the hammer has yet to fall. Incredibly, when far-right incumbent Jair Bolsonaro, in anticipation of his coming defeat at the polls later that year, began preemptively accusing the Brazilian Worker's Party of election fraud against him, the director of the CIA himself privately instructed Bolsonaro to stop questioning the electoral system.[1235] In January 2023, a coup was attempted, but appears to have been undertaken without coordination with any external forces, or even any real organization or plan. Thousands of demonstrators

1230 Nina Lakhani, "Did Hillary Clinton Stand by as Honduras Coup Ushered in Era of Violence?," *The Guardian,* August 31, 2016.

1231 Daniel Ramos and Santiago Limachi, "Supporters of Bolivia's Morales March with Coffins of Dead Protesters," Reuters, November 21, 2019.

1232 Reuters Staff, "Bolivia Returns $350 Mln to IMF after 'irregular and Onerous' Loan," *Reuters,* February 18, 2021.

1233 Guaidó, in fact, did not even manage to call a new election, even though Maduro challenged him to do so. (MercoPress, "Maduro Challenges Guaido to Call Elections," February 20, 2019.)

1234 "Colombia Presidential Candidate Petro Says Gang Planned to Kill Him on Campaign Trail," *Reuters,* May 2, 2022.

1235 Gabriel Stargardter and Matt Spetalnick, "Exclusive: CIA Chief Told Bolsonaro Government Not to Mess with Brazil Election, Sources Say." *Reuters,* May 5, 2022.

stormed the Supreme Court and the presidential palace in the capital of Brasília, calling for the military to intervene and reinstate Bolsonaro; but Bolsonaro himself had already left the country over a week earlier. Neither the Brazilian military nor the Western press mobilized to support the rioters, who were eventually arrested or dispersed.[1236] The aimlessness and incompetence of the would-be revolutionaries mirrored the even-less-successful "Operation Gideon" of 2020, in which the private military company Silvercorp USA had clumsily attempted to depose President Maduro.

It is possible that U.S. machinations were behind the first successful coup against the second Pink Tide—the arrest and removal of Castillo in December 2022—but of this writing, the evidence has not yet come to light. The coup was both abrupt and unexpected—even by the Peruvian left, which had almost seemed more dissatisfied with Castillo than the comprador opposition.[1237] Though the fallout of the coup against Castillo is still developing as of this writing, the similarities to the coup against Morales in 2019 are significant. Massive protests in Peru by workers, peasants, and indigenous communities mirrored the uprising in Bolivia that had followed the fall of Morales, and the new President Boluarte[1238]

1236 Anthony Faiola and Marina Dias, "Bolsonaro Backers Storm Congress, Court, Presidential Office in Brazil's Capital," *Washington Post,* January 8, 2023.

1237 When he took office in July of the previous year, Castillo appointed a radical cabinet of communists, rural organizers, and other left-wing politicians; in the spirit of Castillo's campaign, his new Marxist-Leninist prime minister, Guido Bellido, began threatening foreign natural gas companies with nationalization (Marcelo Rochabrun, "Peru PM Warns Gas Sector: Pay Higher Taxes or Face Nationalization," *Reuters,* September 26, 2021). At the same time, however, Castillo publicly walked back his campaign rhetoric, promising not to nationalize or expropriate the mining sector (Paul Harris, "Castillo Says 'No Nationalisation' of Mining," *Mining Journal,* September 22, 2021). Two weeks later, Castillo gave in to the opposition's objections to Bellido and asked him to resign ("Perú: 3 claves para entender la sorpresiva renuncia de Guido Bellido a la presidencia del Consejo de Ministros" [Peru: 3 keys to understanding the surprising resignation of Guido Bellido to the presidency of the Council of Ministers], *BBC News Mundo,* October 6, 2021). In the first six months of his presidency, Castillo appointed four different cabinets, continually moderating his policy to please a right wing that was never satisfied, and deferring the agenda of a left wing that was never realized. Less than a year after being sworn in, Castillo had disappointed his peasant base, barely survived two impeachment votes, and was asked to resign from Perú Libre, his own political party, who accused him of "implementing the losing neoliberal program." [Vladimir Cerrón (@VLADIMIR_CERRON), "Por acuerdo unánime del Partido, Comisión Política y Bancada."]

1238 Castillo's vice president, who had previously been expelled from Perú Libre.

declared a state of emergency a week later.[1239] On the other hand, the super-empire had clearly been prepared to strike at Morales. The OAS, backed by the European Union and the Western press, had demanded an audit of the Bolivian election results on the day, and quickly alleged fraud thereafter;[1240] on cue, the Bolivian military seized power immediately.[1241] This does not appear to have been the case with Castillo. His removal from power seems to have caught even the U.S. media by surprise; coverage before the coup was mostly neutral, reporting blandly on the opposition's third attempt at impeachment without any particular condemnation of Castillo or his administration. Peru's compradors appear to have seized upon Castillo's apparent weakness on their own initiative.

With this complex exception of Peru, it seems that the age of easy coups d'état is over. The super-empire is in retreat—or at least has completely changed its strategy. Overall, whether the U.S. government's new relatively muted response has been determinative or not, the new Pink Tide has been far more expansive than the first, encompassing not just South America but Mexico, Honduras, and Panama; it has spread throughout the region more than twice as fast and with even more dramatic results, disrupting even Colombia's long succession of brutal right-wing compradors.

What explains the new U.S. policy in the Americas? The most obvious answer is that the situation in Europe has commanded the super-empire's full attention. To lessen the burden of the West's boycott of Russian oil, for example, the U.S. pursued a limited détente with Venezuela, easing oil sanctions and partially unfreezing its assets.[1242] The anti-neoliberal left in Latin America is therefore taking great advantage of a historically unique opportunity—but one that may be fleeting. As the case of Peru has shown, despite a less aggressive U.S., the comprador establishment remains deeply entrenched—perhaps even more so than before. Gone are the days of Chávez and his landslide victories. During the first Pink Tide,

---

1239 Marco Aquino and Kylie Madry, "Peru President Urges Congress to Bring Elections Forward amid Deadly Protests," *Reuters,* December 17, 2022.

1240 BBC, "Bolivia Election: Protests as Evo Morales Officially Declared Winner," *BBC,* October 25, 2019.

1241 Only months later, after the coup had already succeeded, did researchers at the Massachusetts Institute of Technology eventually prove that the audit had been bogus (John Curiel and Jack R. Williams, "Bolivia Dismissed Its October Elections as Fraudulent. Our Research Found No Reason to Suspect Fraud," *Washington Post,* February 27, 2020).

1242 Regina Garcia Cano, "Venezuela's Gov, Opponents Resume Talks; US Eases Sanction," *AP News,* November 26, 2022.

Lula was elected president of Brazil twice in a row, each time with over 60% of the vote; a marked contrast with his recent return to power, which he achieved by the slimmest of margins, only 51% to Bolsonaro's 49%. Petro's victory came with a mandate of only 3%, and Castillo's by less than a single percentage point.

If Castillo's performance had been unsatisfactory to the Peruvian peasantry, President Gabriel Boric's has been no less underwhelming for the Chilean working class, who after a year of intense rioting to compel a referendum voted in record numbers to draft a new constitution by an overwhelming margin of 78%;[1243] though Boric promised that "If Chile was the cradle of neoliberalism, it will also be its grave,"[1244] he did virtually nothing to marshal public support for the new constitution or combat the flood of misinformation by its right-wing opponents.[1245] Chile's Interpreta Foundation reported tens of thousands of messages on social networks by the end of 2021, amplified by conservative politicians during the drafting process, spreading a manufactured narrative that the new constitution would change the flag, national anthem, and even the name of the country.[1246] As the plebiscite neared, more extreme falsehoods circulated, including viral rumors that the constitution would abolish all private property and allow abortions in the ninth month of pregnancy; by July of 2022, two-thirds of Chileans polled reported seeing some form of misinformation.[1247] Without its own champion or organized support, the new constitution was eventually rejected by over 60% of voters, and

---

1243 Jennifer M. Piscopo and Peter Siavelis, "Chile Voted to Write a New Constitution. Will It Promise More than the Government Can Deliver?" *Washington Post,* October 30, 2020.

1244 Fabian Cambero, "Former Protest Leader Boric Seeks to Bury Chile's 'neoliberal' Past," *Reuters,* November 17, 2021.

1245 In fact, even in the face of the plebiscite's sinking popularity, Boric seemed unconcerned with the result, indicating that the government would simply try again if it failed (Ciara Nugent, "Read the Transcript of TIME's Interview With Chile's President Gabriel Boric," *TIME,* August 31, 2022). Months after the plebiscite was rejected, Boric announced that the next draft should be written by the legislature instead. (Juan Martinez, "Chilean President Urges New Constitution to Be Drafted by Elected Body," *The Rio Times,* December 2, 2022). Meanwhile, the original neoliberal constitution remained in effect.

1246 Fundación Interpreta, "Las cuentas detrás de las fake news sobre la modificación de los símbolos patrios en la Convención Constitucional" [The accounts behind the fake news about the modification of the national symbols in the Constitutional Convention], *Interpreta,* November 30, 2021.

1247 Reuters, "Misinformation Spreads on Social Media in Chile Ahead of Vote on New Constitution," *NBC News,* August 29, 2022.

Boric's own approval rating mirrored the plebiscite, sinking to an average of 30% by the end of April as he was widely perceived to have no real economic plan for the country.[1248]

Unless it can deliver something tangible for Latin America's development, the second Pink Tide may recede even faster than the first. Argentina, where far-right demagogue Javier Milei was elected president in 2023, may prove the harbinger of its demise. But possibly, Boric has learned from this debacle and from Castillo's fate. In April 2023, he announced the creation of a new state-owned lithium mining company. *Reuters* called it a "shock move"[1249] and the Chilean business federation SOFOFA registered its "surprise,"[1250] even though this very policy had been one of Boric's campaign promises in 2021[1251]—as if, perhaps, the comprador establishment had never expected him to actually follow through.

Latin America must develop, if not to proletarian rule, then at minimum to the national-bourgeois stage before it can become an independent "pole"; it must first control its own natural resources, develop its infrastructure, and lessen its economic dependence on the United States. Considerable obstacles to this remain; Boric's policy, for example, did not yet affect *already existing* private lithium operations in Chile, which at the time were one-quarter of the world's total production.[1252] The nationalization of Mexico's lithium reserves is also a step toward this future, yet harnessing the incredible value of these resources for the benefit of Mexico will not be easy. As of 2022, the Mexican government had no operating lithium mines nor any experience mining lithium.[1253] The experience of Bolivia's MAS is an object lesson—for nearly fifteen years, the Bolivian government pursued fully independent development of its lithium deposits with very little progress, and thereafter changed

---

1248 Eva Vergara and Daniel Politi, "Chile's Boric Attempts Relaunch as Honeymoon Ends Abruptly," *AP News,* May 9, 2022.

1249 Alexander Villegas and Ernest Scheyder, "Chile Plans to Nationalize Its Vast Lithium Industry," *Reuters,* April 21, 2023.

1250 Ryan Dube, "Lithium Miners Slump as Chile Unveils State-Led Policy," *Wall Street Journal,* April 21, 202.

1251 Gabriel Boric Font (@GabrielBoric), "El litio es el mineral del futuro, usado en millones de aparatos electrónicos. Chile no puede cometer nuevamente el histórico error de privatizar los recursos y para esto crearemos la Empresa Nacional del Litio, generando empleos en los yacimientos y un sello chileno al producto."

1252 Ryan Dube, "Lithium Miners Slump as Chile Unveils State-Led Policy."

1253 Associated Press, "Mexico in Talks with Mining Companies about Lithium."

course to partner with the PRC for the necessary technical expertise to mine it in large quantities.[1254]

The PRC's role in the development of Latin America has already become fundamental. The PRC is now South America's largest trading partner, and may soon be all of Latin America's as well. The PRC is forging closer ties to historically-distant Central American and Caribbean governments; in 2023, Honduras became the latest country in the region to establish diplomatic relations with the PRC, leaving only seven that had not. In 2021, the Jamestown Foundation warned that U.S. financial policy was having the effect of U.S. banks "de-risking" their ties to the central banks of Caribbean countries, and thereby pushing their governments toward using the yuan as a trade currency rather than the dollar.[1255] According to *Forbes* in 2022, China Eximbank had "vaulted itself into the ranks of the region's leading lenders," loaning the equivalent of over $100 billion in Latin America. A total of twenty Latin American countries have signed on to the Belt and Road Initiative,[1256] and Chinese construction companies are building highways, railways, ports, and power plants throughout the region.[1257] Meaningful regional unity, which a geopolitical "pole" or "common front" surely requires, can only be forged with adequate connective infrastructure.

As with many such projects in the periphery, Chinese funding for Latin American infrastructure is often secured after Western financiers consistently refuse to take similar risks. Argentina's Cauchari Solar Plant, for example, one of the largest solar farms in South America with a planned capacity of 500 megawatts, was built with a loan from China Eximbank after local officials had been turned down by potential lenders in the U.S. and Europe.[1258] Latin America may eventually become a "pole," but the quickest road to such a future lies through China.

1254 Thomas Graham, "Bolivia's Dream of a Lithium Future Plays out on High-Altitude Salt Flats," *The Guardian,* January 25, 2023.

1255 Rasheed Griffith, "How U.S. Banks Push the Caribbean Toward China," *China Brief* 21, no. 17 (September 10, 2021).

1256 Milton Ezrati, "China's Latin America Move," *Forbes,* November 7, 2022.

1257 Ciara Nugent and Charlie Campell, "The U.S. and China Are Battling for Influence in Latin America, and the Pandemic Has Raised the Stakes," *TIME,* February 4, 2021.

1258 Cassandra Garrison, "On South America's Largest Solar Farm, Chinese Power Radiates," *Reuters Graphics,* April 23, 2019.

Bipolarity

As of this writing, the likeliest candidate, aside from the PRC, to become a "pole" in a new multipolar world is one Amin did not consider credible in 2006. The position of Putin—and of many who regard the intervention in Ukraine as a historical turning point—appears to be that the Russian Federation, at the very least, has now at last stood up and become the center of one such pole. Therefore, it must be asked, to what degree can Russia presently determine its own destiny?

By the end of the summer of 2023, it became clear that the Russian Army would not be defeated in Ukraine. The Ukrainian counteroffensive, upon which the West placed much hope accomplished next to nothing against its highly entrenched adversary. The Western press at last began to admit that the Armed Forces of Ukraine were in far greater difficulty than previously imagined. In September, for example, the *Financial Times* printed a resigned editorial by a Western military expert estimating that victory was not possible until 2025.[1259] A few months later, an article in the *Wall Street Journal* deemed Western leaders' theretofore unshakeable belief in Russia's swiftly impending defeat to be "magical thinking."[1260] The harsh and unprecedented sanctions placed upon the Russian Federation have also failed. The Russian economy ultimately shrank by only 1.2% in 2022[1261] and rebounded in 2023, with the government projecting net growth. According to the *Financial Times*, the oil cap has proved ineffective.[1262] In terms of military industrial capacity, Russian arms production has thus far outpaced the West. The Russian defense industry is booming, along with the restaurant market, construction, and domestic investment, according to an op-ed in the *Washington Post* at the end of November.[1263]

However, as mentioned in Chapter Four, Russia's success has come at a high price. In order to establish their defensive line and gain the upper hand, Russian forces retreated from Kharkov and Kherson in late 2022,

---

1259 Richard Barrons, "Ukraine Cannot Win against Russia Now, but Victory by 2025 Is Possible," *Financial Times*, September 2, 2023.

1260 Eugene Rumer and Andrew S. Weiss, "It's Time to End Magical Thinking About Russia's Defeat," *Wall Street Journal*, November 16, 2023.

1261 "Russian economy shrank by 1.2% in 2022, less than previously thought - stats service," *Reuters*, December 29, 2023.

1262 David Sheppard et al., "Almost No Russian Oil Is Sold below $60 Cap, Say Western Officials," *Financial Times*, November 14, 2023.

1263 Mikhail Zygar, "In Russia, the Shift in Public Opinion Is Unmistakable," *Washington Post*, November 28, 2023.

giving up territory that the Russian Federation has claimed as its own soil and will likely only with a bloody and grueling campaign be recaptured. Russia's eventual posture of patiently consolidating its territorial gains indicate that a kind of frozen conflict may continue for years. Meanwhile, the Russian Federation's closest allies have themselves come under siege. Iran, whose drone technology the Russian Armed Forces have relied upon, has simultaneously experienced a severe economic crisis and instability, and Azerbaijan has taken the opportunity to seize territory from Russia's ostensible ally Armenia, which has since undertaken joint military exercises with the U.S.[1264] Russia's northern neighbor Finland has joined NATO, and Sweden, formerly neutral, is also expected to eventually join as of this writing. Russia has largely been cut off from the Western financial system, and any hope of future trade and economic integration with Europe has been lost, perhaps for good. According to Gazprom, natural gas exports to the EU in 2022 were only half their volume in 2021.[1265] Russia's export capacity to Europe has been greatly reduced after the destruction of the Nord Stream pipelines and the closure of the Yamal pipeline through Poland; presently, Russia can supply Europe only through Ukraine and through the lesser-capacity TurkStream pipeline under the Black Sea.

Meanwhile, the Russian's economic reliance on the PRC has vastly increased. Russia soon recovered what it had lost in Europe by increasing trade with other Asian countries, including India, Iran, and Türkiye—but with none so much, by far, as China. Almost immediately after the Russian intervention in Ukraine, Gazprom signed a contract to prepare for the construction of a new natural gas pipeline through Mongolia to China.[1266] In August, Chinese custom statistics reported a 60% increase in spending on Russian goods since 2021—mostly a disproportionate volume of natural gas and oil, which was being sold at a steep discount.[1267] The turmoil within its own economy has also compelled the Russian Federation to purchase more and more manufactured goods from China.

1264 "US Completes Joint Military Exercise in Armenia," *Al Jazeera,* September 20, 2023.

1265 Reuters, "Gazprom Says Russian Gas Deliveries to EU Are down 48% This Year," *Reuters,* September 7, 2022.

1266 Grace Dean, "Russia Said It's Pushing Ahead with Building a Massive Natural-Gas Pipeline to China as Western Sanctions Rock Its Economy," *Business Insider India,* March 1, 2022.

1267 Harry Dempsey and Sun Yu, "China's Independent Refiners Start Buying Russian Oil at Steep Discounts," *Financial Times,* May 3, 2022.

Within a few months, Chinese cars tripled their market share in Russia, and Chinese smartphones now account for more than two-thirds of all sales.[1268] Yuan-ruble trading overtook dollar-ruble trading by volume on the Russian stock market for the first time in history, according to RT.[1269] The longer the conflict in Ukraine lasts, the stronger this dependence will likely become.

It is therefore quite difficult to imagine that the "special military operation" in Ukraine could even have been attempted without the existence of Chinese industry and the Chinese market for Russian raw materials. After three decades, the Russian Federation has finally escaped the humanitarian disaster of being the super-empire's comprador only by tying itself inextricably to another power. The Federation is too weak to resist the advance of NATO by itself, just as the Islamic Republic has relied on Chinese investment and support to withstand the weight of Western sanctions. As shown in Chapter Four, the super-empire was determined to destroy national-bourgeois rule in Russia; the Federation's choice to align itself with the PRC was therefore no choice at all. Its ability to maneuver in an increasingly global conflict must also be considered to be afforded by China. In the early 2020s, a wave of rebellions, revolutions, and coups d'état in the Sahel region of Africa replaced several comprador rulers with direct military rule, such as in Niger, Mali, and Burkina Faso, and these new governments are increasingly looking to Russia for assistance against the French and U.S. occupation of their countries—a role that the Federation had not dared to play before now.

If the PRC is the only power in the world capable of making an alternative to super-imperialism possible, then the new emerging world order must be viewed as not yet multipolar but *bipolar*, and one that its current unipolar masters fear even more. According to U.S. Secretary of State Antony Blinken in a speech in May 2022, "China is the only country with both the intent to reshape the international order and, increasingly, the economic, diplomatic, military, and technological power to do it."[1270]

1268 Laura He, "3 Ways China and Russia Are Forging Much Closer Economic Ties," *CNN*, September 15, 2022.

1269 "Yuan Overtakes Dollar on Moscow Exchange," *RT International*, August 18, 2022.

1270 Antony J. Blinken, "The Administration's Approach to the People's Republic of China," U.S. Department of State, May 26, 2022.

CHAPTER TWELVE

The New Cold War

If the world is shifting into a paradigm of bipolarity, of which the two poles are the U.S. and the PRC, it is of greatest importance to determine what the consequences of a conflict between them would be, what might arrest or prevent such a conflict, and, if the conflict is inevitable, why and how the PRC might prevail. The ideologies, intentions, and strategy of these two opposing forces up until the present have already been explored in earlier chapters; but how these are adapting or likely to adapt to bipolarity also remains in question.

Democrats, Authoritarians, or Clashing Civilizations?

"Common membership in a civilization reduces the probability of violence in situations where it might otherwise occur. In 1991 and 1992 many people were alarmed by the possibility of violent conflict between Russia and Ukraine over territory, particularly Crimea, the Black Sea fleet, nuclear weapons and economic issues. If civilization is what counts, however, the likelihood of violence between Ukrainians and Russians should be low. [emphasis added] They are two Slavic, primarily Orthodox peoples who have had close relationships with each other for centuries. As of early 1993, despite all the reasons for conflict, the leaders of the two countries were effectively negotiating and defusing the issues between the two countries. While there has been serious fighting between Muslims and Christians elsewhere in the former Soviet Union and much tension and some fighting between Western and Orthodox Christians in the Baltic states, there has been virtually no violence between Russians and Ukrainians."

—Samuel P. Huntington, "The Clash of Civilizations?"[1271]

1271 Samuel P. Huntington, "The Clash of Civilizations?," *Foreign Affairs* 72, no. 3 (Summer, 1993): 38.

While it is undisputed that the world now stands at the brink of a great power conflict, the *ideological* nature of this confrontation is fiercely debated. Many Western scholars of international relations tend to see current events as a conflict between "democracy" and "authoritarianism"; other approaches ignore ideology altogether, reduce states to self-interested political entities, and consider them subject to an economic determinism, attempting to analyze their behavior only from supposed historical parallels, such as using the term "Thucydides Trap" to warn of a potential conflict between the U.S. and the PRC.[1272] Some variations to these prevailing points of view include the theory that an inevitable "clash of civilizations" is occurring or will soon occur, in which political entities will or should form out of nations or groups of nations on the basis of historical religious or cultural identities. A common flaw of all such theories, however, is their lack of class analysis.

The "democracy vs authoritarianism" dichotomy is perhaps the most tortured and illogical iteration of international relations theory, even though it is the one most favored by the Western press. The idea of democracy is an inspiring and appealing one, yet such approval is not confined to the West: surveys by the Latana Democracy Perception Index Report indicate that over three-quarters of people in China and Vietnam—two countries considered among the most "authoritarian" in the world by the Western press—considered their own country to be democratic, while less than half in the United States—supposedly the leader of the "democratic" world—believed the same.[1273] In contrast, it is difficult to imagine "authoritarianism" as a coherent ideology—or indeed as anything besides a crude label the press might affix to an "other" whose actual beliefs and motivations it does not care to try to understand or illuminate. "Authoritarians" certainly do not feel the comradeship with one another that might be expected. The West labels the Islamic Republic of Iran and the Kingdom of Saudi Arabia as "authoritarian," yet they have engaged in bitter and bloody proxy conflicts against one another throughout the region for decades (a rivalry that has only recently been resolved with the aid of Chinese diplomacy).[1274]

The actual relative benefit that "democracy" has brought those living within what the Western press considers the "democratic" camp is likewise

---

1272 Graham Allison, "Thucydides's Trap Has Been Sprung in the Pacific," *Financial Times*, August 21, 2012.

1273 Latana, "Democracy Perception Index Report 2022," 10.

1274 Mentioned earlier in Chapter Six.

very dubious, even according to its own surveys. Polls published by Pew Research in 2020 prior to Russia's intervention in Ukraine, for example, indicated that a large majority of Ukrainians were dissatisfied with the way democracy was working in Ukraine, and were not significantly more satisfied than Russians were with democracy in Russia, despite the current conflict between Ukraine and Russia purportedly being the front line of a global struggle between democracy and its opposite.[1275] (As mentioned in Chapter Seven, Putin himself is also remarkably popular for such an "authoritarian," with an approval rating that has ranged from over 60% before the intervention in Ukraine[1276] to over 80% during the intervention, according to the *New York Times*.)[1277]

Moreover, no coherent definition of "democracy" seems able to accurately predict conflicts and international relationships. The Latana Report ranked Hungary near the lowest in terms of its citizens' perception of how democratic their political system is, even though Hungary is a member of NATO, supposedly a military alliance that stands for the defense of democracy.[1278] Also in NATO is Türkiye, which also holds regular national elections, purportedly a signature element of democracies, yet President Recep Tayyip Erdoğan was featured in the *Atlantic* alongside Putin and Xi as a "bad guy" of global "authoritarianism" in 2021.[1279] Neither are purported democrats above alliances with purported authoritarians. Israel, often praised by the Western press as "the only democracy in the Middle East" (despite also being condemned by much of the world for being an apartheid state and for its genocidal assault on Gaza since the attacks of October 7, 2023), presently supports Azerbaijan against Armenia, though the latter is consistently ranked considerably higher on Freedom House's ratings of countries and territories' democratic governance.[1280] China, home to one-fifth of the world's entire population and clearly the most important player outside the "democratic" camp in global affairs, "stands out as an outlier and does not fit the theoretical predictions of Western

1275 Aidan Connaughton, Nicholas Kent, and Shannon Schumacher, "How People around the World See Democracy in 8 Charts," Pew Research Center, February 27, 2020.

1276 Ilya Arkhipov, "Putin's Approval Rating Slips Amid Covid Surge, Ukraine Tensions," *Bloomberg,* December 2, 2021.

1277 Ivan Nechepurenko, "Faced with Foreign Pressure, Russians Rally around Putin, Poll Shows," *New York Times,* March 31, 2022.

1278 Latana, "Democracy Perception Index Report 2022," 9.

1279 Anne Applebaum, "The Bad Guys Are Winning," *The Atlantic,* November 15, 2021.

1280 Freedom House, *Countries and Territories.*

political science," according to a 2018 article in *American Affairs* based on a multitude of independently-conducted surveys of the population.[1281] So many exceptions, asterisks, and qualifications are necessary for the "democracy versus authoritarianism" model to apply that by comparison, Ptolemy's reliance on convoluted geometric "epicycles" to justify the theory that the Earth was the center of the universe seems reasonable.

Similarly, the philosophy of "Eurasianism"—notably championed by Russian political philosopher Aleksandr Dugin—cannot easily be applied to the present world in a consistent manner. The Eurasian civilization, supposedly originally formed from the "merger" of Turkic and Slavic ethnic groups,[1282] would, through a broad continental alliance between Islam and Orthodox Christianity, create the conditions for resistance to the hegemony of the Atlanticist bloc of Western Europe and North America. While a strategic alliance has emerged between Russia and Iran, elsewhere within the region, alliances have not conformed to such religious or cultural lines. Iran and Azerbaijan, presumably natural allies due to their demographic majorities of Shia Muslims, have remained at odds; relations between Serbia (majority-Orthodox) and Bosnia and Albania (majority-Muslim) have scarcely warmed since the 1990s. In 2022, during the Russian intervention in Ukraine, Kyrgyzstan and Tajikistan—both members of the Collective Security Treaty Organization (CSTO), presumably the nucleus of the Eurasian alliance—attacked each other in a series of military clashes along the border. By the summer of 2022, even as Germany sent military aid to the Russian Federation's enemies in Ukraine, trade between Germany and key CSTO member Kazakhstan nearly doubled.[1283] A "Eurasian" bloc is clearly forming, yet its contours correspond more to *realpolitik* and localized rivalries than any particular unifying ethnic or religious dimension. The PRC, the most important economic partner to virtually every country mentioned above, is certainly not dominated by Islamic or Orthodox culture.

While the theory of "civilizations" is concerned exclusively with the expression of ancient cultural formations, it is itself an extremely modern theory. Its progenitor, American political scientist Samuel P. Huntington (whose epigraphic quote succinctly demonstrates the predictive power

---

1281 Wenfang Tang, "The 'Surprise' of Authoritarian Resilience in China," *American Affairs Journal* II, no. 1 (Spring 2018): 112.

1282 Aleksandr Dugin, *Foundations of Geopolitics* (Arktogeja, 1997), sec. Neo-Eurasianism: 6.1 Eurasian passionarity Lev Gumilev.

1283 Alan Crawford and Nariman Gizitdinov, "Putin's War Is Deepening a Tussle for Influence in Central Asia," *Bloomberg,* September 15, 2022.

of his theory) first proclaimed his "clash of civilizations" thesis back in 1992. What is meant by a "civilization"? According to Huntington:

> A civilization is a cultural entity. Villages, regions, ethnic groups, nationalities, religious groups, all have distinct cultures at different levels of cultural heterogeneity. The culture of a village in southern Italy may be different from that of a village in northern Italy, but both will share in a common Italian culture that distinguishes them from German villages. European communities, in turn, will share cultural features that distinguish them from Arab or Chinese communities. Arabs, Chinese and Westerners, however, are not part of any broader cultural entity. They constitute civilizations. A civilization is thus the highest cultural grouping of people and the broadest level of cultural identity people have short of that which distinguishes humans from other species. It is defined both by common objective elements, such as language, history, religion, customs, institutions, and by the subjective self-identification of people.[1284]

Thus, while a plethora of *nations*[1285]—many hundreds, at least—exist in today's world, they are in fact sub-categories of a handful of larger civilizational entities. Huntington identifies "seven or eight" major civilizations in the world ("Western, Confucian, Japanese, Islamic, Hindu, Slavic-Orthodox, Latin American and possibly African")[1286] while Dugin includes a ninth "Buddhist" civilization. In Dugin's own conception of civilizational theory, he predicted that the "poles" of a multipolar world would eventually correspond exactly to these civilizations.[1287] Dugin's 1997 work *Foundations of Geopolitics* considered a bipolar world to be a necessary intermediate step toward multipolarity:

1284 Huntington, "The Clash of Civilizations?," 23-24.

1285 In 1913, in what is commonly considered the foundational Marxist definition of a nation, Joseph Stalin called it ". . . a historically constituted, stable community of people, formed on the basis of a common language, territory, economic life, and psychological make-up manifested in a common culture." (J. V. Stalin, "The Nation.")

1286 Huntington, "The Clash of Civilizations?," 25.

1287 According to Dugin's thesis: "we can answer at once the fundamental question about how many poles a multipolar world must have. The answer: *as many as there are civilizations.*" [Aleksandr Dugin, *The Theory of a Multipolar World* (Aktos Media Ltd., 2020), sec. Civilization as Actor: Large Space and Politeia: Huntington's Theory: The Introduction of the Concept of Civilization.]

...the main geopolitical task of the West at this stage is to prevent the very possibility of forming a large-scale geopolitical bloc of continental volume, which could be comparable in one way or another to the forces of Atlanticism. This is the main principle of U.S. military-political doctrine, as articulated in Paul Wolfowitz's report. In other words, the West most of all does not want a return to bipolarity. That would be fatal for it.

Neo-Eurasianism, based on the interests of the "geographical axis of history," asserts the exact opposite of the West. The only way out of this situation can be only a new bipolarism, since only in this direction could Eurasia gain the prospect of genuine geopolitical sovereignty. *Only a new bipolarity can subsequently open the way for such multipolarity*... [emphasis added][1288]

In 2012, however, once it had become clear that China, not Russia, would inevitably be the center of his prophesied "new bipolarity," Dugin firmly rejected bipolarity of any sort, calling it "ideologically impossible" under the impression at that time that "the U.S. and NATO have pulled so far ahead that no country is capable of symmetrical competition with them militarily, strategically, economically, or technically)."[1289] Among his "six points" describing the qualities of a multipolar world:

The multipolar world *does not propose a return to a bipolar system,* since today there exists neither strategically nor ideologically a force capable of opposing alone the material and spiritual hegemony of the contemporary West and its leader, the U.S. There must be more than two poles in a multipolar world.[1290]

The mere existence of the PRC, in fact, represents a serious problem for this philosophy. Dugin's theory of the multipolar world's poles as vaguely-defined "civilization" entities is sharply contradicted by the PRC's inter-"civilizational" multiculturalism; China presently incorporates not only the "Confucian" civilization but a large portion of the nascent "Buddhist" civilization as well as several Turkic and Russian

---

1288 Aleksandr Dugin, *Foundations of Geopolitics*, sec. Neo-Eurasianism: 6.3 Towards a new bipolarity.

1289 Aleksandr Dugin, *The Theory of a Multipolar World*, sec. Introduction: Multipolarity Is Not Bipolarity.

1290 Aleksandr Dugin, *The Theory of a Multipolar World*, sec. Introduction: Summary.

minority groups ("Islamic" or "Eurasian" civilizations).[1291] All such civilizational groups are no longer clashing, but thriving together within China in peace, united most fundamentally on the basis of *class*.[1292]

Consequently, the type of "civilizational" mixture enabled by the PRC is considered an unwelcome aberration. Dugin's influence over actual Russian policy has of course been highly exaggerated by the Western press, and by the late 2010s, Dugin himself recognized the necessity of the Russia-PRC partnership.[1293] Yet fundamentally, any class-based alliance is contradicted by his vision that "the elites and masses belonging to one or another civilization must recognize their shared civilizational identity, the significance of which should be weightier than the significance of class identity."[1294] Alliances between civilizations, for the purposes of defeating Western hegemony, are desirable and even necessary according to this worldview, yet class solidarity between civilizations cannot be imagined. Marxist analysis, according to Fanon, "should always be slightly stretched every time we have to do with the colonial problem";[1295] but to Dugin, Marxism's "burdensome dogmas"[1296] are to be cast aside entirely. "For some civilizations," Dugin writes, "material prosperity and capitalist forms of economy are acceptable and desirable, but for other civilizations it is possible that they are not at all so."[1297]

Though Dugin's opposition to Western imperialism is the basis for his demonization by the Western press, it is yet an anti-imperialism bereft of anti-capitalism, the exact inverse of the deficiency shown by the social-democratic Western left.[1298] Without a class analysis, it may be relatively easy to imagine different civilizations, represented by sovereign countries or blocs of countries, peacefully coexisting in their own

1291 Aleksandr Dugin, *The Theory of a Multipolar World*, sec. Civilization as Actor: Large Space and Politeia: The Poles of a Multipolar World / List of Civilizations.

1292 See Chapter Nine for a detailed analysis of the development of Chinese ethnic minorities, and Chapter Eight for an exploration of the PRC's minority policies.

1293 Cyril Ip, "How 'Putin's Rasputin' Alexander Dugin Changed His Mind about China," *South China Morning Post*, August 29, 2022.

1294 Aleksandr Dugin, *The Theory of a Multipolar World*, sec. Theory of a Multipolar World and Other Paradigms of IR: The Relevance of Marxism and Neo-Marxism to the TMW.

1295 Fanon, *The Wretched of the Earth*, 40.

1296 Aleksandr Dugin, *The Theory of a Multipolar World*, sec. Hegemony and its Deconstruction: Deconstructing the Will to Power.

1297 Aleksandr Dugin, *The Theory of a Multipolar World*, sec. Theory of a Multipolar World and Other Paradigms of IR: The Relevance of Marxism and Neo-Marxism to the TMW.

1298 See Chapter Five.

spheres apart from the rest of the world—Latin American and Islamic civilizations, for example, would appear to have no particular animosity or reason to be in conflict with one another.

The antagonism that exists between *classes*, however, cannot be reconciled by multipolarity alone. Capitalists not only cannot exist without workers of their own nation to oppress, but they also cannot exist without dispossessive accumulation and the relentless drive to expand once domestic markets are exhausted and thus super-exploit the people of *other* nations. If unchecked, this class antagonism will likely therefore evolve again into some version of imperialism. The abolition of this oppression can only come about as the result of a global world-historical class struggle.

The Soviet Strategy

Chapters One through Five showed that the United States is the strongest center of capitalist power in the world; Chapters Six through Ten showed that the PRC is the strongest center of proletarian power in the world. Though the super-empire's mechanisms of exploitation and control have developed since the inter-imperialist rivalry era, financial capital still dominates the West, and its fundamental tendency that Lenin identified a century ago—to ever expand and ever increase its profits—is likewise unchanged. There is indeed a Thucydides Trap—not one determined merely by the military and economic power of states, but also by their class character. In order to grow, the Western bourgeoisie *must* eventually subdue China. If it cannot do so by subversion, sabotage, and trade manipulation, it will try to do so by force. The super-empire's reaction can be delayed, if it can profit first by subjugating other victims (such as the Russian Federation and its other national-bourgeois enemies), but the world is finite, and as far as we know, the rate of extraction cannot increase much further; the most efficient paradigm of dispossessive accumulation yet discovered—neocolonialism—is already prevalent nearly everywhere.

A conflict therefore *is* inevitably coming, a death-struggle between the American financial capitalist and the Chinese peasant/worker that will span the entire planet. If the PRC declines to defend itself, it will be destroyed; but if the financial oligarchy cannot destroy the PRC, it will lose its own control over class society. Were the PRC an empire, the new Cold War would not fundamentally threaten capitalist rule; victory would simply mean one gang of capitalists replacing another, just as new, ascendant empires have absorbed old, decaying ones throughout history. But the *Chinese* capitalists do not control finance in their own country, the workers do, and they are not required by their class interest to seek profit and exploitation at others' expense. A Chinese victory thus has the potential to be another paradigm shift—a progression between stages of history.

We have been here before. The bipolar world of the original Cold War, dominated by the United States and the Soviet Union, displayed exactly this dynamic, and the Soviet Union was defeated utterly. It would seem wise to avoid the same situation that has historically led to disaster; but this can only happen if the two superpowers cooperate in avoiding kinetic, economic, or proxy conflict, and the United States almost certainly will not. An examination of the Soviet Union's errors, the errors of contemporary anti-imperialists, and of any qualitative differences between the conditions it faced in the twentieth century and those presently faced by the PRC, is therefore essential to predicting its surest path to victory.

The PRC currently enjoys a relatively better position than the Soviet Union at its height. It has a considerably larger share of the global economy and total world population, as well as far greater international trade leverage. Even more importantly, unlike during the First Cold War, it has pursued close cooperation with the Russian Federation despite the differences in the ruling class of each country. The infamous Sino-Soviet Split, which set the two largest socialist countries at odds with one another, has not continued into the twenty-first century, and the super-empire's open hostility toward both Russia and China make that chapter of history unlikely to repeat itself in the near future.[1299] Political strategy, however, may still ultimately be the most decisive factor in the Second Cold War.

In the first months after the October Revolution, Lenin wrote:

…until the world socialist revolution breaks out, until it embraces several countries and is strong enough to overcome *international imperialism*, it is the direct duty of the socialists who have conquered in one country (especially a backward one) not to accept battle against the giants of imperialism. Their duty is to try to avoid

---

1299 If any surviving socialist country is able to learn from its twentieth-century nationalist mistakes, which led not only to the Sino-Soviet Split, but to war between the PRC and the Socialist Republic of Vietnam, it is the PRC. Today, relations between the PRC and the SRV are cordial and continuously improving.

battle, to wait until the conflicts between the imperialists weaken them *even more*, and bring the revolution in other countries even nearer...

...one must be able to calculate the balance of forces and *not help* the imperialists by making the battle against socialism easier for them when socialism is still weak, and when the chances of the battle are manifestly *against* socialism.[1300]

The fledgling Russian Soviet Republic, which at first had controlled only the urban centers of Moscow and St. Petersburg, could not fight the forces of every imperialist power at once; indeed, the key to its survival was not war against them, but extricating itself from the First World War as quickly as it could.[1301] For the next two decades, it followed Lenin's strategy, seeking to make peace and détente with the imperialists while it was still weak and they were still strong. Great sacrifices were made to consolidate and defend the revolution within the Soviet Union, to appear harmless before the capitalist world, and to sow discord between the empires, which were not yet united. The Second World War seemed to vindicate this strategy; as the imperialist governments of France and the UK deliberately "appeased" Nazi Germany in the hopes that it would destroy socialism in Europe for them, the Soviet Union's maneuvering succeeded in broadening the war, such that even while encircled by Germany and the Empire of Japan, it did not face their might alone. As a result of inter-imperialist conflict, the Soviet Union and its sphere of influence expanded, bringing revolution and proletarian rule to Eastern Europe, China, Mongolia, and Korea.

Yet the Second World War was also the last inter-imperialist war. The Soviet leadership became the victim of its own success, believing that the same strategy would work again under the next stage of imperialism, which at that point had not been identified. In 1952, Joseph Stalin confidently dismissed any objections to the contrary:

After the first world war it was believed that Germany had been finally put out of action, just as certain comrades now think that Japan and Germany have been finally put out of action. Then, too, it was also said—the press dinned forth that the USA had placed Europe on a dole, that Germany could no longer rise to her feet,

---

1300 Vladimir Lenin, *"Left-Wing" Childishness* (1918).
1301 See Appendix C for a more detailed analysis.

that from now on there could be no war among the capitalist countries. Yet in spite of this Germany revived and rose to her feet as a great power within some 15 to 20 years after her defeat, having broken out of bondage and set out upon a course of independent development. It is typical in this regard that none other than Britain and the USA should have helped Germany to revive economically and to raise her economic war potential. Of course, the USA and Britain, though helping Germany to revive economically, in so doing intended to direct the revived Germany against the Soviet Union, to use her against the country of socialism. However, Germany directed her forces in the first place against the Anglo-French-American bloc. And when Hitler Germany declared war on the Soviet Union, the Anglo-French-American bloc not only failed to join with Hitler Germany, but, on the contrary, was obliged to enter into a coalition with the USSR against Hitler Germany.

Consequently, the capitalist countries' struggle for markets and the desire to crush their competitors turned out in actuality to be stronger than the contradictions between the camp of capitalism and the camp of socialism.

The question is, what guarantee is there that Germany and Japan will not again rise to their feet, that they will not try to wrest themselves from American bondage and to live their own independent lives? I think there are no such guarantees.

But it follows from this that the inevitability of wars among the capitalist countries remains.[1302]

Stalin did not live to correct this error, and his successors also failed to recognize it, even as the Cold War's imperialist bloc increasingly became not less but more united against socialism.[1303] In 1956, the Soviet Union officially adopted the policy of "peaceful coexistence" with the capitalist empires. Similarly, Deng advocated a foreign policy of "keeping a low profile"—which, after the collapse of the socialist bloc and the total encirclement of the remaining socialist countries, succeeded in keeping the Party in power at the cost of integration with the capitalist world—and ever since his passing, the PRC has officially forsworn seeking any form

---

1302 J. V. Stalin, "Inevitability of Wars Among Capitalist Countries" in *Economic Problems of Socialism* (Moscow: Foreign Languages Publishing House, 1952), 32–37.

1303 See Chapter One.

of hegemony and has scrupulously followed its self-imposed principles of non-interference in other countries' internal political affairs. Yet it is now obvious from the remainder of twentieth century history that inter-imperialist war was *not* inevitable.

During the 1980s, such conflict did seem a real possibility, as the Japanese economy—already the world's second largest—gained unprecedented strength, just as Stalin predicted. Japan's rate of foreign direct investment, a mere $2.3 billion in 1980, grew exponentially throughout the decade, to over $50 billion in 1990.[1304] Japan's singular flavor of capitalism, with heavy government intervention and the continual reinvestment of profit,[1305] had been an enormous success; even during the Soviet Union's twilight years, Stalin's prophecy appeared to be on the cusp of fulfillment.

The socialist remnant therefore eyed these developments keenly. Wang Huning, a highly influential future member of the Chinese Politburo, viewed the growing U.S.-Japan animosity as all-important; in 1991, in a conclusion to his first-hand analysis of U.S. society, he wrote that "[t]he shadow of the Empire of the Sun is looming over the United States." Japan, according to Wang, had regained something approaching hegemony in East Asia, commanding significant investments in Taiwan and the Republic of Korea. During his visit, he carefully observed a widespread American fear of the Japanese:

The Japanese now have control over the U.S. economy, and many Americans are worried about it. In the first seven months of 1988, Japan spent $9 billion on foreign companies, several of which were American companies. American markets and companies fell to the Japanese.

"Japan's aggressive *katana*," Wang reasoned, "has been pointed directly at the United States."[1306] At the beginning of the 1990s, however, the Japanese stock market crashed. In 1996, Japan's GDP growth plummeted, never exceeding a 3% increase in any year (except 2010, as of

---

1304 World Bank, "Foreign Direct Investment, Net Outflows (BoP, Current US$) - Japan."

1305 This system, sometimes called "Japan Inc." in the West, or "capitalism from above" by economists such as Michio Morishima, was remarkably similar in form, though not in political economy, to the PRC's current model.

1306 Wang Huning, *America Against America* (independently published, 1991), 344–46.

this writing) ever since.[1307] What began as Japan's "Lost Decade" became referred to by some as the "Lost 30 Years" as stagnation persisted long into the twenty-first century.[1308] What happened?

As described in Chapter Two, the super-empire's structural adjustment policies typically aim to *devalue* peripheral countries' currencies, thus increasing the rate of unequal exchange to the imperialist countries in the core. This works because the victim countries are near the bottom of the economic value chain, and must sell their commodities—raw materials or intermediate goods—to the same small coterie of buyers (such as Apple or Sony, in the case of the electronics industry), who set the prices. Between two countries at the *top* of the value chain, each of which sells manufactured products to Western populations at large, a different sort of sabotage is needed. According to Hudson:

> What was so remarkable about dollar devaluation—that is, an upward revaluation of foreign currencies—is that far from sig-naling the end of American domination of its allies, it became the deliberate object of U.S. financial strategy, a means to enmesh foreign central banks further in the dollar-debt standard.[1309]

Economists generally consider the Plaza Accord of 1985—in which the second-tier imperialist powers, i.e. Japan, Germany, France and the United Kingdom, agreed to intervene in currency markets to *appreciate* their respective currencies against the dollar—to be a strong contributing factor in Japan's asset price bubble. The Accord was ostensibly designed to balance trade by protecting domestic U.S. manufacturing, which was being undersold by cheap Japanese consumer goods; as the Japanese yen strengthened, these goods became more expensive, allowing U.S. industry to compete. In the first quarter of 1986, Japanese companies began losing ground in the U.S. market, threatening to send Japan into recession; to prevent it, the Bank of Japan increased lending by cutting short-term interest rates, leading to a severe inflation of real estate prices.

Defenders of the Plaza Accord maintain that it was not *intended* to hamstring the Japanese economy; Germany, after all, had appreciated the

---

1307 World Bank, "GDP Growth (Annual %) - Japan."
1308 池田信夫 (Nobuo Ikeda), "「失われた30年」に向かう日本" [Japan Heading for the 'Lost 30 Years'].
1309 Michael Hudson, *Super Imperialism: The Origin and Fundamentals of U.S. World Dominance* (Pluto Press, 2003).

deutschmark at the same time, and did not experience such a disastrous bubble. Yet the Accord also specifically targeted Japanese real estate in a unique provision, obliging its government to "[increase] private consumption and investment through measures to enlarge consumer and mortgage credit markets."[1310] The BOJ's response had in fact been heavily encouraged by the Accord; the crisis in Japan was likely neither an accident, nor some vicissitude of the "free market," but the outcome of deliberate sabotage.

The asset price bubble seems a severe contrast to the U.S. real estate bubble that caused the Great Recession in 2008. How could a similar crisis set Japan's economy back *decades*? The Japanese recovery was so slow, in fact, that the new term "zombie lending" was coined in economics, describing the phenomenon of government regulators' forbearance in allowing banks to continue lending to firms that had become insolvent. The BOJ cut interest rates again, to less than a single percent, ostensibly hoping to eventually stimulate its way out of the slump with unusually cheap loans.

The cure for zombie lending, in fact, is large infusions of new capital, which were not forthcoming. German economist Richard Werner posited that the BOJ's managers deliberately prevented the bank from printing money, which would have greatly aided the recovery; their objective in doing so, he surmised, was to unravel "Japan Inc." and cause a long-term neoliberalization of the Japanese economy "virtually identical with the goals demanded by the United States."[1311] [1312] Regardless of whether the BOJ was complicit, coerced, or simply incompetent, Western financial institutions ignored the crisis; there would be no bailout and no Marshall Plan under super-imperialism. To guarantee the stability of the West's outposts in East Asia, and to provide a bulwark against the spread of socialism, the Japanese capitalist class had been given the rare opportunity to

---

1310 Announcement the Ministers of Finance and Central Bank Governors of France, Germany, Japan, the United Kingdom, and the United States (Plaza Accord).

1311 Richard Werner, *Princes of the Yen: Japan's Central Bankers and the Transformation of the Economy* (Routledge, 2003), 177.

1312 This managerial clique, according to Werner, had originated with BOJ Governor Eikichi Araki, who in 1946 had been indicted for war crimes allegedly committed during the Japanese occupation of China. In 1952, however, "almost straight from being under investigation for war crimes" Araki was mysteriously appointed ambassador to the United States, and subsequently *again* became Governor of the BOJ in 1954 (Richard Werner, 149–50).

develop and join the club of exploiters, but they would *never* be allowed to challenge their benefactors. The needed example was set.

During the brief U.S.-Japan trade war, Japanese corporations were dismayed to see that the deck was stacked against them. "With increasing regularity," reported the *New York Times* in 1992, "American companies are demanding, and winning, large royalty payments from Japanese companies for the use of patented technology." Hundreds of millions of dollars in profit, accumulated from the blood and sweat of wage-labor exploitation via the infamously harsh Japanese work ethic, were wiped out in instants as U.S. courts sided with U.S. capitalists almost every time. In April, Sega was shaken down for $33 million by a Los Angeles jury; the same year, in separate lawsuits, two Japanese camera manufacturers were made to pay Honeywell a total of nearly $200 million. According to the Bank of Japan, domestic corporations paid over $3 billion more in royalties than they received in 1991.[1313] U.S. arrogance in dealing with Japan heightened; in 1994, the *New York Times* revealed that the CIA and State Department had paid millions of dollars to the right-wing Liberal Democratic Party during the Cold War, financing half a century of LDP dominance of Japanese politics.[1314] [1315] In September 1995, news emerged that a U.S. Navy soldier and two Marines stationed in Japan had kidnapped and raped a 12-year-old Okinawan girl, triggering a wave of outrage throughout the country. The next LDP prime minister (Ryutaro Hashimoto) succeeded Murayama a few months later.

The LDP's monopoly on power was broken only once afterward, when the new center-left Democratic Party of Japan won a majority in the Diet in 2009. During his campaign, Prime Minister Yukio Hatoyama pledged to close just one U.S. Marine Corps airbase in Okinawa, rather than relocate it to a less-populated part of the island according to an earlier agreement negotiated by an LDP government. In March 2010, six months into his ministry, he expressed hopes that President Obama would meet with him to negotiate.[1316] Over the following two months, Obama

---

1313 Andrew Pollack, "Japanese Fight Back As U.S. Companies Press Patent Claims," *New York Times,* September 5, 1992.

1314 Tim Weiner, "C.I.A. Spent Millions to Support Japanese Right in 50's and 60's," *New York Times,* October 9, 1994.

1315 Just as with the secret State Department memo on the Cuban embargo mentioned in Chapter Two, the U.S. government waited only until the Soviet Union was dead and buried before declassifying these records.

1316 "Hatoyama Unlikely to Meet Obama to Resolve Dispute," *The Korea Herald,* March 30, 2010.

showed no willingness to visit Japan; instead, in May, Hatoyama was forced, over a phone call, to agree to the U.S. terms to relocate rather than close the airbase.[1317] Humiliated, a few weeks later Hatoyama resigned in disgrace at his failure to fulfill his promise, and in the next general election, the LDP returned to power in a landslide. In a later interview with journalist Tim Shorrock, Hatoyama recounted an intense pressure campaign against his policy from not only U.S. officials but LDP-aligned Japanese bureaucrats who were "always trying to please the U.S., trying to guess what they wanted and acting proactively on that."[1318] The airbase was never closed, nor even yet relocated as of this writing. Japan is still host to over 50,000 U.S. troops, an occupation currently financed by the Japanese government itself, which pays over $1 billion each year to keep their bases operational.[1319]

The experiences of Japan are the clearest evidence that the inter-imperialist unity that outlived even the Soviet Union is in no danger. There would be no inter-imperialist war in the latter twentieth century, and one is not likely in the twenty-first. The greatest conflict between capitalist empires of the super-imperial era resembled nothing so much as the United States pointing a gun at an unarmed man. There is no reason to believe that the unprecedented unity among empires in the face of a socialist enemy that was a feature of First Cold War will not also be a feature of the Second, especially not now that the super-empire and neocolonialism are fully entrenched throughout the world. The PRC is therefore no more likely than was the Soviet Union to win simply through patience.

As described earlier in Chapter Eleven, the severing of the Nord Stream was in no country's self-interest but the United States' (and Norway's); pipelines, railroads, bridges, ports, and other transport infrastructure of the kind that the PRC has been patiently and methodically building throughout the periphery are all vulnerable. What takes years to build can be destroyed in moments; without its own military and soft-power influence, the PRC's long-term geopolitical strategy[1320] will soon be at a tremendous disadvantage, and it may lose what it has so painstakingly gained.

1317 Reuters Staff, "Hatoyama, Obama to Talk on Futenma Air Base: Report," *Reuters,* May 25, 2010.

1318 Tim Shorrock, "Mike Pence and Japanese Leader Shinzo Abe Rain on South Korea's Olympics Parade," *The Nation,* February 14, 2018.

1319 Hiroshi Asahina, "Japan Greenlights $8.6bn to Host U.S. Troops," *Nikkei Asia,* March 26, 2022.

1320 See Chapter Six.

In any war, hot or cold, the advantage usually lies with the side that takes the initiative. Though the PRC is still rising economically, militarily, and in every other respect, the United States has consistently acted first, through trade wars, diplomatic maneuvering, propaganda, and other provocations. It has retained its military outposts in Korea and is expanding them throughout the Pacific, securing new arrangements with the Philippines[1321] and Papua New Guinea;[1322] it is pushing Japan, once again ruled by the LDP, to re-arm; it continues to push Taiwan to purchase more weapons; in 2023, in unprecedented provocations toward China's neighbor, the DPRK, a nuclear-armed U.S. submarine visited a port in southern Korea for the first time in July,[1323] and a U.S. Air Force B-52 bomber landed in a southern Korean airbase for the first time in October.[1324] The Cold War blocs are re-forming, and the PRC is the *de facto* leader of the opposition whether the Party is ready or not. The outcome of the Second Cold War will depend heavily upon whether and in what fashion the PRC will take on this mantle of leadership.

Post-Primacy Adaptation

What, then, is the strategy the United States is undertaking in the Second Cold War? The ultimate goal of the U.S. is clear—the elimination of China's challenge to its hegemony—but how it intends to accomplish this is not so obvious. Now let us examine the internal and external contradictions of the U.S., itself, and what obstacles its ruling class faces in its plans to maintain its dominance over the world.

It is evident that the U.S. is attempting to rebuild its domestic manufacturing base, which since the 1990s had been decreasing as a percentage of global manufacturing. As of 2022, according to a report by McKinsey, the number of manufacturing firms and plants in the U.S. had seen a 25% decline since 1997,[1325] yet in the years just prior, manufacturing jobs had the largest rate of increase since the 1980s, and the total industrial

---

1321 U.S. Department of Defense, "Philippines, U.S. Announce Locations of Four New EDCA Sites," April 3, 2023.

1322 Ryo Nakamura and Rurika Imahashi, "U.S. Military to Use Papua New Guinea Naval Base for 15 Years," *Nikkei Asia,* July 19, 2023.

1323 Martha Raddatz and Luis Martinez, "ABC News Exclusive: Inside the U.S. Nuclear Ballistic Missile Submarine in South Korea," *ABC News,* July 20, 2023.

1324 Chae Yun-hwan, "U.S. Strategic Bomber B-52 Lands at S. Korean Air Base for 1st Time," *Yonhap News Agency,* October 17, 2023.

1325 "Delivering the U.S. Manufacturing Renaissance," McKinsey & Company, August 29, 2022.

workforce became larger than it was before the 2008 financial crisis and accompanying Great Recession.[1326] [1327] A downturn in the first quarter of 2023 shows that steady growth is still elusive, but a surge of demand for the defense industry's output is expected, and as Europe further de-industrializes,[1328] the United States plans to further re-industrialize.

There is a careful intent behind this new industrial renaissance rooted in geopolitical maneuvering. The U.S. government's protectionism is targeting quality over quantity. In 2022, the CHIPS and Science Act was enacted, allocating billions in loans, grants, and tax incentives for domestic U.S. microchip production. A few months later, Taiwan Semiconductor Manufacturing Company Limited (TSMC), the world's most valuable computer chip manufacturer, announced an expansion of its U.S. operations, promising to open a new factory in Arizona that would produce 3-nanometer node semiconductor chips, then the most advanced type of computer chip in production anywhere.[1329] If successful, the United States' economic reliance upon Taiwan—which hinges upon Taiwan's status as the world's most advanced semiconductor foundry with 92% of all sub-10-nanometer manufacturing capacity, as of 2021[1330]—will be vastly reduced, meaning that in any future confrontation with the PRC over its wayward province, the U.S. would lose little by sacrificing Taiwan, if by doing so the U.S. might also damage its rival.

Officially, the U.S. government refers to the new protectionism as "friend-shoring," which purportedly boosts the resiliency of global supply chain networks by decoupling them from any countries that are not "allies and partners." Yet thus far, the only country whose industrial base is expanding to provide this resiliency is the United States; even as U.S. Treasury Secretary Janet Yellen promoted "friend-shoring" in a speech before Korean technology conglomerate LG in Seoul in July 2022, the fruits of these "exchanges" included LG's new lithium-ion battery manufacturing capacity in Michigan, Hyundai's new electric vehicle plants

1326 Chris Isidore and Christine Romans, "Made in America Is Back, Leaving U.S. Factories Scrambling to Find Workers," CNN, October 10, 2022.

1327 Although not quite larger than its previous high in 2019, before the COVID-19 pandemic began. (Bureau of Labor Statistics, "Union Members—2020," 8.)

1328 See Chapter Eleven.

1329 Emma Kinery, "TSMC to up Arizona Investment to $40 Billion with Second Semiconductor Chip Plant," *CNBC*, December 6, 2022.

1330 Antonio Varas, Raj Varadarajan, Jimmy Goodrich, and Falan Yinug, *Strengthening the Global Semiconductor Supply Chain in an Uncertain Era*, (Boston Consulting Group / Semiconductor Industry Association, April 2021).

in Georgia, and another chip plant in Texas from Samsung, the world's *second*-largest advanced semiconductor manufacturer.[1331] Once this process is far enough along, any new proxy wars in eastern Asia during the Second Cold War will be no skin off the super-empire's nose; instead of threats to its economic performance and profits, such conflicts will become opportunities to inflict casualties upon the PRC and its allies, just like in the wars in Korea and Vietnam during the latter twentieth century. Just as with Europe, the super-empire is also seeking to drain its eastern appendages of their most valuable capital and transform them into disposable pawns.

Industrial redevelopment is only one facet of the super-empire's wide-ranging restructuring, however. Less obvious but just as crucial are the adaptations being made to its military apparatus. In 1992, a secret document detailing the U.S. government's plan for its new reign as the leader of the world's unipolar empire was leaked to the *New York Times*; dubbed the "Wolfowitz Doctrine" after its architect U.S. Defense Secretary Paul Wolfowitz, it described the United States' foremost priority as to ensure that no rivals to U.S. power—either regional or global—would develop.[1332] For a quarter of a century, the super-empire ran roughshod over the world in an orgy of death and destruction for the sake of profit; yet now it has acknowledged that the Wolfowitz Doctrine has finally failed, and the PRC's ascension to becoming a new global rival cannot be prevented. In 2017, a report published by the U.S. Army War College concluded that the United States would soon lose its position as the world's sole superpower, identifying an impending "volatile and uncertain restructuring of international security affairs in ways that appear to be increasingly hostile to unchallenged U.S. leadership."[1333] The report called this new period "post-U.S. primacy" and advised the Department of Defense to take measures to "secure access to the global commons and strategic regions, markets, and resources" and "create, preserve, and extend U.S. military advantage" in response.[1334] In particular, the report stated:

1331 Su-Lin Tan, "Yellen Says the U.S. and Its Allies Should Use 'Friend-Shoring' to Give Supply Chains a Boost," *CNBC,* July 19, 2022.

1332 Patrick E. Tyler, "U.S. Strategy Plan Calls for Insuring No Rivals Develop," *New York Times,* March 8, 1992.

1333 Nathan P. Freier, Christopher M. Bado, Christopher J. Bolan, and Robert S. Hume, *At Our Own Peril: DoD Risk Assessment in a Post-Primacy World* [monograph] (Army War College Press, June 29, 2017), xv.

1334 Nathan P. Freier et al., xvi.

... the post-primacy reality demands a wider and more flexible military force that can generate advantage and options across the broadest possible range of military demands. To U.S. political leadership, maintenance of military advantage preserves maximum freedom of action. Further, it underwrites yet another bedrock principle of American defense policy—nuclear and conventional deterrence. *Finally, it allows U.S. decision-makers the opportunity to dictate or hold significant sway over outcomes in international disputes in the shadow of significant U.S. military capability and the implied promise of unacceptable consequences in the event that capability is unleashed.* [emphasis added][1335]

The flood of 40,000 new U.S. troops into Europe in 2022 and the plans to construct new military facilities in the Philippines announced in 2023[1336] must be evaluated in the context of this unambiguous statement of intent. All around the world, the global U.S. occupation forces are not declining but becoming further concentrated. During the GWOT the U.S. army had used individual brigades for small counter-insurgency operations; in 2021, the U.S. Army Training and Doctrine Command issued new guidelines for the reorganization of U.S. battle operations, re-combining the brigades into divisions for large-scale combat operations.[1337] In October of 2022, the U.S. Congress proposed granting the Pentagon wartime procurement powers, greatly increasing the budget for munitions. An analyst from CSIS remarked that the numbers involved were far greater than were needed to resupply the Armed Forces of Ukraine, and instead indicated that Congress was concerned with "building stockpiles for a major ground war in the future."[1338]

In short, the reorientation of the U.S. military following the dissolution of the Soviet Union described in Chapter Two is now happening in reverse; but in both instances, total military spending *increased*. Simultaneously, the scale of the U.S. military's covert operations has also expanded. Between 2017 and 2020, over $300 million was spent on the secretive "127e" program that arms, trains, and provides intelligence

---

1335 Nathan P. Freier et al., 48.

1336 Sui-Lee Wee, "U.S. to Boost Military Role in the Philippines in Push to Counter China," *New York Times*, February 3, 2023.

1337 LTG Theodore D. Martin (featured presenter), *WayPoint in 2028 – Multidomain Operations*, Army University Press video [14:00], December 3, 2021.

1338 Joe Gould and Bryant Harris, "Lawmakers Seek Emergency Powers for Pentagon's Ukraine War Contracting," *Defense News*, October 17, 2022.

to foreign proxy forces for combat operations against enemies of the U.S.—a tenfold increase from the program's initial 2005 budget.[1339] The United States is no longer specializing in counter-insurgency, but neither is it abandoning the covert realm; it now seeks to *foster* insurgency rather than counter it.

In 2021, Elbridge A. Colby, former U.S. Deputy Assistant Secretary of Defense for Strategy and Force Development and the lead architect of the Department of Defense's National Defense Strategy, published a roadmap for U.S.-PRC policy titled *The Strategy of Denial: American Defense in an Age of Great Power Conflict*. The book was praised by members of Congress, former U.S. defense officials, and numerous media establishment figures, and selected as one of the top ten books of the year by the *Wall Street Journal*. Colby writes, as a central thesis, that:

> Physical force, especially the ability to kill, is the ultimate form of coercive leverage. While there are other sources of influence, such as wealth, persuasiveness, and charisma, they are all dominated by the power to kill. One with the ability to kill another can, if willing, escalate any dispute to that level and thus prevail. Although hard power is not the only form of power, it is dominant if effectively employed; hard power always has the capacity to dominate soft power. Left unaddressed, might trumps right. Therefore, to protect its interests, the United States must be especially concerned about the use of physical force.[1340]

Given that the United States no longer enjoys what Colby calls a "preponderance of power" in the world, he asserts that in order to prevent an "unfavorable balance of power" from forming against it, it is necessary for the U.S. to maintain its ability to kill any opponent, including and especially the PRC.

The likelihood of any other state, even a "hegemonic power," ever attacking the United States, Colby acknowledges, is "rather remote" given the United States' nuclear arsenal, isolated geographic position, and enormous resources available for defense. Instead, according to Colby, this extreme militant position toward China should be adopted merely

---

1339 Nick Turse and Alice Speri, "How the Pentagon Uses a Secretive Program to Wage Proxy Wars," *The Intercept,* July 1, 2022.

1340 Elbridge A. Colby, *The Strategy of Denial: American Defense in the Age of Great Power Conflict* (Yale University Press, 2021), chap. 1.

because the PRC's growing commercial and trading bloc could cause the "erosion of America's economic power";[1341] in other words, the U.S. must be ready and willing to destroy any country that might undermine in any way its position as the dominant exploiter of the world, as well as any allies of such a country, any of its strategic partners, or any of its neighbors.

Even if it has the ability to "kill" China, however, before the super-empire can do so, it must first ensure that it will not itself be killed by the PRC's counter-stroke. The principle of mutually-assured destruction, which during the First Cold War prevented any intentional open military conflict between NATO and the Warsaw Pact, still applies in the new era; but in the terms of its military strength and nuclear deterrent, the PRC's relative position lags behind the Soviet Union's during the twentieth century. The PRC's conventional navy and air force are vastly outmatched by the United States; as of 2022, the People's Liberation Army Navy had only two operational aircraft carriers while the U.S. Navy had eleven. According to the International Campaign to Abolish Nuclear Weapons, behind the Russian Federation and the United States, the size of the PRC's arsenal was a distant third at 350 warheads, less than 10% of the size of the U.S. arsenal. If the super-empire succeeds in somehow neutralizing the Federation, the PRC will be overwhelmingly outgunned in any potential nuclear conflict. Even if combined with the strength of the DPRK, the PRC would still be outmatched by even the super-empire's nuclear-powered junior partners (France, the UK, and Israel).[1342]

Upon first glance, any strategy involving nuclear confrontation would seem catastrophically irrational. The PRC's nuclear arsenal, if deployed with the intention, is nonetheless more than powerful enough to destroy all human civilization and perhaps even all human life—the ultimate deterrent to military aggression. Yet elements within the U.S. government, defense industry, and press are still seeking some way to weaken it. "The U.S. Should Show It Can Win a Nuclear War" a *Wall Street Journal* op-ed headline advised in April 2022.[1343] In a report issued to the U.S. Air Force Global Strike Command in 2020, the Louisiana Tech Research Institute advised an expansion and upgrade of U.S. nuclear weaponry

---

1341 Colby, *The Strategy of Denial*, chap. 1.

1342 International Campaign to Abolish Nuclear Weapons, "The World's Nuclear Weapons."

1343 Seth Cropsey, "The US Should Show It Can Win a Nuclear War," *Wall Street Journal*, April 28, 2022.

not to preserve its own deterrent but to attain *nuclear superiority*. "The United States has never been content with a mere second-strike capability" wrote national security strategist and former CIA officer Matthew Kroenig; "Like with North Korea, the United States retains the ability to impose much more significant costs on China, and Chinese nuclear experts fear that Washington may even be able to deny China's deterrent with a nuclear first strike on China's nuclear forces."[1344] One year earlier, the Pentagon advised the development of a new, technologically advanced missile defense system reminiscent of the Cold War-era Strategic Defense Initiative.[1345] If the United States can deploy even a rudimentary missile defense system, the Western capitalist oligarchy will not hesitate to accept the risk of a few million Americans' deaths as acceptable "collateral damage" in exchange for removing the PRC's deterrent.

Economic Decoupling

Nuclear apocalypse or open warfare, however, are not the only ways to kill. China's dominance of global manufacturing is presently its best defense against the super-empire's aggression; the economies of the United States and China are presently so intertwined that the "termination shock" to the U.S. of abruptly severing ties to its largest trading partner would bring total economic ruin, severe shortages of basic goods, and potentially social chaos or even mass starvation. Such a disruption would seriously threaten the capitalist oligarchy's rule and rate of profit.

The super-empire must therefore reverse course and first "decouple" itself from its enemy before it can attempt to land a killing blow. The scale and complexity of the global economy, as well as China's increasingly central role within it, makes this a protracted and extremely difficult process. Indeed, the challenge for the super-empire is not merely separating the U.S. trade from China and developing its own industry, but separating the vast array of global supply chains of raw materials and intermediate manufacturing from China as well. In this endeavor even the United States' junior imperialist partners have proven reluctant to cooperate and have required the U.S. to apply an increasing amount of coercion to produce the desired results. The government of Germany, in one example,

---

1344 Stephen Blank, *Guide to Nuclear Deterrence in the Age of Great-Power Competition* (Louisiana Tech Research Institute, 2021), 37–39.

1345 Geoff Brumfiel, "Trump Unveils Ambitious Missile Defense Plans," *NPR, All Things Considered,* January 17, 2019.

openly expressed a desire to maintain its trade relations with the PRC in November of 2022, when Chancellor Scholz became the first G7 head of state to visit China since the outbreak of the COVID-19 pandemic.[1346] In 2023, President Macron made a similar visit, and French multinational energy corporation TotalEnergies began accepting payment for liquified natural gas in yuan (rather than dollars) for the first time.[1347]

In fact, from a general overview of China's economic integration with the super-empire, it would seem that decoupling has thus far been a colossal failure. The United Kingdom, in another example, has not reduced trade with China but expanded it; between 2018 and 2021, the value of Chinese imports to the UK rose by 66%.[1348] Foreign direct investment in China from the super-empire's lieutenants has been increasing, with Germany and the Republic of Korea providing the greatest amounts of new capital, followed by Japan and the UK.[1349] Some of the most dramatic successes of decoupling—for example recent trade disputes between the PRC and Australia—have been the result of policy changes by the PRC, not Western governments. By the end of 2021, the Australian wine industry's sales in China were reduced by 97%—yet this annihilation was not caused by Australia shifting to new markets, but by tariffs issued by the PRC in unofficial retaliation for Australia's ban on Huawei and its continued political antagonism towards Beijing.[1350] Overall, exports from Australia to China in fact *increased* by 24% in the same year.[1351]

This contradiction is evident even at the highest levels. In 2022, the chair of the Switzerland-based multinational wealth manager UBS—the largest private bank in the world—assured a financial forum in Hong Kong that global bankers were "very pro-China" and open to making further investment.[1352] Despite the State Department's rhetoric and the

1346 Olaf Scholz, "We Don't Want to Decouple from China, but Can't Be Overreliant," *Politico,* November 3, 2022.

1347 Andrew Hayley, "China Completes First Yuan-Settled LNG Trade," *Reuters,* March 28, 2023.

1348 BBC, "China Overtakes Germany as UK's Top Import Market," *BBC,* May 25, 2021.

1349 Ben Jiang, "German Optical Giant Zeiss Breaks Ground on US$25 Million Plant in Suzhou in Vote of Confidence in China," *South China Morning Post,* October 21, 2022.

1350 "Trade Dispute With China Puts Australian Wine Industry In a Precarious Position," *Wine Enthusiast,* updated September 28, 2022.

1351 Weizhen Tan, "Australia's Exports to China Are Jumping despite Their Trade Fight," *CNBC,* October 27, 2021.

1352 Hudson Lockett et al., "Global Bankers 'Very pro-China', Says UBS

recent exchanges of tariffs, even the Western financial oligarchy itself, or at the very least a significant faction of it, still sees China as a source of profit in the near future. If even the masters of the super-empire are not in favor of pursuing it, then "decoupling"[1353] is *not* dead on arrival, but *not yet even seriously attempted.*

When, then, will rhetoric become reality? Most likely, the Western bourgeoisie have recognized that decoupling will be a long-term and multistage process. They cannot shun Chinese imports until the reinvigoration of U.S. domestic industry has begun to bear fruit; they will therefore continue doing business in the meantime with sheathed knives and a smile. There are certain strategic sectors, however, where decoupling will grant the super-empire the greatest immediate advantage for the lowest risk; it is in *these* areas, and not in a general sense, that decoupling is being actively pursued.

In October 2022, the U.S. Department of Commerce announced new sanctions on China's computer chip industry, forbidding exports of advanced technology to China and restricting all "U.S. persons" from being employed at semiconductor facilities in China.[1354] Soon after, both Japan and the Netherlands—home to the largest manufacturers of chip-making equipment, Tokyo Electron and ASML—moved to comply with the new export controls.[1355] This shift did not take place immediately, but over the course of two months—during which time the U.S. strongarmed its "allies" by threatening to ban the sale of *any* foreign products to China that contained U.S. technologies.[1356]

It is now clear that the U.S. government will not succeed in preventing mainland China's computer chip industry from catching up with TSMC and Samsung, nor even significantly prolong the gap's existence. In September 2023, within a year of the application of sanctions, a teardown of the newest of Huawei phone revealed that China's top chipmaker, Semiconductor Manufacturing International Corp., had already achieved

---

Chair," *Financial Times,* November 2, 2022.

1353 Or at least, *economic* decoupling—see Chapter Eight for an analysis of decoupling in other areas.

1354 U.S. Department of Commerce, Bureau of Industry and Security, U.S. Mission China, "Commerce Implements New Export Controls on Advanced Computing and Semiconductor Manufacturing Items to the People's Republic of China (PRC)," October 7, 2022.

1355 Takashi Mochizuki, Cagan Koc, and Peter Elstrom, "Japan to Join US Effort to Tighten Chip Exports to China,"*Bloomberg,* December 12, 2022.

1356 Cagan Koc, Eric Martin, and Jenny Leonard, "Netherlands Plans Curbs on China Tech Exports in Deal With US," *Bloomberg,* December 7, 2022.

7-nanometer capability.[1357] It is also clear, however, that the U.S. has power to decouple an entire industry when it chooses to do so, and the leverage to compel third parties to fall in line in a matter of months. The PRC's appeals to the World Trade Organization over the chip sanctions, even if successful, will have no effect on the decoupling process. In December 2022, the WTO officially ruled in the PRC's favor in the dispute over U.S. metal tariffs from a few years prior, judging that the U.S. was in violation of international trade rules; the U.S. government promptly responded that it would maintain the tariffs anyway.[1358] The U.S. government is both willing and able to break its own rules the moment those rules cease to serve its interests, and no institution, country, or other power in the world is yet capable of stopping it.

In summary, what can be observed of the present foreign and economic policy of the United States reveals that it has four major long-term strategic goals:

1. To significantly slow China's technological development
2. To isolate the PRC from its current or potential allies, partners, and neighbors
3. To provoke the PRC into a costly and destructive proxy war in East Asia
4. To remove the PRC's nuclear deterrent

In the first goal, which it has recently pursued most urgently, it has already failed, and in the second, it is also failing. The Russian Federation—whose defeat and subjugation would have allowed the super-empire to encircle the PRC—has proved more resilient than expected, and in general the periphery is growing more friendly to the PRC, rather than less. Success in the third and fourth goals appear increasingly remote—but this is not by any means an assurance that the U.S. will not try. As of this writing, hundreds of thousands of lives have been lost in Ukraine; Taiwanese and Korean lives are certainly no less cheap to the Western oligarchy, and when nuclear powers are involved, military action of any kind has the potential to escalate to global proportions. The great danger of our time is therefore less that the U.S. may succeed in preserving its

---

1357 Vlad Savov and Debby Wu, "Huawei Teardown Shows Chip Breakthrough in Blow to US Sanctions," *Bloomberg,* September 3, 2023.

1358 Bryce Baschuk, "WTO Says Trump's Metals Tariffs Broke Rules as U.S. Rejects Findings," *American Journal of Transportation,* December 14 2022.

hegemony, but in how many people its government still has the power to kill in its attempts to do so.

Unequal Exchange in Ghanaian Gold Mining

Proceeding from the example of Apple's iPhone 6 given in Chapter Two, this appendix will estimate one of the more hidden forms of unequal exchange involved in the extraction of raw materials for its production (or, increasingly, as Apple itself shifts to recycling, the production of similar products). Often, lower down in the supply chain, labor exploitation becomes more severe and more difficult to quantify; the type of precious metals needed to construct the iPhone are extracted most cheaply through "artisanal" or small-scale mining with hand tools in the periphery, in mineral-rich countries such as Peru, Ghana, Mali, and the Democratic Republic of the Congo, where the global relations of imperialism enforce extremely low wages and sometimes even slave labor.[1359]

According to a detailed investigation by journalist Brian Merchant in 2017, a single iPhone 6 contained only about one dollar's worth of raw materials (excluding plastics) by weight, which required mining approximately 34 kilograms of ore. A trace amount of gold (0.014 grams, or about 0.0005 ounces) accounted for $0.56 and required mining 18 kilograms[1360] out of those 34.[1361] According to a report on field surveys conducted in 2012 by the International Labor Organization, over 56 tonnes of gold were estimated to be produced annually by artisanal gold miners in Ghana, who extracted an average of two ounces (about 57 grams) each per year (i.e. about eleven iPhones' worth per day),[1362] which at a global

---

1359 In 2016, artisanal mining supplied livelihoods to over one hundred million people worldwide [Armah *et al.*, "Working Conditions of Male and Female Artisanal and Small-Scale Goldminers in Ghana: Examining Existing Disparities," *The Extractive Industries and Society* 3, no. 2 (April 2016)]. Gold and cobalt, the most expensive materials in the iPhone 6 by weight, can be and are also mined profitably in the core where labor power is more expensive, but only with advanced mechanization.

1360 Assuming that the gold is extracted via hard-rock mining, presently the most common type of gold mining worldwide.

1361 Merchant, "Everything That's Inside Your IPhone," *VICE*, Aug 15, 2017.

1362 International Programme on the Elimination Of Child Labour (IPEC), *Analytical Studies on Child Labour in Mining and Quarrying in Ghana* (International Labour Organization, May 2013), ix.

market price of $1,411 per ounce[1363] would garner about $7.73 of *revenue* (not wages) per worker per day.[1364]

The chronic undervaluation of Ghana's gold exports (which according to a study by Ghana's Institute of Statistical, Social and Economic Research garnered less than 90% of the global market price between 2011 and 2017)[1365] is driven by this artisanal mining industry and consequent gold smuggling, which further reduces the total cost of the production, further reduces the wage of the gold miner, and deprives the state of Ghana of tax revenue on these exports that might be spent on development that could directly or indirectly increase its workers' standard of living. The average Ghanaian artisanal gold mine *worker* earns only a few dollars per day.[1366]

Thus if the Ghanaian gold miner were compensated fairly, then his wages, and consequently Ghana's below-market export price of gold, would increase, and if the margins in the remainder of the supply chain are unchanged, this increase could only come by increasing the retail price or reducing the profit collected through the sale of the iPhone (or similar product). In core countries, such as Canada and Australia, which also mine large amounts of gold annually, the gold mining process involves a much greater amount of constant capital (e.g., technologically advanced mining equipment) that enables mines to extract the same amount of gold with a much smaller amount of human labor—both less quantitatively,[1367] less

---

1363 World Bank, "World Bank Commodities Price Data (The Pink Sheet) December 2014," 2.

1364 Ghana is used as an example due to its status as the Africa's largest producer of gold. The opacity of supply chains makes determining how much of Apple's gold was actually sourced from Ghana in 2014 difficult. Though today, Apple has "reformed" its supply chain to source gold from South America and from recycled electronics, Ghanaian gold is still part of a multitude of similar products.

1365 "Ghana Loses over $2bn in Taxes to Undervaluation of Gold Exports," *Ghanaian Times,* January 28, 2022.

1366 This is in fact considerably higher than the average income of a Ghanaian agricultural worker, who earns less than one dollar per day. For this reason, a drop in the price of gold typically has no effect on the size of the population of artisanal miners. (Artisanal Gold Council, "The Effect of Changing Gold Prices on Artisanal Mining.")

1367 Canada, for example, produced about 193 tonnes of gold in 2021 (World Gold Council, "Global Mine Production") while employing roughly only 17,200 total workers mining both gold and silver (IBISWorld, "Gold & Silver Ore Mining in Canada – Employment Statistics 2005–2028"). If approximately one million Ghanaians can produce 56 tonnes in a year, Canadian miners would be no less than two hundred times more productive. It is the height of absurdity to imagine that a Canadian miner somehow works two hundred times harder than a Ghanaian miner;

arduous and dangerous qualitatively, and compensated at much higher rates[1368]—but still resulting in a profit.[1369] Even as the periphery's single largest producer of gold, Ghana has no leverage whatsoever to demand a higher price; therefore the core receives a very large quantity of gold from it each year that is both cheaper than market prices and required virtually no expenditure of capital due to artisanal mining. This savings in *capital* expenditure is not directly reflected in the recorded profit margin of the iPhone or other high-tech devices, yet is accomplished by super-exploiting the Ghanaian worker.

---

the discrepancy can only be (in part) the result of vast differences in constant capital. As the remainder of this book shows in greater detail, it is a key objective of the super-empire to obstruct the victim country's access to—and independent control over—capital of this nature.

1368 The average base compensation for a Canadian gold miner advertised on Indeed in 2022 was around 355 Canadian dollars, or about 260 U.S. dollars, per day. (Indeed, "Miner Salary in Canada.")

1369 Canadian gold is of course still more expensive than Ghanaian gold, but the amount produced cheaply in the periphery is not sufficient to meet total global demand, so more expensive gold can also be profitably sold.

Unequal Exchange between Africa and China

"We are certainly not against marketing and trading. On the contrary, we are for a widening of our potentialities in these spheres, and we are convinced that we shall be able to adjust the balance in our favour only by developing an agriculture attuned to our needs and supporting it with a rapidly increasing industrialisation that will break the neo-colonialist pattern which at present operates." [emphasis added]

—Kwame Nkrumah, 1965[1370]

Köhler's formula for unequal exchange between countries is used here to update his findings. For the sake of consistency, Köhler's original results from 2009 will be reproduced, and then the same formula will be applied to data from 2016, the most recent year for which the IMF's World Economic Outlook Database included the same statistical indicators referenced by Köhler.[1371]

The table below shows Köhler's "distortion factor," or the values of the selected countries' currencies compared with the dollar, based on the ratio of each country's GDP per capita at purchasing power parity (PPP) to its GDP per capita in current U.S. dollars in 2009. With the exception of individual African countries and the addition of Russia, the list is the same chosen by Köhler to display a wide range of data.[1372]

1370 Nkrumah, *Neo-Colonialism, the Last Stage of Imperialism* (1965), 9.

1371 Attempts to quantify unequal exchange for more recent years may require different statistical indicators, and thus possibly encounter the same problem as Köhler, who in pioneering his formula could not directly compare his conclusions with Amin's. The development of new or updated formulas is therefore best attempted by more qualified specialists such as Köhler or Hickel.

1372 Gernot Köhler, *Estimating Unequal Exchange: Sub-Saharan Africa to China and the World* (Oakville: Sheridan College, 2022), table. 1.

Gross domestic product and currency values in 2009[1373]

Country or Region	Total GDP (million USD)	GDP per capita (USD)	GDP per capita (at PPP)	Distortion factor *d*
Timor-Leste	590	543	2522	4.65
India	1235975	1031	2941	2.85
"Sub-Saharan Africa" (IMF)	885245			1.98*
"Sub-Saharan Africa" (UN)	942128			1.98**
China	4908982	3678	6567	1.79
Russia	1229227	8694	14920	1.72
Brazil	1574039	8220	10514	1.28
United States	14256275	46381	46381	1.00
United Kingdom	2183607	35334	34619	0.98
Germany	3352742	40875	34212	0.84
Luxembourg	51736	104512	78395	0.75

*Mean average of the distortion factors for the group of 44 African countries defined by the IMF.[1374] In 2009, this group included Eritrea, but excluded Sudan, Djibouti, and Mauritania.

**Mean average of the distortion factors for the group of 46 African countries defined by the UN International Trade Statistics Yearbook.[1375] In 2009 this group included Sudan, Djibouti, and Mauritania, but excluded Eritrea.

These values match Köhler's; using the same statistical indicators in the World Economic Outlook Database, the corresponding data for 2016 is given below:

1373 World Economic Outlook Database, "Report for Selected Countries and Subjects: April 2010 (Brazil, China, Germany, India, Luxembourg, Russia, Democratic Republic of Timor-Leste, United Kingdom, United States)."

1374 World Economic Outlook Database, "Report for Selected Countries and Subjects: April 2010 (IMF-Defined Sub-Saharan Africa)."

1375 World Economic Outlook Database, "Report for Selected Countries and Subjects: April 2010 (UN-Defined Sub-Saharan Africa)."

Gross domestic product and currency values in 2016[1376]

Country or Region	Total GDP (million USD)	GDP per capita (USD)	GDP per capita (at PPP)	Distortion factor *d*
Timor-Leste	2498	2102	4187	1.99
India	2256397	1723	6616	3.84
"Sub-Saharan Africa" (IMF)	1411495			2.7*
"Sub-Saharan Africa" (UN)	1504258			2.62**
China	11218281	8113	15399	1.9
Russia	1280731	8929	26490	2.97
Brazil	1798622	8727	15242	1.75
United States	18569100	57436	57436	1.0
United Kingdom	2629188	40096	42481	1.06
Germany	3466639	41902	48111	1.15
Luxembourg	59468	103199	104003	1.01

*Mean average of the distortion factors for the group of 45 African countries defined by the IMF.[1377] In 2016, this group included Eritrea and South Sudan, but excluded Sudan, Djibouti, and Mauritania.

**Mean average of the distortion factors for the group of 46 African countries defined by the UN International Trade Statistics Yearbook.[1378] In 2016, this group included Sudan, Djibouti, and Mauritania, but excluded Eritrea and South Sudan. Note that it also included the British territory of Saint Helena, but statistics for Saint Helena were not tracked by the IMF database and it is therefore not included in this average.

Immediately obvious are the changes brought on by the increase in the value of the dollar compared with other currencies. Not only did the distortion factors for the African and the BRICS countries all increase, *including* China's, but the factors for European countries increased as well. However, the *relative* gap between Africa and China, and between Africa and Europe, widened considerably, suggesting that the "drain," or transfer value, from Africa to those countries also grew. To calculate the transfer value between two countries (or groups of countries) in 2009, Köhler used the following equation:

$$T = \frac{d_1}{d_2}X - X$$

where T is the transfer value, X is the volume of exports from the lower-wage country to the higher-wage country, d_i is the distortion factor for

---

1376 World Economic Outlook Database, "Report for Selected Countries and Subjects: April 2017 (Brazil, China, Germany, India, Luxembourg, Russia, Timor-Leste, United Kingdom, United States)."

1377 World Economic Outlook Database, "Report for Selected Countries and Subjects: April 2017 (IMF-Defined Sub-Saharan Africa)."

1378 World Economic Outlook Database, "Report for Selected Countries and Subjects: April 2017 (UN-Defined Sub-Saharan Africa)."

the lower-wage country, and the d_2 is the distortion factor for the higher-wage country. The results of this calculation for 2009 are given below:

Exports and transfer values from "Sub-Saharan Africa" (as defined by the UN) in 2009[1379]

Destination	Export volume (million USD)	Transfer value from IMF region (million USD)	Transfer value from IMF region (% of GDP)	Transfer value from UN region (million USD)	Transfer value from UN region (% of GDP)
"Developed economies" (UN)	145170	142267*	16.07	142267*	15.1
China	37784**	4011	0.45	4011	0.43

*The UN International Trade Statistics Yearbook relied upon by Köhler does not use the IMF's "Advanced economies" grouping, and the IMF's database does not use the UN's "Developed economies" grouping, leading him to estimate this result by assuming an average distortion factor of 1.

**The UN yearbook also lacks data for China as an individual recipient of trade. This number is Köhler's estimate of 75% of the export volume from the UN's SSA region to the UN's "Eastern Asia" region, which was 50379 million USD in 2009.

When the values in the fourth column are rounded to the nearest tenth of a percent (16.1% and 0.5% to the "Advanced economies" and China respectively) Köhler's results are reproduced exactly.[1380] Another limitation of Köhler's method is apparent, however. While the IMF did not consider Sudan to be part of "Sub-Saharan Africa," the United Nations (which aggregated the volume of exports X) did, leading to different GDP totals for the region depending on which definition is used. Thus while Sudan did not significantly alter the region's average distortion factor—and by extension its transfer values—in 2009, the transfer values are lower as a percentage of the total regional GDP than if Sudan is excluded. Rounding similarly, Köhler's "low estimate" (assuming an average distortion factor of 1.00 for the "developed economies") for the transfer value from the African countries to the "Developed economies" of the world should therefore be slightly lower at 15.1% of total GDP, and the transfer value to China also lower at 0.4%.

Using the new UN International Trade Statistics Yearbook, but the same indicators and approximations for trade volumes as before, the results for 2016 are as follows:

1379 United Nations Department of Economic and Social Affairs, Statistics Division, "International Trade Statistics Yearbook, 2009. Volume I, Trade by Country," 22–23.

1380 Köhler, *Estimating Unequal Exchange,* table 7.

Exports and transfer values from "Sub-Saharan Africa" (as defined by the UN) in 2016[1381]

Destination	Export volume (million USD)	Transfer value from IMF region (million USD)	Transfer value from IMF region (% of GDP)	Transfer value from UN region (million USD)	Transfer value from UN region (% of GDP)
"Developed economies" (UN)	130954	222622	15.77	212145	14.1
China	30000	12632	0.89	11368	0.76

The relative strength of the yuan did indeed increase unequal exchange from Africa to China, but not so dramatically. By 2016, the transfer values to both China and the "Developed economies" grew, yet the transfer value to China was still comparatively tiny, 0.76% of the region's GDP; even according to the less-accurate estimate (i.e. including Sudan's exports but excluding its GDP and distortion factor), the transfer to China remained lower than 1% of regional GDP.

The other limitations of Köhler's method identified by Hickel et al. apply here as well.[1382] Since China has continued to prosper since 2016, it would also seem this transfer value may have continued to grow, even if it cannot be consistently measured against Köhler's original estimate. The volume of trade recorded for the two years, however, suggests that contrary to the popular conception that China is the fastest-growing trading partner to Africa, *total exports* from Africa to China—as well as exports from Africa to the "Advanced" or "Developed" economies—are not increasing.

The World Bank's more detailed trade statistics between 2009 and 2020[1383] reveal that China's status as nearly every country's primary trading partner is based far more on exports *from* China *to* Africa, which skyrocketed during this time period. The average yearly rate of increase in China's share of the African region's total export value, however, was

---

1381 United Nations Department of Economic and Social Affairs, Statistics Division, "International Trade Statistics Yearbook, 2016. Volume I, Trade by Country," 22–23.

1382 See Chapter Two.

1383 It must be noted that though the data tracked by the World Bank's World Integrated Trade Solution is not directly comparable to the UN yearbooks', given not only possible differences in data collection or aggregation, but also the fact that the World Bank uses yet *another*, distinct definition of "Sub-Saharan Africa" (including Eritrea, Sudan, South Sudan, and Mauritania, but excluding Djibouti).

-0.2%.[1384] Since the end of the commodities boom of the early 2000s, the proportion of all African exports received by China has remained constant at about 14%.

Similarly, the share received by the World Bank's best approximation of the "Advanced" or "Developed" economies—the combination of its North America and Europe & Central Asia regions—steadily declined during the same time period, though this decline was driven entirely by North America; Europe's share, though still the largest overall at around 28%, remained more or less constant. Instead, the World Bank-defined region with the largest and most consistent increase in the share of total exports from countries in "Sub-Saharan Africa" was "Sub-Saharan Africa" itself, which by 2020 received a quarter of all exports from African countries[1385]—very likely a sign of the continent's industrialization and improving connective infrastructure.

1384 Since the value of trade between countries can vary considerably from year to year, a method of estimating the average increase over a longer period is needed.

1385 World Integrated Trade Solution (WITS), "Sub-Saharan Africa Export Partner Share in Percentage All Countries and Regions between 2009 and 2020."

How the Bolshevik Revolution Was Won

Continuing from Chapter Three's analyses of armed struggle, this appendix will strive to place the Bolshevik Revolution in its appropriate historical and geopolitical context, which in 1917 was the First World War and the inter-imperialist rivalry stage defined in Chapter One.

Eventually, the old European empires, relentlessly driven to expand by finance capital, were only able to do so at the expense of each other's territory, making global conflict inevitable. A complicated network of alliances led nearly all of Europe to enter the First World War on one of two opposing sides. Victory would ensure imperial expansion, while defeat would mean the loss of some or all colonial possessions. The stakes for the capitalist class were therefore enormous. When the Russian provisional government was overthrown by the Bolsheviks, Russia's imperialist allies—primarily France, the United Kingdom, and the United States—were much more anxious about how the revolution would affect the progress of the war than the possible emergence of a new economic system that could fundamentally challenge bourgeois rule. Many, in fact, did not even conceive of such a thing. Though the bourgeoisie are typically quite class-conscious (those wielding power in class society are always well aware of their own interests and of those who do not share them) they did not seriously consider the possibility that Marxism was anything other than a long-discredited theoretical dead end.

Thus not only was "[t]he front of capital [pierced] where the chain of imperialism [was] weakest,"[1386] but the novelty of the proletariat seizing state power worked in the Bolsheviks' favor. Unaware of the true danger to capitalist empire that socialism represented, the bourgeois press remained optimistic even as Petrograd turned red and Russia descended into civil

---

1386 In his work *Foundations of Leninism*, Joseph Stalin argued that under the new stage of imperialism described by Lenin, proletarian revolution would not necessarily occur in the countries where capitalism had developed the most, but wherever in the world the forces of imperialism could be most easily defeated. (J. V. Stalin, *Foundations of Leninism*, chap. 3.)

war. In the days after the Bolsheviks stormed the Winter Palace, the paper of record dutifully printed predictions that they would not hold power for long,[1387,1388] and spilled much ink boosting hopes that a "strong man" or a new monarchy would arise instead.[1389,1390] Only after an initial counterrevolution failed and the days became weeks did the headlines became more directly critical of the Bolsheviks, but mostly on the grounds of their suspected ties to Germany, and not because they were communists.[1391] Even as late as January of 1918, the *New York Times* printed that the Allied Powers were willing to recognize the new Bolshevik government, if it would keep Russia in the war on their side.[1392,1393] Only after the Bolsheviks had negotiated a peace with the Central Powers in March of 1918 did the Allied Powers actually invade Russia.

The Allied intervention in the Russian Civil War must therefore be analyzed in the context of the prevailing relations of world imperialism. Unlike the interventions in Korea and Vietnam in the latter part of the twentieth century, during the Russian Civil War the Western empires were

---

1387 "BELIEVE RUSSIAN CRISIS TEMPORARY; Washington and Embassy Officials Expect Bolsheviki Rule to Be Short," *New York Times,* November 10, 1917.

1388 "WASHINGTON HOPEFUL OF RUSSIA'S FIGHTING: Separate Peace Not Expected—Financial Help From Allies to Continue—Radicals Not Regarded as Permanently in Control—Kerensky's Weakness Deplored," *New York Times,* November 11, 1917.

1389 "HOPE STRONG MAN WILL RULE RUSSIA: Zemstvos' Agent Here and Herman Bernstein Agree That Kerensky Must Go," *New York Times,* November 9, 1917.

1390 "RUSSIA'S STRONG MAN: From One Who Believes He Will Soon Appear," *New York Times,* November 30, 1917.

1391 This was a persistent theme throughout the next several months: "Lenine Anti-American as Well as Pro-German," *New York Times,* November 18, 1917; "KEEP RUSSIA IN TURMOIL; German Agents Busy Among Working Classes and Peasants," *New York Times,* November 23, 1917; "RUSSIA'S 'FREEDOM' MADE IN GERMANY: Revolution Prepared by Berlin Long Before the War, Dr. Vesnitch, Serb Envoy, Says," *New York Times,* January 1, 1918; "GERMANS RUNNING RUSSIA?—THEODORE MARBURG," *New York Times,* January 19, 1918; "BOLSHEVIKI AIDED AT THE OUTSET BY GERMAN GOLD: Alleged German Offical Documents Published by Paris Paper Reveal Plot," *New York Times,* February 9, 1918; "CLEVER PROPAGANDA BROKE DOWN RUSSIA: Germans Circulated a Newspaper in the Prison Camps and Russian Trenches," *New York Times,* March 10, 1918.

1392 "ALLIES NOW MAY RECOGNIZE LENINE; Attitude of Powers Modified as Result of Peace Conference Failure," *New York Times,* January 4, 1918.

1393 "WASHINGTON WATCHES EVENTS IN RUSSIA; Bolsheviki May Gain Recognition If They Decide to Remain in the War," *New York Times,* January 5, 1918.

not united, and their policies were not yet fully oriented along anticommunist lines. Instead, the primary war goals of the invaders were to revive the eastern front against Germany, and to prevent the Central Powers from seizing any resources from the fracturing Russian Empire. If their class enemies the Bolsheviks needed to be overthrown in order to accomplish those goals, so much the better; but this was only one possible means to those ends, and no serious attempt was made to pursue it once those ends had been otherwise achieved.

The forces of counterrevolution—the White *Armies*, plural—thus remained divided, poorly supported, and proved ultimately surmountable by the superior organization of the Red Army. After the Central Powers surrendered, most Allied forces left Russia within a year—before the Civil War had been decisively concluded and before their armies deployed against Germany had even finished demobilizing. Altogether, the Allied invasion consisted of fewer than 300,000 troops and took less than 2% casualties, few of which were suffered by the Western empires. The majority of Allied combat deaths in the Civil War were in fact Czechoslovakian. The combined peak totals of French, British, and U.S. troops in Russia barely exceeded 70,000—and their collective total casualties were only about seven hundred men, clear evidence that they saw relatively little actual combat with the Red Army.[1394] Of the each country's invasion force, Japan's was the most numerous, remained in Russia the longest, and left the most reluctantly—but rather than strangling Bolshevism in its crib, the rising Empire of Japan's primary goal was simply to expand its own sphere of influence by grabbing a piece of Russia for itself. In the final analysis, the Bolsheviks' victory in the Civil War owed much to the great powers' failure to take them seriously.

It is clear that if these conditions are ever to be replicated, the global relations of imperialism must first return to the inter-imperialist rivalry stage. Whether this could come about as a consequence of a retreat or "split" of the super-empire, or whether such a reversion is even possible, is unknowable. At first glance, given recent world events, such a transformation does not appear inconceivable; yet as shown in Chapters Eleven and Twelve, a return to the Cold War stage is both preferable to the oppressed peoples of the world, and more likely.

1394 Meredith Reid Sarkees and Frank Wayman, *Resort to War: 1816–2007* (CQ Press, 2010).

Unemployment in the Xinjiang Uyghur Autonomous Region

As noted in Chapter Eight, while the Chinese government admitted at the time that minority unemployment in the XUAR during the 2000s and early 2010s was quite high, official statistics did not record exactly how high. In 2008, Minority Rights Group International (MRG) claimed that the total Uyghur unemployment rate in Xinjiang was as high as 70%;[1395] though MRG did not explain how this figure was calculated, this appendix will attempt to corroborate it from other demographic data, and broadly estimate if it has improved or not in the years since then.

A crucial limitation to such an estimate is not knowing the size of the *total labor force* in rural China. The China Statistical Yearbook defines the labor force as "the population aged 16 and over who are capable of working, are participating in or willing to participate in economic activities, including employed and unemployed persons."[1396] This definition is broadly universal, being also used by organizations such as the OECD, the International Labor Organization, and the U.S. Bureau of Labor Statistics.[1397] An individual who does not have a job or is not making an attempt to find one is therefore considered not part of the labor force and therefore not "unemployed." At the time of MRG's report, a majority of Xinjiang's population was rural (and an even larger majority of that rural population are Uyghur), and unemployment statistics are not broken down by ethnic group, leaving rural areas as the best proxy for statistics on Uyghur unemployment; however, unemployment in rural areas is not recorded by the government's statistical yearbooks either.

1395 Minority Rights Group International, "World Directory of Minorities: Uyghurs," 3.

1396 China Statistical Yearbook 2014, "Explanatory Notes on Main Statistical Indicators."

1397 A study published by the BLS in 2000 found that when unemployment rates in the U.S. and Canada were calculated using each other's statistical method, they differed by less than 1% in either direction; between the U.S. and several European countries, this discrepancy was even smaller. (Sorrentino, "International Unemployment Rates: How Comparable Are They?," 3.)

Nevertheless in 2013, the year before the Party announced the new targeted poverty alleviation program, almost 73% of Xinjiang's population was between the ages of 15 and 64,[1398] which is internationally considered the working age.[1399] The rural population totaled about 12.6 million,[1400] and for the end of the year, the CSY reported that just over half a million people in rural Xinjiang were either engaged in private enterprises or self-employed.[1401] Even if only *half* the working-age population were in the labor force,[1402] the rural unemployment rate in Xinjiang would have been well over 80%—higher even than MRG's figure. If the actual unemployment rate were any less than *50%*, it would mean the labor force in rural Xinjiang would have been smaller than one in ten working-age people in 2013—by itself a clear symptom of extreme poverty. According to a labor report by the government of Hotan Prefecture (which has an overwhelmingly Uyghur population) 600,000 workers still had no jobs or farms in 2017—which amounted to 40% of the local workforce and over one-quarter of the entire population.[1403]

Though they are sufficient to show the massive scale of the problem, the wide range of these estimates and the number of assumptions involved limits their usefulness. To measure whether the economic conditions faced by the Uyghur people have since improved or by how much, a comparative analysis is called for, especially if it can be done within the same sets of data.

1398 China Statistical Yearbook 2014, "2-11 Age Composition and Dependency Ratio of Population by Region (2013)."

1399 The average age at which Chinese workers actually retire, however, was still much lower at 54, according to the *Economist* in 2021 ("At 54, China's Average Retirement Age Is Too Low," June 26, 2021).

1400 China Statistical Yearbook 2014, "2-7 Total Population by Urban and Rural Residence and Birth Rate, Death Rate, Natural Growth Rate by Region (2013)."

1401 269,000 people in rural Xinjiang were engaged in private enterprises (either as workers or employers) [China Statistical Yearbook 2014, "4-8 Number of Engaged Persons in Private Enterprises at Year-End by Region (2013)"], and 240,000 were self-employed [China Statistical Yearbook 2014, "4-9 Number of Self-Employed Individuals at Year-End by Region (2013)"]. Numbers are rounded to the thousands.

1402 The U.S. labor force, by comparison, is relatively stable at around 62% of the total population. Between 2013 and 2022, the seasonally adjusted labor force participation rate in the U.S. varied between a minimum of 60.1% and a maximum of 63.7% [U.S. Bureau of Labor Statistics, "Data Retrieval: Labor Force Statistics (CPS)"].

1403 Huo et al., "Research on Population Development in Ethnic Minority Areas in the Context of China's Population Strategy Adjustment," *Sustainability* 12, no. 19 (2020).

The neighboring province of Gansu, though smaller than Xinjiang by land area, is nonetheless quite similar in other respects. In 2013, the total population of the XUAR was about 90% of that of Gansu, a similar proportion of which was rural;[1404] yet rural Gansu had almost twice as many jobs as rural Xinjiang.[1405] In terms of wealth and income, both regions are quite poor in comparison with the rest of the country, though Gansu is not a minority autonomous region.

Between 2013 and 2021, both regions saw increasing urbanization,[1406] but also a tremendous rise in rural employment. The 2022 CSY reported a total of nearly six million jobs in the countryside of the XUAR and nearly seven million in Gansu, increases of over one thousand percent and six hundred percent, respectively.[1407] Assuming a constant labor participation rate of 61%, rural unemployment would have fallen from over 90% to the low double digits in the XUAR and almost vanished altogether in Gansu. In China overall, it would have fallen from over 80% to less than 10%.

Region	Year	Rural population*	Total population*	Rural employed persons*	Increase from 2013 (%)	Estimated rural employment rate** (%)
XUAR	2013	1257	2264	51	—	6.6
XUAR	2021	1107	2589	586	1051	86.8
Gansu	2013	1546	2582	97	—	10.3
Gansu	2021	1162	2490	693	612	97.8
China	2013	62961	136072	7473	—	19.5
China	2021	49835	141260	27879	273	91.7

*Units of 10,000.

**Employment rate is calculated in the same way as earlier in this appendix, but assuming a total labor force of 61% of the total population for selected years.

1404 China Statistical Yearbook 2014, "2-7 Total Population by Urban and Rural Residence and Birth Rate, Death Rate, Natural Growth Rate by Region (2013)."

1405 407,000 people in rural Gansu were engaged in private enterprises (either as workers or employers) [China Statistical Yearbook 2014, "4-8 Number of Engaged Persons in Private Enterprises at Year-End by Region (2013)"] and 566,000 were self-employed [China Statistical Yearbook 2014, "4-9 Number of Self-Employed Individuals at Year-End by Region (2013)"]. Numbers are rounded to the thousands.

1406 China Statistical Yearbook 2022, "2-7 Total Population by Urban and Rural Residence and Birth Rate, Death Rate, Natural Growth Rate by Region (2021)."

1407 China Statistical Yearbook 2022, "4-3 Number of Employed Persons by Region (End of 2021)."

Evidently, the New Deal in Xinjiang, described at greater length in Chapter Eight, was neither restricted to Xinjiang, nor particularly remarkable in China overall during the late 2010s. Though the Western press has made great efforts to conflate it with a supposed attempt to destroy the Uyghur cultural identity, it is clear that the very same phenomenon has also transformed Gansu, which was and is over 90% Han. It seems that "targeted poverty alleviation" is exactly that. It has targeted not any particular ethnic group, nor minorities in general, but the poor—both Uyghur and Han alike.

Acknowledgements

Writing is typically a solitary craft. The immersion into a topic that is required to produce anything worthwhile is not often shared, but whenever and to whatever degree that immersion is shared is precious. The author therefore extends the most thanks to Dr. Rongbo Hu, Mohamed Khougali, Alice Malone, Sheena Sisk, and Nathan Barton.

This book was written for a global audience, but by a Westerner and thus ultimately from a Western perspective. Much reading and investigation was done to inform its descriptions of social and economic conditions across the world, all of which are necessary to form a coherent and useful analysis of the world-economy; but no amount of study, travel, or immersion can replace the first-hand experience of those who have lived lifetimes in each area of study. When dealing with any country not his own, the author is bound to make the errors of a foreigner—and for their help in correcting such errors, thanks are due to Rohito M., Sun Feiyang, Rune Agerhus, Zhao DaShuai, and others too numerous to name. Any remaining mistakes are the author's own.

For her excellent work in editing this manuscript, the author thanks Diana Collier; for their exemplary efforts in fact-checking and proofreading, the author thanks Daisy Zhao, Michael Carr, Boris Barkanov, Vicente Quintero, and Shawn Adelman.

Thanks also to those who selflessly donated their time to reading early drafts of this manuscript and offered constructive criticism, among them Professor Jason Hickel, Professor Joshua Pollock, Basil Hackworth, Roderic Day, Andrew Westerman, and Richard Pope.

The sources and information referenced in this book required considerable time and effort to gather, but thanks are due to all those who aided in that process, offered advice, or published related material themselves, including Kimberly Miller, Dr. Stuart Gilmour, Dr. Barry Sautman, David Fishman, the Quantitative Debunking team, and others again too numerous to name.

Bibliography

For reasons of length, a complete bibliography could not be produced here, but can be found online at https://kyletrainemoji.substack.com/

Abrahamian, Ervand. *A History of Modern Iran*. Cambridge: Cambridge University Press, 2008.

Abrams, A. B. *Immovable Object: North Korea's 70 Years at War with American Power*. Atlanta: Clarity Press, Inc., 2020.

Achcar, Gilbert. "On the 'Arab Inequality Puzzle': The Case of Egypt." *Development and Change* 51, no. 3 (March 17, 2020). https://doi.org/10.1111/dech.12585.

Acker, Kevin, Deborah Brautigam, and Yufan Huang. *Debt Relief with Chinese Characteristics*. Working Paper. China Africa Research Initiative, June 2020. https://static1.squarespace.com/static/5652847de4b033f56d2bdc29/t/60353345259d44 48e01a37d8/1614099270470/WP+39+-+Acker%2C+Brautigam%2C+Huang+-+Debt+Relief.pdf.

Adeniran, Adedeji, Mma Amara Ekeruche, Chukwuka Onyekwena, and Thelma Obiakor. "Estimating the Economic Impact of Chinese BRI Investment in Africa." Special Report. South African Institute of International Affairs, June 21, 2021. https://saiia.org.za/research/estimating-the-economic-impact-of-chinese-bri-investment-in-africa/.

Adserà, Alicia, Francesca Dalla Pozza, Sergei Guriev, Lukas Kleine-Rueschkamp, and Elena Nikolova. "Transition from Plan to Market, Height and Well-Being." IZA Discussion Papers. Bonn, Germany: Institute of Labor Economics (IZA), September 2019. https://www.iza.org/publications/dp/12658/transition-from-plan-to-market-height-and-well-being.

Ahmed, Saifuddin, and Jörg Matthes. "Media Representation of Muslims and Islam from 2000 to 2015: A Meta-Analysis." *International Communication Gazette* 79, no. 3 (April 1, 2017): 219–44. https://doi.org/10.1177/1748048516656305.

Alvaredo, Facundo, Lucas Chancel, Thomas Piketty, Emmanuel Saez, and Gabriel Zucman. "Global Inequality Dynamics: New Findings from WID.World." NBER Working Paper Series. Cambridge, Massachusetts: National Bureau of Economic Research, April 2017. https://www.nber.org/system/files/working_papers/w23119/w23119.pdf.

Amin, Samir. *Beyond U.S. Hegemony? Assessing the Prospects for a Multipolar World*. Translated by Patrick Camiller. New York: Zed Books Ltd., 2006.

———. *Delinking: Towards a Polycentric World*. Translated by Michael Wolfers. English Edition. London: Zed Books Ltd., 1990.

———. "Samir Amin: How to defeat the Collective Imperialism of the Triad." Exclusive interview for Katehon." *Kana'an Online,* January 9, 2016. https://kanaanonline.org/en/2018/08/17/samir-amin-how-to-defeat-the-collective-imperialism-of-the-triad-an-exclusive-interview-for-katehon/.

———. "China 2013." *Monthly Review* 64, no. 10 (March 1, 2013). https://monthlyreview.org/2013/03/01/china-2013/.

Amnesty International. "'Like We Were Enemies in a War': China's Mass Internment, Torture, and Persecution of Muslims in Xinjiang." Amnesty International, June 10, 2021. https://xinjiang.amnesty.org/wp-content/uploads/2021/06/ASA_17_4137-2021_Full_report_ENG.pdf.

Ansari, Ali M. "The Myth of the White Revolution: Mohammad Reza Shah, 'Modernization' and the Consolidation of Power." *Middle Eastern Studies* 37, no. 3 (July 1, 2001): 1–24. https://doi.org/10.1080/714004408.

Armah, Frederick Ato, Sheila A. Boamah, Reginald Quansah, Samuel Obiri, and Isaac Luginaah. "Working Conditions of Male and Female Artisanal and Small-Scale Goldminers in Ghana: Examining Existing Disparities." *The Extractive Industries and Society* 3, no. 2 (April 1, 2016): 464–74. https://doi.org/10.1016/j.exis.2015.12.010.

Arrighi, Giovanni. "World Income Inequalities and the Future of Socialism." *New Left Review* 1, no. 189 (Sept./Oct. 1991). https://newleftreview.org/issues/i189/articles/giovanni-arrighi-world-income-inequalities-and-the-future-of-socialism.pdf.

Artisanal Gold Council. "The Effect of Changing Gold Prices on Artisanal Mining." Non-profit organization. 2022. https://artisanalgold.org/the-effect-of-changing-gold-prices-on-artisanal-mining/.

Atta-Asamoah, Andrews. "Proceed with Caution: Africa's Growing Foreign Military Presence." Institute for Security Studies, August 27, 2019. https://issafrica.org/iss-today/proceed-with-caution-africas-growing-foreign-military-presence.

Avedon, John F. "Tibet Today: Current Conditions and Prospects." *HIMALAYA* 7, no. 2 (1987): 1–10.

Behdad, Sohrab. "Winners and Losers of the Iranian Revolution: A Study in Income Distribution." *International Journal of Middle East Studies* 21, no. 3 (1989): 327–58. https://doi.org/10.1017/S0020743800032542.

Better Cotton Initiative. "2020 Annual Report." Annual Report. Better Cotton Initiative, September 2021. https://bettercotton.org/wp-content/uploads/2021/09/BCI-2020AnnualReport.pdf.

Biglaiser, Glen, and Ronald J. McGauvran. "The Effects of IMF Loan Conditions on Poverty in the Developing World." *Journal of International Relations and Development* 25, no. 3 (September 1, 2022): 806–33. https://doi.org/10.1057/s41268-022-00263-1.

Bluhm, Richard, Axel Dreher, Andreas Fuchs, Bradley Parks, Austin Strange, and Michael Tierney. "Connective Financing: Chinese Infrastructure Projects and the Diffusion of Economic Activity in Developing Countries."

Working Paper. Williamsburg, Virginia: AidData at the College of William & Mary, September 11, 2018. https://www.aiddata.org/publications/connective-finance-chinese-infrastructure-projects.

Brautigam, Deborah. "A Critical Look at Chinese 'Debt-Trap Diplomacy': The Rise of a Meme." *Area Development and Policy* 5, no. 1 (2020): 1–14. https://doi.org/10.1080/23792949.2019.1689828.

———. *The Dragon's Gift: The Real Story of China in Africa.* New York: Oxford University Press Inc., 2009.

Bray, Sean. "Corporate Tax Rates around the World, 2021." The Tax Foundation. December 9, 2021. https://taxfoundation.org/publications/corporate-tax-rates-around-the-world/.

B'Tselem. "Planning Policy in the West Bank." Last updated February 6, 2019. https://www.btselem.org/planning_and_building.

Bucsky, Péter, and Tristan Kenderdine. "The Ferghana Valley Railway Should Never Be Built." Washington, D.C.: Middle East Institute. March 17, 2020. https://www.mei.edu/publications/ferghana-valley-railway-should-never-be-built.

Busch, Berthold, Björn Kauder, and Samina Sultan. "Wer finanziert die EU? Nettozahler und Nettoempfänger in der EU" [Who finances the EU? Net contributors and net recipients in the EU]. IW-Report. Cologne: German Economic Institute, November 2, 2022. https://www.iwkoeln.de/en/studies/berthold-busch-bjoern-kauder-samina-sultan-net-contributors-and-net-recipients-in-the-eu.html.

Carlson, Elwood, and Sergey Tsvetarsky. "Birthweight and Infant Mortality in Bulgaria's Transition Crisis." *Paediatric and Perinatal Epidemiology* 14, no. 2 (April 2000): 159–62. https://doi.org/10.1046/j.1365-3016.2000.00242.x.

Carnegie Endowment for International Peace. "Sanctions Decade: Assessing UN Strategies in the 1990s." Non-profit organization. *Carnegie Endowment for International Peace* (blog), April 18, 2000. https://carnegieendowment.org/2000/04/18/sanctions-decade-assessing-un-strategies-in-1990s-event-50.

Castro, Fidel. *Fidel Castro Speaks on Marxism-Leninism: Dec. 2, 1961.* PRISM: Political & Rights Issues & Social Movements Collection. New York: Fair Play for Cuba Committee, 1962. https://ucf.digital.flvc.org/islandora/object/ucf%3A5073.

Cereseto, Shirley, and Howard Waitzkin. "Economic Development, Political-Economic System, and the Physical Quality of Life." *American Journal of Public Health* 76, no. 6 (1986): 661–66. https://doi.org/10.2105/ajph.76.6.661.

Chen, Ting, and James Kai-sing Kung. "Busting the 'Princelings': The Campaign Against Corruption in China's Primary Land Market." *The Quarterly Journal of Economics* 134, no. 1 (February 2019): 185–226. https://doi.org/10.1093/qje/qjy027.

Cheng, Enfu, and Lu Baolin. "Five Characteristics of Neoimperialism." *Monthly Review*, May 1, 2021. https://monthlyreview.org/2021/05/01/five-characteristics-of-neoimperialism/.

Children Underground. Documentary Film. Childhope International, 2001.

Childs, Geoff, Melvyn C. Goldstein, Ben Jiao, and Cynthia M. Beall. "Tibetan Fertility Transitions in China and South Asia." *Population and Development Review* 31, no. 2 (June 2005): 337–49.

Chimere-dan, O. "Apartheid and Demography in South Africa." *Etude de La Population Africaine (African Population Studies)*, no. 7 (April 1992): 26–36. https://doi.org/10.11564/7-0-419.

Clarke, M. E. *Xinjiang and China's Rise in Central Asia - A History*. Taylor & Francis, 2011. https://books.google.com/books?id=xXSrAgAAQBAJ.

Collins, Chuck. "Updates: Billionaire Wealth, U.S. Job Losses and Pandemic Profiteers." *Inequality.org*, May 6, 2022. https://inequality.org/great-divide/updates-billionaire-pandemic/.

Colby, Elbridge A. *The Strategy of Denial: American Defense in the Age of Great Power Conflict*. New Haven and London: Yale University Press, 2021.

Committee to Protect Journalists. "Journalists Imprisoned." NGO. Committee to Protect Journalists, December 1, 2021. https://cpj.org/data/imprisoned/2021/?status=Imprisoned&cc_fips%5B%5D=CH&start_year=2021&end_year=2021&group_by=location.

Concerning Violence - Nine Scenes From the Anti-Imperialistic Self-Defense, 2014.

Cong, Lin William, Haoyu Gao, Jacopo Ponticelli, and Xiaoguang Yang. "Credit Allocation Under Economic Stimulus: Evidence from China." *The Review of Financial Studies* 32, no. 9 (September 2019): 3412–60. https://doi.org/10.1093/rfs/hhz008.

Coronil, Fernando, and Julie Skurski. "Dismembering and Remembering the Nation: The Semantics of Political Violence in Venezuela." *Comparative Studies in Society and History* 33, no. 2 (1991): 288–337. https://doi.org/10.1017/S0010417500017047.

The Coup. "Repo Man." Track 12 on *Genocide & Juice*. Wild Pitch Records, 1994.

Crawford, Neta C., and Catherine Lutz. "Human Cost of Post-9/11 Wars: Direct War Deaths in Major War Zones: Afghanistan & Pakistan (Oct. 2001–Aug. 2021); Iraq (March 2003–Aug. 2021); Syria (Sept. 2014–May 2021); Yemen (Oct. 2002–Aug. 2021) and Other Post-9/11 War Zones." Costs of War. Watson Institute of International and Public Affairs at Brown University, September 1, 2021. https://watson.brown.edu/costsofwar/figures/2021/WarDeathToll.

Credit Suisse Research Institute. "Global Wealth Report 2014." October 2014. https://web.archive.org/web/20141016002346/https://publications.credit-suisse.com/tasks/render/file/?fileID=60931FDE-A2D2-F568-B041B58C5EA591A4.

———. "Global Wealth Report 2021." June 2021. https://www.credit-suisse.com/about-us/en/reports-research/global-wealth-report.html.

Crescenzi, Riccardo, and Nicola Limodio. "The Impact of Chinese FDI in Africa: Evidence from Ethiopia." London: Institute of Global Affairs at the London School of Economics and Political Science, January 2021. https://www.lse.ac.uk/iga/assets/documents/research-and-publications/FDI-in-Ethiopia-Crescenzi-Limodio.pdf.

Cunningham, Edward, Tony Saich, and Jessie Turiel. "Understanding CCP Resilience: Surveying Chinese Public Opinion Through Time." Harvard Kennedy School, Ash Center for Democratic Governance and Innovation, July 2020. https://ash.harvard.edu/publications/understanding-ccp-resilience-surveying-chinese-public-opinion-through-time.

Curtis, Glenn E. "Foreign Economic Relations." In *Russia: A Country Study*, edited by Glenn E. Curtis. Washington, D.C.: U.S. Government Publishing Office for the Library of Congress, 1996. http://countrystudies.us/russia/67.htm.

Curtis, Mark. *The New Colonialism: Britain's Scramble for Africa's Energy and Mineral Resources.* London: War on Want, July 2016. https://www.waronwant.org/sites/default/files/TheNewColonialism.pdf.

Curtis, Mark, and Tim Jones. *Honest Accounts 2017: How the World Profits from Africa's Wealth.* Global Justice Now and partners. Second edition, July 2017. https://www.globaljustice.org.uk/wp-content/uploads/2017/07/honest_accounts_2017_web_final_updated.pdf.

Daum, Werner. "Universalism and the West: An Agenda for Understanding." *Harvard International Review* 23, no. 2 (Summer 2001): 19–23.

Deych, T. L. "China in Africa: A Case of Neo-Colonialism or a Win-Win Strategy?" *Outlines of Global Transformations: Politics, Economics, Law* (2019): 63–82. https://doi.org/10.23932/2542-0240-2018-11-5-119-141.

Dong, Ensheng, Hongru Du, and Lauren Gardner. "An Interactive Web-Based Dashboard to Track COVID-19 in Real Time." *The Lancet: Infectious Diseases* 20, no. 5 (May 1, 2020): 533–34. https://doi.org/10.1016/S1473-3099(20)30120-1.

Dugin, Aleksandr. *Foundations of Geopolitics.* Moscow: Arktogeja, 1997. https://www.maieutiek.nl/wp-content/uploads/2022/05/Foundations-of-Geopolitics.pdf.

———. *The Theory of a Multipolar World.* Translated by Michael Millerman. London: Arktos Media Ltd., 2020.

Earp, Madeline. "In China, a Debate on Press Rights." Beijing: Committee to Protect Journalists, October 19, 2010. https://cpj.org/reports/2010/10/in-china-a-debate-on-press-rights/.

Easter, Gerald M. *Capital, Coercion, and Postcommunist States.* Ithaca and London: Cornell University Press, 2012.

Economist Intelligence. "Worldwide Cost of Living 2019." EIU, 2019. https://www.eiu.com/public/topical_report.aspx?campaignid=WCOL2019.

Emmanuel, Arghiri. *Unequal Exchange: A Study of the Imperialism of Trade.* Second Printing. New York and London: Monthly Review Press, 1972.

El-Erian, Mohamed A. "VI Mexico's External Debt Policies, 1982–90." In *Mexico: The Strategy to Achieve Sustained Economic Growth*, 98. Occasional Papers. International Monetary Fund, 1992. https://www.elibrary.imf.org/view/books/084/04618-9781557753120-en/ch06.xml.

Elliott, Mark. "The Case of the Missing Indigene: Debate Over a 'Second-Generation' Ethnic Policy." *The China Journal* 73 (January 1, 2015): 186–213. https://doi.org/10.1086/679274.

Ellner, Steve. *Rethinking Venezuelan Politics: Class, Conflict, and the Chávez Phenomenon*. Boulder, Colorado: Lynne Rienner Publishers, Inc., 2008.

———. "The Radical Potential of Chavismo in Venezuela: The First Year and a Half in Power." *Latin American Perspectives* 28, no. 5 (September 2001): 5–32.

Enache, Cristina. "Wealth Taxes in Europe." The Tax Foundation, April 19, 2022. https://taxfoundation.org/net-wealth-tax-europe-2022/.

Food and Agriculture Organization of the United Nations. "Global Forest Resources Assessment 2020." Main report. Rome: Food and Agricultural Organization of the United Nations, 2020. https://www.fao.org/3/ca9825en/CA9825EN.pdf.

Forster, Timon, Alexander E. Kentikelenis, Thomas H. Stubbs, and Lawrence P. King. "Globalization and Health Equity: The Impact of Structural Adjustment Programs on Developing Countries." *Health Inequalities: The Emerging Field of Comparative Cross-National Research on Social Inequalities in Health* 267 (December 1, 2020): 112496. https://doi.org/10.1016/j.socscimed.2019.112496.

Fanon, Frantz. *The Wretched of the Earth*. Translated by Constance Farrington. New York: Grove Press, 1963.

Freedom House. "Countries and Territories." Democracy Scores. Freedom House, 2023. https://freedomhouse.org/countries/nations-transit/scores.

Friedman, George. *The Next 100 Years: A Forecast for the 21st Century*. New York: Doubleday, 2009.

Fundación Interpreta. "Las cuentas detrás de las fake news sobre la modificación de los símbolos patrios en la Convención Constitucional (The accounts behind the fake news about the modification of the national symbols in the Constitutional Convention)." Fundación Interpreta, November 30, 2021. https://plataformacontexto.cl/contexto_factual/las-cuentas-detras-de-las-fake-news-sobre-la-modificacion-de-los-simbolos-patrios-en-la-convencion-constitucional/.

G5iO. "How the Uyghur Issue Has Been Framed Across Global Media - A Snapshot." Analytics and Projections. Islamabad: Islamabad Policy Research Institute, September 2021. https://g5io.org/g5-content/uploads/2021/11/G5iO-How-the-Uyghur-Issue-Has-Been-Framed-Across-Global-Media-A-Snapshot.pdf.

Galeano, Eduardo. *Open Veins of Latin America*. Translated by Cedric Belfrage. 25th Anniversary. New York: Monthly Review Press, 1997. https://library.uniteddiversity.coop/More_Books_and_Reports/Open_Veins_of_Latin_America.pdf.

Gardner, Matthew, and Steve Wamhoff. "55 Corporations Paid $0 in Federal Taxes on 2020 Profits." Institute on Taxation and Economic Policy, April 2, 2021. https://itep.org/55-profitable-corporations-zero-corporate-tax/.

Gluschenko, Konstantin. "Costs of Living and Real Incomes in the Russian Regions." MPRA Paper. Novosibirsk State University: Institute of Economics and Industrial

Engineering of the Siberian Branch of the Russian Academy of Sciences, January 30, 2022. https://mpra.ub.uni-muenchen.de/111774/.

Gohlke, David, Yan Zhou, Xinyi Wu, and Calista Courtney. "Assessment of Light-Duty Plug-in Electric Vehicles in the United States, 2010–2021." U.S. Department of Energy, November 2022. https://publications.anl.gov/anlpubs/2022/11/178584.pdf.

Goldstein, Melvyn C. *A History of Modern Tibet. Vol. 4: In the Eye of the Storm: 1957–1959.* Oakland: University of California Press, 2019.

Goldstein, Melvyn C., Ben Jiao (Benjor), Cynthia M. Beall, and Phuntsog Tsering. "Fertility and Family Planning in Rural Tibet." *The China Journal*, no. 47 (January 2002): 19–39. https://doi.org/10.2307/3182072.

Goldstein, Melvyn C., and Cynthia M. Beall. "Change and Continuity in Nomadic Pastoralism on the Western Tibetan Plateau." *Nomadic Peoples*, no. 28 (1991): 105–22.

———. "China's Birth Control Policy in the Tibet Autonomous Region: Myths and Realities." *Asian Survey* 31, no. 3 (March 1991): 285–303. https://doi.org/10.2307/2645246.

———. "The Impact of China's Reform Policy on the Nomads of Western Tibet." *Asian Survey* 29, no. 6 (June 1989): 619–41. https://doi.org/10.2307/2644756.

———. "The Remote World of Tibet's Nomads." *National Geographic* Vol. 175 (January-June 1989).

Gratius, Susanne. "Assessing Democracy Assistance: Venezuela." Project. Assessing Democracy Assistance. World Movement for Democracy and Fundación para las Relaciones Internacionales y el Diálogo Exterior (FRIDE), May 2010. https://web.archive.org/web/20110813085612/http://centrodealerta.org/documentos_desclasificados/fride_report_on_funding_in_.pdf.

Han, Yawen, and David Cassels Johnson. "Chinese Language Policy and Uyghur Youth: Examining Language Policies and Language Ideologies." *Journal of Language, Identity & Education* 20, no. 3 (May 2021): 183–96. https://doi.org/10.1080/15348458.2020.1753193.

Hasmath, Reza, and Jennifer Hsu. *China in an Era of Transition: Understanding Contemporary State and Society Actors.* New York: Palgrave Macmillan, 2009.

He, Xianjie, Oliver M. Rui, and Tusheng Xiao. "The Price of Being a Billionaire in China: Evidence Based on Hurun Rich List," July 10, 2012. https://doi.org/10.2139/ssrn.2102998.

Henneberg, Sabina. "The Libyan National Transition Council." Chapter 4 in *Managing Transition: The First Post-Uprising Phase in Tunisia and Libya*, by Sabina Henneberg. Cambridge University Press, 2020. https://doi.org/10.1017/9781108895729.004.

Hickel, Jason, Christian Dorninger, Hanspeter Wieland, and Intan Suwandi. "Imperialist Appropriation in the World Economy: Drain from the Global South through Unequal Exchange, 1990–2015." *Global Environmental Change* 73 (March 1, 2022): 102467. https://doi.org/10.1016/j.gloenvcha.2022.102467.

Hickel, Jason, Dylan Sullivan, and Huzaifa Zoomkawala. "Plunder in the Post-Colonial Era: Quantifying Drain from the Global South Through Unequal Exchange, 1960–2018." *New Political Economy* 26, no. 6 (November 2, 2021): 1030–47. https://doi.org/10.1080/13563467.2021.1899153.

Hong Kong Legislative Council Research Office. *Socioeconomic Implications of Home Ownership for Hong Kong.* Research Brief Issue no. 2 (2020–2021). Hong Kong: Legislative Council Secretariat, March 1, 2021. https://www.legco.gov.hk/research-publications/english/2021rb02-socioeconomic-implications-of-home-ownership-for-hong-kong-20210301-e.pdf.

Horn, Sebastian, Bradley C. Parks, Carmen M. Reinhart, and Christoph Trebesch. "China as an International Lender of Last Resort." NBER Working Paper No. 31105. Cambridge, Mass.: National Bureau of Economic Research (NBER). March 28, 2023. https://www.aiddata.org/publications/china-as-an-international-lender-of-last-resort.

Hsieh, Chang-Tai, and Zheng (Michael) Song. "Grasp the Large, Let Go of the Small: The Transformation of the State Sector in China." NBER Working Paper. Cambridge, Mass.: National Bureau of Economic Research, March 2015. https://doi.org/10.3386/w21006.

Huang, Tianlei, Nicolas Véron, and David Xu. "The Private Sector Advances in China: The Evolving Ownership Structures of the Largest Companies in the Xi Jinping Era." Working Paper. Peterson Institute for International Economics, March 2022. https://www.piie.com/sites/default/files/documents/wp22-3.pdf.

Hudson, Michael. *Super Imperialism: The Origin and Fundamentals of U.S. World Dominance.* Second Edition. London and Sterling, Virginia: Pluto Press, 2003.

Huntington, Samuel P. "The Clash of Civilizations?" *Foreign Affairs* 72, no. 3 (1993): 22–49. https://doi.org/10.2307/20045621.

Huo, Jinwei, Xinhuan Zhang, Zhiping Zhang, and Yaning Chen. "Research on Population Development in Ethnic Minority Areas in the Context of China's Population Strategy Adjustment." *Sustainability* 12, no. 19 (2020). https://doi.org/10.3390/su12198021.

Hu, Angang, Hu Linlin, and Chang Zhixiao. "China's Economic Growth and Poverty Reduction (1978–2002)," 2005. https://doi.org/10.1057/9780230505759_3.

Hyde, Sarah. *The Transformation of the Japanese Left: From Old Socialists to New Democrats.* First edition. London: Routledge, 2009. https://www.taylorfrancis.com/books/mono/10.4324/9780203874356/transformation-japanese-left-sarah-hyde.

Innocenti Research Centre. "A Decade of Transition." Regional Monitoring Report. UNICEF, 2001. https://www.unicef-irc.org/publications/313-a-decade-of-transition.html.

International Commission of Jurists. "Tibet: Human Rights and the Rule of Law." International Commission of Jurists, December 1997. https://www.icj.org/

wp-content/uploads/1997/01/Tibet-human-rights-and-the-rule-of-law-thematic-report-1997-eng.pdf.

International Energy Agency. "Electric Car Registrations and Sales Share in China, United States, Europe and Other Regions, 2016-2021." Paris: International Energy Agency, October 26, 2022. https://www.iea.org/data-and-statistics/charts/electric-car-registrations-and-sales-share-in-china-united-states-europe-and-other-regions-2016-2021.

——. "Solar PV Global Supply Chains." Special Report. Paris: International Energy Agency, 2022. https://www.iea.org/reports/solar-pv-global-supply-chains/executive-summary.

International Programme on the Elimination Of Child Labour (IPEC). "Analytical Studies on Child Labour in Mining and Quarrying in Ghana." International Labor Organization, May 1, 2013. https://www.ilo.org/ipec/Informationresources/WCMS_IPEC_PUB_25875/lang--en/index.htm.

Jacoby, Erich H. "Cuba: The Real Winner Is the Agricultural Worker." *CERES: FAO Review* 2, no. 4 (August 1969): 26–33.

James, Jaq. "Amnesty International & Human Rights Watch's Forced Xinjiang Labour Claims: Junk Research or Noble Cause Corruption?" Working Paper. CO-WEST-PRO Consultancy, August 13, 2022. http://www.cowestpro.co/uploads/1/9/9/7/19974045/cowestpro_2-2022_-_aug.pdf.

Jansson, Johanna. "The Sicomines Agreement: Change and Continuity in the Democratic Republic of Congo's International Relations." SAIIA Occasional Paper. South African Institute of International Affairs, November 1, 2011. https://saiia.org.za/research/the-sicomines-agreement-change-and-continuity-in-the-democratic-republic-of-congo-s-international-relations/.

——. "The Sicomines Agreement Revisited: Prudent Chinese Banks and Risk-Taking Chinese Companies." *Review of African Political Economy* 40, no. 135 (March 1, 2013): 152–62. https://doi.org/10.1080/03056244.2013.762167.

Jayaram, Kartik, Omid Kassiri, and Irene Yuan Sun. "Dance of the Lions and Dragons: How Are Africa and China Engaging, and How Will the Partnership Evolve?" McKinsey & Company, June 2017. https://www.mckinsey.com/~/media/mckinsey/featured%20insights/middle%20east%20and%20africa/the%20closest%20look%20yet%20at%20chinese%20economic%20engagement%20in%20africa/dance-of-the-lions-and-dragons.pdf.

Jiang, Shigong. "A History of Empire Without Empire." In *After Tamerlane: The Global History of Empire Since 1405*, edited by Sun Feiyang and Nia Frome. Translated by Roderic Day. Red Sails, 2021. https://redsails.org/jiang-on-empire/.

Jones, Bart. *Hugo!: The Hugo Chávez Story from Mud Hut to Perpetual Revolution.* Hanover, New Hampshire: Steerforth Press, 2008.

Jones, Lee, and Shahar Hameiri. "Debunking the Myth of 'Debt-Trap Diplomacy': How Recipient Countries Shape China's Belt and Road Initiative." Research Paper. London: Chatham House, August 19, 2020. https://www.chathamhouse.org/2020/08/debunking-myth-debt-trap-diplomacy.

Kautsky, Karl. "Ultra-Imperialism." *Die Neue Zeit*. September 11, 1914. https://www.marxists.org/archive/kautsky/1914/09/ultra-imp.htm.

Kennedy, Scott, and Qin (Maya) Mei. "Measurement Muddle: China's GDP Growth Data and Potential Proxies." *Big Data China*. Center for Strategic & International Studies, September 13, 2023.   https://bigdatachina.csis.org/measurement-muddle-chinas-gdp-growth-data-and-potential-proxies/.

Kley, Dirk van der. "Chinese Companies' Localization in Kyrgyzstan and Tajikistan." *Problems of Post-Communism* 67, no. 3 (May 3, 2020): 241–50. https://doi.org/10.1080/10758216.2020.1755314.

Köhler, Gernot. "Estimating Unequal Exchange: Sub-Saharan Africa to the World." In *Accounting for Colonialism: Measuring Unjust Enrichment and Damages in Africa,* edited by Richard F. America. Palgrave Macmillan, 2023. https://doi.org/10.1007/978-3-031-32804-6_14.

Kolenikov, Stanislav, and Anthony Shorrocks. "A Decomposition Analysis of Regional Poverty in Russia." WIDER Discussion Paper. Helsinki: The United Nations University World Institute for Development Economics Research (UNU-WIDER), October 2003. https://www.econstor.eu/bitstream/10419/53118/1/376632895.pdf.

Kopparam, Raksha. "The Federal Reserve's New Distributional Financial Accounts Provide Telling Data on Growing U.S. Wealth and Income Inequality." Washington Center for Equitable Growth, August 22, 2019. https://equitablegrowth.org/the-federal-reserves-new-distributional-financial-accounts-provide-telling-data-on-growing-u-s-wealth-and-income-inequality/.

Kratz, Agatha, Allen Feng, and Logan Wright. "New Data on the 'Debt Trap' Question." Rhodium Group, April 29, 2019. https://rhg.com/research/new-data-on-the-debt-trap-question/.

Kushi, Sidita, and Monica Duffy Toft. "Introducing the Military Intervention Project: A New Dataset on U.S. Military Interventions, 1776–2019." *Journal of Conflict Resolution* 67, no. 4 (April 2023): 752–779. https://doi.org/10.1177/00220027221117546.

Kuznetsov, A. V. "Direct Investment from Russia Abroad: Changes since 2018." *Herald of the Russian Academy of Sciences* 91 (November 2021): 700–707. https://doi.org/10.1134/S1019331621060162.

Kvangraven, Ingrid Harvold. "A Dependency Pioneer – Samir Amin." Chapter 1 in *Dialogues on Development Volume 1 – On Dependency*, edited by Ingrid Harvold Kvangraven, Maria Dyveke Styve, and Ushehwedu Kufakurinani. Institute for New Economic Thinking, 2017. First edition. https://www.researchgate.net/publication/317603001_A_Dependency_Pioneer_-_Samir_Amin.

Lakmeeharan, Kannan, Qaizer Manji, Ronald Nyairo, and Harald Poeltner. "Solving Africa's Infrastructure Paradox." McKinsey & Company, March 6, 2020.   https://www.mckinsey.com/business-functions/operations/our-insights/solving-africas-infrastructure-paradox.

Landry, David. "The Risks and Rewards of Resource-for-Infrastructure Deals: Lessons from the Congo's Sicomines Agreement." *Special Issue on Mining Value Chains,*

Innovation and Learning 58 (October 2018): 165–74. https://doi.org/10.1016/j. resourpol.2018.04.014.

Latana. "Democracy Perception Index Report 2022." https://latana.com/ democracy-perception-index-report-2022/.

Lenin, Vladimir Ilyich. *The Impending Catastrophe and How to Combat It.* Marxists Internet Archive, 1917. https://www.marxists.org/archive/lenin/works/1917/ ichtci/11.htm.

———. *Imperialism, the Highest Stage of Capitalism.* Moscow: Progress Publishers, 1963. https://www.marxists.org/archive/lenin/works/1916/imp-hsc/.

———. *"Left-Wing" Childishness.* Translated by Clemens Dutt and Robert Daglish. Marxists Internet Archive, 1918. https://www.marxists.org/archive/lenin/ works/1918/may/09.htm.

———. *"Left-Wing" Communism: An Infantile Disorder.* Translated by Julius Katzer. Marxists Internet Archive, 1999. https://www.marxists.org/archive/lenin/ works/1920/lwc/index.htm.

———. *Lenin Collected Works.* 4th English Edition. Volume 31. Moscow: Progress Publishers, 1965. https://www.marxists.org/archive/lenin/works/cw/index.htm.

———. "A Letter To G. Myasnikov." Letter to Gavril Myasnikov. August 5, 1921. https://www.marxists.org/archive/lenin/works/1921/aug/05.htm.

———. *The Tax in Kind (The Significance Of The New Policy And Its Conditions).* Translated by Yuri Sdobnikov. Marxists Internet Archive, 1921. https://www. marxists.org/archive/lenin/works/1921/apr/21.htm.

———. "To the Russian Colony in North America." Translated by Bernard Isaacs. *Russky Golos* no. 2046, January 10, 1923. https://www.marxists.org/archive/ lenin/works/1922/nov/14b.htm.

———. "What the 'Friends of the People' Are and How They Fight the Social-Democrats, Part III." In *What the "Friends of the People" Are and How They Fight the Social-Democrats.* Marxists Internet Archive, 1894. https://www. marxists.org/archive/lenin/works/1894/friends/06.htm.

Lehr, Amy. "Addressing Forced Labor in the Xinjiang Uyghur Autonomous Region." CSIS Brief. Center for Strategic & International Studies, July 2020. https:// csis-website-prod.s3.amazonaws.com/s3fs-public/publication/200730_Lehr_ XinjiangUyghurForcedLabor_brief_FINAL_v2.pdf.

Leibold, James. "Planting the Seed: Ethnic Policy in Xi Jinping's New Era of Cultural Nationalism." *China Brief* 19, no. 22 (December 31, 2019). https://jamestown.org/program/ planting-the-seed-ethnic-policy-in-xi-jinpings-new-era-of-cultural-nationalism/.

Левада-Центр(LevadaCenter). "СТРУКТУРА И ВОСПРОИЗВОДСТВО ПАМЯТИ О СОВЕТСКОМ СОЮЗЕ" [Structure and Reproduction of the Memory of the Soviet Union]. Левада-Центр (Levada Center), March 24, 2020. https://www. levada.ru/2020/03/24/struktura-i-vosproizvodstvo-pamyati-o-sovetskom-soyuze/.

Li, Cheng. "Preparing For the 18th Party Congress: Procedures and Mechanisms." *China Leadership Monitor*, 2012.

Li, Minqi. "China: Imperialism or Semi-Periphery?" *Monthly Review* 73, no. 3 (July 1, 2021). https://monthlyreview.org/2021/07/01/china-imperialism-or-semi-periphery.

Linn, Amy. "The Navajo Nation's Horrendous Roads Keep Killing People and Holding Students Hostage, but Nothing Changes." *Center for Health Journalism.* University of Southern California, 2020. https://centerforhealthjournalism.org/resources/lessons/navajo-nation-s-horrendous-roads-keep-killing-people-and-holding-students-hostage.

Lintner, Bertil. "The United Wa State Army and Burma's Peace Process." *Peaceworks.* United States Institute of Peace, April 29, 2019. https://www.usip.org/publications/2019/04/united-wa-state-army-and-burmas-peace-process.

Liu, Xiang. *Strategies of the Warring States.* Translated by Kyle Ferrana. Accessed November 23, 2023. https://zhanguoce.5000yan.com/32913.html.

Losurdo, Domenico. "Flight from History? The Communist Movement between Self-Criticism and Self-Contempt (1999)." Translated by Charles Reitz. Red Sails, January 10, 2021. https://redsails.org/flight-from-history/.

Louisiana Tech Research Institute. "Guide to Nuclear Deterrence in the Age of Great-Power Competition." Bossier City, Louisiana: Louisiana Tech Research Institute, October 2020. https://atloa.org/wp-content/uploads/2020/12/Guide-to-Nuclear-Deterrence-in-the-Age-of-Great-Power-Competition-Lowther.pdf.

Luxemburg, Rosa. "Protective Tariffs and Accumulation." Chapter 31 in *The Accumulation of Capital*, edited by Dr. W. Stark. Translated by Agnes Schwarzschild. Marxists Internet Archive, 2003. https://www.marxists.org/archive/luxemburg/1913/accumulation-capital/ch31.htm.

MacroPolo. "Boon or Boondoggle? The Cost and Benefit of China's Bullet Trains." Chicago: The Paulson Institute, 2022. https://macropolo.org/digital-projects/high-speed-rail/.

Magioncalda, William. "A Modern Insurgency: India's Evolving Naxalite Problem." Center for Strategic & International Studies, April 8, 2010. https://csis-website-prod.s3.amazonaws.com/s3fs-public/legacy_files/files/publication/SAM_140_0.pdf.

Mao, Zedong. "Analysis of the Classes in Chinese Society." Foreign Languages Press, March 1926. In *Selected Works of Mao Tse-tung: Vol. I.* Marxists Internet Archive. https://www.marxists.org/reference/archive/mao/selected-works/volume-1/mswv1_1.htm.

———. "On Protracted War." Lecture, May 1938. In *Selected Works of Mao Tse-tung: Vol. II.* Marxists Internet Archive. https://www.marxists.org/reference/archive/mao/selected-works/volume-2/mswv2_09.htm.

Marx, Karl. *Capital. A Critique of Political Economy. Volume I: The Process of Production of Capital.* Edited by Frederick Engels. Translated by Samuel Moore and Edward Aveling. Moscow: Progress Publishers, 1887. https://www.marxists.org/archive/marx/works/1867-c1/index.htm.

———. *Critique of the Gotha Programme*. 1875. Marxists Internet Archive. https://www.marxists.org/archive/marx/works/1875/gotha/ch04.htm.

———. *The Eighteenth Brumaire of Louis Bonaparte*. Chapter 1. 1852. Translated by Saul K. Padover from the German edition of 1869. Marxists Internet Archive. https://www.marxists.org/archive/marx/works/1852/18th-brumaire/ch01.htm.

———. *The Eighteenth Brumaire of Louis Bonaparte*. Chapter VII. 1852. Translated by Saul K. Padover from the German edition of 1869. Marxists Internet Archive, 1869. https://www.marxists.org/archive/marx/works/1852/18th-brumaire/ch07.htm.

———. "Theses On Feuerbach." 1845. Translated by Cyril Smith and Don Cuckson. Marxists Internet Archive. https://www.marxists.org/archive/marx/works/1845/theses/index.htm.

Marx, Karl, and Friedrich Engels. *The German Ideology*. 1845. Marxists Internet Archive. https://www.marxists.org/archive/marx/works/1845/german-ideology/ch01b.htm.

McFaul, Michael. "Ukraine Imports Democracy: External Influences on the Orange Revolution." *International Security* 32, no. 2 (2007): 45–83.

McKinsey & Company. "Delivering the U.S. Manufacturing Renaissance." August 29, 2022. https://www.mckinsey.com/capabilities/operations/our-insights/delivering-the-us-manufacturing-renaissance.

———. "The Rise and Rise of the Global Balance Sheet: How Productively Are We Using Our Wealth?" Special Report. November 15, 2021. https://www.mckinsey.com/industries/financial-services/our-insights/the-rise-and-rise-of-the-global-balance-sheet-how-productively-are-we-using-our-wealth.

McMann, Kelly M. "Central Asians and the State: Nostalgia for the Soviet Era." The National Council for Eurasian and East European Research, February 16, 2005. https://www.ucis.pitt.edu/nceeer/2005_818_09_McMann.pdf.

Minority Rights Group International. "World Directory of Minorities: Uyghurs." July 2008. https://www.justice.gov/sites/default/files/eoir/legacy/2014/02/19/Uyghurs.pdf.

Moseley, William G., Judith Carney, and Laurence Becker. "Neoliberal Policy, Rural Livelihoods, and Urban Food Security in West Africa: A Comparative Study of The Gambia, Côte d'Ivoire, and Mali." *Proceedings of the National Academy of Sciences* 107, no. 13 (March 25, 2010). https://doi.org/10.1073/pnas.0905717107.

Mupepele, Léonide. "Etude d'évaluation de la mise en œuvre de la convention de collaboration relative au développement d'un projet minier et d'un projet d'infrastructures en RD Congo Projet SICOMINES" [Evaluation study of the implementation of the collaboration agreement relating to the development of a mining project and an infrastructure project in the DR Congo SICOMINES Project]. Kinshasa: Initiative pour la Transparence dans les Industries Extractives (ITIE), November 2021. https://congominespdfstorage.blob.core.windows.

net/congominespdfstorage/RAPPORT%20D'EVALUATION_PROJET%20 SICOMINES_Version%20Finale.pdf.

National Endowment for Democracy. "2008 Independent Auditor's Report." January 15, 2009. https://www.ned.org/docs/08annual/PDFs/AR_Financials08.pdf.

———. "Annual Report 1989." https://www.ned.org/docs/annual/1989%20NED%20 Annual%20Report.pdf.

———. "Annual Report 1995." https://www.ned.org/docs/annual/1995%20NED%20 Annual%20Report.pdf.

Nkrumah, Kwame. *Handbook of Revolutionary Warfare*. New York: International Publishers, 1968. https://consciencism.files.wordpress.com/2018/08/handbook-of-revolutionary-warfare-a-guide-to-the-armed-phase-of-the-african-revolution-copy.pdf.

———. *Neo-Colonialism, the Last Stage of Imperialism*. London: Panaf Books, 1965. https://www.marxists.org/subject/africa/nkrumah/neo-colonialism/neo-colonialism.pdf.

Núñez Tenorio, J. R. *Estrategia y Táctica: ¿Cómo hacer? ¿Cuál es la salida?* [Strategy and Tactics: How to do it? What is the way out?]. Second edition. Caracas: Fondo Editorial de la Asamblea Nacional William Lara, 2014.

Obobisa, Emma Serwaa, Haibo Chen, Emmanuel Caesar Ayamba, and Claudia Nyarko Mensah. "The Causal Relationship Between China-Africa Trade, China OFDI, and Economic Growth of African Countries." *SAGE Open*, December 21, 2021. https://doi.org/10.1177/21582440211064899.

Obokata, Tomoya. "Contemporary Forms of Slavery Affecting Persons Belonging to Ethnic, Religious and Linguistic Minority Communities." United Nations Human Rights Council, July 19, 2022. https://undocs.org/A/HRC/51/26.

Oliveros, Luis. "Impacto de las Sanciones Financieras y Petroleras sobre la Economia Venezolana" [Impact of Financial and Oil Sanctions on the Venezuelan Economy]. Washington, D.C.: Washington Office on Latin America, October 2020. https://www.wola.org/2020/10/new-report-us-sanctions-aggravated-venezuelas-economic-crisis/.

大西　広 (Onishi, Hiroshi). "「ウイグル問題」に関する西側キャンペーンを検証する" [Examining Western Campaign on 'Uyghur Issue']. 社会主義理論研究 1, no. 1 (November 25, 2021): 6–20. https://doi.org/10.51058/sost.1.1_6.

O'Toole, Randal. "The High-Speed Rail Money Sink: Why the United States Should Not Spend Trillions on Obsolete Technology." Policy Analysis. Cato Institute, April 20, 2021. https://www.cato.org/policy-analysis/high-speed-money-sink-why-united-states-should-not-spend-trillions-obsolete.

Pantsov, Alexsander V., and Steven I. Levine. *Deng Xiaoping: A Revolutionary Life*. New York: Oxford University Press, 2015.

Parenti, Michael. *Blackshirts and Reds: Rational Fascism and the Overthrow of Communism*. San Francisco: City Lights Books, 1997. https://archive.org/details/michael-parenti-blackshirts-and-reds.

Parker, David. "Privatization in the European Union: A Critical Assessment of Its Development, Rationale and Consequences." *Economic and Industrial Democracy* 20, no. 1 (February 1, 1999): 9–38. https://doi.org/10.1177/0143831X99201002.

Parodi, Carlos A., Elizabeth Van Wie Davis, and Elizabeth Rexford. "The Silent Demise of Democracy: The Role of the Clinton Administration in the 1994 Yemeni Civil War." *Arab Studies Quarterly* 16, no. 4 (1994): 65–76.

Patnaik, Utsa, and Prabhat Patnaik. "The Drain of Wealth." *Monthly Review* 72, no. 8 (February 1, 2021). https://monthlyreview.org/2021/02/01/the-drain-of-wealth/.

Peerenboom, Randall. "Assessing Human Rights in China: Why the Double Standard." *Cornell International Law Journal* 38, no. 1 (2005): 72–172.

Pfeifer, Karen. "How Tunisia, Morocco, Jordan and Even Egypt Became IMF 'Success Stories' in the 1990s." *Middle East Report*, no. 210 (1999): 23–27. https://doi.org/10.2307/3012499.

P.F.L.P.: Popular Front for the Liberation of Palestine. *Strategy for the Liberation of Palestine*. 1969. http://pflp-documents.org/documents/PFLP_StrategyforLiberationofPalestine1969.pdf.

Popov, Vladimir. "Mortality and Life Expectancy in Post-Communist Countries." Dialogue of Civilizations Research Institute, June 5, 2018. https://web.archive.org/web/20190705210652/https://doc-research.org/2018/06/mortality-life-expectancy-post-communist/.

Prendergast, John. "Blood Money for Sudan: World Bank and IMF to the 'Rescue.'" *Africa Today* 36, no. 3/4 (1989): 43–53.

Qiao Collective. "Attacks on Xinjiang and Beyond." Media. Qiao Collective, 2021. https://www.qiaocollective.com/attacks-on-xinjiang.

Raiffeissen Research. "CEE Banking Sector Report." Raiffeissen, June 2015. https://web.archive.org/web/20151123062842/http://www.rbinternational.com/eBusiness/services/resources/media/829189266947841370-829189181316930732_829602947997338151-1078945710712239641-1-2-EN-9.pdf.

———. "CEE Banking Sector Report 2020." Raiffeissen, November 2020. https://www.raiffeisenresearch.com/servlet/NoAuthLibraryServlet?action=viewDocument&encrypt=b0bc1dfb-a056-4e1e-95ea-11c305f117e5&mime=HTML.

Ruser, Nathan, James Leibold, Kelsey Munro, and Tilla Hoja. "Cultural Erasure: Tracing the Destruction of Uyghur and Islamic Spaces in Xinjiang." Policy Brief. Australian Strategic Policy Institute, September 24, 2020. https://ad-aspi.s3.ap-southeast-2.amazonaws.com/2020-09/Cultural%20erasure_0.pdf?VersionId=NlJYOaEV6DF3IfupGsdb73xtX0wCNokg.

Roberts, Geoffrey. "'Now or Never': The Immediate Origins of Putin's Preventative War on Ukraine." *Journal of Military and Strategic Studies* 22, no. 2 (December 12, 2022): 3–27.

Robinson, Michael Edson. *Korea's Twentieth-Century Odyssey*. Honolulu: University of Hawaii Press, 2007. https://archive.org/details/koreastwentieth00robi/page/119/mode/2up.

Rudelson, Justin Ben-Adam. *Oasis Identities: Uyghur Nationalism Along China's Silk Road*. Columbia University Press, 1997. https://books.google.com/books?id=DMU8Ue0HECcC.

Russian Federation and People's Republic of China. "China-Russia: Joint Declaration on a Multipolar World and the Establishment of a New International Order." *International Legal Materials* 36, no. 4 (1997): 986–89. https://doi.org/10.1017/S0020782900015138.

Salehi-Isfahani, Djavad. "Poverty and Income Inequality in the Islamic Republic of Iran." *Revue Internationale Des Études Du Développement* N° 229 (April 6, 2017): 113. https://doi.org/10.3917/ried.229.0113.

———. "Rising Poverty and Falling Living Standards in Iran in 2020." *Tyranny of Numbers,* August 28, 2021. Economics blog. https://djavadsalehi.com/2021/08/28/rising-poverty-and-falling-living-standards-in-iran-in-2020/.

Sarkees, Meredith Reid, and Frank Wayman. *Resort to War: 1816–2007*. Data Set. Washington, D.C.: CQ Press, 2010. https://correlatesofwar.org/data-sets/COW-war.

Sautman, Barry. "Affirmative Action, Ethnic Minorities and China's Universities." *Pacific Rim Law & Policy Journal* 7, no. 1 (January 1988): 77–116.

———. "Is Tibet China's Colony: The Claim of Demographic Catastrophe." *Columbia Journal of Asian Law* 15, no. 1 (September 1, 2001). https://doi.org/10.7916/cjal.v15i1.3205.

———. "'Cultural Genocide' and Tibet." *Texas International Law Journal* 38 (2003): 173–247.

———. "Ethnic Policies: China vs. U.S. and India." *The Adelaide Review*, September 10, 2013. https://www.adelaidereview.com.au/latest/opinion/2013/09/10/ethnic-policies-china-vs-us-and-india/.

———. "Is Xinjiang an Internal Colony?" *Inner Asia* 2, no. 2 (2000): 239–71.

———. "Paved with Good Intentions: Proposals to Curb Minority Rights and Their Consequences for China." *Modern China* 38, no. 1 (January 1, 2012): 10–39. https://doi.org/10.1177/0097700411424563.

———. "Scaling Back Minority Rights?: The Debate about China's Ethnic Policies." *Stanford Journal of International Law* 46 (June 1, 2010): 51–120.

Scheiring, Gábor, Aytalina Azarova, Darja Irdam, Katarzyna Doniec, Martin McKee, David Stuckler, and Lawrence King. "Deindustrialisation and the Post-Socialist Mortality Crisis." *Cambridge Journal of Economics* 47, no. 2 (March 2023): 341–372. https://doi.org/10.1093/cje/beac072.

Schmidt, Dirk. "Tibetan Language Readability & Literacy." University of Wisconsin-Madison, 2017. http://dx.doi.org/10.17613/M6VW98.

Schultz, Kristen. *Tropical Versailles: Empire, Monarchy, and the Portuguese Royal Court in Rio De Janeiro, 1808–1821*. New York: Routledge, 2001.

Scissors, Derek. "Deng Undone: The Costs of Halting Market Reform in China." *Foreign Affairs* 88, no. 3 (2009): 24–39.

Scott, James and Carie Steele. "Assisting Democrats or Resisting Dictators? The Nature and Impact of Democracy Support by the United States National Endowment for Democracy, 1990–99." *Democratization* 12, no. 4 (2005): 439–60. https://doi.org/10.1080/13510340500225947.

———. "The Assessment on Human Rights in Xinjiang by the United Nations Office of the High Commissioner for Human Rights: A Critical Analysis." Working Paper. CO-WEST-PRO Consultancy, July 20, 2023. https://www.cowestpro.co/cowestpro_4-2023_-_jul.pdf.

———. "The Australian Strategic Policy Institute's Uyghurs for Sale Report: Scholarly Analysis or Strategic Disinformation?" Working Paper. CO-WEST-PRO Consultancy, September 8, 2022. http://www.cowestpro.co/uploads/1/9/9/7/19974045/cowestpro_1-2022_-_sept.pdf.

Seeley, J. R. *The Expansion of England: Two Courses of Lectures*. Cambridge: Cambridge University Press, 1883.

Sison, Jose Maria. Specific Characteristics of People's War in the Philippines. Answers to Guide Questions from ND Online School of Anakbayan-Europe. June 27, 2021. http://bannedthought.net/Philippines/CPP/Sison/2021/Sison-SpecificCharacteristicsOfPeoplesWarInPhilippines-2021-06-27.pdf.

———. "The Filipino People's Revolutionary Armed Struggle for National and Social Liberation in the Past 50 Years." Communist Party of the Philippines, March 28, 2019. https://web.archive.org/web/20191206043046/https://cpp.ph/statement/the-filipino-peoples-revolutionary-armed-struggle-for-national-and-social-liberation-in-the-past-50-years/.

Smith, Stansfield. "Is Russia Imperialist?" *Monthly Review*, January 2, 2019. https://mronline.org/2019/01/02/is-russia-imperialist/.

Smits, Jeroen, and Iñaki Permanyer. "The Subnational Human Development Database." *Scientific Data* 6, no. 190038 (2019). https://doi.org/10.1038/sdata.2019.38.

Sorrentino, Constance. "International Unemployment Rates: How Comparable Are They?" *Monthly Labor Review* 123, no. 6 (June 2000): 3–20.

Stalin, J. V. *Foundations of Leninism*. Marxists Internet Archive, 2008. https://www.marxists.org/reference/archive/stalin/works/1924/foundations-leninism/.

———. "Inevitability of Wars Among Capitalist Countries." In *Economic Problems of Socialism*. Moscow: Foreign Languages Publishing House, 1952. https://soviethistory.msu.edu/1947-2/cold-war/cold-war-texts/stalin-on-the-inevitability-of-war-with-capitalism/.

————. "The Nation." In *Marxism and the National Question*. Vienna: 1913. Marxists Internet Archive. https://www.marxists.org/reference/archive/stalin/works/1913/03a.htm#s1.

St. John, Ronald Bruce. "The Changing Libyan Economy: Causes and Consequences." *Middle East Journal* 62, no. 1 (Winter 2008): 75–91.

Starrs, Sean. "American Economic Power Hasn't Declined—It Globalized! Summoning the Data and Taking Globalization Seriously." *International Studies Quarterly* 57, no. 4 (December 1, 2013): 817–30. https://doi.org/10.1111/isqu.12053.

Sultan, Hend ElMahly Mahhoud, and Degang Sun. "China's Participation in the Conflict Resolution in Sudan and South Sudan: A Case of 'Creative Mediation.'" *Briq* 1, no. 2 (Spring 2020): 7–23.

Sussman, Gerald, and Sascha Krader. "Template Revolutions: Marketing U.S. Regime Change in Eastern Europe." *Westminster Papers in Communication and Culture* 5, no. 3 (2008): 91–112. https://doi.org/10.16997/wpcc.95.

Sustainable Bus. "Electric Bus, Main Fleets and Projects around the World." July 12, 2022. https://www.sustainable-bus.com/electric-bus/electric-bus-public-transport-main-fleets-projects-around-world/.

Sylvaire, Debongo Devincy Yanne, Wu Hua Qing, Chang He Ran, Diane Laure Kassai, Nzabana Vincent, Djossouvi Adjoa Candide Douce, Osei-Kusi Frank, et al. "The Impact of China's Foreign Direct Investment on Africa's Inclusive Development." *Social Sciences & Humanities Open* 6, no. 1 (2022). https://doi.org/10.1016/j.ssaho.2022.100276.

Szymczak, Pat Davis. "Tengizchevroil Production Rebounds After Antigovernment Protests Curtailed." *Journal of Petroleum Technology*, January 10, 2022. https://jpt.spe.org/tengizchevroil-production-rebounds-after-antigovernment-protests-curtailed.

Tang, Wenfang. "The 'Surprise' of Authoritarian Resilience in China." *American Affairs* 2, no. 1 (February 20, 2018): 101–17.

Tax Foundation. "Historical U.S. Federal Individual Income Tax Rates & Brackets, 1862–2021." August 24, 2021. https://taxfoundation.org/historical-income-tax-rates-brackets/.

————. "Taxes in Hungary." Accessed 2022. https://taxfoundation.org/country/hungary.

Tharappel, Jay. "Why China's Capital Exports Can Weaken Imperialism." *World Review of Political Economy* 12, no. 1 (April 1, 2021): 27–49. https://doi.org/10.13169/worlrevipoliecon.12.1.0027.

Thomas, Cooper. "Bombing Missions of the Vietnam War: A Visual Record of the Largest Aerial Bombardment in History." StoryMaps, 2017. https://storymaps.arcgis.com/stories/2eae918ca40a4bd7a55390bba4735cdb.

To Sell a War. Documentary film. Canadian Broadcasting Corporation, 1992. https://www.youtube.com/watch?v=yaR1YBR5g6U.

Torregrosa-Hetland, Sara, and Oriol Sabaté. "Income Tax Progressivity and Inflation during the World Wars." *European Review of Economic History* 26, no. 3 (July 23, 2022): 311–39. https://doi.org/10.1093/ereh/heab020.

Toussaint, Éric. "The Mexican Debt Crisis and the World Bank." *Committee for the Abolition of Illegitimate Debt*, August 4, 2020. https://www.cadtm.org/The-Mexican-debt-crisis-and-the-World-Bank.

———. *Your Money or Your Life! The Tyranny of Global Finance*. First edition. London: Pluto Press, 1999.

Tucker, Jasmine. "Native American Women Need Action That Closes the Wage Gap." National Women's Law Center, September 2021. https://nwlc.org/wp-content/uploads/2020/09/Native-Women-Equal-Pay-2021.pdf.

UN Human Rights Council. *Report of the Independent International Fact-Finding Mission on Myanmar.* UNHRC 39th Session, UN Doc A/HRC/39/64 (September 12, 2018). https://www.ohchr.org/sites/default/files/Documents/HRBodies/HRCouncil/FFM-Myanmar/A_HRC_39_64.pdf.

UN Office of the High Commissioner for Human Rights. *OHCHR Assessment of Human Rights Concerns in the Xinjiang Uyghur Autonomous Region, People's Republic of China.* August 31, 2022. https://www.ohchr.org/sites/default/files/documents/countries/2022-08-31/22-08-31-final-assesment.pdf.

Valdés, Nelson P. "Health and Revolution in Cuba." *Science & Society* 35, no. 3 (Fall 1971): 311–35.

Vicziany, Marika. "State Responses to Islamic Terrorism in Western China and Their Impact on South Asia." *Contemporary South Asia* 12, no. 2 (June 1, 2003): 243–62. https://doi.org/10.1080/0958493032000147690.

Vine, David. "Lists of U.S. Military Bases Abroad, 1776–2021." Washington, D.C.: American University Library. Online resource posted on August 4, 2023. https://doi.org/10.17606/7em4-hb13.

Vine, David, Cala Coffman, Katalina Khoury, Madison Lovasz, Helen Bush, Rachael Leduc, and Jennifer Walkup. "Creating Refugees: Displacement Caused by the United States' Post-9/11 Wars." *Costs of War.* Watson Institute of International and Public Affairs at Brown University, August 19, 2021. https://watson.brown.edu/costsofwar/files/cow/imce/papers/2021/Costs%20of%20War_Vine%20et%20al_Displacement%20Update%20August%202021.pdf.

Wallerstein, Immanuel. *Historical Capitalism*. New York and London: Verso, 2011.

———. *The Capitalist World-Economy: Essays by Immanuel Wallerstein*. First edition. Cambridge: Cambridge University Press, 1979.

———. *The Modern World-System, Volume I: Capitalist Agriculture and the Origins of the European World-Economy in the Sixteenth Century*. New York: Academic Press, Inc., 1974.

Walsh, David, Ruth Dundas, Gerry McCartney, Marcia Gibson, and Rosie Seaman. "Bearing the Burden of Austerity: How Do Changing Mortality Rates in the UK Compare between Men and Women?" *Journal of Epidemiology and*

Community Health 76, no. 12 (December 1, 2022): 1027. https://doi.org/10.1136/jech-2022-219645.

Wang, Huning. *America Against America*. Internet Archive, 1991. https://archive.org/details/america-against-america.

Wang, Mei (Lisa), Zhen Qi, and Jijing Zhang. "China Becomes a Capital Exporter: Trends and Issues." *China's Domestic Transformation in a Global Context* (2015): 315–38.

Weber, Isabella M. *How China Escaped Shock Therapy: The Market Reform Debate*. New York: Routledge, 2021.

Weisbrot, Mark, and Jeffrey Sachs. *Economic Sanctions as Collective Punishment: The Case of Venezuela*. Washington, D.C.: Center for Economic and Policy Research, April 2019. https://cepr.net/images/stories/reports/venezuela-sanctions-2019-04.pdf.

Werner, Richard. *Princes of the Yen: Japan's Central Bankers and the Transformation of the Economy*. New York: Routledge, 2015.

White, Stephen. "The Russian Presidential Election, March 2000." *Electoral Studies* 20, no. 3 (September 2001): 484–89. https://doi.org/10.1016/s0261-3794(00)00053-6.

Whitney, Rich. "U.S. Provides Military Assistance to 73 Percent of World's Dictatorships." *Truthout,* September 23, 2017. https://truthout.org/articles/us-provides-military-assistance-to-73-percent-of-world-s-dictatorships/.

Wood, Tony. *Russia Without Putin: Money, Power and the Myths of the New Cold War*. Brooklyn, New York: Verso, 2018.

Xi, Jinping. *The Governance of China Volume 1*. First edition. Beijing: Foreign Languages Press Co. Ltd., 2014.

———. *The Governance of China Volume 2*. First edition. Beijing: Foreign Languages Press Co. Ltd., 2017.

Xie, Xiang, Yi-Tong Ma, Yi-Ning Yang, Zhen-Yan Fu, Xiang Ma, Ding Huang, Xiao-Mei Li, et al. "Alcohol Consumption and Carotid Atherosclerosis in China: The Cardiovascular Risk Survey." *European Journal of Preventive Cardiology* 19, no. 3 (June 1, 2012): 314–21. https://doi.org/10.1177/1741826711404501.

Xu, Vicky Xiuzhong, Danielle Cave, James Leibold, Kelsey Munro, and Nathan Ruser. "Uyghurs for Sale: 'Re-Education', Forced Labour and Surveillance beyond Xinjiang." Policy Brief. Australian Strategic Policy Institute, March 1, 2020. https://www.aspi.org.au/report/uyghurs-sale.

Zenz, Adrian. "Coercive Labor in Xinjiang: Labor Transfer and the Mobilization of Ethnic Minorities to Pick Cotton." Intelligence Briefing. Newlines Institute for Strategy and Policy, December 2020. https://web.archive.org/web/20220912100905/http://newlinesinstitute.org/wp-content/uploads/20201214-PB-China-Cotton-NISAP-2.pdf.

———. "Sterilizations, IUDs, and Mandatory Birth Control: The CCP's Campaign to Suppress Uyghur Birthrates in Xinjiang." Washington, DC: The Jamestown

Foundation, June 2020. https://jamestown.org/wp-content/uploads/2020/06/Zenz-Internment-Sterilizations-and-IUDs-UPDATED-July-21-Rev2.pdf.

Zhang, Haiyan, and Michael L. Lahr. "Households' Energy Consumption Change in China: A Multi-Regional Perspective." *Sustainability* 10, no. 7 (2018): 1–17. https://doi.org/10.3390/su10072486.

刘仲康, 韩中义, and 古丽夏. "关于正确认识和处理新形势下新疆宗教问题的调查报告" [Investigation Report on Correct Understanding and Handling of Religious Issues in Xinjiang under the New Situation]. 马克思主义与现实 [Marxism and Reality], 2001. https://xueshu.baidu.com/usercenter/paper/show?paperid=b7ddf3f4efd2c3bfe695cdafe0a271fc.

胡鞍钢 and 胡联合. "中国梦的基石是中华民族的国族一体化." 清华大学学报 28, no. 4 (2013): 111–16.

———. "第二代民族政策：促进民族交融一体和繁荣一体" [The Second Generation Ethnic Policy: Promoting National Integration and Prosperity]. 新华文摘, no. 24 (2011): 6.

Index